Nazi Prisoners of War in America

Never before has the *full* story been told of how we kept nearly a half a million Nazi prisoners in 511 POW camps across the country, as well as in hastily converted CCC camps, high school gyms, and local fairgrounds. Even Santa Anita race track was used as a holding area for thousands of incoming *Afrika Korps* captives.

It was America's first experience handling so many foreign prisoners of war, and there were virtually no precedents upon which to form policy. The War Department simply hammered out decisions as problems arose—and there were difficulties aplenty. There were public relations problems, escapes, Nazism in the camps, kangaroo courts, and political murders among the prisoners. Some American camp administrators, in fact, sometimes seemed to favor Nazis over the anti-Nazi German prisoners because the former were more "orderly."

There was a secret Government "re-education plan" and even a top secret proposal, given serious consideration at the highest military level, to allow the enlistment in the U.S. Army of a POW "German Volunteer Corps" to fight the Japanese. More important, hundreds of thousands of Germans were utilized by labor-starved American farmers and businessmen to alleviate the drain of able-bodied workers fighting overseas. German POWs were engaged on projects from lumber production, roadwork, and harvesting crops, to their ironic appearance as contract workers at a kosher meatpacking firm in New Jersey.

There are stories of a Nazi-loving American POW guard (a former Harvard ROTC cadet), who, together with several of his charges, escaped briefly to Mexico, of another camp guard who machine-gunned to death eight Nazis after he'd watched an atrocity film, of an American camp commander who insisted that he be saluted with "Heil Hitler", and of a massive Hitler's birthday demonstration at the Fort Lewis stockade, a Nazi banner atop the flagpole. One escaped German prisoner received a tax rebate from the IRS and opened a bookstore in Chicago. Georg Gaertner, the last German POW, remained at large until 1985, surrendering after reading the hardcover edition of this book.

Illustrated with more than 70 rare photos, many of them never published before, this is the definitive history of one of the most incredible and least known facets of America's participation in the Second World War.

Nazi Prisoners of

ARNOLD KRAMMER

Twenty thousand German prisoners in France before shipment to the United States.
(U.S. Army Photo)

War in America

Scarborough House/*Publishers*

To my mother

Scarborough House/*Publishers*
Chelsea, MI 48118

FIRST SCARBOROUGH HOUSE PAPERBACK EDITION 1991

Nazi Prisoners of War in America was originally published in
hardcover by Stein & Day/*Publishers*.

A small portion of this material appeared in somewhat different form in the
author's articles "When the *Afrika Korps* Came to Texas," published in the
Southwestern Historical Quarterly, and "German Prisoners of War in the United
States," which appeared in *Military Affairs.*

Library of Congress Cataloging-in-Publication Data

Krammer, Arnold, 1941-
   Nazi prisoners of war in America / Arnold Krammer. — 1st
  Scarborough House pbk. ed.
      p.   cm.
   Previously published: New York : Stein & Day, 1979.
   Includes bibliographical references and index.
   ISBN 0-8128-8526-0
   1. World War, 1939-1945 – Prisoners and prisons, American.
  2. Prisoners of war – Germany. 3. Prisoners of war – United States.
  I. Title.
  [D805.U5K7   1991]
  940.54'7273 – dc20
                                     90-22987
                                       CIP

Acknowledgment

When America went to war on December 7, 1941, few could have imagined the profound changes which the next four years would bring. Battles great and small produced heroes and cowards; savage brutality with an occasional glimpse of human dignity; the development of awesome weapons; and millions of prisoners of war. For such prisoners, the war was an entirely different experience from that shared by their comrades at the front. After capture they were processed and shipped thousands of miles to prisoner communities where they carved out new, if temporary, lives for themselves in the midst of their enemies. Some prisoners of war, such as Americans in Japanese hands or Germans captured by the Russians, fared badly and were often fortunate simply to survive. Others, as will be seen, had a much better time in captivity.

It is astonishing how few Americans recall that between 1942 and 1946, nearly 400,000 German war prisoners (not to mention the more than 50,000 Italians and 5,000 Japanese) arrived in the United States from the battlefields of North Africa, Sicily, and Italy, and were held in some 500 prison camps across the country. While in the United States, most of the Germans spent the war years uneventfully, and, in some cases, even enjoyably. They worked, studied, played, escaped on occasion, and sometimes harassed and even killed one another in ideological disputes. There was really no such thing as the "typical" prisoner of war experience in America; the life of a German POW who spent the war years as a PX clerk at Fort Meade, Maryland, for example, in no way compared to that of the POW who picked cotton at Camp Como, Mississippi. While they shared such general experiences as their awe at the size and beauty of the United States, and listless boredom of camp life, the prisoners often recall events and circumstances dissimilar from those in different camps and even in different barracks of the same camp.

A word about the use of the term "Nazi," a subject which is treated in detail later. It is certainly true that not all of the incoming POWs were officially Nazis, i.e., members of the Nazi Party—far from it. Indeed, a sprinkling of them might have been devout anti-Nazis even prior to their capture. One of the central problems of the whole POW program, in fact, was to somehow distinguish the "real" Nazis from the political opportunists, the ardent German nationalists, and the non-political soldiers. The difficulty in applying such political labels is further complicated by the blurring of recollections. Former prisoners who once strongly sympathized with Nazism have often become more vocally democratic as events have receded into the distant past, and their fortunes (or waistlines) have increased. Yet, they were the military representatives of the Third Reich, and to the generation of Americans who captured them, lived near their prison camps, or utilized their farm labor, the German prisoners were simply and unquestionably "Nazis." Hence, its appearance in the title. The many dozens of former German prisoners who co-operated so fully in the preparation of this book will understand.

From among those many former prisoners, several deserve special thanks for their efforts. Heinrich Matthias, in Hamburg; Eberhard Scheel, in Bad Vilbel; and especially Karl Wagner in Gustavsburg and Colonel Alfred Klein in Munich, were unstinting in the detailed recollections and patient explanations which generated a voluminous correspondence over some three years.

My deep appreciation also goes to Freiherr Rüdiger von Wechmar, a former POW at Camp Trinidad, Colorado, who later rose to become the President of the General Assembly of the United Nations; he was kind enough to write the Introduction to the German edition of this study: *PW – Gefangen in Amerika* (Motorbuch Verlag, Stuttgart).

On this side of the Atlantic, the number of people who merit special thanks is somewhat longer. First and foremost, I join the countless scholars who are indebted to the professional archivists at the Hoover Institution of War, Revolution, and Peace at Stanford University; at the Office of the Chief of Military History in Washington, D.C.; and, of course, at the National Archives. To the experts at the latter's Modern Military Branch—William Cunliffe, George Wagner, and Charles Shaughnessy—who guided me through the more than 3,000 boxes of recently declassified documents from the agency in charge of the POW program, the Provost Marshal General's Office, I am especially grateful.

It was at the Modern Military Branch of the National Archives that I learned a basic truth about historical research from Mr. Anthony Brown, there completing his monumental study on wartime intelligence, *Bodyguard of Lies.* "The more you know," noted Brown, "the more people are inclined to talk to you." The accuracy of that observation was borne out in frustrating and often bizarre ways, from cases of former prisoners and American personnel who refused to be interviewed—only to change their minds as the study moved to completion or until after certain other participants were interviewed first; to the natural inclination of archivists to cater to the specialist before the amateur. In only two curious cases did the reverse occur: As this book neared completion, two former POWs (now successful American businessmen) who had enthusiastically contributed their recollections over a period of many months, suddenly and separately demanded that their biographies be purged from the volume "to protect the safety of family and relatives." One can only speculate on the reasons.

The difficulties, however, only illuminate more brightly the generous help provided by so many others. To the following I offer my deep appreciation: Eddie A. White, Andrea Celeste Elbert, Ernest B. Walker, Richard Staff, Donna Newberry, Brian Burrer, and Ron Orth. I am also grateful to my colleagues, Professors Garland Bayliss, Roger Beaumont, Betty Unterberger, and Archivist Charles R. Schultz at Texas A&M University; Howard Mumford Jones at Harvard; Edward Pluth at St. Cloud State College; William G. Moulton at Princeton, Matthew J. Schott at the University of Southwestern Louisiana, T. Hunt Tooley at Erskine College, and Harold Deutsch at the Army War College, for providing both criticism and support in large doses. Support of a different type was provided through grants from the American Council of Learned Societies, and the American Philosophical Society.

The photographs were drawn from a collection obtained through the U.S. Army's outstanding Audio-Visual Activity Office in the Pentagon—a veritable treasure-trove of military history—as well as from the participants in the POW program themselves. The reproduction and enlargement of most of those pictures was the work of various photographic experts: Glen Green, Paul Glenn, and Michael Minoia.

I am indebted to Benton M. Arnovitz, now Editorial Director, Scarborough House/*Publishers,* for his unerring judgment throughout the production of this volume.

Finally, this time, I take this opportunity to thank Jan Smith and young Douglas, for their encouragement and cheerful tolerance in my inevitable preoccupation with this project.

Contents

Introduction

Early morning in a small town. People are eating breakfast, businesses are opening their doors for their first customers, and traffic is coming to life. In the distance one suddenly hears the crisp, guttural commands of military German, and busy townspeople stop to shade their eyes against the bright morning sun and stare at the columns of young men marching through town to harvest crops in the surrounding fields.

A rural town in Germany? A generation of wartime Americans knows better. This scene could have taken place in Algona, Iowa; Cawker City, Kansas; Windfall, Indiana; Clark, Missouri; Cooke, California; Crossville, Tennessee; Robinson, Arkansas, and hundreds of other cities and towns across the United States.

It was the second year of the war—1943—and the American people were adjusting to the scarcity of certain products and the daily influx of war news. The population was exhorted to produce at Stakhanovite levels; rural people were moving to the city to get higher paying jobs in war industry; OPA ration books were the housewives' Bibles; and "Mairzy Doats" was at the top of the charts. Young boys avidly followed the course of the war by shifting pins on their bedroom wall maps; people were amused to find that "Kilroy" (whoever he was) had gotten there ahead of them; and every advertisement reminded the reader to "Buy War Bonds."

No one remained untouched by that second year of the war, but for many Americans the first contact with the military reality of the conflict came with the appearance in their communities of large numbers of German and Italian prisoners of war.

Between the end of 1942 and mid-1946, the American government and its citizens participated in a unique experience. With the outbreak of the Second World War had come the appearance of nearly a half million enemy prisoners of war. They were transported to our shores from the battlefields of North Africa and Italy, often within weeks of their capture. The transport ships unloaded confused and often hostile cargoes. The long lines of young men in tattered, sometimes bloodstained, uniforms were marched on to the docks under heavy guard, their future to be determined by a new prisoner of war program. It was a novel experiment for the United States, which had never held as many war captives in its entire history, much less maintained them within the "Zone of the Interior" during wartime. The hastily constructed program contained enough problems to tax even the War Department's formidable ingenuity.

Few theoretical guidelines compensated for the lack of practical experience. The Army reports and manuals written after the First World War were based on America's experiences overseas and were of little value at home. The Geneva Convention of 1929 was laudable but untested in war and incapable of solving the unique problems which the next global war was to bring. Unexpected problems appeared at every turn. The issue of security and the nation's fear of sabotage, while proving groundless, drained much of the early flexibility of the War Department's plans. Behind the scenes, various governmental agencies negotiated for jurisdiction over different aspects of the prisoners' lives, and, if the situation required further complication, the War Department faced a serious and continual shortage of qualified and experienced personnel.

The prisoners had their own difficulties. German-speaking guards were nearly nonexistent, and the POW-spokesman, whose English was sufficient to maintain communications between his fellow prisoners and the camp administrators, did not always represent the ideological views of his constituents. Ideology would, in fact, become a major issue. Despite the several attempts by the War Department to segregate the hardened Nazis from the less fanatic captives, nearly all of the 155 base camps and 511 branch camps experienced some internal ideological struggle. In some cases, entire camps fell under the control of a minority of obdurate Nazis as the result of terror campaigns, physical intimidation, kangaroo courts, and the rest. Problems also resulted when prisoners were mobilized to fill the depleted ranks of American agricultural labor. And there were escapes.

Yet despite all these difficulties and more, the War Department and the American public rose to the challenge. By the end of the war, the POW program had successfully fed, clothed, housed, entertained, and in many cases even reeducated the hundreds of thousands of men in its care. This success resulted from determined and persistent administrators, continual modification in planning, and a bit of blind luck. Moreover, America's severe labor shortage had been partially alleviated by prisoner labor, and the use of prisoners on nonstrategic military tasks freed substantial numbers of American troops for shipment overseas. Most significantly, the War Department's even-handed and humane treatment of enemy captives assured that American prisoners in German hands would be accorded reciprocal treatment. In fact, this humane treatment may even have shortened the war in Europe by making the prospect of surrender less odious to the resisting German *Wehrmacht*. Former prisoners, many now prosperous German businessmen, can still recall those days now fifty years in the past as "wonderful years" and "the experiences of their lives," an impressive testimony to the program's accomplishments.

This book chronicles those years and attempts to analyze the impact of America's first prisoner of war program.

CHAPTER I

From Capture to Camp

Nearly one year had passed since the attack on Pearl Harbor, and the United States had only 431 enemy prisoners within its borders. Washington had been understandably less concerned about creating the mechanism for caring for prisoners than in pursuing the far more critical task of fighting a global, two-front war. Indeed, with the exception of the reorganization of the War Department and the government's April, 1942, publication of the "Regulations Governing Civilian Enemy Aliens and Prisoners of War," progress on the POW program had been slow and rather tortuous. Governmental agencies and their bureaucracies had spent the year trying to define the hierarchies and areas of responsibility over the prisoners, without the benefit of previous guidelines. The difficulties, moreover, were not entirely restricted to the American government.

Relations between Washington and London concerning wartime administrative matters were far from cordial. Contrary to the official image of fraternal allies, nearly every decision regarding their joint prosecution of the war came about as the result of prolonged and often stormy conflict. Each had its individual philosophy concerning the direction of the war; they did not share intelligence data; chiefs of staff were on the coolest terms; and international conferences were tests of will.[1] Indeed, throughout the war American authorities resisted England's every advance to establish a program of cooperative responsibility, recalling, perhaps, General Fox Cannon's military dictum: "If you have to go to war, for God's sake do it without allies." [2] With regard to the question of prisoners of war, the tension was no less evident. Due to her early entrance into the world war, Britain had been receiving substantial numbers of German and Italian prisoners for more than a year, and the problem was approaching crisis proportions. From Washington's point of view, the United States simply refused to enter into any agreement which might adversely affect its ability to act independently throughout the war. In fact, there were so many areas of administrative conflict and rivalry that the creation of a snug relationship, involving only the matter of prisoners of war, would have been difficult to maintain. Moreover, there were a number of complex legal issues to consider as well as the very distinct possibility that if an agreement were to occur and Britain then mistreated her German captives, the fate of Americans in enemy hands would then be jeopardized. In any event, the newly created Prisoner of War Divison was simply not equipped, in terms of available time or personnel, to maintain a continual liaison with London. Relations over this issue became so cool, in fact, that Whitehall was finally forced to exclaim in exasperation, "It is very hard to understand on this side why, on a matter which is of such vital interest to us, it should prove so difficult even to get agreement in principle from the State Department." [3] Perplexed but undaunted, London continued to press for some measure of cooperation on the prisoner of war issue, especially as Britain's ability to maintain the increasing numbers of her enemy captives on that tiny island were taxed to the breaking point. Finally, in August of 1942, after months of futile efforts by Lord Halifax, London's emissary to the State Department, Washington begrudgingly offered to accept an emergency batch of 50,000 enemy prisoners from Britain.[4]

No one doubted, therefore, that prisoners would eventually be arriving. No one could even guess the ultimate numbers. Any estimate would have to follow a consideration of such unfathomable variables as future battles, the availability of ocean transportation, the attitudes of the commanding officers in the theaters of operation, and the demands for additional manpower at home. An accurate prediction was simply impossible.[5] Thus, the planning would have to continue even as the prisoners arrived, and their arrival was about to begin.

Processing in North Africa

The North African campaign opened in November of 1942 and raged through the spring and summer of the following year, as America's global strategy dictated a major assault into Tunisia. More than 100,000 American troops under Generals Omar Bradley and George Patton joined the British forces under General Bernard Montgomery to continue a gigantic slugging match against General Erwin Rommel's elite *Afrika Korps*. The battles fought across the Mediterranean coasts of Algeria, Libya, and Tunisia were enormously sophisticated and involved the most massive artillery and tank battles in the history of the world. Men died by the thousands—and were taken prisoner by the tens of thousands.

As the German and Italian prisoners poured in from battlefields—wounded, disoriented, in shock—their initial stages of processing consisted of little more than a thorough search for weapons. Few American soldiers at the front lines spoke German, and the verbs and nouns of the moment were spoken in shoves, "Milwaukee Deutsch," and the menacing movement of rifle muzzles. Even when German translators were available, they found that some prisoners—recruited from Poland, Hungary, Serbia, France, Finland, Belgium, Lithuania, Estonia, and the Ukraine—spoke little German themselves. The best thing to do at the moment, therefore, was to simply disarm the long lines of men and move them back out of the combat zone.

Roads to the front lines were perpetually choked with military traffic, as convoys of trucks moved endlessly, bringing fresh troops and ammunition to the battle zone. Since the trucks generally returned empty after unloading their supplies, theater commanders decided to utilize them to take prisoners back to the processing stations. Squabbles over the use of such vehicles for POW evacuation were not uncommon, and at first the prisoner convoys could expect jeers and catcalls from passing columns of men en route to the front. As the campaign moved across North Africa and the tide of battle appeared to be tipping in favor of the Allies, however, resentment against enemy prisoners nearly disappeared. The personal nature of the war had given way to an impersonal resignation that the war was simply a job that had to be done, and as the POWs began to lose their initial fear of mistreatment at the hands of their captors, both sides began to relax. In fact, interest in one another decreased to such a point that in mid-November, 1943, the American reader of *Collier's* magazine might have been astonished to see a photograph showing a long line of captured *Afrika Korps* soldiers marching toward a POW processing center—unguided and unguarded!

The Allied forces still had no idea how many prisoners they might be expected to process, and the hastily built compounds at Oran, Casablanca, and Marrakech were simply expanded to accommodate increased numbers. American Army officials in North Africa were first told by the War Department to prepare for 10,000 German and Italian POWs. Within months, the Provost Marshal General's Office estimated that the appearance of 40,000 POWs would not be unreasonable. Then the estimates rose to 60,000, and by the spring of 1944, the number of prisoners who had arrived in the United States alone surpassed 100,000. Frankly, no one knew where it all would end. At the reception and processing centers of North Africa in the autumn of 1943, prisoners continued to pour in from the front lines. Makeshift POW camps became villages, and villages increased to the size of small towns. As more captives arrived from the Sicilian and Italian campaigns, the prisoner compounds swelled to the bursting point. By the late spring of 1944, the Army found itself handling more German and Italian prisoners than there had been American soldiers in the entire pre-war U.S. Army.

If the capture and initial confinement of these captives seemed difficult, the next step was to be still more difficult. Reception centers were set up in the compounds, and the formal processing began. The prisoners were first run through a cursory medical examination, which would have been familiar to any of the thousands of American draftees and enlistees being trained in the United States. In fairness to the hard-pressed corpsmen, however, it must be noted that seriously wounded prisoners were immediately transferred to military hospitals where they received treatment identical to that received by any wounded American soldier.

Further down the processing line, the POWs were assigned serial numbers which they used throughout their internment. The numbers consisted of two components. The first component of the serial number designated the theater in which the prisoner had been captured. For example, the number 81 meant North Africa; 5 indicated the Western Defense Command; and 31 meant the European Theater. Directly following this number came a letter indicating the country in whose army the prisoner had served. A German soldier captured in North Africa would therefore carry the first component of 81G–; an Italian captured in Europe would have the designation of 31I–; an Austrian taken in Europe would be assigned 31A–, and so forth. The second component was the individual number, assigned consecutively, to the POW upon his capture. Thus, a veteran of Rommel's *Afrika Korps* captured in North Africa might have the serial number: 81G–5379.[6]

Thousands of prisoners, however, were transported to camps in the United States before a serial number could be assigned. This generally occurred when a sudden attack necessitated their swift removal from the area, or a home-bound American vessel became available unexpectedly. For those men processed in the United States, the system was somewhat different. The first component contained three symbols: the number of the Army Service Command—numbered 1 to 9—representing the military districts into which the United States was divided, "W" for War Department, and the first letter of the country for which the prisoner served. Thus, an incoming POW from North Africa who found himself being processed in Oklahoma or Texas was assigned the number 8WG–1234.[7] These numbers were of major importance since many prisoners had similar or identical names, or their names had been misspelled or incorrectly copied, Thus, the army of POWs, like armies anywhere, moved on serial numbers and forms.

And the forms came next. Each prisoner was required to fill out a three-page form (a variation of the Army's Basic Personnel Record),[8] which requested his personal and medical history, fingerprints, serial numbers, an inventory of personal effects, and information about his capture as noted on the tag still hanging from his tunic.[9] This form became his permanent record, and copies were forwarded to the International Red Cross and Swiss authorities so that the prisoner's family could be immediately informed about his fate. With the completion of these forms, he became an official prisoner of war. Considering the large numbers of enemy captives who were herded through these reception centers, often under chaotic conditions only hours or days after battles in which both sides had fought brutally and tenaciously, the process was remarkably smooth. Yet a number of glaring errors occurred regularly enough to indicate several problems which would plague the POW experience throughout the rest of the war.

The first major difficulty was a severe lack of interpreters and foreign language clerk-typists. Most of the military's competent German- and Italian-speaking personnel were quickly absorbed by military intelligence units and related segments of the war effort. They were used to interrogate high-ranking enemy officers, monitor enemy radio signals, and interpret and create propaganda. They were not easily released for the decidedly less important task of registering prisoners of war. As a result, the prisoners were sometimes able to take advantage of the language barrier and playfully ignore the commands or confuse the registration process. In more serious cases, prisoners with sufficient motivation and luck were able to change ranks or identities. One prisoner's photo, for example, would be placed on another's forms, while a third POW added his fingerprints, and so on. Important officers or prisoners with valuable intelligence information were theoretically able to slip through the registration net simply because the guards and clerk-typists were unable to penetrate the language smokescreen and, out of frustration, would wave the culprit through. The War Department understood the problem but was simply unable to improve the ratio of translators to prisoners until later in the war.[10]

Moreover, problems arising from the lack of interpreters did not end in North Africa. German-speaking personnel were even more scarce in the United States than overseas. Camp commanders found themselves in the difficult position of having to maintain their compounds, often containing as many as 8,000 or 10,000 prisoners, with the aid of a single translator. According to an investigation by the *New York Herald Tribune* on April 13, 1944, "Only one officer at Camp Breckenridge [Kentucky] speaks German, . . . a situation duplicated at 194 other POW camps." As a result, the local American POW authorities had to turn for help to the very people they were trying to control: the prisoners. The only two options available to camp commanders were either to rely on English-speaking prisoners, whether Nazis or anti-Nazis, or to simply forget about the prisoners and allow them to run themselves. Under these circumstances, the Army's reliance on English-speaking prisoners to run the POW camps was clearly the better choice, although the danger of heavy Nazi influence was a calculated risk which often backfired.

Another difficulty in the early stages of the POW program concerned the attitudes and the caliber of the American soldiers themselves. The average GI involved in the hauling or processing of POWs was one who, by lack of qualifications, was not needed elsewhere. Linguists were sent into intelligence units; combat engineers and demolition experts were utilized elsewhere; highly-prized code and communications men were sent to special units; administrators, supply officers, snipers, priests, mechanics and drivers, weapons experts and armorers, doctors and corpsmen: each of them had a special usefulness to the military. Everybody of value to the war effort had a place, though as any veteran can testify, the Army's evaluation of one's specialty and potential skills seldom coincided with one's own.

Those soldiers with few qualifications of value to the war effort were assigned to low-priority areas in the backwater of the war, one such area being the POW program. And most of them knew it. Consequently, the American soldier in the POW program generally viewed his role as that of custodian, far from the "guts and glory" of the front lines. Often torn by conflicting emotions, those involved in the processing of prisoners were understandably grateful for the safety of serving in an area removed from the danger and discomfort of the front, yet they often regretted not fulfilling the heroic expectations of their youth. Even when they approached their task with enthusiasm and efficiency, they found themselves restricted by a vague, chivalrous, and outdated code of regulations: the Geneva Convention written in 1929, which even the War Department had difficulty sorting out.

As a result, the average American soldier, more often than not, viewed the prisoners of war as a source of war souvenirs: medals, decorations, daggers, and pistols. These souvenirs became proof of their close contact with the enemy, sought-after trophies for the folks back home, and highly-prized items for sale to new recruits. The incoming prisoners were searched repeatedly for any piece of Nazi equipment which might have escaped the notice of the previous searchers. Luger and Walther pistols, of course, were instantly snatched by their triumphant new owners, as were ceremonial SS daggers. Even the wounded were fair game. German Sergeant Reinhold Pabel, wounded in the chest at the Volturno River during the Italian campaign, vividly recalled that "as soon as the stretcher had been placed on the floor, a bunch of souvenir hunters ripped some of my decorations off my blouse. After they had done so, they asked me if I had any objections. I kept my mouth shut." Weeks later, after a long and difficult boxcar journey across North Africa, "they dumped us into another makeshift camp near

Long lines of newly captured German prisoners move to the collection points in the rear areas. *(U.S. Army Photo)*

The incoming prisoners move past a rudimentary checkpoint before further evacuation to the rear. *(U.S. Army Photo)*

The prisoners are thoroughly searched for contraband, military information, and sometimes just souvenirs. *(U.S. Army Photo)*

These German prisoners turned out to be Soviet Georgians and Mongolians. *(U.S. Army Photo)*

Some 10,000 German prisoners remain in this enclosure until ocean transports become available to take them to England or the United States. *(U.S. Army Photo)*

Whether processed in the United States or overseas, the prisoners were first held in large holding pens at a Port of Embarkation . . . *(U.S. Army Photo)*

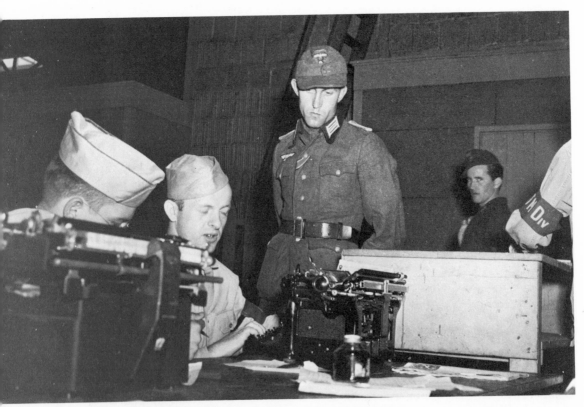

Their records were completed. . . . *(U.S. Army Photo)*

They were fingerprinted. . . . *(U.S. Army Photo)*

Their belongings disinfected with DDT. . . . *(U.S. Army Photo)*

11

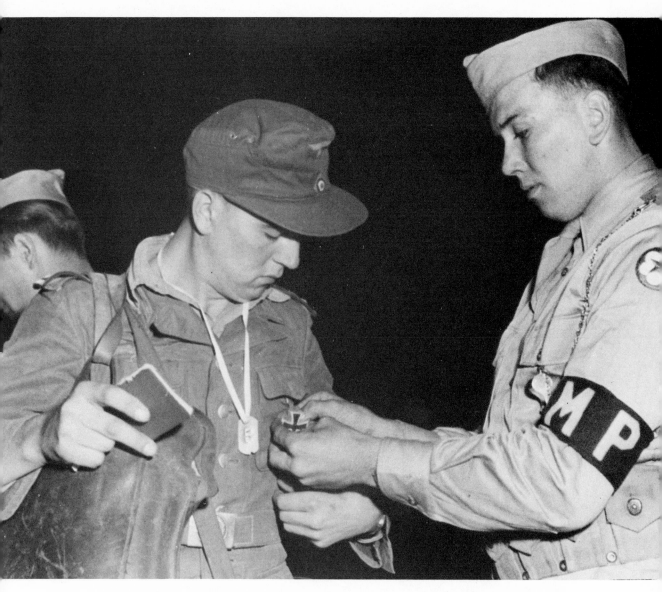

This German prisoner learned too late that he should have kept his Iron Cross out of sight. *(U.S. Army Photo)*

Oran . . . [and almost immediately] . . . in a businesslike manner, they rifled our pockets for personal effects. In the afternoon, I got the shock of my life when we were searched all over again. . . ." [11] Even worse than being stripped of one's medals and service ribbons, bristles a former German paratrooper and POW, Henry Kemper, was the fact that "these acts of thievery were committed in full view of their American officers." [12]

Pistols and medals were one thing; they were strictly military souvenirs and fair game regardless of which army represented the captives and which the captors. A more serious problem arose when guards confiscated the prisoners' documents, which might have been instrumental in their processing. Most important among the papers, which were sometimes grappled from the prisoners, was the *Soldbuch*. The *Soldbuch*, a contraction of the German "soldier's book," was a 15-page booklet carried by every German enlisted man and officer, infantry or air force. In effect, these booklets were condensed Basic Personnel Files and contained not only such personal data as weight, height, birthdate, birthplace, parental information, vaccinations, and eye examinations, but also information about military training, units, transfers, duties, and promotions. The inside cover of the *Soldbuch* carried a photograph of the owner and his signature. More than an aid in the registration of the prisoners, these booklets often contained helpful information for interrogators and intelligence analysts; at the very least, these documents could prevent a high-ranking prisoner or potentially dangerous captive from intentionally slipping undetected through the registration net. The random confiscation of documents and of *Soldbuchs* was not in any way condoned by the American authorities. Military documents of any nature came under the control of the intelligence services and were sacrosanct. The *Soldbuchs*, in particular, were to be confiscated only by interrogators and used for screenings, after which the documents were sealed in envelopes and passed from commanding officer to commanding officer to accompany the prisoners as they were shipped to their final camps. In the end, however, the random confiscation of these booklets by souvenir-hungry American guards needlessly made the War Department's efforts more difficult and led to registration problems whose results would continue to crop up even in the American camps.

The final and most important problem which emerged during the early stage of prisoner processing was America's failure to plumb the degree and intensity of the prisoners' ideological feelings and to segregate those prisoners whose attachment to Nazism was transitory and opportunistic from those whose beliefs were deep-seated and unalterable. Instead, only the most superficial division of enemy personnel took place: Army personnel were separated from air force, and officers from enlisted men. Nazis were imprisoned with anti-Nazis from this early stage of processing as well as throughout the war, seriously hampering all future experiments to introduce "democratic reeducation" into the POW camps. During the first several days after capture, the prisoner—any prisoner—exhibits a universal disorientation which must be immediately exploited by his captors for military information or for purposes of future reeducation. Once he is allowed to regain his psychological bearings, the initial advantage is lost. If, in addition, the now stable POW is able to dominate his less ideological comrades (in this case, anti-Nazis), any future efforts to alter his ideological makeup would be extremely difficult. American authorities took only the most visibly rabid Nazis, a total of only 4,500 by 1945, and interned them at Alva, Oklahoma, while the most visibly dedicated anti-Nazis, 3,300 in number, were shipped to Fort Devens, Massachusetts and Camp Campbell, Kentucky. Although a program was later initiated to "democratize" the hundreds of thousands of prisoners in American camps, the best opportunity to segregate the various shades of political ideology had passed, and totalitarian reinforcement was allowed to take place.

It would, at this point, be well worth examining the British model of prisoner of war care for several reasons. However strained the relationship, Britain was still America's closest wartime ally and acted as the transfer agent for the thousands of POWs captured in North Africa and shipped to the United States. More importantly, England had been in the war two years longer than the United States and had established a pattern of prisoner care which Washington might well have considered.

All prisoners coming to British custody, for example, were immediately registered at collecting points in North Africa before being passed on to holding camps prior to shipment to Britain. All ranks were issued strict orders regarding the treatment of POWs, and while every British soldier was instructed to remember that the Geneva Convention was of paramount importance, "it may be necessary to adopt special measures." The tying of hands or feet of prisoners under combat conditions, for example, was considered an "operational necessity" if it was required to protect British troops, prevent the destruction of important intelligence papers, or to protect the captives themselves from random battle casualty.[13] Of critical importance, the regulations noted, "there should be no fraternization with a prisoner of war." [14] The result produced a more disciplined and, interestingly, more respectful prisoner of war community than that held by the American authorities,

The British system of registering incoming prisoners was based on completion of an Army Form W 3000, not unlike the American military's Basic Personnel File, and copies of the registration forms were forwarded by air to a Central Prisoner of War Information Bureau in London to the Swiss and Spanish Consuls and the International Red Cross Committee. As with other facets of Allied prisoner of war regulations, London's meticulous care to properly and swiftly inform the responsible international agencies of each prisoner's capture was designed to insure similar treatment by the enemy toward British captives. It was not surprising, therefore, that Britain became deeply concerned with Washington's delay in forwarding the AFW 3000 forms of the many thousands of British-captured German prisoners which had been turned over, by the agreement of 1942, to American custody. American-owned POWs, transshipped from Tunisia to the United States on November 24, 1943, for example, were diverted to Canada before they had completed their AFW 3000 forms, which, in turn, led to an official protest to London by the Swiss. The horrified British authorities immediately exchanged a number of priority telegrams with their ambassador in Washington to inform the American Government that such negligence "would provide the German Government with a pretext for penalizing British POWs in their hands."[15] London was also annoyed with Washington's failure to continue the British process of segregating prisoners, which not only separated Nazis from non-Nazis but distinguished between German nationals and, hopefully, the more easily salvageable Austrians. Once turned over to the American military for shipping and housing, however, the prisoners were reunited and remained together throughout the war.[16]

In October and November of 1943, however, these problems were of little interest to either the prisoners or the American authorities. The registration of the prisoners was continuing as smoothly as could be expected, and all the participants had reason to be pleased with their experiences.

The Atlantic Crossing

The next step was the trip to the United States. From collection areas across North Africa, the newly registered prisoners were funnelled by the trainloads toward embarkation points at Casablanca, Morocco, and Oran, Algeria. Here they remained in reception centers, reading books donated by the American, International, or German Red Cross, writing letters home, or simply pacing about the camp grounds. The length of their wait, of course, depended on the availability of shipping to the United States, usually a returning Liberty ship or an empty ocean vessel. When a returning ship finally appeared, the embarkation process shifted quickly into high gear in order to move the milling prisoners out of the area and link up with other ships forming convoys across the Atlantic.[17]

Authority on board ship was maintained by American military police, although the day-to-day discipline was enforced by the German officers and NCOs, who were soberingly tough on their own men. The slightest infraction of rules resulted in a severe dressing down or confinement to quarters on bread and water. It was as if the German officers were reasserting themselves after a prolonged period of separation, drawing the German army together again. There was certainly no question in anyone's mind that all their military instincts remained intact. Second Lieutenant Yvonne E. Humphrey, an Army nurse assigned to care for the POWs on one such transatlantic convoy, noted that their idea of discipline was indeed extreme. "If a soldier failed to salute a superior with sufficient snap he would be severely reprimanded or perhaps confined to quarters. One young German, who violated the wartime regulation by throwing something overboard—in this case, nothing more instructive to the enemy than apple peelings—was instantly thrown into solitary confinement on bread and water for three days. . . . Their officers came close to arrogance. You felt rather than saw the great loathing inside them for all things democratic and American." [18] The most fanatically political among them fully expected to see the major cities of the United States in ruins, bombed and devastated by the *Luftwaffe*, and often exhibited a sort of perverse pleasure in believing that they would be the men who would be in America to greet the invading German armies. On the other hand, the enlisted German personnel remained cheerful and cooperative, accepting the tasks assigned to them by their officers with enthusiasm. They worked in the galley, cleaned the ward rooms, and painted everything which did not appear to be alive.

Regardless of their attitudes, however, they were treated with courtesy and even some warmth by the American guards. They were fed as well as their captors and supplied with cigarettes, writing paper, and a selection of books to occupy their trip. When the facilities on the prisoners' ships were particularly plush, the men received correspondingly better treatment. One such transatlantic crossing, described in every luxuriant detail by the *Washington Daily News* on June 10, 1943, noted with some outrage that the Germans slept in cabins (as opposed to the cramped conditions of the cargo holds), dined on ice cream and stewed plums, played shuffleboard on deck, and staged boxing and wrestling exhibitions for the American wounded traveling on board. "An American soldier, just about recovered from his wounds," lamented the *Daily News,* "looked down at the empty swimming pool and said wistfully: 'Gee, I wish the prisoners would ask for some water in the pool, so we can all have a swim.' "

One tradition remained unchanged from the processing stage in North Africa, however, and Nurse Humphrey recounts the continuation of what was becoming an apparently endless occurrence. "Many of our boys were eager to acquire some of the buttons, buckles, and insignias of the German officers to take home as trophies. The Germans accepted this idea with tolerant amusement and a little scorn." [19] It appears that the further the prisoners were from the front lines, the more vociferous the souvenir hunters. American soldiers all along the route from processing center to POW camp were painfully aware that their contact with the POWs was as close to the war as they would probably get, and the further back along the line, the more frustrated, and hence, the more anxious to garner some physical evidence of their participation.

The Atlantic crossing of the POW convoys was generally uneventful. With the exception of very rare probes by enemy fighters and submarines, the journeys became routine, and throughout the war not one ship carrying prisoners was sunk by the enemy. The most difficult problem with which the POWs had to contend was frequent seasickness and inadequate exercise and ventilation, a condition familiar to any American soldier transported overseas. Unlike American GIs, who received little sympathy from their hard-bitten noncoms for their plight, however, the POWs were able to complain loudly and effectively to the Swiss Legation, which protected German interests. In any case, the six-week journey from the North African collection areas ended at one of the two American Ports of Embarkation—Camp Shanks, New York, or Norfolk, Virginia—from which the next and last stage of the journey would take place.

As long as the prisoner-of-war program was operated solely by the Army, as it generally was up to this point, confusion was kept to a minimum. But with the appearance of the POWs in the United States, various new agencies were now drawn into the program to pursue their separate areas of jurisdiction and control. Seldom would such fragmentation be more evident than in the early alignment of departments and divisions involved in receiving and transporting these arriving German and Italian prisoners. The Quartermaster's Office, for example, was responsible for collecting, storing, and eventually returning the prisoners' personal possessions as well as disinfecting their clothing upon their arrival stateside. The commanding general of the Port of Embarkation, for his part, was responsible for deciding which ships would be unloaded in what order and whether the unloading should be accomplished by ferrying the men in from the ship or docking it directly at the pier. The Military Police, meanwhile, had the responsibility for interpreting orders to the disoriented herds of POWs, escorting them through the bureaucratic maze, and guarding them en route to their camps. The Chief of Transportation and railroad officials, of course, had to be kept informed about the arriving prisoners, the number of men, the number of railroad cars required, security precautions, and prisoner destinations. To complicate matters still further, the intelligence community, via the Director of the Intelligence Division of the Port of Embarkation, maintained a watchful eye over the list of incoming prisoners, detaining and interrogating those POWs whose value had been somehow overlooked during their first screenings and reporting all pertinent information to the Security Division of the Office of Chief of Transportation.[20] Such information was vital if proper security was to be maintained. Each new shipment of prisoners, through the early months of the spring of 1943, led to a series of hectic agency meetings as liaison officers tried to coordinate the separate responsibilities of each group.

It is worth mentioning that Britain, unlike the United States, systematically interrogated each arriving batch of prisoners regardless of their rank or suspected information. The resulting system centered in a collection of nine interrogation depots in England. The most famous was the "London Cage," a large house on the corner of Kensington Park Gardens and Bayswater Road, where teams of the Prisoner of War Interrogation Section (PWIS), mostly British Army sergeants of German-Jewish stock who spoke fluent German and understood the prisoners' mentality, extracted crucial information from the most hardened U-boat captains, SS officers, and *Luftwaffe* leaders with remarkable success. According to Colonel A. P. Scotland, Commandant of the London Cage, information was gained with the least amount of physical degradation by an agent posing as a prisoner from the same town or by applying psychological pressure.

> Playing on the German prisoners' fear of the Russians was another technique said to be successful. At the London Cage a Russian-speaking interpreter, wearing a KGB uniform, would sit in on the interrogation of recalcitrant prisoners. And if his presence failed to frighten the prisoner, the ostentatious stamping of the prisoner's file with "NR" usually did. To the prisoner's query as to what "NR" meant the reply was "Nach Russland" (to Russia).[21]

The fear of being shipped to Russia was evidently enough to break down the prisoner's resistance rapidly. No such blanket interrogations occurred when the prisoners arrived in the United States. Instead, the prisoners were placed aboard trains to begin their journeys to the camps.

The Journey to Prison Camps

The experiences shared by the overwhelming majority of POWs are best described by Reinhold Pabel, a chronicler of these pre-camp experiences. The date is January 2, 1944, and the *Empress of Scotland* had just finished unloading its cargo of prisoners.

> And so we went ashore at Norfolk, Va., in the morning hours. After going through the customary delousing process we marched to the railroad station. There were immediate shouts of "Man, oh, man!" and "How about that?" when we followed orders to board the coaches of a waiting train. Most of us had always been transported in boxcars during the military service. These modern upholstered coaches were a pleasant surprise to everyone. And when the colored porter came through with coffee and sandwiches and politely offered them to us as though we were human beings, most of us forgot . . . those anti-American feelings that we had accumulated. . . .
>
> The guards at each end of the coaches had strict orders not to take chances with us. Whenever someone had to go to the washroom he was expected to raise his hand like a schoolboy in class so the guard could . . . accompany him safely to the head of the car. . . . It all looked very amusing to me and I kept thinking what a beautiful confusion one could create by conspiring with a number of the boys in the coach to raise their hands simultaneously. What would the guards have done?
>
> No matter how divided we prisoners might have been in our opinion of America, we were nearly all quite curious to find out . . . what the United States would really be like. . . .
>
> Enroute through Virginia and Kentucky we pressed our noses against the windowpanes to take in the sights. The first impression we had was the abundance of automobiles everywhere. . . [22]

The transportation of prisoners to their new homes, despite the bureaucratic difficulties behind the scenes, was a successful and most often startling and educational experience for those unfamiliar with the breadth and beauty of the country.

A number of prisoners, however, were not pleased. In the many weeks since their capture, the prisoners, reinforced by the return to strict military discipline at the hands of their own officers, began to reorient themselves to their new situation. Earlier anxieties about the intentions of their captors,

Several thousand German prisoners en route to their new camps in the United States come up on deck for a few hours of sunshine and ocean air. *(U.S. Army Photo)*

German prisoners under heavy guard aboard a British vessel. *(Imperial War Museum)*

First look at America, as German prisoners move down the gangplank at the North River Terminal, New York. *(U.S. Army Photo)*

An American interpreter instructs a group of incoming POW officers about their rights and responsibilities under the Geneva Convention. *(U.S. Army Photo)*

The German prisoners climb into the trains waiting to take them to their permanent camps. *(U.S. Army Photo)*

During the long trips across country, the prisoners were often skeptical about the lack of bomb damage which their propaganda had alleged; and always impressed at the size and beauty of the U.S. *(U.S. Army Photo)*

about their destinations and personal safety, were rapidly fading only to be replaced by the prisoners' determination to make the best of a bad situation and to exploit the weaknesses of their captors wherever possible. Complaints to the Swiss authorities increased. They referred to everything from discomfort at being forced to sleep in a sitting position during the trip to the intrusion of the porters bringing coffee. Others grumbled that their train routes were contrived to confuse them or avoid the devastated areas which the *Luftwaffe* must surely have created. One complaint of this type, registered by a Hans Galhard, as soon as he arrived at his new home at Camp Trinidad, Colorado, described the "brutalizing" train ride in the following manner: "The journey lasted about one hundred hours. In that time we were hardly allowed to move. The consequences were indigestion and blood pressure of the severest type. And then the watch! In each coach were two men with automatic pistols and two men armed with clubs. They transported us like the lowest criminals about which they seem to have plenty of experience in this country." [23]

One former prisoner, Henry Kemper, went so far as to charge the American authorities with committing atrocities against the transported POWs. "We were put into box cars on the train trip from New York to Arkansas 60 to 100 men per car. It was a long and terrible ride. All we had to eat was orange jam, which they deliberately gave us to make us sick. The Americans knew what effects the orange jam had on our empty stomachs. They had previous experience at this. Everybody had diarrhea. A few of the older men died—how many I don't know—I just saw them throw the dead bodies off the train." [24] Such charges are extremely rare, however, and unsubstantiated. While it is certainly possible that during the many hundreds of wartime POW train rides across the United States some prisoners experienced discomfort; that such discomfort was intentional governmental policy is ludicrous.

To prevent this minority of prisoners from exploiting their available rights, guards and military police were warned against the "insidious danger of soft, sticky, sentiment, or maudlin, marshmallow friendliness." [25] Those Americans who dealt with the POWs were cautioned to remember that "the good-looking youth . . . with such charm, was the same murderous maniac who fashioned the booby trap that blew American soldiers into bloody bits; the same Hitler youth who had kicked in a peasant's face in the name of the Fuehrer." The model guard, they were reminded, believed that "You don't have to be cruel to these guys, but you have to show them they're not going to get away with anything. If you start feeling sorry for them and soften up, they take advantage of you right away. We don't have to be mean, but we're going to have to be plenty hard-boiled!" [26] With the exception of the troublesome minority of complaining prisoners, however, and an accidental train wreck in Virginia on September 16, 1943,[27] the shipment of incoming POWs to their camps was quite routine.

Camp Location and Construction

Prisoners were now pouring into the United States by the thousands as the Allies broke the back of Rommel's *Afrika Korps* in November, 1943, and began the campaigns across Sicily and up the Italian boot. Despite the continual difficulties resulting from a lack of qualified linguists and from the War Department's initial failure to segregate the anti-Nazis from the Nazis, the prisoner internment process was beginning to operate with a well-oiled efficiency. Washington was wisely learning from the experiences of the past year and continually refined the procedures involved in moving captured prisoners from the battlefields, through the various bureaucratic stages, to their camps in the United States.

There had been, in fact, little preparation for the temporarary housing of prisoners-of-war during the first year of the war. The nation's primary consideration, of course, was that of national defense, and the question of POWs was simply something that would have to take care of itself. The problem could no longer be put off, however, not with thousands of men coming in from the battlefields of North Africa, and the Provost Marshal General's Office was galvanized into action. On September 15, 1942, the Provost Marshal General submitted a program of camp construction to the Joint Chiefs of Staff to care for the first 50,000 POWs who were then due to arrive via the British. Immediate needs, it was decided, would be filled by using every abandoned Civilian Conservation Corps camp built during the Depression to provide rural employment for an army of unemployed young men as well as unused sections of regular military bases, fairgrounds, auditoriums, and, if necessary, tent cities. Even the famed Santa Anita racetrack was turned into a POW holding area.[28] The CCC camps were perfect for housing POWs. They were built as barracks constructed by necessity near rural work projects, and, most important, empty and available. Moreover, they were located mainly in the South and Southwest, far from the critical war industries of the Midwest and the Eastern seaboard. In rural areas they could be better contained and guarded, and by placing the majority of POW camps in the lesser populated sections of the country, in an area commanded by the Fourth, Seventh, and Eighth Service Commands (encompassing 18 states, from Arkansas and Alabama, across Georgia, Mississippi, Louisiana, to Wyoming, Nebraska, Oklahoma, Colorado, and

Texas), officials minimized the terrifying specter of escaped Nazis sabotaging and raping their way across the United States.

On September 15, 1942, the War Department also opened a number of military posts, which had some extra space, to contain prisoners. These included Camp Forrest, Tennessee (capacity for 3,000 prisoners); Camp Clark, Missouri (3,000); Fort Bliss, Texas (1,350); Fort Bragg, North Carolina (140); Fort Devens, Massachusetts (1,000); Fort Meade, Maryland (1,680); Fort Oglethorpe, Georgia (948); Camp McCoy, Wisconsin (100); Fort Sam Houston, Texas (1,000); Camp Shelby, Mississippi (1,200); and Fort Sill, Oklahoma (700).

Such emergency measures, it was estimated, could satisfy about 75 percent of the immediate needs. In an effort to make up the difference for the estimated 144,000 POWs whose appearance was already assured, the Provost Marshal General called for a massive $50 million construction program to build the necessary camps.[29] By the end of 1942, Army Service Forces commanders were being approached to sell vacant land to the government and the Corps of Engineers began to survey possible locations.

In the location of campsites and their construction, the War Department, Corps of Engineers, Provost Marshal General's Office, and Army commanders were guided by a number of principles. First and foremost was the literal interpretation of the Geneva Convention of 1929. Unlike England, for example, which made adjustments in the guidelines when the situation demanded, or the Soviet Union, which made absolutely no pretense of following any international guidelines, the United States followed the Geneva Convention to the letter. Prisoner-of-war camps, for example, had to be constructed to standards of an American camp. The Geneva Convention was taken so seriously that in camps which did not have enough barracks space to house both the prisoners and the guards, compelling the POWs to live in tents temporarily, the guards were ordered by the camp commanders to live in tents as well, while the barracks remained empty![30]

Security was the most pressing concern with which the War Department had to contend. Washington was understandably sensitive—no less than the residents of those towns whose areas were being considered for future campsites—to the placement of large numbers of hardened Axis captives across the country. Regulations stipulated, therefore, that all POW camps should be as isolated and as heavily guarded as possible. Emergency wartime measures further directed that the camps could not be located within a blackout area extending about 170 miles inland from both coasts, a 150-mile-wide "zone sanitaire" along the Canadian and Mexican borders, or near shipyards, munitions plants, or vital industries. As a result, two-thirds of the base camps (containing approximately three-fourths of the prisoners) would be located in the south and southwest regions of the country; one-fifth of the base camps (containing one-eighth of the POWs) would be in the middle west; and the remaining camps, one-sixth of the total (containing a tenth of the total number of prisoners), would be scattered throughout the east and west regions of the United States.[31] By July of 1944, there were 98 such base camps across the United States. The total reached 155 by the end of the war.

The Corps of Engineers considered the ideal base campsite to be an area of approximately 350 acres, five miles from a railroad. In the interest of seclusion, the camp could not be located less than 500 feet from any important boundary or public thoroughfare.

> In addition to the essential provision of an adequate water supply and electric power, it was important for reasons of security that portions of a site to be included within compounds should be of an even terrain without abrupt breaks in contour but with a moderate overall slope for surface drainage . . . all trees, shrubs, and tall grasses must be removed between compound buildings and perimeter patrol road to effect adequate security. . . .[32]

New camps were constructed in accordance with a standard layout plan and were designed to contain between 2,000 and 4,000 prisoners. The camp was divided into four main compounds of approximately 500 to 750 men each, and each compound, in turn, consisted of four barracks with about 150 men each as well as a mess hall, workshop, canteen, infirmary, administrative building, and recreation hall. The barracks were designed for utility rather than comfort. They were 20 feet by 100 feet and consisted of a concrete slab floor and a cheaply-built 2' × 4' structure covered by tar paper or corrugated tin. Inside were rows of cots and footlockers and a potbellied stove in the center aisle. Walkways and gravel roads ran throughout the camp, and a wide, flat area, beyond the compound buildings, served as a combination inspection ground, processing center, and soccer field. The camp at large housed a hospital, chapel, and showers and laundry tubs with unlimited hot and cold running water. The addition of a post office, a warehouse, and utility area completed the standard layout of the prisoner of war camp. The only differences between these camps and normal Army training centers, in fact, were the watch towers with auxiliary power searchlights, the two chain-link fences—ten feet high and eight feet apart, which surrounded the entire camp—and the single chain-link fence which isolated each individual compound. Indeed, many Americans felt that the camps were too good for the prisoners, and local communities often grumblingly referred to the POW camp outside of town as "The Fritz Ritz."

A temporary prisoner of war camp at Fort Sam Houston, Texas. *(U.S. Army Photo)*

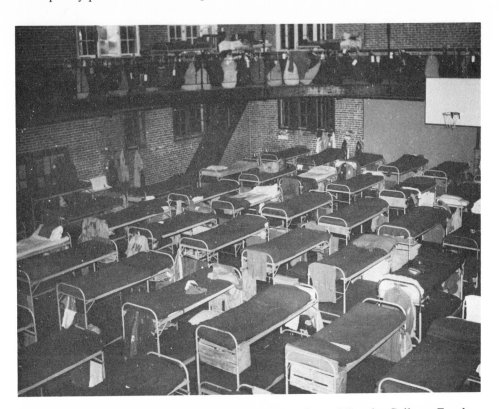

This temporary camp was established in the gymnasium of Eureka College, Eureka, Illinois. *(U.S. Army Photo)*

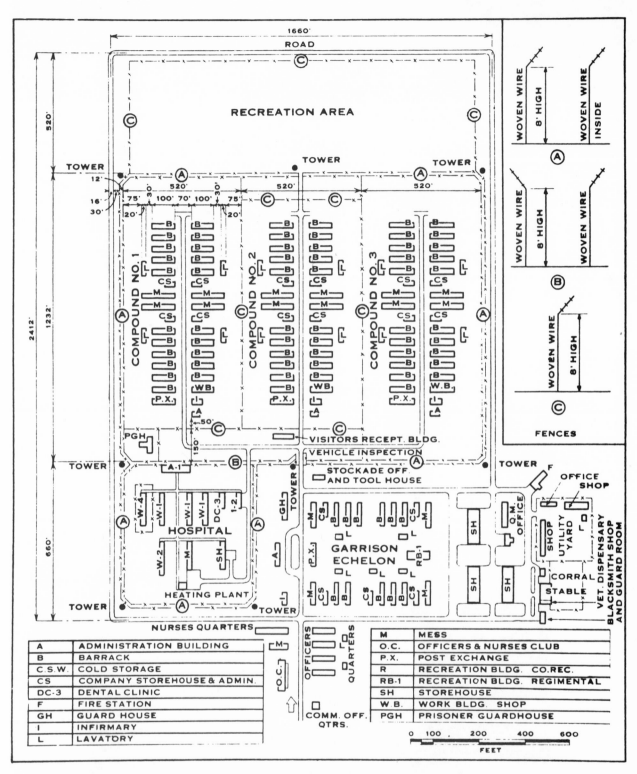

Standard layout for a camp of 5,000 POWs. (*The Military Engineer*)

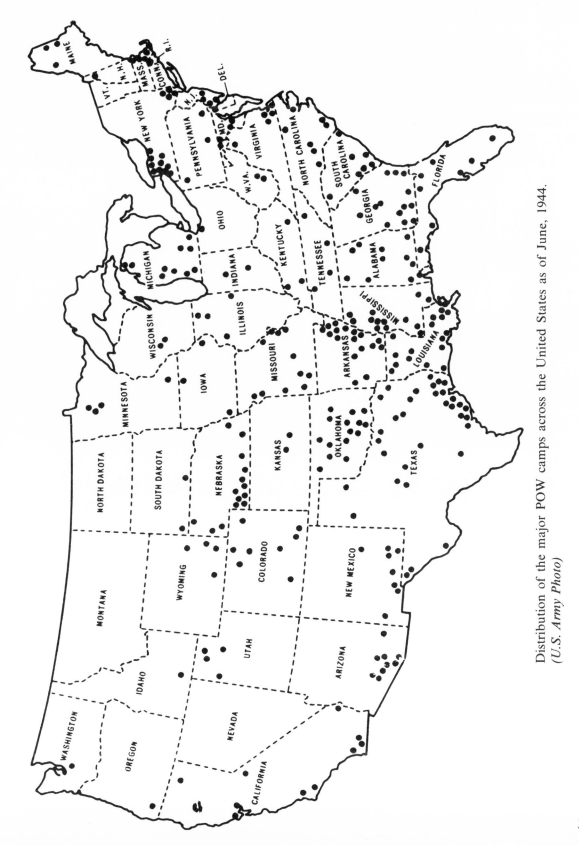

Distribution of the major POW camps across the United States as of June, 1944. (*U.S. Army Photo*)

31

PRISONER OF WAR BASE CAMP ORGANIZATION CHART AND STATEMENT OF FUNCTIONS

PRISONER OF WAR BASE CAMP ORGANIZATION CHART

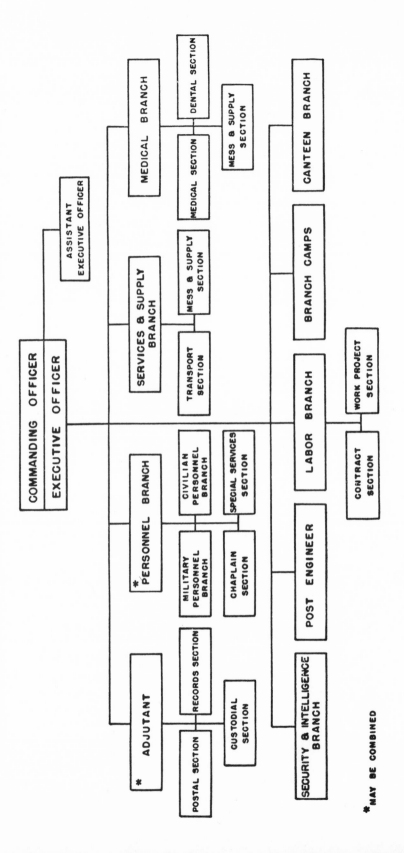

*MAY BE COMBINED

(U.S. Army Photo)

Unlike the American system where the campsites were chosen by representatives of the Provost Marshal General's Office and the Corps of Engineers, the British War Office polled each of England's seven military commands—EASTCO, NORCO, SOUTCO, SCOTCO, WESTCO, SECO and USTED—for their advice, given certain restrictions, on the location of camps within their commands. The camps were much smaller than their American counterparts, generally none larger than 500 prisoners, and the satellite hostels, a maximum of three attached to each camp, contained between 50 to 70 POWs. A large number of prisoners were billeted on farms or contracted to small businesses, and the farmer or employer was required to provide suitable lodging and facilities which complied with the standards of the Geneva Convention. The camps were smoothly run according to a remarkably complete 50-page government manual, *Orders For Prisoner of War Camps in the United Kingdom*, and while the POW community was considerably smaller than that held by the United States, it was remarkably disciplined and civilized.[33]

In both the United States and Britain, German officers and enlisted men were generally maintained in different camps, and barracks for the former were constructed to provide at least 120 square feet of living space per man, while those for enlisted men were built to provide only 40 square feet per man. Moreover, officers were allowed accommodations for their enlisted orderlies and aides-de-camp. In those prison camps which contained both officers and enlisted men, the prisoners were segregated into separate commands as directed by the Geneva Convention, although the PMGO was sensitive to the enlisted prisoner's need to retain his military chain of command not only because the Geneva Convention required it but as the most logical channel through which the American authorities could maintain control. As a result, the War Department stipulated that every group of about 3,000 prisoners would have direct access to a hierarchy of about 32 of their own officers. With some variations in camp size and structure, most of America's 155 main prisoner of war camps looked remarkably similar.

There was, however, an exception. One large compound at Camp Clinton, Mississippi, and several others at different installations were used to house the nearly 40 German generals and 3 admirals who were held in the United States during the war, and their rank and influence demanded special attention. A detailed memorandum from the Special War Problems Division of the Department of State advised camp commanders in contact with such high-ranking captives to remember that a German general's status and prestige in Germany far exceeded that of an American general in this country; it noted the political influence which men such as von Hindenburg, von Ludendorff, von Seeckt, and others had in directing the course of German affairs. "Sometime after the end of hostilities," the memo cautioned, "the German generals will be repatriated . . . and several or all of them are likely to exercise considerable influence on Germany's life regardless of the type of German Government which then may be in existence." It would therefore be to the interest of the United States that "there should be among the returned German prisoner of war officers a strong contingent of generals who have strong and favorable impressions of *this* country to counter the effects of the propaganda which we assumed was being used on the equal number of German generals in Russian captivity, even if, perhaps, it should not be possible to make all of them 'friendly' toward the United States." Commanders were instructed, therefore, to take particular care in dealing with such prisoners, treating them with the deference due their positions, actual and potential. Educational material and films by the Office of War Information were to be made available to these prisoners, and to emphasize the enormous economic strength and industrial power of the American war effort, they were to be taken on tours of shipyards or major ordnance depots. Their itineraries were also to include trips to cultural areas, "e.g., Mt. Vernon or Williamsburg, a university, a religious institution, a modern American high school, et cetera, which are distinctly 'American.' "

With regard to the administrative staff of such special camps, it was strongly recommended that the post of Camp Commander be assigned to a retired American general, preferably a graduate of West Point with a strong sense of military tradition and courtesy, and, if possible, "with service in various parts of the world . . . and with wide interests who can converse interestingly. An able executive officer assigned to his staff . . . a man possessing a special understanding for the educational opportunities in the generals' compound . . . a man with tact, consideration, and insight . . . could take care of the bulk of the work connected with the other aspects of the prisoner of war camp." The few guards necessary were to be unmatched in character and appearance; the camp educational officer was to serve as the interpreter; and, in accordance with any general's specific request, a prisoner of war officer was to be assigned to their compound to teach them the English language systematically. German POW priests and ministers for the camp "should be selected with special care, keeping in mind the fact that religious guidance by its very nature is anti-Nazi," a rather uninformed view of German church history in light of the ardent religious support for Hitler's National Socialist regime. In what was an additional departure from the normal POW camp program, each general was to be given a radio of his own "in order that no possible extremist among them . . . may keep any one of them from listening to American news broadcasts of his personal choice." [34]

The most representative of these generals' camps (in actuality, one compound at the large POW installation of Camp Clinton, Mississippi) contained ten German generals, including one four-star, two three-star, and three two-star generals: such luminaries as General Ludwig Cruewell, General Gustav von Vaerst, General Gotthard Frantz, General Karl Buelowins, General Willibald Borowietz, and the prize of the North African campaign, General Jürgen von Arnim. The total capacity of the compound was 63 officers, physicians, and adjutants; it consisted of a number of wooden houses under spreading old trees scattered over a large area to allow the inhabitants the feeling of privacy and seclusion. POW gardeners helped maintain the various flower and vegetable gardens, and nearly each officer had a pet of some variety. The houses of the generals were each equipped with a new refrigerator. A large prison library was available, and the generals were allowed to attend soccer games, shows, and concerts provided by the lower ranked German prisoners of war at the other end of their camp.

On the other hand, most of the men were middle-aged, some ill or wounded, and like prisoners anywhere longed to return to their families. They baked in summer and froze in winter. Moreover, they were sharply divided into two groups. Those captured early were known as *"Afrikaner"*— veterans of the Afrika Korps who put up a clean fight, but lost early in the war. The *"Afrikaner"* were led by the hard-nosed von Arnim. The second group arrived after June 1943 from Italy or France and were called *"Französen;"* while they could gloat about being captured later, thus being braver, the *"Französen"* had few illusions about the outcome of the war. They had experienced the shortages and bombing raids, and many had participated in atrocities on the Eastern front. The *"Französen"*, whose spokesman was the amiable old von Neuling, were more cooperative; the *"Afrikaner"* were largely unrepentant Nazis. None of this mattered. Washington decided that the generals were of no value and, unlike the British who doted on their elite captives, the nearly forty generals were simply forgotten for the rest of the war.[35]

It quickly became evident to the War Department, however, that large base camps, whether for officers, enlisted men, or special camps for generals, would not be sufficient, and that an additional type of camp was necessary. A network of branch camps was created in order to house the more than 100,000 POWs who would work in private industry ranging from logging, meat packing, and mining to railroads, foundry work, and agriculture. The risks involved in frequent transportation had to be minimized. The existence of these branch camps was entirely dependent on the requirements of the designated work project, and they, therefore, were enormously diversified in capacity and layout. Over 500 such camps were constructed across the country, usually varying from 250 to 750 prisoners. They consisted of every variety of housing from mobile units and tentage, to enable the POW workers to follow harvests and road building, to municipal facilities and private homes [36] for those working as blacksmiths, mechanics, and upholsterers. Initially, the prisoners were utilized exclusively by the military, on or near military installations. Incoming POWs were tested and classified according to aptitudes, skills, and training, and with the exception of those prisoners who were visibly antagonistic or untrustworthy, the information was duly noted in their records. The Service Command in charge controlled the local disposition and use of the laborers, and as requisitions for workers with specific skills came in to the Personnel Control Unit of the individual Service Commands from other POW camps or military installations, the laborers were shipped out on temporary jobs. Prisoners with needed skills could be transferred anywhere and at any time that military or agricultural needs arose, and branch camps were made available or temporarily erected for just that purpose. The arrangement proved remarkably successful. Business leaders and chambers of commerce were invited to petition the War Department for the use of prisoner of war labor with a number of stipulations regarding their pay and safeguards as guaranteed by the Geneva Convention. Once the business community's initial fears of mass escapes or brutal murders by the captives proved to be absolutely groundless, petitions for POW labor began to flow into Service Command offices.

Camp Administration

Prisoner of war camps were classified as Class I installations, and, as such, were placed under the control of the commanding general of the Service Command in whose area the camp was located rather than under the direct control of the Provost Marshal General. This was a compromise decision which resulted from months of bureaucratic bickering. It placated the Service Command generals at the expense of establishing a command hierarchy. This decision ironically placed at a difficult distance the very office responsible for the POW program.

A noticeable complication in leadership and responsibility occurred when a prisoner of war camp happened to be located on a military post, as were a majority of them. The camp commander in charge of the POWs was directly responsible to the post commander, on whose installation his prisoners were held, and who, in turn, was responsible to the service commander. The problem was that the camp commander, on matters of the prisoners of war, could bypass the post commander and deal directly with the service command headquarters, which led to a dual administration and a host of command jealousies. Post commanders, after all, had not asked to have POW camps placed on their installations, and they often let their annoyance at the imposition be known. For their part, camp commanders did not ask to have their POWs thrust into the installation, but once so ordered, resented the competition and meddling into their affairs by the post commander. Both jealously guarded their avenues to the service commander and the War Department, as well as the day-to-day movement of authority in their own fiefdoms. As the war years progressed, most of these problems diminished, but such administrative friction remained a potential problem in all further prisoner of war programs.[37]

If the administrative picture appears complex at the upper echelons of the prisoner of war program, it was even more convoluted at the camp level. The camp commander delegated authority to, and received advice from, a host of administrative specialists who shared in the smooth daily efficiency of the camp. The camp commander's personal adjutant, for example, handled the writing of a camp history, routine administrative matters of the POW camp, correspondence, budgetary problems, and so forth; the Stockade Control Officer maintained discipline and was responsible for general maintenance; a Supply Officer was in charge of providing the tools, bedding, and clothing which are guaranteed by the Geneva Convention to be of the same high quality as that issued to the troops of the retaining power; a Medical Officer tended to the health needs of the prisoners; a Canteen Officer was charged by Article 12 of the same Convention with providing, at the local market price, food products and ordinary objects; a Work Projects Officer served as a liaison with agencies and private firms utilizing prisoner labor; and, finally, an Intelligence Officer was responsible for all facets of camp security, the censorship of prisoners' mail, and liaison with the Department of Justice.[38] The operating efficiencies of the many prisoner of war camps varied as widely as the relationships between the different members of the administrative teams.

Two additional military structures need to be considered at this point, one within the prisoner community and the other within the camp administration. According to the guarantees of Article 43 of the Geneva Convention, "in every place where there are prisoners of war, they shall be entitled to appoint agents entrusted with representing them directly with military authorities and protecting Powers." Thus, the prisoners were allowed, indeed requested, to elect a spokesman through whom the camp community could voice their grievances and requests. The camp spokesman was almost always the highest ranking prisoner available, although a number of camps bestowed only token leadership on these officers, choosing, instead, to put forward a more aggressive or ideologically appealing candidate. The responsibilities of these spokesmen were multifaceted. In addition to acting as the conduit between the prisoners and the camp commander, the spokesman was empowered by the Geneva Accords to represent the prisoners in meetings with members of the Swiss Legation and with such humanitarian agencies as the International Red Cross Committee and the YMCA. The American authorities were enormously sensitive to the periodic findings of the Swiss Legation and the IRCC, not only because their representatives were guaranteed unrestricted access to the POWs by Article 88 but because any findings by these agencies of American mistreatment of POWs would almost certainly bring immediate retaliation against American prisoners in German hands. In short, it was within the spokesman's control to influence the treatment of thousands of American captives in distant German camps— a power of no small significance—and although the spokesmen held their positions, theoretically, at the discretion of the camp commander, the leverage was often on the side of the prisoners. The prisoner-spokesman's influence moved in the other direction as well, for while they were theoretically forbidden to exercise any authority over their fellow prisoners, the camp commanders frequently used the POW leaders to maintain military discipline. The primary concern of every camp commander, above all else, was the assurance to his superiors and to local townspeople that quiet and orderly discipline prevailed. There could be no mass escapes or riots. If internal discipline could be maintained through prisoner leaders, who spoke the language and understood the Teutonic mind, and at the same time, reduce the number of required guards, all the better.

The final group in the camp hierarchy whose involvement in the prisoner of war program was of major importance was the guard contingent. When the POW program began in earnest in 1942, only 36 military escort companies (325 men per company) had been activated. But with the decision to accept 50,000 POWs from the British, the Provost Marshal General immediately requested the activation of an additional 32 MP companies to bring the ratio of guards to prisoners to one American guard company per every 1,000 prisoners (one guard for every three prisoners). It became the responsibility of each camp commander to determine the strength of the security his camp required based on its size, terrain, and proximity to populated centers. Some camps used watchdogs, others relied on the construction of numerous towers and continuous surveillance, and still others used periodic four-man patrols within the compounds.

This early preoccupation with security, however, especially in view of the surprisingly low escape rate and the pressing need for combat soldiers overseas, led both Major General Brehon Somervell, Commander of the Army Service Forces, and Brigadier General B.M. Bryan, Jr., Assistant Provost Marshal General, to voice their irritation over their overcautious camp commanders. "Our principal concern," Bryan declared, "should be that of weighing work done against reasonable risk; in other words, we should take a calculated risk." [39] Camp administrators in the Seventh Service Command, for instance, were told in no uncertain terms by the Assistant Provost Marshal to "let the prisoners do everything!" [40] This policy of "calculated risk" resulted in larger reductions of American guard personnel, the majority of whom were transferred to combat units for action in France. As predicted, the escape rate did not greatly increase. Some camps, during 1944 and 1945, increased the ratio of guards to POWs to as high as 1:10 and even 1:15 with little difficulty, while others experimented with random patrols, unsupervised work details, and, in limited cases involving higher-ranking POW officers, a parole system based on their word of honor. POWs in the United States, together with the processing centers and transportation networks, were completely supervised by less than 47,000 American personnel, a commendable ratio of 1:9.[41]

From the government's point of view, this was a beneficial trend. The War Department was caught in a crunch, after all, since it was absolutely essential to send every available man overseas so that the maximum pressure could be put on the enemy at the earliest moment. Every man who was physically qualified for combat duty was shipped out, and only those unfit for overseas duty were available to guard prisoners of war. The resulting problems, however, were twofold: the first, which will be discussed later in some detail, was that the American personnel were often replaced by "trustworthy German prisoners" who sometimes turned out to be far less than trustworthy. In a large number of camps, the most vocal element of the prisoner population—Nazis—generally stepped forward to fill the personnel void, leading to well-grounded public charges that the American POW program was, in fact, helping to foster Nazism in the camps. The second problem resulting from the withdrawal of qualified American personnel concerned the quality of the men who remained.

While it was deemed vital to American interests that the prisoners' contact with American personnel and way of life result in a positive attitude, the Army Service Forces were often compelled to use "superfluous"—or unqualified—personnel: those declared physically or psychologically unfit; recently retired officers and those destined for a terminal or "dead-end" appointment; combat veterans recycled home; and raw recruits. An American enlisted man, recently transferred from overseas combat, for example, who may have had friends wounded or killed, would certainly be less than cheerful toward his former enemies and therefore an obstacle to the smooth operation of the camp. The selection of new draftees, although not yet exposed to the emotional rigors of combat, might fare no better since they might be unduly sympathetic toward the prisoners or disgruntled at being placed in a low priority job as the exciting war years were passing them by. In nearly every POW camp administration, among the decreasing number of dedicated and conscientious American personnel, could be found those enlisted men with chronic psychological, legal, alcoholic, or physical difficulties. Guard morale was often so poor that the War Department was prompted to issue its commanders the following warning: "If U.S. personnel remark with any justification: 'We may as well be the ones wearing the 'PW,'' or 'We would be better off if we were the prisoners,' then the danger signal is flying." [42] The War Department could not have been deeply surprised, for example, when Private Clarence V. Bertucci, a guard at Fort Douglas, near Salina, Utah, reportedly went berserk and machine-gunned eight German POWs to death in their sleep. The Camp Commander, Colonel Arthur J. Ericsson, was perplexed at the guard's motives on that night of July 8, 1945—more than a month after the war in Europe had ended—though he admitted that Bertucci "had twice been tried before a summary court-martial . . . sentenced to hard labor . . . and had been in several Army hospitals in the last year."[43] The guards were further alienated from their prisoners by the language barrier. Indeed, at several camps in the Southwest, the English language was itself a scarcity, as personnel vacancies were filled by groups of National Guardsmen whose primary language was Spanish. Though it is important to emphasize that the quality of the guards varied greatly from camp to camp, even the official historian of the Army Service Forces, John Millett, was himself forced to admit that the prison camp commands "tended to be a dumping ground . . . for field grade officers who were found to be unsatisfactory." [44]

This deteriorating situation was finally brought to the public attention in late 1944 by the respected James H. Powers of the *Boston Globe*. His sharp criticism that the whole POW question involved a test of national will for which American personnel were "less than proficient," [45] astonishingly brought frank agreement from Bernard Gufler of the State Department Special War Problems Division. He agreed that "no effort seems to have been made to train either the officers or the guard personnel for their highly specialized work." [46] The prisoners, he continued, were often exposed to the most comic and least efficient side of their captors. While there is no accurate measure of these criticisms, the War Department, particularly the Provost Marshal General's Office, launched an immediate series of conferences for AFS service commands in 1943 and 1944 (which were of questionable value); a reference manual resulting from the conferences, which was far more successful; and three-week training programs beginning in October, 1944, at Fort Sam Houston, Texas, and Fort Custer, Michigan.

Because the British Government could afford to limit its camps to 500

POWs, their need for guards and administrative staff was understandably smaller. Standardized by a War Office directive of July 19, 1941, the maintenance of the three sizes of British POW camps was designated as follows: camps of 200 POWs were to have 27 administrative staff members and 70 guards (total 97); camps of 300 POWs had 27 and 86 (113); and the largest camps were allowed a staff of 28 men and 106 guards (134).[47] The most important point about camp personnel, however, was the War Office's particular care in the quality of the guards. In contrast to American policy, British prisoner of war personnel (provost sergeants, wardens, and guards) "will not suffer from more than one of the following disabilities: flat feet, varicose veins, stiffness of joints, defective eyesight, or low weight. . . . The object of these restrictions is to ensure that guards are reasonably efficient." Since, from the beginning, the British POW program hierarchy ran directly from the Prisoner of War Division in the War Office to the National Commands, each of the seven military districts was made responsible for the camps in its area. As early as November 16, 1940, the War Office instructed all Commands that "security of the camps remain the responsibility of your Command. . . . We expect an immediate report on all men, suitability for their duties, number to be replaced . . . and such reports will continue until all unsuitable personnel have been replaced." [48]

While Great Britain's experience in the processing and care of their prisoners of war was, indeed, highly successful, it must be remembered that their total POW community did not exceed 175,000 men—less than half as many as were held in the United States. On the other hand, Washington made little effort to draw upon its ally's experience, even where the methods were clearly applicable. Motivated by a reluctance to enter into any web of agreements in which Washington would be the dependent party, and the belief that an American POW program was to be uniquely American, the War Department strode confidently forward by itself. Despite America's initial shortsightedness in preparing for the prisoners of war, the slow adjustment from planning the custody of evacuees and enemy aliens to captured POWs, the tangled network of bureaucratic hierarchies, the lack of language specialists and trained personnel, and the vast diversity of camp conditions and philosophies of leadership, the first POW operation in American history appeared to be working. By the war's end, the War Department and the PMG's Office had managed to operate and maintain a surprisingly efficient POW program.

The thousands of incoming prisoners—disoriented, disillusioned, many wounded, most happy to be out of war—knew nothing, of course, about these problems. Only six or eight weeks removed from the battlefields of North Africa and Sicily, POWs were pouring into the United States. From the summer of 1943, they poured in at the rate of between 10,000 and 20,000 prisoners per month. Even if the POWs had been aware of the difficulties their hosts were encountering in organizing the first prisoner of war program in its history, they would not have been immediately concerned. As the German officers and enlisted men were rolling inland from Ports of Embarkation, sitting two abreast in the rhythmically lurching coaches while disinterested MPs patrolled the aisles, their central preoccupation concerned their destination: The Camp.

CHAPTER **II**

Life Behind Barbed Wire

The Allied successes in North Africa through the summer and fall of 1943 sent the numbers of incoming POWs soaring. From a total of 5,007 prisoners in April, the number quickly rose to 80,558 in July, 130,229 by August, and 163,706 in September and still the prisoners continued to pour in. The camp construction program was being frantically pursued by the Provost Marshal General's Office and the Corps of Engineers, and the War Department was wrestling with the requirements and availability of administrative and security personnel. A mixed lot of prisoners was coming in from the battlefields of North Africa. Many of them were hardened Nazis, some were wounded and in pain, and most were simply grateful to be safely out of the war. What they had in common, at that moment, was a deep anxiety about the conditions awaiting them at their new camp homes. As the POW trains left the Ports of Embarkation, local communities in whose midst the prisoners would soon be housed were also growing anxious.

The citizens of El Reno, Oklahoma, first learned of plans for building the Fort Reno prisoners' camp from their local newspapers on January 7, 1943. Local engineers and contractors were delighted to learn that they were needed to construct the $500,000 series of compounds on a hundred-acre tract of the Army's Fort Reno Military Post, and building activity moved feverishly through to completion in April. The local population then waited for the next two months for some official word regarding the nationality and number of POWs to which their community and new camp would play host. On July 1, a Fort Reno news release announced that while the camp had originally been designed for 2,500 Nisei Japanese, recent Allied victories in North Africa now dictated that the arriving prisoners would be Germans. Quickly afterward a guard detachment of the 435th Military Police Company, 3 officers and 130 enlisted men fresh from a special police training program in Michigan, arrived by train at Fort Reno. Now both the townspeople *and* the Military Police settled down to wait. And then on July 8, 1943, with little warning, the *El Reno American* headlined the arrival of the "FIRST BATCH OF HUN CAPTIVES," and the *Afrika Korps* had come to

Oklahoma.[1] At newly constructed prisoner of war camps across the South and Southwest and, eventually, in almost every state in the Union, the same scene was being enacted.

Camp Arrival

When the first trainloads of prisoners arrived, entire towns turned out to watch. At Mexia, Texas, in the eastern hill country of the state, townspeople lined up along Railroad Street to stare, awestruck, at the seemingly endless stream of German prisoners who disembarked from the train: 3,250 men in short pants, desert-khaki uniforms, and the large-billed cloth caps and goggles which came to symbolize Rommel's elite. "The line of prisoners stretched the full three miles out to the camp!" a long-time resident recalled. "Remember that we were a town of only 6,000 people, and we had just seen our population increased by 50%—and they were foreigners on top of it!" [2]

Yet the arrival of 4,000 or even 8,000 captive Germans at rural towns across the country was a minor event compared to the number of prisoners which appeared at some of the country's larger camps. If the citizens of Mexia were startled, consider the scene at the small village of Crossville, Tennessee, population 2,000. It had been one year since their city commissioner, M. E. Dorton, had received a wire from Fourth District Congressman Albert Gore announcing a $3 million War Department project for their community. Part of that project turned out to be a military installation. Now the people of Crossville were about to learn who the inhabitants were. In mid-August of 1943, the entire citizenry turned out at the little brick railroad station as the special trains rolled in from the east. They watched in silence as 15,000 Germans and Italians emerged from the coaches and stood milling about, blinking in the bright Tennessee sunlight. "The majority of the Germans are from Rommel's once dreaded *Afrika Korps*," reported an observer from *American Magazine*. "There are fliers, parachute men, artillerymen, panzer men from the German tank divisions. Some of them wear the gaudy uniforms, faded and rumpled now, of high ranking officers. Many of them are still deeply burned from the African sun; some who cruised beneath the ocean until a depth bomb brought them up, are pale and blonde." [3] Hastily assembled into ranks by watchful guards, the prisoners at the Crossville Station were herded toward a convoy of waiting trucks and buses to be transported to the nearby former CCC camp which was to be their new home for the duration of the war.

Interestingly, almost all communities adjusted quickly to the camps in their midst. In fact, despite the initial shock, the majority of the townspeople were surprisingly optimistic about their new neighbors. They had already had several months to get accustomed to the idea since the War Department and the Corps of Engineers had previously announced the location of each site. Furthermore, it was clear that the Army had provided sufficient security to prevent any mass escapes, and it certainly appeared that the government was leaving little to chance. Those people who still remained anxious were quickly soothed by the government's continual assurance that the POWs would be used as laborers in local businesses and on nearby farms. Even small businessmen, whose firms were not large enough to profit from the sudden availability of raw labor, swiftly saw the advantages of steady purchases by the guards and high-ranking prisoners. Perhaps the most basic explanation for this unexpectedly optimistic acceptance of the thousands of nearby prisoners of war was the sheer novelty of the situation. How often, after all, had something like this occurred in these small communities?

In almost every community, however, a small minority of citizens was outraged at the thought of having Nazis in their midst, especially while their sons and husbands were overseas fighting Nazism.

> I only met one such person [recalls former First Lieutenant William Arthur Ward, today a top administrator of Texas Wesleyan College], but it was enough to make me take the matter seriously. As the medical supply officer at Camp Brady [Texas], I once had to escort a group of about 30 POWs to Camp Polk, Louisiana. While waiting for our military bus in Stephenville [Texas], I bought cokes for all the guards and POWs. To my shock, the woman behind the counter at the general store went wild; she yelled and cursed, accused me of sympathy for the enemy, and damn near physically hit me. It was an unnerving experience.[4]

The Director of the Prisoner of War Division, Colonel Francis E. Howard, confided to a reporter from *Collier's* magazine that he had received literally hundreds of letters every week. "About half echo the thoughts of one man who advised: 'Put them in Death Valley, chuck in a side of beef, and let them starve to death.'"[5] It was a feeling that was certainly understandable in light of the war hysteria, the weekly casualty reports in the newspapers, and the dreaded arrival of the War Department telegram. As the war progressed, however, even this minority came to realize, if not appreciate, the logic behind the POW program and the potential advantage of the prisoners to labor-starved farmers.

If the local communities were reasonably pleased with the arrangement thus far, the prisoners seemed just as pleased with the general efficiency of the registration process. After the POWs were marched into camp and receipts for the men were signed, they were directed to the reception barracks for processing. Ideally, there was to be no opportunity for contact between the new arrivals and those men already in the camp in order to prevent the exchange of documents or to allow low morale to spread from the old inmates to the optimistic newcomers. But such precautions varied widely from camp to camp. Moving quickly and efficiently, the new prisoners filled out identification forms, went through their second medical examination, and then were subject to close search of their belongings.

When the 15,000 new arrivals at Camp Crossville spread out their personal possessions for inspection, *American Magazine*'s Beverly Smith described the process:

As their packs are spread out you see all the curious variety of possessions which a soldier clings to throughout bombing, machine-gunning, and shellfire. Pictures of wife, family, children. A letter-writing kit. Skin lotion against African sun and insects. A pair of prized carpet slippers. Toilet papers always. Shaving kit. Sometimes a phonograph record carrying a favorite tune. . . . One handsome German pilot of the Luftwaffe, shot down over Algiers, has a little toy monkey. . . . I saw one German tank lieutenant with an unopened 5-pound can of German butter which no peril of field, fire, or flood had caused him to relinquish. . . .

The inspection of baggage is the first real contact the prisoners have with the American officers and men who administer the camp. The prisoners were grim and impassive at first. Then, as the Americans treated them pleasantly, handled the prized possessions carefully, and amiably joshed them along about some of their unusual possessions, I could see even the sternest of the Nazi officers relax, smile, and chuckle. There was something deeper here. These prisoners now knew that they would be decently treated.[6]

Unlike the more security-conscious British POW camps, the American War Department allowed the incoming prisoners to retain most of their personal effects—with several exceptions. Personal letters were examined and returned at the discretion of the camp commander, and all money held by the POW was surrendered and placed in an envelope bearing his name and identification number and held for the remainder of the war. Without hard currency, it was reasoned, the prisoner would have a difficult time escaping; he would be unable to bribe guards or buy civilian clothes or train tickets, and for that reason all future POW wages were paid in nonnegotiable canteen coupons for use in the camp PX.[7] Further down the line, the prisoners were issued dark blue work clothes, since their German uniforms were to be reserved for use during their leisure hours. A large, white "PW" was stenciled on the back of each shirt and coat to identify them as prisoners of war and, if necessary, provide a target for the guards in the event of their escape.[8] In addition to the work clothes, the POWs were issued:

1 belt	1 pair shoes
2 pair cotton trousers	4 pair socks
2 pair wool trousers	4 pair drawers
1 pair gloves	4 undershirts
1 wool coat	1 raincoat
1 overcoat	1 wool shirt

Finally, at the end of the processing day, the prisoners were lined up for inspection and officially welcomed by the camp commander. The American officer usually explained his philosophy of prisoner care in a gruff soldier-to-soldier speech, or a more conciliatory let's-be-friends-and-make-the-most-of-a-bad-situation talk.[9] He then traditionally introduced his subordinates and outlined the most important regulations regarding damage to property, precautions against fires, and maintenance of sanitary conditions, medical and dental inspections, the rules governing the length and legibility of letters to their families, and the punishment for escape. With the completion of the speech, the POWs were dismissed to locate their bunk assignments, thus ending their first day in their new homes.[10]

The Typical Day

The daily schedules in prisoner camps across the country were nearly identical. Reveille took place at 5:30, bunks were made, and prisoners were ready for breakfast at 6:00. By 6:30, the POWs had finished and were marched back to their barracks to shave and shower, clean the barracks, and police the area. At 7:30, the prisoners began their work projects in the camps or—after the national work program was established—boarded trucks to be taken to nearby farms or factories. At noon the POWs generally ate their bag lunches out in the fields, their backs propped up against trees. They were back at work at 1:00. At about 4:30 in the afternoon, the farmer or factory supervisor began to gather his tools, and the prisoners were loaded back into their trucks for the trip back to camp. Following a shower and change of clothes, usually into their German uniforms, the prisoners ate dinner between 6:00 and 7:00, after which the remainder of the evening was at their disposal.[11] While the schedules and work tasks varied with the size of each camp and the type of labor involved, the War Department took special pains to adhere to or exceed every requirement of the Geneva Convention.

One of the most pleasant surprises to greet the new camp inmates was the quality and quantity of their food. No matter how late in the day the prisoners arrived, it was an unwritten policy to end their first day with a big meal—to feed them after their long train ride, of course, but more than that to impress the POWs with the good treatment they could expect. In fact, one of the major factors in the treatment of German prisoners of war which served to protect the interests of Americans being held in enemy camps was the manner in which the German POWs were fed. While German prisoners in Russian camps were often reduced to eating rats and drinking melted snow, German POWs in the United States, from the moment they arrived in this country, sat down to better meals than they would have enjoyed in their mothers' kitchens at that moment. A standard bill of fare at Camp Clinton, Mississippi, for May 12, 1944, for example, was as follows:

Breakfast	Corn Flakes
	Cake or Bread
	Marmalade
	Coffee, Milk
	Sugar
Lunch	Potato Salad
	Roast Pork
	Carrots
	Icewater
Supper	Meat Loaf
	Scrambled Eggs or Boiled Eggs
	Coffee
	Milk
	Bread [12]

Furthermore, each camp was required by the Geneva Convention to maintain a canteen where, during certain hours, the prisoners could purchase additional foodstuffs, sweets, crackers, soft drinks, and locally grown produce at the prevailing market price. In some camps even beer and light wines were permitted at the prisoner's own expense.[13]

Not only did the American authorities provide the German prisoners with a diet as good as that enjoyed by American troops at home—and far better than American troops at the front who lived on C-rations and K-rations and had no canteen privileges—but, amazing as it seems, the diet was eventually even tailored to their tastes. Prisoners had complained not that the quality or quantity was deficient, but that their prison menus did not reflect national tastes. The government agreed. Colonel Martin Tollefson, then Director of the Prisoner of War Division of the Office of the Provost Marshal General, noted that because of the great differences between the dietary preferences of the German, Italian, and Japanese prisoners, American rations did not satisfy them. This fact led to the waste of food. If prisoners were to receive food more to their liking, the government reasoned, they would eat more and throw away less. Tollefson continued:

> It thus became necessary to provide each camp with prisoner-of-war menus suitable to the needs, habits, and tastes of the respective prisoner groups. The War Department, through the offices of the Quartermaster General, Surgeon General, and Provost Marshal General, spared no efforts in providing necessary, adequate, and appropriate foods without waste.[14]

Captivated by the argument of food conservation, Washington notified the camp authorities on July 1, 1944, that POW menus could be altered to suit the tastes of the inmates. At the same time, however, the directive cautioned the camp commanders that "under no condition was the cost of the ration furnished prisoners of war to exceed that authorized for American troops." [15] Within weeks the German prisoners were receiving meals not unlike any they might have eaten in pre-war Germany, featuring substantial portions of pork and pigs' knuckles, wurst, and fish soups. Italian POWs, more than 53,000 of whom were held in the United States, were also covered by the food directive and began receiving menus offering frequent portions of spaghetti and a diet heavily seasoned with paprika, onions, and olive oil.[16] Within a very short time, the dietary conditions in American camps had reached such levels that John Mason Brown, the Director of the Internees Section of the Department of State, could boast that "in many camps the prisoners have asked the German Red Cross through the Swiss representatives to keep food and tobacco in Germany because they are not needed by prisoners held in this country." [17]

Other aspects of life behind the barbed wire followed a well-ordered pattern. The prisoners were still soldiers captured in the line of duty and were treated as soldiers by the Geneva Convention. While their present circumstances were not what they might have envisioned for themselves when they first marched gallantly off to war, they were still in the German Army. As such, their camp social structure duplicated the military hierarchy of the German Army. Officers exercised the same authority they had before capture, a privilege guaranteed them by the Geneva Convention. They continued to receive their regular military salaries and were not required to do manual labor. If their rank permitted, they were provided with a valet or aide-de-camp from among the POW enlisted men. German officers lived in their own compounds within the camps and remained aloof from the enlisted men at all times. While many of them pursued the same leisure activities as did their lower ranked comrades—taking courses; attending concerts, movies, and plays; and so forth—participation was strictly segregated. The infrequent contact between the two groups was normally confined to strolling groups passing each other, and such a scene saw the enlisted men snap to attention while the officers would casually return the salute without even a pause in their stride.

Discipline within the camp was maintained by the prisoners themselves, and only in the case of an infrequent sit-down strike or a politically-motivated scuffle were the American guards sent in. Sergeants, as in any army, controlled the enlisted men and were, in turn, responsible to the officers for the conduct of their men. Prisoners were required by the Geneva Convention to salute all American officers, though German officers had to salute only American officers of equal or higher rank. Generally speaking, were it not for the barbed wire fences and the presence of American guards around the perimeter of the camp, the scene might have resembled an ordinary *Wehrmacht* training camp in Germany.

Recreation

From the moment the prisoners arrived in the United States, both captors and captives knew that there would have to be daily diversions and an eventual program of work projects to occupy the prisoners' time. Psychologically, the incoming POWs displayed a universal problem. Unless men are put to work by their captors or otherwise occupied, a variety of explosive symptoms will rapidly appear. The prisoner soon finds himself at a loss to occupy his endless days and begins to dwell on his fate and the circumstances which brought it about. Time becomes leaden in confinement, and memoirs of imprisoned people are filled with the limitless devices which are created to break the monotony. Prisoners carve chess pieces out of soap; others juggle mathematical tables in their minds, make handicrafts out of available material, or bet on cockroach races; and some simply lose their sanity. When no systematic work projects are available, the unoccupied prisoner develops a well-documented syndrome which sees his raging frustration channelled into emotional depression and deep despondency. He sees himself as the "forgotten man," abandoned by his country and despised by his captors. He becomes alternately withdrawn or surly and complaining.

The captured soldier, however, has an additional option not available to civilian internees or convicted criminals. He has built up in himself, through training and experience, the frame of mind necessary to make it possible to tolerate the rigors of combat and aggression. One of the final alternatives to the unoccupied soldier, therefore, is the use of deep-seated aggression as a *raison d'être,* and in a POW camp, that reason for existence may take the form of escapes, kangaroo courts, or sabotage.[18] From the prisoners' point of view, therefore, if there had been no work available, to paraphrase the proverb, it would have been necessary to invent it. As it happened, however, the War Department had already authorized a wide selection of recreational camp activities and was hard at work creating the guidelines for a nationwide labor program to be implemented in the very near future.

Camp activities were generally left to the discretion of the camp commanders, but ultimately they depended on the enthusiasm and variety of talents of the prisoners themselves. Sports were the most popular pastime, especially the invariable soccer matches found in every POW camp. Any family out for a Sunday drive along U.S. Highway 6 near Atlanta, Nebraska, for example, could stop to watch the POWs enthusiastically kicking a soccer ball across the field, while hundreds of wildly cheering fellow POWs supported their favorite team. At Camp Opelika, Alabama, Alfred Klein recalls that:

> Sports started right after breakfast, and our camp had a whole slate of outstanding teams in soccer, handball, volleyball, etc. Athletic activities were taken very, very seriously. The Camp Championships, especially in soccer and handball, were so exciting that even our guards participated as cheerleaders from their towers and attended the games on weekends with their families shouting from the sidelines. Many of our athletes, as a matter of fact, went on to sports careers in Germany after their release.[19]

Next to sports, the most popular pastime was the production of plays and theatrical performances. Every camp had a makeshift theater, usually at one end of the mess hall, in which the POWs performed everything from uproariously funny skits with burly men cavorting about in women's clothing to highly sophisticated three-act plays complete with props and orchestration. When a reporter from the *Kansas City Star* toured Camp Trinidad, Colorado, he was escorted by the commander, Lieutenant Colonel Lambert B. Cain, to a front row seat for a recital of Goethe's "Faust"—a performance complete with the strains of cathedral music and chorals, and the pealing of chimes—all from a recording. A crudely built electrical system, fashioned from tin cans, controlled the lighting fixtures. Ceiling light fixtures were made by using inverted glass jars.[20] Any Friday or Saturday night, the prisoners at any large POW camp would have been treated to a theatrical performance of some sort; laughing at a little skit set in a French café; hooting and wolf-whistling at a group of hairy and muscular men in Polynesian grass skirts; or listening in rapt attention as Cyrano de Bergerac wooed lovely Roxanne from beneath her balcony. Although the performances were directed for the camp population at large, German officers and American camp administrators were always preferential guests, and the occasional visits by representatives of the War Department, Swiss Legation, YMCA, or International Red Cross were heralded by impressive evenings.

In addition to skits and plays, the POWs were quick to organize choral groups, and a prisoner Music Committee in each camp went about recruiting talented musicians from among the inmates to form a camp orchestra. Instruments ranging from violins to drum outfits were purchased out of profits from the prisoner-run camp canteen or received as gifts from the War Prisoners' Aid Committee of the YMCA. A representative list of the musical performances, submitted in a report by Colonel T. B. Birdsong, Commanding Officer of POW Camp Shelby, Mississippi, as of August 31, 1944, was as follows:

CONCERTS

Date	Orchestra	Musicians	Location	Audience
1-30-44	Piano	2 men	Rec. Hall	90 men
2-13-44	Piano/Violin	2 men	Rec. Hall	120 men
2-20-44	Piano/Violin	2 men	Rec. Hall	180 men
2-27-44	Variety	6 men	Mess Hall-F	250 men
3-05-44	Variety	7 men	Rec. Hall	200 men
3-05-44	Variety	5 men	Mess Hall-H	260 men
3-19-44	Co. E.F.G.H.	24 men	Heidelberg Platz	500 men
3-26-44	Co. A & B	12 men	Rec. Hall	200 men
4-09-44	Camp Orchestra	35 men	Amphitheatre	1200 men

4-23-44	Camp Orchestra	34 men	Tin Shop	380 men
5-01-44	Camp Choir	36 men	Music Stand	1000 men
5-28-44	Camp Orchestra	32 men	Amphitheatre	900 men
6-30-44	Co. F & G	16 men	Music Stand	200 men
7-02-44	Dance Orchestra	14 men	Music Stand	700 men
7-09-44	Brass Orchestra	20 men	Hindenburg Platz	300 men
7-16-44	Small Orchestra	18 men	Sports Area	800 men
7-16-44	Piano Solo	1 man	Outside Theatre	960 men
7-16-44	Co. A & B	10 men	Mess Hall-B	200 men
7-16-44	Dance Orchestra	9 men	Hindenburg Platz	300 men
7-24-44	Small Orchestra	12 men	Amphitheatre	800 men
7-30-44	Camp Orchestra	17 men	Outside Theatre	960 men
8-13-44	Dance Orchestra	10 men	Outside Theatre	960 men
8-20-44	Camp Orchestra	17 men	Music Stand	380 men

It is a cultural schedule which would do justice to any large urban area, much less a camp community of 2,773 men! Moreover, these musical activities in no way exhausted the recreational alternatives available to the prisoners of war.

Every POW camp had a library of German and English books, donated by the War Prisoners' Aid Committee of the YMCA or purchased out of the camp canteen profits. The libraries ranged in size from a few dozen dog-eared books at Angel Island POW Camp in San Francisco Bay to the substantial collection of more than 9,000 volumes at Camp Dermott, Arkansas.[21] Each camp library also subscribed to several dozen copies of at least three newspapers; generally, *The New York Times* and two local papers. The POWs were initially skeptical about the facts they read concerning America's high productivity, domestic freedom, and war news. And the American camp personnel were initially skeptical also, although their concern centered on the vital military information which the pro-Nazi POWs might somehow signal back to Germany. By the spring of 1944, however, both sides had thoroughly relaxed and by all accounts generally accepted the truthfulness of the camp newspapers at face value. The POWs continued to be amazed at the openness of the news reports, a frankness that would serve as an early part of the "reeducation" program to follow. If nothing else, the newspapers were avidly sought by the prisoners as an aid to learning English. By the summer of 1944, the War Department felt comfortable enough with the newspaper program to authorize camp subscriptions for the New York-based *Neue Volkszeitung*, an outspoken German-language paper, often critical of American policies.

In addition to the plays, musical performances, and library facilities, the larger POW camps maintained a film library, and movies were shown often. Nearly every camp purchased its 16mm projector from its canteen profits during the spring of 1944 and showed a selection of eight to ten rented movies to the inmate population as often as 40 times a month.[22] An average selection of rented films included six or seven American films, which were first previewed by the camp authorities and translated to the POW audience by an "approved" (anti-Nazi) prisoner, and one or two closely reviewed German films. Interestingly, the American films, and especially cartoons, were far more popular with the prisoners than the "sanitized" German films, and outdoor shows were often attended by as many as 1,000 men. In November, 1944, the Special War Problems Division of the State Department lifted these burdens from the shoulders of the individual camp administrators and issued a directive, listing 24 "acceptable" motion picture performances for all prisoner of war camps across the country. By 1945 the POWs were enjoying such evenings as:

Performance #13:   *Sports:* "Tigers of the Deep"
                   Educational: "Pittsburgh: Steel Town"
                   Feature: "The Great Victor Herbert"
Performance #21:   *Cartoon:* "Andy Panda Goes Fishing"
                   Scientific: "Fire, the Red Poacher"
                   Feature: "The Gentlemen from West Point" [23]

As Hollywood produced a sufficient supply of anti-Nazi motion pictures through 1944 and 1945, the prisoners began to receive a steady diet of such films as "The Seventh Cross," "The Moon is Down," "Watch on the Rhine," and "Tomorrow, the World." Those prisoners who showed a particular spark of enthusiasm for what was in essence a reeducation program were treated to the Office of War Information's "Why We Fight" series. In any case, motion pictures formed a substantial diversion for the German prisoners.

Of equal importance, both as a diversion and later as an instrument in the reeducation program, was the publication of camp newspapers. The War Department had come to the realization, early in the POW experience, that the publication of such camp papers would not only occupy the men but might serve in other ways. They were an excellent means of transmitting information to the prisoners—changes of regulations, upcoming events, even war news—if they did not serve to increase prisoner resistance. At the same time, the papers could be monitored by the authorities as an accurate barometer of the prisoners' mood and morale. Moreover, once the reeduca-

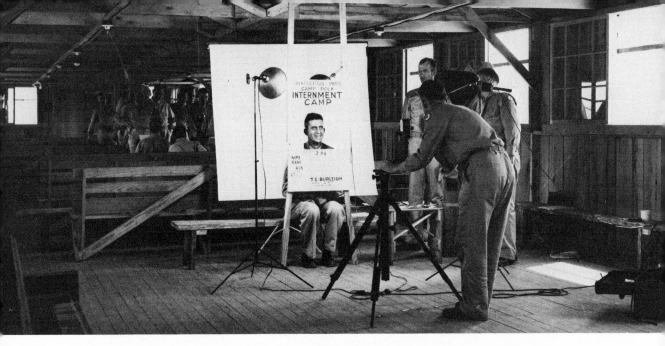

Prisoner identification photos are taken at Camp Polk, Louisiana. *(U.S. Army Photo)*

All personal property had to be accounted for, and with the exception of currency, was returned to the prisoners. *(Alfred Klein)*

HEADQUARTERS
ARMY SERVICE FORCES
Prisoner of War Camp
Camp Rucker, Alabama

201. KLEIN, Alfred   (PW)   Date ___3 JAN 1946___

SUBJECT: Prisoner of War Personal Property

TO   : Whom it may concern.

    1. This letter will acknowledge that prisoner of war
KLEIN, Alfred   , ISN _4 WG-73562_ , has the following property in his possession:

        a. 1 Ring, silver   f. 1 Tobaccopouch
        b. 1 Fountainpen   g.
        c. 2 Automaticpencils   h.
        d. 4 Billfolds   i.
        e. 1 Cigarettcase   j.

    2. The above property could not be stamped due to it's
shape, design or nature (musical instruments, tools etc.)

                            J.E. Daugherty
                            1st Lt., AUS
                            Custodial Officer of
                            Prisoner of War Property

                    ARMY SERVICE FORCES
                    Fourth Service Command
                    Headquarters, Prisoner of War Camp
Camp Rucker, Ala.   Date 3/1/46
                    Personal Property of
(PW) _Klein, Alfred_ ISN 4 WG-73562
            Name
Ownership verified by _R.K. Bird_ 1st Lt.
                        Name   Rank

A typical POW camp, this at Camp Polk. October, 1943. *(U.S. Army Photo)*

The prisoners quickly settled
into their new surroundings,
complete with American pin-up girls.
Camp Blanding, Florida.
(U.S. Army Photo)

German Mess Sergeant checks supplies at the POW mess hall. Camp Swift, Texas. *(U.S. Army Photo)*

Sunday afternoon soccer championship game. *(UPI)*

57

At the POW-operated Post exchange. *(UPI)*

Since the use of currency
was forbidden, the prisoners
used these canteen coupons
for all purchases.
(Alfred Klein)

German prisoners at Camp Evelyn, Michigan, enjoy a moment of relaxation at the camp canteen. *(U.S. Army Photo)*

Three members of the *Afrika Korps* enjoy the "Pause That Refreshes" at Aliceville POW camp in Alabama. *(U.S. Army Photo)*

In addition to the camp band at Mexia, Texas, there was also a full string orchestra as well as a popular dance band. *(Eberhard Scheel)*

"A Festival in Venice," part of the variety show put on by the German prisoners at Camp Polk, Louisiana. *(U.S. Army Photo)*

tion program got underway, these papers would serve as an experiment in democracy which allowed the inmates to write anything they pleased without fear of censorship or retaliation. Within a very short time, every camp in the country began publishing its own newspaper. Camp Shelby put out the *Mississippi Post;* Camp Carson, Colorado, *Die PW Woche (The PW Weekly);* Camp Campbell, Kentucky, *Der Europaer (The European);* Camp Crossville, Tennessee, *Die Brücke (The Bridge);* Camp Houlton, Maine, *Der Wachter (The Watchman);* and so forth. Camp Maxey's (Texas) literary-minded prisoners published no less than three newspapers: *Echo, Der Texas Horchposten (The Texas Listening Post),* and *Deutsche Stimme (The German Voice).*[24] Written entirely by the prisoners and mimeographed on the camp machine, these papers were surprisingly sophisticated, carrying such things as poetry and short stories; crossword puzzles and word games; a weekly calendar of events; sports news; announcements of plays, concerts, and films; technical articles ranging from anatomy to photography; clever cartoons and comic strips; and, finally, a page of classified ads. They were remarkable efforts by the prisoners, an outlet for talent which might easily have been directed toward less acceptable channels and a continuous diversion for men behind barbed wire.

In addition to these recreational programs, every large camp, and the majority of the smaller ones, allocated several large rooms in the camp's warehouse or utility building for use as a craft center. At Camp Shelby, Mississippi, for example, the craft center was used by the prisoners for woodcraft, metalcraft, leathercraft, papercraft, painting, and drawing. Those prisoners who wanted to sell their handicraft articles were able to do so through the post exchange, and periodically the men organized a camp exhibition with prizes drawn from the canteen fund.[25] Many of these camp sales and exhibitions at Camp Holabird, Maryland, Fort Du Pont, Delaware, and Camp Como, Mississippi, for instance, became local social events for the civilians in nearby communities. Every camp also had a recreation room complete with several ping-pong tables, a dozen chess boards, packs of playing cards, bingo sets and an inevitable phonograph. Camp Campbell's (Kentucky) recreation room boasted a collection of 50 phonograph records ranging from "Home on the Range," "Missouri Waltz," and "Whistling Cowboy," to "Tuxedo Junction," "Friendly Tavern Polka," and "Can't Get Indiana Off My Mind." [26] The most popular record at Campbell, as well as at nearly every other camp, was Bing Crosby's "Don't Fence Me In." Most of these recreational items, as well as the handicraft tools, were either donated by the German Red Cross, the National Catholic Welfare Council, the War Prisoners' Aid Committee of the YMCA or purchased out of the camp's canteen fund.[27] These recreation rooms were enormously popular with the young Germans, especially those for whom the other activities held little attraction.

The most interesting and far-reaching camp program was its educational curriculum. The question of classroom facilities was first raised by the inmates themselves almost immediately after arriving in camp. The camp authorities saw no reason to prevent the men from studying, especially since English was the subject most eagerly sought, and after receiving the authorization from the War Department, they set up classes in every camp. Since a large number of the prisoners had been civilian teachers, carpenters, watchmakers, lawyers, mechanics, bank clerks, and the like, the POW camps had a large reservoir of talent upon which they could draw to teach the classes. The prisoners elected a Study Leader, who was responsible for establishing the camp's educational curriculum, and by the end of 1943, literally every large camp in America boasted courses in English, Spanish, German literature, shorthand, commerce, chemistry, and mathematics. As faculty made themselves available, camps were able to offer unique courses to their populations. At Camp Clinton, Mississippi, for instance, prisoners were offered courses in the history of the American Indians, Chinese culture, and the plants of the United States.[28] At Camp Crossville, Tennessee, POWs were given piano lessons, and at Camp Campbell, Kentucky, they could even take a course on the symbolism of the American Funnies.[29] Reinhold Pabel recalls:

> At Camp Ellis, Illinois, I decided to take full advantage of the educational facilities which were provided.
> I got together with some other linguistically inclined men for small classes in foreign languages. Among others, we purchased a Persian Linguaphone Course and learned enough to be able to read and listen to excerpts from the *Rubaiyat* in the original. I concentrated my efforts finally on Russian and completed two correspondence courses in that language with the University of Chicago Extension Division. Sometime later, I conducted two Russian courses for beginners for my fellow prisoners, making up my lessons myself and mimeographing them for class use.[30]

With Teutonic thoroughness, the camp courses demanded continued attendance, the students took notes and participated in classroom discussions, and examinations were followed by final grades.

So successful were these courses, and so technically competent, that on May 19, 1944, the Reich Ministry of Education offered full high school and university credit for courses taken by German prisoners in the United States. In a 12-page edict, transmitted through the auspices of the German Red Cross, POWs were informed that 15 major German and Austrian universities, from the Universities of Bonn, Berlin, and Kiel, to the Polytechnic Institutes of Danzig, Dresden, and Graz, would accept their grades at face value. The Reichsminister detailed the process by which the POWs could obtain any of the five successive academic or vocational degrees, including instructions on the number of faculty members on each type of examination board.[31] While Germany's Eastern Front lay in shambles and the Allies poised for the most massive invasion in the history of the world against Normandy, the German Reich took the time to supply their POWs with official booklets to note their educational progress in the United States! Issued by no less an authority than the Army High Command (OKW), the 40-page *Studiennachweis für Kriegsgefangene (Evidence of Study for War Prisoners)* booklet described the German grading system and demanded that each POW professor authenticate the course and grade for each POW student. These booklets were to serve as certified transcripts and were, in fact, accepted by German universities at face value.[32]

If the prisoners found that their camp "universities" failed to offer courses in a particular subject, however, they had an additional option. The Office of the Provost Marshal arranged to allow prisoners whose camps were located near American universities to take extension courses! Thus, POWs at Houlton, Maine, took extension and correspondence courses through the University of Maine; at Camp Pine, New York, through Syracuse University; at Meade, Maryland, they took courses through Johns Hopkins; at McCoy, Wisconsin, from the University of Wisconsin; and across the United States, the German prisoners studied at 103 different universities and technical colleges.[33]

As a result of these educational opportunities, no small number of men in American camps graduated from German universities after finishing part of their undergraduate work at such institutions as "The University of Blanding, Florida," "The University of Como, Mississippi," or "The University of Polk, Louisiana." Alfred Klein, for example, returned to Germany where he remained in the service, rose to the rank of Lieutenant Colonel, and is, at present, head of the Air Warfare Department at the German Air Force Academy (Fürstenfeldbruck)—thanks, in part, to his wartime education. A former *Afrika Korps* officer and prisoner at Camp Trinidad, Colorado, the aristocratic Freiherr Rüdiger von Wechmar studied journalism at the University of Minnesota. As a direct result of these studies, states Baron Wechmar, he had little difficulty in landing post-war employment, first as a reporter with the German News Agency in Hamburg, and later as the chief of Bureau of the United Press in Bonn.[34] Another former POW, Heinrich Matthias, went on to become a prosperous banker in Germany; Dr. Karl Janish rose to become a Justice of the Austrian Supreme Court; Walter Horst Littman became a Senior Chemist in the German Department of Defense.[35] All gratefully acknowledge their POW training, as do hundreds of others. While there is no way of knowing how many POWs became dedicated fans of the Michigan Wolverines, the Wisconsin Badgers, or the Texas Longhorns, many prisoners of war returned to Germany with a substantially improved education.

Some prisoners with spare time pursued personal hobbies or made handicrafts on their own. Officers, in particular, were fond of gardening, and what they did not grow, they purchased in town. At the Mexia internment camp, for instance, German officers were permitted to order flowers from local florists, which they did to the tune of 50 dollars a day, and kept their quarters filled with them. Other POWs built walnut furniture. Some painted murals on the walls of the theater, mess halls, and hospitals. A few prisoners in each camp spent their time locating and visiting with relatives, usually long-time naturalized American citizens.

At Camp Grant, Illinois, a group of talented artists painted oil portraits of such German figures as Frederick the Great, Field Marshal Rommel, Bismarck, and Hindenburg, which they sold to a steady stream of appreciative guards and souvenir-hungry townspeople.

At Camp Carson, Colorado, the prisoners recreated a bit of the Fatherland by building an authentic beer garden for use during their off-hours. The beer garden was complete with chairs, tables, and decorations made in the camp woodcraft shop. With the new beer garden, indoor and outdoor sports, woodworking shop, theater, school classes ranging from grade school to college, camp newspaper *(Die PW Volke),* and the stage plays written and produced by the prisoners, Camp Carson's commander, Lieutenant Colonel Eugene N. Frakes, was able to report: "Morale in the camp is unbelievably high." [36] Little wonder.

Prisoners held near Halloran General Hospital, Staten Island, devoted their spare time to a sizable victory garden, which the Army Service Forces proudly announced would provide vegetables for 650 German POWs for the entire year.[37]

A former German physicist, interned at Camp Trinidad, Colorado, wasted little time in reconstructing his prewar Berlin laboratory, "a Rube Goldberg affair, dials spinning, chimes sounding, and a pen scratching crazy lines on a chart. . . ." [38]

At Camp Hearne, Texas, the Germans painstakingly constructed concrete replicas of old German castles—waist high—down to the detailed

Models were especially popular. *(Imperial War Museum)*

A display of art projects made by prisoners at Camp Grant, Illinois. *(U.S. Army Photo)*

An English class at Camp Blanding, Florida. The "professors" are fluent in English, many having visited or lived in the U.S. before the war. *(U.S. Army Photo)*

A selection of the courses offered at just one camp. *(National Archives)*

```
                    Prisoner of War Camp
                  Kriegsgefangenen-Lager
                        Rupert, Idaho


          This Certificate of Achievement is awarded to:

                      Zeugnis


              Werner . RICHTER . 8WG-13333 ....

Who has successfully comple-        Hat in dem fuer Kriegsgefan-
ted a course  in USA History        gene in Rupert, Idaho statt-
USA Civics,USA Geography and         findenden Kursen in USA Ge-
English for Prisoners of War         schichte,USA Buergerkunde  ,
Conducted at PW Camp Rupert,         USA Laenderkunde und Englisch
Idaho.                               mit Erfolg teilgenommen.
In witness thereof the under-        Beglaubigt hiermit durch die
signed have hereunto set their       Unterzeichneten
names the:                           den:


                   .11 January. 1946
```

Arthur T.YATES Capt. CMP .
(Name)   (Rank)
Compound Commander.
Lagerkommandeur

Georg KUEHL Cpl, 9 WG 7546   Ludwig DIEDERICH Cpl. 81G 302811
(Name)   (Rank)   (Name)   (Rank)
PW Director of Studies   Acting Camp Spokesman
Unterrichtsleiter fuer
Kriegs Gefangene

The academic courses were so thorough as to offer "graduation certificates."
(Werner Richter)

The officer to the left,
a former professor in Berlin,
shows off his wind and
weather recording device,
all constructed of scrap material.
(Wide World Photos)

A happy reunion between a POW
at Camp Campbell, Kentucky,
and his two sisters,
now naturalized U.S. citizens.
(U.S. Army Photo)

A funeral service being held
in the Chapel at Ft. Custer,
Michigan, for a German prisoner.
(U.S. Army Photo

The prisoners at Camp Como, Mississippi, line up to take books out of the library. *(National Archives)*

There were flowers, a wedding cake, and a best man—but no bride—as this POW (second from left in front) marries his sweetheart in Germany by proxy. *(UPI)*

turrets and moats, and a curious visitor to the old camp site can still examine a medieval little schloss rising just above the weedtops in a corner of the empty landscape where the camp used to be.[39]

One enterprising German spent his entire three years at Mexia, Texas, making a clock out of scrap materials, using two Coca Cola bottles for weights. It actually kept perfect time.[40]

On very rare occasions, and usually as the result of a camp visit by a representative of the American Red Cross, YMCA, or local charity, the prisoners would rally to a charitable cause with admirable enthusiasm. On February 27, 1945, for example, a group of Germans at Camp Campbell, Kentucky, contributed $3,800 to the American Red Cross, money which the men had saved from their 80¢ per day canteen coupons and which was converted to currency by the War Department to honor the prisoners' gesture.[41]

German prisoners at Eglin Field, Florida, outraged at their government after viewing a series of atrocity films, were moved to contribute the substantial sum of $2,371 to American war charities.[42] At the tiny branch camp of Marked Tree, Arkansas, the entire population of 120 Austrian-born prisoners celebrated the fall of Vienna to Allied forces by the spontaneous donation of $176 to the American Red Cross.[43] Such projects occurred from time to time in about 10 percent of the POW camps.

Finally, on rare occasions, a prisoner might be allowed to occupy himself with interests outside of the camp. German officers with good camp records were eligible, at the discretion of the camp commander, to be placed on limited parole. The officer was placed on his word of honor not to escape or wander more than five miles from the camp, and was to be accompanied by an unarmed American officer. Usually such paroled German officers simply spent a Sunday walking through the woods, or birdwatching in the early morning hours. One surprising exception, recounted by author John Moore, concerned five hardened submarine officers who were evidently allowed to travel to their new homes at Camp Blanding, Florida, pretty much on their own. They spent the several days on the train dressed in American uniforms, with small Nazi lapel pins, chatting amiably with fellow passengers, who had little idea that the men were prisoners of war on parole.[44]

Not all of the projects which occupied the prisoners were strictly legal, and in every prisoner of war community, dozens of minor schemes were hatched weekly. Some men spent their spare time accumulating hard currency in the event of escape, and these men seldom passed up an opportunity to cajole small change from the guards and sell handcrafted souvenirs to local townspeople.

Reinhold Pabel was one of the few inmates whose preoccupation with currency led to his successful escape from Camp Grant, Illinois. In his search for money, Pabel recalls that

> Mac [one of the guards] was quite anxious to obtain a souvenir made by prisoners. One day I somehow managed to secure a neatly done wood carving and showed it to Mac. His eyes lit up instantly and he asked eagerly:
> 'What do you want for it?'
> 'Not much,' I replied. 'Since we are friends, I'll let you have it for five bucks.' . . .
> He eyed me suspiciously:
> 'What do you want the cash for? You can't spend it anyhow. And it is against orders, you know' . . .
> I argued: 'Look at it this way, Mac. I assume you want this genuine POW-made carving as a souvenir, right?'
> 'Yeah, of course!'
> 'O.K. And I want a five-dollar bill as a souvenir, so I shall be able to show my grandchildren something to prove that I really was in America once. In other words: souvenir for souvenir. Fair enough?'
> This did the trick. He handed me a crisp shiny greenback and I shoved this first contribution to my escape fund in my pocket, trying to appear as casual as possible about the whole transaction while my heart cried out in exuberant joy: 'I've got it! I've got it! I've got it!' [45]

That the government's policy regarding currency inside the camp was well-founded is borne out by Pabel's eventual escape, his disappearance into the mainstream of life in Chicago, and the F.B.I. manhunt, which did not end until his capture and deportation in 1953!

There was no end to the number of clandestine preoccupations which took place in the POW communities. Some men collected cigarettes, the universal currency of army camps, prisons, and closed institutions the world over; [46] others tried to counterfeit canteen coupons; and still others devised political plots—to be discussed in detail in a later chapter—ranging from efforts to make radio contact with the Fatherland, through the secret publication of anti-Semitic flyers, to the establishment of kangaroo courts and "death committees."

One of the more harmless and most popular pastimes, however, concerned alcohol. Many camps, at the discretion of the Service Forces commanding officer and the camp commander, made light wine and 3.2 "near-beer" available to the inmates, though on a tightly rationed basis, and with a close eye on public opinion. When public opinion periodically rose to protest the "coddling" of the prisoners of war causing the end to the sale of beer, POWs across the country rose to meet the challenge by making whiskey. Making whiskey required a bit of planning and patience. First the Germans collected oranges, apples, potatoes, and the raisins that they had picked out of the raisin bread at breakfast. To this they added their hoarded sugar rations. Then they added yeast, which they obtained from the prison baker in exchange for packs of cigarettes. POW John Schroer at Camp Rucker recalls: "From the size of the bread on the breakfast table each morning, I could tell if the yeast content was low; if it was," he laughs, "I knew that somewhere in camp a large batch of whiskey was being processed." [47] These ingredients were combined, and the mixture was allowed to ferment in the sun. The results, according to a number of former prisoners, were potent and sometimes even palatable. Despite the efforts of the American guards to locate the contraband moonshine in monthly sweeps through the barracks, the alcohol often went undiscovered until raucous laughter and slurred singing brought the guards on the run. Eventually, when the guards felt that the situation was getting out of hand, a surprise raid on the camp chapel would generally yield several jars of fermenting liquid hidden in the altar.

That the altar would have been used to hide contraband was a general commentary on the initial importance of religion among the German prisoners of war. Neither Protestantism nor Catholicism, the two major religions of Germany, had been of any significance in halting the Nazi movement. Since Nazism became, in essence, Germany's secular religion and since one cannot serve two masters, it was understandable that only a minority of the incoming German POWs admitted to any strong religious convictions. For many of the men, however, two independent forces would bring about a major change. The first, already discussed, concerned the large blocks of unoccupied time which the prisoners now found on their hands. It was, for many, a time for thought and reflection about their lives: about their childhood, their wartime experiences, and their futures. They were, in effect, severed from the Fatherland, and with the loss of one master, it was natural, perhaps, that many would turn to another. The second factor, not one to be underestimated, was the fervor with which American religious organizations approached the POWs. In the words of Chaplain John Dvorovy, of the Provost Marshal General's Office:

> Religious work among German prisoners of war has been pioneer work. ... The blessings with which this important work has been crowned is due to the fact that army chaplains have unselfishly given of their time and energy to the task of reclaiming souls for God's kingdom. They have been carrying forward the banner of true religion under the most trying conditions and circumstances. Personal feelings and preju-

dices had to be set aside. They have been preaching the simple but effective truth of Christ's Gospel as a power of God unto salvation. . . .

The effective work of the Chaplains Corps in prisoner of war camps has not only aided thousands of these prisoners to see their own doctrine, but has also turned many of them to the worship of the true God. . . .[48]

Civilian church agencies also combined deep humanitarianism with a war-time crusade to provide the POWs with an alternative to Nazism, and for many of the inmates the alternative was welcomed. Organizations such as the War Relief Services, National Catholic Welfare Council, Lutheran Commision for Prisoners of War, War Prisoners' Aid of the YMCA, World Council of Churches, and the Ecumenical Commission for Chaplaincy Service to Prisoners of War deluged camp chaplains with religious books, pamphlets, and other items necessary to a successful religious program. The American Bible Society, for example, donated tens of thousands of Bibles—printed in German—to the POWs,[49] and the Federal Council of Churches of Christ in America went so far as to import two prominent Swedish clergy-men to work with German prisoners of war in the United States and Canada.[50]

For all the promise of reclaiming the souls of German youth, the American Army chaplains in the POW camps were, in many ways, as regulated as the inmates they were to help. It was not enough for the chaplain to simply be there; he had to converse with the POWs in German or work through a politically reliable prisoner-interpreter. If there were priests or ministers among the Germans, it was the camp chaplain's respon-siblility to establish a "working relationship" and to "cultivate his trust and confidence." Every item of religious literature and all reading material, in German or English, had to be cleared first through the camp Intelligence Office as well as the Stockade Office. Among the many instructions for chaplains assigned to POW camps, issued at the Army Chaplain's School, were the following bits of advice:

> Conduct *religious services.* Preach on Gospel texts and avoid political propaganda. No matter how subtle, they will catch on. . . .

And finally, the new chaplains were admonished:

> . . . not to let the assignment to a PW Camp frighten you. Your fears that you might be slugged or decapitated will be found to have been groundless.[51]

However difficult the task, periodic surveys of the prisoners by various church organizations, supported by the growing demand for religious literature, indicated that, indeed, the Germans were responding to the religious program. One six-month survey indicated an increase of a whopping 31 percent in the church attendance of both faiths.[52] Whether any of the inmates were present to keep an eye on the fermenting contraband hidden inside the altar is not known.

Prisoner Reaction

Life in the POW camp was not entirely unpleasant, it appears, nor without some diversions. Certainly it was a prison, and regardless of its advantages (in comparison, for example, with a POW camp in Russia), it contained captured enemy soldiers, walled off from society, and far from home. Days were often dreary and monotonous; hopes rose and fell as war news filtered through the camp; and cliques of hardened Nazis often made life difficult for the community at large.

Yet, many former POWs today recall that these years contained some of the most enjoyable moments in their early lives. Some recall the humor in having hidden contraband eggs under a loose floorboard in Mexia (Texas) internment camp only to wake up to find nearly 50 noisy chicks scampering through the barrack.[53]

At Camp Foley, Alabama, a group of POWs remember when they were entrusted to return a farmer's automobile and were stopped by the Alabama police for speeding along a country road. "I still remember the expressions on those two highway patrolmen when they finally caught up with us," chuckles Alfred Klein. "They started to write out speeding tickets when they realized we were POWs. They were absolutely speechless! I still laugh about it today." [54] Another former prisoner, John Schroer—today a successful businessman in Los Angeles—fondly remembers the many months he spent on the loading docks at Montgomery, Alabama. "Most of the time we moved things like flour and canned goods from the warehouses to the trains," he recalls. "But several times a week, we found ourselves loading beer—and the guards always encouraged us to break a case or two. Since we couldn't ship them, of course, we all sat down in the shade together and drank the beer." [55]

Certainly, camp life was often difficult, but on the other hand, there was plenty to keep the men occupied. When asked about the number of escapes from his camp at Fort Lee, Virginia, Colonel Philip K. Moisan explained to the reporter from the *Washington Post* that they had not yet had a successful escape. Why? "Hell, you couldn't drive some of those fellows out!"

While the first arrivals at camps were far more politically hardened than those who would follow, the prisoners seemed surprisingly content with their new surroundings. In Camp Grant, Illinois, POW Reinhold Pabel recalls:

> We found our first permanent home. Our shelters were regular army barracks, clean and fairly roomy, with plenty of showers, and a PX, well-stocked with merchandise. What a world of difference between these quarters and those inadequate facilities in Africa!
>
> The "old" inmates of the camp showered us upon our arrival with ice-cream bars, candy, cigarettes and other goodies. When we gathered in the mess halls for our first dinner at camp, we at first suspected that the Yanks wanted to make fun of us. Such a menu: soup, vegetables, meat, milk, fish, grapes, coffee and ice cream! Never before in our military career had we been served a meal like that.[56]

Excerpts from routinely censored POW letters from Camp Trinidad, Colorado, indicate a similarly enthusiastic impression:

> I have never as a soldier, been as well off as I am here; we are being treated very decently—much better than we were by our own officers. I write you this quite openly because it is the truth and I don't want you to get a false impression of the Americans. [Obergefr. Josef Sworsky, June 22, 1943]

> There is room for approximately 2000 men here. The wooden barracks are all equipped with electric lights and individual cots with quilts. The wash-room and showers may be used at any hour. The food is excellent and plentiful. Particular attention is given to the state of our health. . . . After everything we went through it is just like a rest-cure to be here. [St. Gefr. Hans Jahnichen, June 20, 1943][57]

Similar contentment was voiced to the Swiss authorities by new prisoners at dozens of other camps.

A portion of the new prisoners, as might be expected, were not pleased with their new surroundings, and the security officer at each camp, in an effort to head off potential security problems, noted such complaints during the routine censoring of all POW mail. Ironically, a sample of these complaints could be found in letters from the previously lauded Camp Trinidad:

> ... And now the camp! We are here 14 days and still have no tables nor chairs. We are given only empty promises. The Americans cannot organize the least thing. ... They fear us "Bad Nazis" so much, but this fear only fills us with pride. The living quarters are better not mentioned. ... Now you have an idea how things are run in "God's" country. [Zahlmeister Hans Gelhard, Camp D, June 16, 1943]

> It seems to me that things are not going as smoothly in America as they did in England. ... The heat is so intense one dares not to venture outside. ... We get less food than we did in England. There is nothing for us to read, not even newspapers. This section of the country is fit only for Indians and not for white men. ... [Karl Tomola, Camp A, June 28, 1943]

> ... I do not think I can reconcile myself to the conditions which prevail here. ... Many promises made and none maintained. Up to the present we neither have a chair nor a table—no lamp in the room, only a bulb. A case-like contraption is called a clothes-closet; it is put together with boards and burlap. ... Yesterday we caught a rattlesnake almost 3 feet long. ... [Oberleutnant Bernhard Vandamme, Camp C, June 28, 1943]

A small number of hardened Nazis misinterpreted the War Department's indulgence and humanitarianism as weakness. One prisoner from the *Afrika Korps* declared to an interpreter that the Americans could congratulate themselves for giving the best food and best-constructed barracks to the Germans. "Because," he announced, "when Germany wins the war, this will make at least one good point in your favor." [58] Another newly arrived prisoner, Heinz Pachter, recalls of his comrades at Camp Livingston, Louisiana:

> They instantly thought all of this was a sign of weakness. They had not been transported in cattle trucks, they had received white bread, this American white bread that they called "cake." (They came from a country where there was only black bread, ration bread.) So they thought: "if you give us this good bread, it is only to coax us, to corrupt us. If you are treating us so well, it is because you are afraid of losing the war." [59]

Such skepticism was shared by only a small minority of the prisoners, however, and one can assume that to these men, every act of kindness would have been misinterpreted in a similar way.

Pleased or displeased with their new surroundings, the thousands of incoming prisoners began the process of settling into their daily routine. It cannot be overemphasized, however, that the procedures, climate, and efficiency of each American camp was unique. For example, the experiences of POWs at Camp Grant, Illinois, who worked in the Sycamore Preserve and Marmalade plant, in no way resembled the conditions encountered by the prisoners who picked cotton in the 110° heat of Camp Mexia, Texas, or harvested sugarcane near Camp Livingston, Louisiana.

In attempting to create a positive environment for the prisoners, the War Department was driven by the highest motives. By taking such special care, Washington was, hopefully, insuring that Americans in enemy hands would receive the best possible treatment and that contented POW laborers would work harder, thus shortening the war and saving lives. In retrospect, Washington was correct. At the end of the war, returning American POWs who had been held by the Germans substantiated that as poorly as American prisoners had been cared for in German camps, in comparison with their German counterparts in the United States, they were always better off than the French, and certainly, Russian prisoners in their midst.

In 1943 and 1944, however, the American public could not yet understand Washington's motives in protecting American prisoners in enemy hands by indulging captured Nazis. The public was concerned only with the war effort: Patriotic citizens were urged to conserve food and essential items, ration books and automobile stickers became the passports to daily necessities, and personal sacrifices were willingly endured as Americans answered the continuous call for higher productivity. War news had become a daily bill of fare, and every newsreel, radio broadcast, and magazine advertisement brought home to each American the personal nature of the struggle. As news reports began to note the care being lavished upon the unknown numbers of enemy prisoners in their midst, a tremor of resentment swept the country. Despite the logic of the War Department's efforts to provide for its prisoners, Washington had sorely misgauged American public opinion. A short flash of indignation swept the reading public in 1943, as evidenced by several letters to *The New York Times* demanding a review of Washington's food policies within the POW camps.[60] But as long as food was still reasonably available to the general public, rationed or not, Americans were only moderately annoyed. Nor would there be an outcry during 1944. However, by 1945, an increased food shortage across the United States was instantly reflected in a rash of public hostility and newspaper investigations which, in turn, made up a large segment of the general charges against the War Department's POW program, known simply as "coddling." But in 1943, as the first trainloads of prisoners were exploring the nooks and crannies of their unfamiliar camps, and adjusting to the first few days of their prisoner routines, 1945 seemed a long way off.

If the 380,000 German prisoners of war in the United States thought that they had as much diversion as they could possibly handle, they were about to be surprised by what the government had in store for them. A nation-wide work program, designed to alleviate the severe domestic labor shortage and to relieve American military personnel for shipment overseas, was already in progress.

CHAPTER III

The Labor Program

Within a year of the beginning of the war, the domestic labor market was already feeling the pinch of the war effort. The military draft was draining the nation's manpower pool, and the prospects of filling the massive production quotas appeared dim. The country, in effect, was caught in a crunch. On the one hand, production demands were continually on the increase: Factories which manufactured airplanes, munitions, or anything else critical to the war effort worked around the clock; "overtime" became standard. On the other hand, the Armed Forces were drafting every available man; recruiting drives and posters appealed to many whom the draft had not yet taken, and labor quickly felt the shortage. By 1942, the federal government had already begun recruiting foreign workers from Mexico, Jamaica, and the Bahamas to supplement dwindling farm labor; but this trickle could not even begin to match the drain. The government finally ordered a long-overdue draft exemption status for "essential" farm and factory workers in March, 1943, but the situation was already dangerously out of balance. Even the Secretary of Agriculture, Claude R. Wickard, implied that the situation was critical.[1] It was at this very moment that hundreds of thousands of German and Italian prisoners of war were settling into their daily routines of camp life. The answer suddenly became clear: Fill the dwindling industrial and farm labor ranks with incoming prisoners of war!

The POW Labor Program

The Geneva Convention of 1929 specified that the prisoners could, indeed, be required to work for the benefit of their captors. In fact, American prisoners in German and Italian POW camps had already been put to work to fill similar gaps in diminishing labor forces. Both Washington and Berlin turned to the most obvious solution to identical problems. In both capitals, the central guidelines were provided by the Geneva Convention, which established the basic criteria for the treatment and use of prisoners on both sides of the Atlantic. Within the third section of Part III of the Convention were the Articles, numbers 27 to 34, which were to form the backbone of the POW work program. Article 27 established the three central rules of POW labor: Officers were not to be used for labor unless they specifically requested to work; noncommissioned officers were required to perform supervisory labor only; and belligerents could only employ prisoners who were physically fit.

The details were discussed in Articles 28, 29, and 30. Article 28, for instance, charged the detaining country with the responsibility to maintain, treat, care for and pay prisoners employed by individual contractors. Article 29 reiterated the instructions of the earlier Article 27 regarding the physical fitness of working prisoners with the added instruction that even the prisoner who was physically fit might be physically unsuited for a particular type of work. Article 30 was concerned with the working hours of the prisoners. The duration of the daily work, including the travel to and from the work site, could not be "excessive" and could not exceed the number of hours worked by civilian employees in the same region performing the same job. Moreover, each prisoner was allowed a rest period of 24 consecutive hours every week, preferably on Sunday.

The next two Articles, 31 and 32, regulated the kinds of labor which could be undertaken and the conditions under which the prisoners could work. Article 31 stated that prisoners could not furnish labor that was directly related to war operations such as the manufacture of arms or munitions or the transportation of materials intended for units in combat. Article 32 noted again that prisoners were not to be made to participate in dangerous or unhealthy work. Article 33 listed the conditions and responsibilities for prisoner of war detachments; labor detachments had to have the same sanitary, food, and medical conditions found in the prisoner of war camp. The responsibility for the application of these conditions lay with the camp commander. Finally, Article 34 dealt with the wages for prisoner of war labor, which were to be fixed by agreements between belligerents. This Article also outlined the need for a method of payment (either scrip or currency), the manner in which the prisoner obtained his pay, and a system by which the prisoner could save money until his repatriation.[2]

For all its logic and complexity, however, the Geneva Convention was still only a collection of general guidelines written during peacetime nearly 14 years earlier. A vast number of problems which were merely academic in 1929 became very real considerations in 1943. For example, it was understood that prisoners were not to be employed in the manufacture of military hardware (i.e., tanks) since they were directly related to war operations. Could they, however, be employed in the scrap iron industry, whose products would eventually be turned into tanks? Could quarry work be considered dangerous or unhealthy? Could a prisoner claim to be "unsuited" to pick cotton or collect garbage? Hundreds of new questions were raised as the issue of POW labor was thrashed out, and whatever the international representatives at Geneva had failed to contemplate in 1929, American policy-makers were swift to bring into existence in 1943.

In the final analysis the Geneva Convention was entirely open-ended. It was dependent on the captors' interpretation of nearly every major point, from the definitions of "fitness" and "dangerous work" to civilian labor conditions and wage standards.

It was clear, therefore, that before the prisoners could be put to work, the government would have to predict as many future problem areas as possible and establish policy with regard to each. Slowly, through the winter of 1942, the government set about hammering out a future guide for POW labor. Questions of interpretation of the Geneva Convention were referred to a newly created Prisoner of War Employment Reviewing Board in the War Department. On those occasions when the Reviewing Board could not agree on a solution, the matter was sent to the PMGO and the Judge Advocate General's Office for final adjudication.

Moreover, the final report not only had to follow the guidelines set down by the Geneva Convention but had to take into consideration such factors as the reaction of organized labor to the sudden employment of non-union workers. Most importantly, the final guidelines had to establish a policy which would not jeopardize American prisoners in German hands. After months of meetings between high-ranking military and governmental representatives, the final statement was completed on January 10, 1943, and published as "The War Department Policy with Respect to Labor of Prisoners of War." After dozens of pages of analysis of each Geneva Convention article dealing with POW labor, the directive simply concluded:

> . . . any work outside the combat zones not having a direct relation with war operations and not involving the manufacture or transportation of arms or munitions, and not unhealthful, dangerous, degrading, or beyond the particular prisoner's physical capacity, is allowable and desirable.[3]

There it was in a nutshell: what was not disallowed was allowed. This War Department policy, as broadly defined, was clear and acceptable to all parties. The German POWs would be utilized for a wide variety of tasks, both civilian and military, with particular emphasis on filling the dire domestic labor shortage caused by the recruitment of able men into the Armed Forces. The key word throughout the War Department directive was that prisoners were to be used for "essential" work, defined as work which had to be done whether or not there were any prisoners of war to do it. Since the nation was at war, the most essential work revolved around the military.

Labor on Military Installations

The key to military-related POW labor was, of course, that it freed American soldiers for service overseas. Every GI involved in the routine maintenance and operational tasks common to any large military base, the War Department reasoned, was a warrior wasted. Thus with the government's decision on January 10, 1943, to utilize POW labor, German prisoners were immediately moved to fill a wide variety of menial and clerical jobs within their own compounds, and on Army, Navy, and Army Air Corps bases across the nation. The emphasis was always on relieving American personnel to be shipped overseas, and a glance at the Camp Shelby (Mississippi) prisoner roster for the week of September 14, 1944, provides a representative illustration of the tasks assigned:

A. Inside Stockades	Number of POWs
POW Company Overhead	64
Hospital	4
Compound Overhead	6
Personnel Office	22
Police & Prison Clerks	10
Infirmary Orderlies	14
Fly Detail	3
Bugler	2
HQ Post Office	1
Music Director	1
Dental Clinic Aides	6
Canvas Repair	4
Tinsmiths	8
Mosquito Control	8
Sub-total	153

B. Outside Stockade	Number of POWs
Mechanics, J. Area	111
CE Tailors	33
Shoe Repair	27

Reclamation	10
Farms	388
Laundry	97
QM Bakery	24
Roads	20
Carpenters	36
Coal Yard	5
Malaria Control	10
Draftsmen	3
Car Washing	5
Painters and Sign Painters	19
Plumbers	15
Post Dump	6
Yard Detail, J. Area	13
Camp PX Detail	2
QM Subsistence Dty Whse	5
C & E Classification	5
Electric Grass Mowers	2
Grounds Maintenance	14 [4]
Sub-total	850
Total	1,003

By mid-1944, German POWs had quietly and efficiently moved into practically every type of job existing at military reservations. No small number of American troops, en route home from overseas combat assignments, were startled and often angered to find themselves being handed their furlough papers by a POW receptionist. Local communities around POW camps, on the other hand, quickly adjusted to the "familiar spectacle of columns of gray or denim-clad POWs swinging along in the precise easy rhythm achieved only by men familiar with marching since childhood."[5] Not an especially unpleasant way to wait out the war years. Moreover, they were paid.

The POWs received the maximum rate of 80 cents a day in addition to the 10 cents which every enlisted prisoner got for the purchase of toothpaste, shoe polish, razor blades, handkerchiefs, and tobacco at the camp canteen. The War Department even established a savings program for the thrifty, through which they could receive hard currency upon their repatriation to Germany after the war.[6] Officer prisoners, by contrast, were not required to work but received salaries anyway. Lieutenants received $20.00 per month; Captains, $30.00; and Majors through Generals, $40.00. Lest one assume that such salaries were in any way excessive, it must be noted that American POW officers in Germany received a slightly higher amount:

Second Lieutenants	72 Reichsmarks or $28.80
First Lieutenants	81 Reichsmarks or $32.40
Captains	96 Reichsmarks or $38.40
Majors	108 Reichsmarks or $43.20
Lieutenant Colonels	120 Reichsmarks or $48.00
Colonels	150 Reichsmarks or $60.00

While these salaries were more liberal than those paid to German officers in American camps, they were subject to deductions for all food and clothing used by the American officers. So, in reality, American officers in German POW camps probably fared no better financially than the German officers captured by the U.S. Army.[7] Since War Department regulations (and common sense) prevented hard currency from falling into the hands of our prisoners, both officers and enlisted men were paid in scrip, redeemable upon repatriation.

Despite the apparent ease with which the prisoners accepted their tasks in and around the camps, once the alternatives were made sufficiently clear, the War Department was still quite uneasy. The very thought that German combat veterans, only months removed from the battlefields of North Africa, would be running amuck on American military bases sent shivers down the Army's collective spine. Consequently, security during the first several months of the military work program was excessive, often involving nearly as many guards as prisoners. To protect the security of installations under these new circumstances, the assignment of POW employment was at first closely regulated by a Priority Board, appointed by the post commander, which tried to weigh the record of each POW against the sensitivity of the task for which he was being considered. By September and October of 1943, however, the surprisingly small number of incidents, combined with the Army's continued need for American soldiers for other purposes, caused the War Department to let down its guard. Slowly, the prisoners were allowed to work without constant supervision. "I remember a number of occasions when I was set to work at Fort [Camp] Rucker, Alabama," says Alfred Klein, "and the guard would ask me to hold his rifle until he had climbed in or out of the truck. Almost as an after-thought, he would ask me to hand it up to him a few minutes later."[8]

Although the level of security was relaxed, the tempo of work was not.

Camp commanders were continually reminded that their task was vital to the overseas war effort. The harder their POWs worked, the more GIs could be cycled to the front. Every incident or slowdown in the military work program, therefore, was a direct (and dangerous) drain on the struggle against Nazism. Thus, when the Army Service Forces' official *Handbook for Work Supervisors of Prisoners of War* was distributed to all concerned American personnel, guards and supervisors were exhorted: "Be aloof, for the German respects firm leadership. Allow them to rest only when necessary. DRIVE!" [9] The War Department's feelings about the maximum use of POW labor in the military sector were perhaps most succinctly capsulized by American Lieutenant General Wilhelm D. Styer, Commanding General, AFWESPAC, who grunted: "We must overcome the psychology that you cannot do this or that. . . . I want to see these prisoners work like piss ants!" [10] And work they did.

In paid work on military installations alone, the POWs performed 90,629,233 man-days of labor during the period from early 1943 to the end of December, 1945. During 1944 alone, when prisoner labor on military posts was at its highest level, the War Department estimated that even if the pay had been as high as $4.00 per day, prisoner labor was worth approximately $70 million. For the entire three years from 1943 to 1946, the military labor of the POWs was estimated to be as high as $131 million.[11] And that in no way measured the value of freeing thousands of American personnel for the war effort overseas. Yet POW labor on military installations made up only a portion of the total labor program.

Contract Labor

The situation with regard to civilian labor, especially in agriculture, was deteriorating rapidly as the American work force felt the drain of the war effort. In October, 1942, the employed labor force of the United States, exclusive of 5.3 million in the Armed Forces, numbered 52.4 million persons. During the previous year, 3.3 million people had been drawn from the labor force to fill the ranks of the Armed Forces, and in November, 1942, the War Department predicted a total Armed Forces objective of 10.6 million men by the end of 1943. In an ominous 11-page memorandum stamped "SECRET," the Planning Committee of the War Production Board reported to its Chairman, Donald M. Nelson:

> . . . unless non-war production is curtailed below the levels necessitated by shortages of critical facilities and materials, we need 1.7 million

more workers in war production and civilian employment than are now available. This estimate assumes a war production program which has been cut back to limits of feasibility as dictated by shortages of materials and facilities. . . . Plans for building our total armed strength to 10.6 million by the end of 1943 require that we reach 9.8 million by October, an increase from . . . this year of 4.5 million. Thus, the total drain on our manpower resources during the coming year (October to October) will amount to 6.2 million persons. . . .[12]

The obvious answer to this manpower problem was to expand the prisoner work program to fill the gaping chasm in the civilian labor sector.

If the War Department's original decision to use POW labor on military posts had been difficult to work out, the expansion of such labor into the civilian sector was absolutely tortuous. Through the early months of 1943, there followed a succession of more than a dozen meetings between the Provost Marshal General's Office, the War Manpower Commission, the Department of Agriculture, and the Industrial Personnel Division of the Army Service Forces. These organizations sought to work out an acceptable policy of POW civilian-labor use. The agencies wrestled with such issues as the competition of POW labor with "free" (American) labor; the wages to be paid and the costs to the employer of "nuisance factors" such as the hidden expenses of security, interpreters, and possible espionage; the difference between "essential" and "non-essential" tasks; and the bureaucratic process by which employers could apply for laborers and pay for their services. Private industry did not intend to be excluded from these decisions, and the government agencies were quickly inundated with requests for immediate labor aid or the relaxation of certain regulations by pressure groups, congressional lobbyists, and representatives of powerful organizations such as the American Sugar Cane League.[13] Finally, in April, 1943, the War Department announced that POW labor would be made available to the civilian sector, an announcement which was hailed by farmers across the country. Unfortunately, it took some time for the proper bureaucratic procedures to be established and for a sufficient number of prisoners to arrive in the United States. In fact, not until the fall of 1943 did the War Department, the War Manpower Commission (WMC), and the War Food Administration finally manage to work out a satisfactory method of making the POW labor available.

Initially, the War Department and the War Manpower Commission outlined a strict procedural arrangement which first divided society's need into two broad priorities: military installations, as always, retained the first claim to prisoner labor for "essential work" on the war effort; only then did the Army agree to contract out the remaining prisoners for industrial and agricultural needs.[14]

Then came the complications. In order for potential employers to draw upon the labor available through this second category, they had to receive a Certification of Need from the War Manpower Commission. The employer was directed to submit his request to the local employment office of the WMC, detailing the particulars of the work project and providing the necessary assurance that every normal source of labor had been exhausted. In addition, the potential employer had to convince the local agent of the War Manpower Commission that the hiring of POW labor would not lead to a lowering of wages or a decline in working conditions which would be detrimental to returning American workers. Finally, the employer had to assure the government that the prisoners' rights were not being violated, and that wages and working conditions were equal to that of local free labor.[15] Once these specifications had been met, the certification was approved, and the request was passed on to local military officials, who turned to the Department of Agriculture's Extension Service to determine the number of POWs required to complete the task. (In some areas of the country, the WMC refused to allocate POW labor in groups of less than 20 men. The farmer took 20 or more prisoners at one time or none at all.) [16] When the bureaucracy eventually released its approval, the employer and the War Department entered into a contract for the use of POW labor, which could not exceed three months duration. Only after all of these steps had been completed could the prisoners of war finally begin work. Sound difficult? Imagine how frustrating it must have seemed to a labor-starved farmer who lived, perhaps, within a mile or two of a POW camp bulging with thousands of willing and healthy workers.

It should be noted that as exasperating as these regulations and delays may have been to the labor-starved employer, the government's central concern was, as always, the welfare of the POWs, and through them, the safety of the American POWs in German hands. Yet, whatever the motivation, the end result was that the POWs received fair wages and good treatment. Prisoners continued to receive the War Department's original wage of 80 cents per day, and since employers were pledged to pay the prevailing rate of "free" labor in that area, the difference was paid into the Federal Treasury to support the POW program. When certain areas of agriculture required more than the normal eight-hour workday, the WMC authorized the initiation of an incentive pay plan, by which hard workers were rewarded with increased pay while laggards received less. The minimum wage was still 80 cents per day, but under the incentive plan, a hard working prisoner could earn as much as $1.50 a day, payable as always in canteen coupons. In its effort to protect both the prisoner-laborer and the reputation of the program abroad, as well as to prevent an atmosphere of exploitation which might spill over to American labor after the war, the WMC was no less concerned about working conditions. Since the use of POW labor was closely scrutinized by the Swiss representatives, the War Department took great care to promote maximum productivity and safety. Before approving a work project, for example, an on-the-job determination was generally made by a representative of the Army or the WMC to assess the suitability of the work, the physical condition of the prisoners involved, and the training and safety devices necessary. In projects which involved some normal hazards—lumber work or quarrying, for instance—the POWs were provided with hard-toed shoes, goggles, gloves, and all the safety equipment used by non-POW labor in the same jobs.[17] As with the earlier military-labor program, POW officers were not required to work, and non-commissioned officers could be used only for supervisory work unless they specifically volunteered to work. In any case, the labor crisis in the United States was growing more critical by the week; labor-starved farmers across the country were responding to the new program with enthusiasm, and the prisoners were going to work.

The POWs could only relieve the labor shortage, however, if they could be efficiently transported to the work sites. Since it was obviously impractical to shuffle camp populations which often averaged between 8,000 to 12,000 prisoners, the answer was to distribute the men to smaller camps nearer the potential work sites. Thus began the branch camp network, ultimately a total of 511 small satellite camps which provided POW labor where it was most needed. In the state of Arkansas, for example, the three huge base camps—Chaffee, Robinson, and Dermott—eventually supplied POW la-borers to 30 branch camps. The largest camp was at Wynne with a population of 732 Germans; the smallest at Knoble held only 91. Reflecting the overwhelming use of the prisoners as agricultural workers, 26 of these camps were located in Arkansas's richest farming area, the alluvial plain of the Mississippi Delta.[18]

Regardless of the state in which the prisoners were located, they were used, first and foremost, to harvest crops. In Louisiana, for example, prisoners were used to plant and harvest rice, cotton, and sugarcane (harvesting more than 246,000 acres of cane in 1944 alone).[19] In Missouri, prisoners of war harvested potatoes, shucked oats, and wheat. They harvested tomatoes in Indiana, potatoes and sugar beets in Nebraska, wheat and seed crops in Kansas, and more than 1,075,000 stacks of peanuts on 58,000 acres in Georgia. In Pennsylvania, the prisoners were used primarily for nursery and orchard work; in Maryland they harvested fruit, corn, hay, grain, and tobacco; in Maine they harvested over 4,890,000 bushels of potatoes in 1945 alone; in New York State they harvested and helped process over 2 million tons of fruits and vegetables; in Illinois they cut asparagus; and in Texas the POWs gathered pecans, picked peaches and figs, and harvested record amounts of cotton. In Mississippi, in the three months from October to December 1943, the POWs picked over 6,675,000 pounds of cotton seed; and in Idaho, they harvested sugar beets, fruits, and vegetables. Spinach growers of Muskogee County, Oklahoma, used German prisoners from nearby Camp Gruber to harvest more than 4,000 acres during the single month of December, 1943.[20] And so it went across the country. From the end of 1943 to early 1946, war captives were employed on every major agricultural crop in nearly every state in the union.

Despite the original bureaucratic confusion in obtaining POW labor and the normal skepticism of farmers, opposition dwindled as experience with the use of POWs increased. Even though the War Manpower Commission continued to shift prisoners from nonessential tasks to agriculture, and additional Mexican and Jamaican workers were imported,[21] the agricultural demands for the prisoners constantly exceeded the supply, a situation that existed through the end of the war. The rush for POW labor, motivated as much by the increasing enthusiasm of American farmers for the prisoners as by the continuing domestic labor shortage, eventually tipped the balance between the number of POWs allocated to military work and the number working in agriculture. For the first time, on November 22, 1944, more prisoners—74,000—were involved in agriculture than the 69,899 on military installations; [22] and November 1, 1945, the number of captives working in agriculture had risen to 115,369.[23] For its part, the War Department made every effort to reduce the more difficult obstacles facing the nation's farmers in their effort to obtain prisoner labor while maintaining an anxious eye on the rising opposition of organized labor and on the effects of POW labor on the "free" labor sector. Farmers were often encouraged to apply for "group contracts," pooling their labor requirements in order to hasten the War Manpower Commission's final authorization. Farmers still complained, however, that the procedure was too complicated, slow, and restrictive, and in March, 1944, the War Department allowed the Agricultural Extension Service of land grant colleges in most states to act as the official arbiter between labor-starved farmers and POW camp authorities. Although this relationship, and the procedures and regulations which it established, varied widely from state to state—and, sometimes from county to county within a state—the paperwork and lag time were substantially reduced. By the end of the war, rural communities which were located near POW branch camps could often obtain groups of German laborers with little more difficulty than a telephone call to the camp commander.

In addition to the bureaucratic complexities, there were several other difficulties, not the least of which continued to be the language barrier. Rural farmers were as unlikely to speak German or Italian as Army personnel, but at the same time, the harvesting of wheat or the cutting of asparagus required a minimum of communication. Moreover, the prisoners were often anxious to work, many having had rural backgrounds themselves, and they made an effort to understand the farmer's instructions that they would not have made for a prison camp guard. Still, the language problem was there, and the resulting difficulties were more often humorous than not. One day in the spring of 1944, an American sergeant was marching a group of prisoner-laborers the several miles from a farm near Bastrop, Texas, to the prisoner compound in Camp Swift and found himself groping in his vocabulary for the German equivalent of "Halt!" (which happens to be "Halt!") He threw up his arm to stop them, and the entire platoon of prisoners came to attention, shot their arms upward, and chorused, "Heil Hitler!" [24]

Another difficulty concerned the lack of training with which the prisoners often faced their tasks. Prisoners in New England and across the Middle West had little difficulty learning how to harvest wheat, apples, or corn, but in the South and Southwest, where a majority of the prisoners were located, it was a different story. Most of the German prisoners had never seen a stalk of cotton, and according to one Huntsville, Texas, farmer, the Germans did not know "a stalk of cotton from a goddam cockleburr." [25] As a result of this inexperience, the prisoners did not do well in the vast cottonfields of Louisiana, Mississippi, and Texas, seldom picking as much poundage as would have been required of "free" labor. While their results improved with the introduction of a government-sponsored "incentive program," which enabled especially productive prisoners to earn up to $1.50 per day, their overall level of production was disappointing.[26] In other areas of agriculture, however, where the prisoners may have had some earlier experience to draw upon, or where the tasks required little skill and explanation, the Germans did exceptionally well. Farm associations and county extension agents made every effort to increase POW productivity in areas other than cotton by providing short training courses for the POW laborers. In Utah, for example, the Extension Service conducted training schools to instruct the prisoners in the proper thinning of sugar beets and the picking of fruits and tomatoes. In Illinois, an illustrated mimeographed leaflet entitled "Snap Sweet Corn Easier and Faster" was translated into German and distributed to all sweet corn growers using POW labor.[27] The majority of prisoners were reasonably receptive to these efforts, and in most areas their production approached that of American labor.

During the earliest stages of the government's program to ease the labor shortage by the allocation of war prisoners, the issue of security was of paramount concern. The Army, no less than the anxious farmer and businessman, was obsessed by fears of mass escapes and by visions of hordes of Nazis killing and running amuck. Their fears, however, proved groundless. From the moment that small groups of German prisoners began to appear on American farms during the fall of 1943, it was apparent that the prisoners were not going anywhere. Unlike American captives in Germany who could escape to neutral Sweden or Switzerland, and who often had the help of the French underground, German prisoners in the United States found little political sympathy among American citizens, and even if they did escape there was no place for them to go. Thus, from the beginning, the prisoners were resigned, and the Army was enormously grateful. When groups of POWs left their camps in the morning to work on local farms, they were generally accompanied by a single camp guard who watched over their activities throughout the day. While the number of military personnel that guarded the prisoners varied according to the size of the task and the number of guards available, the average work party was composed of one guard for every ten prisoners. By mid-1944, with prisoner escapes a highly infrequent occurrence, it was not unusual for the same guard to oversee a group of 50 to 90 working prisoners. Around Fort Riley, Kansas, German POWs were not guarded at all. The Army explained its "perimeter" system: "Soldiers in cars patrol the general area of the farms. If a prisoner should disappear the farmer is instructed not to stop work to search for him or to bring the others in. He is to notify the prison camp and the guards in cars will be alerted and look for the missing man." The Army contended that the prisoners worked better unguarded, and noted proudly that only one POW had attempted to escape during the entire previous year and he was picked up within a mile of the farm.[28] On a few occasions, when a farmer needed only three or four prisoners for yard work or house painting, no guard even accompanied the captives. In some areas of the country, security became so lax that some of the guards slept while the prisoners worked; others dismantled and cleaned their rifles; and still others simply assigned one of the prisoners to hold the heavy weapon.[29] In one instance, the POWs had so much freedom that handpicked German prisoners working in Louisiana were allowed to enjoy unguarded weekends in New Orleans.[30]

The relationship between the prisoners and the farmers who employed them was generally one of mutual and genuine admiration. Farmers who utilized German captives have consistently described them as "cooperative," "well-mannered," "intelligent," and "good natured." A Louisiana sugar planter recalls that the prisoners assigned to his plantation were not only fine workers, but they even invited him to visit their Camp Thibodaux to view some Christmas decorations they had made.[31] At Camp Houlton, Maine, the commanding officer received a steady flow of letters from various contractors who had utilized POW labor expressing in glowing terms their thanks for the cooperation and high value of the prisoners.[32] An east Texas farmer, Lloyd Yelverton, stated: "They were just the best bunch of boys you ever saw in your life. You enjoyed being around them." [33] In the farming community of Peabody, Kansas, an Army representative was forced to caution farm wives against further incidents of sewing the prisoners' clothing, transporting them to and from town, or baking them cakes and cookies.[34] " 'It's a pity,' mused the big Negro perched on the tractor . . . as he gazed across the cotton fields at the German prisoners complacently harvesting cotton, 'that nice young folks like them has to get in sech devilment that they has to chop cotton so far from home.' " [35] In the main, the prisoners felt the same about the farmers for whom they worked. "Working on the farms in southern Alabama, near Camp Foley," writes Alfred Klein, "we established an excellent personal relationship with the farmers. We were even, in some cases, treated to meals in the farmer's house. How deep this relationship went may be seen from the fact that when my wife and I returned to Alabama for a visit in 1959, I was even invited to join the community's prestigious Elberta Social Club." [36]

As always, there was a minority of prisoners that remained dissatisfied. Some disliked being forced to work, but those engaged in chopping cotton (which the Germans called *baumwolle,* "tree wool") were particularly resentful. Their animosity not only centered on what they considered to be "woman's work" or "low class" labor, but, in an odd twist of logic, considering Germany's racial policies, the prisoners also claimed to resent the exploitation of their "fellow" black farm workers. A Corporal Hein Severloh, at Camp McCain, Mississippi, bitterly complained:

We picked cotton the length of the Mississippi. I'm an agriculturalist, and I know how to handle hard work, but there it was truly very, very hard. It was terribly hot, and we had to bend over all day. We had nothing to drink. . . . There were a great number of Blacks on the plantation. They required us to gather 100 lbs. of cotton a day; but of the Blacks, they demanded two or three times more. . . . For them it was worse than for us. And you have to see how they lived. Their farms: very ugly, very primitive. These people were so exploited. . . . [37]

From Corporal Willibald Bergmann, at Camp Sheridan, Illinois:

Me, I was in peas; picking and the canning factory. The farmers liked me, and wanted me to stay after the war, but I wasn't sure. . . . I met some old people of German origin one day, and these poor old people told me: "We feel alone here. It's sad. It's too big. If we could, we would walk back to Germany on foot. . . ." And the Blacks! They were always saying: "We are just like you: Prisoners; Oppressed; Second-class men. . . ." [38]

From Corporal Hans Gurn, Camp Roswell, New Mexico:

There was a plumber who came to work in the camp. His name was Gutierrez, and he was Mexican. . . . He was a very nice guy. When he went to the barbershop, he stood in the corner, he did not move, and, as he was "colored," he had to wait until all the Whites were done. You know, things like that upset us very much. . . .[39]

And finally:

I was in a camp near Miami in Florida. I was one of the scavenger commandos; every morning we went to gather the garbage in the city. . . . People of German origin were the least nice to us. . . . Those who helped us the most, on the contrary, were the Jews. . . . Ah, the Jews and the Blacks.[40]

The issue of race discrimination in the United States remained the continued target of many German prisoners [41] and would become a source of keen embarrassment to the War Department during later efforts to "democratize" the POWs. Yet as deplorable as such discrimination was, the fact that it was exploited by the soldiers of a government which was, at that moment, exterminating people by the millions, was ludicrous.

Prisoner of war labor was used to a lesser extent in a large variety of other industries as well. Nearly 22,000 POWs were used in logging, lumbering, and pulpwood production, largely in the southern wood-producing states, the Appalachian region, and northern Michigan and Minnesota. In the area of food processing, the prisoners worked in canning plants in New

York State and the northern Illinois-Wisconsin-Michigan area at such places as the Quaker Oats Plant in Rockford and the California Packing Corporation plants in Dekalb and Rochelle, Illinois. At Springdale, Arkansas, the prisoners became particularly adept at picking grapes for Welch's Grape Juice Company.

More than 4,000 prisoners worked in foundries, and between 1,000 and 3,000 prisoners worked in quarries and in open pit mines. POWs were shipped wherever their labor was needed for major tasks and minor; and German prisoners of war were utilized for jobs which ranged from helping local Boy Scouts pick up bundles of old newspapers from the curbs of Huntsville, Texas, to their ironic but far from unenjoyable assignment as kosher meatpackers in Farmington, New Jersey.[42] Prisoners were even dispatched on a voluntary basis for emergency flood control work along the Mississippi River in May of 1943, saving an estimated 1,000 acres of rich Missouri farmland from imminent flooding. Despite the initial fears of both employers and government agencies concerning POW sabotage and escapes (both of which were present but negligible), reports appear to be unanimous in their praise of POW labor. In three industries, however, labor union problems arose.[43]

Union Reaction to POW Labor

The first problem area was that of meatpacking. The demand for meat during the war for American troops overseas and for lend-lease shipments to our Allies had increased dramatically. Yet available civilian labor generally preferred the relative comfort of defense work to the unpleasant conditions associated with stockyards and slaughterhouses, and the meat packing industry was caught on the horns of a dilemma. On the one hand, labor was desperately needed and increasingly unavailable; on the other, it was feared that the use of POW labor would invite the most potentially devastating effects of sabotage or disease.[44] The Surgeon General, Provost Marshal General's Office, and the War Manpower Commission, understandably cautious, delayed making a final decision on the problem pending a full investigation. Even as the investigation continued through the summer months of 1943, the labor situation grew more critical until in November, representatives of the War Food Administration urged the Undersecretary of War, Robert P. Patterson, to press on with the allocation of POW labor regardless of the consequences.

Opposition then appeared from a new direction: The Chicago Meat Institute, representing the meatpacking industry, decried the utilization of

German prisoners aid waste paper drive at Fort Devens, Massachusetts. *(UPI)*

Prisoners from Camp Funston working in the wheat fields near Peabody, Kansas. *(U.S. Army Photo)*

Two POWs from Camp Lufkin, Texas, cut and trim logs near Pollack, Texas, for use as pulpwood. *(U.S. Army Photo)*

Thousands of olives are being stuffed with Spanish sweet peppers by German prisoners at a cannery near Alvin, Texas. *(U.S. Army Photo)*

After V-E Day, the German prisoners were allowed to work on war-related tasks. Here they dip carbines into cosmoline for overseas shipment as other POWs dry the weapons with air pressure. *(U.S. Army Photo)*

Prisoners repairing army
vehicles at the Post Motor Pool,
Fort Story, Virginia.
(National Archives)

An army of POWs repairing American Army uniforms at Fort George Meade,
Maryland. *(National Archives)*

APPENDIX D

CERTIFICATION OF NEED FOR EMPLOYMENT OF PRISONERS OF WAR

CERTIFICATION OF NEED FOR EMPLOYMENT OF PRISONER OF WAR

To: Commanding General,
_____ Service Command

Attention: _____

The_____certifies that:

1. The employer to whom this certificate is issued and whose name, address and place of business are listed below, has need for the labor hereinafter described for essential work at his establishment or farm.

a. Name of employer_____

b. Address of employer_____
_____

c. Type of business_____

d. Location of work (if not at above address)_____
_____

e. Labor needed: From _____ to _____
                        (date)   (date)
   For period of approximately_____ days - months
                              (number) (cross out one)
f. Detail of type of work, number of prisoners, and wage rates:

Number needed	Occ. Title and Code for Industry or Nature of Work Done for Agric.	Man Days or Hours Required	Unit of Work	Prevailing wage per unit

g. If at piece rate, average
   civilian labor will complete_____units per day.
                              (number)
h. The employer usually furnished the following services free of charge to civilian labor: *
_____

i. The employer_____supply transportation to and from
              (will or will not)
   the prisoner-of-war enclosure.

j. The employer_____provide the noonday meal.
              (will or will not)
k. Length of work day in this locality
   for this type of work is customarily_____hours.
                                          (number)

*Enter, if appropriate, one or more of the following: transportation to and from work; noon meal; housing accommodations.

AGO 647A

2. Conditions of employment offered by this employer are not less favorable than those for other workers in the same or similar employment at this establishment or farm, or less favorable than those prevailing in the locality for similar work.

3. The prevailing wage, or price per unit, certified above is that paid to free labor in this locality for this type of work. (For agricultural work, the prevailing wage, or price per unit, certified by the State Director of Extension may be based on public hearings conducted by County Farm Wage Boards.)

4. It has been impossible to secure the necessary workers for this employer through an active campaign of recruitment which has taken into account not only all persons normally engaged in the activities listed above, but also potential workers from other fields of activities.

5. The employer is willing to use through contract with the Government, the labor of prisoners of war detained by the United States of America and in the custody of the War Department. It is the understanding of the undersigned that such contract will follow substantially War Department contract Form No. _____ and that amount to be paid and conditions stated in the contract will be in accord with those certified in this statement.

INDORSEMENTS

I. Approval of the above certificate is recommended:

_____   _____
        (signature)   (title)

_____   _____
        (date)   (address)

II. The above certificate is approved:

_____   _____
        (signature)   (title)

_____   _____
        (date)   (address)

III. The labor certified above has been determined to fall in priority_____

_____   _____
        (signature)   (title)

_____   _____
        (date)   (address)

AGO 647A

(U.S. Army Photo)

Certificate of Credit Balance
for
Prisoner of War

Date
Datum ___JUL 1 5 1945___

This is to certify that ___KLEIN, Alfred___ Sold. ___4WG- 73 562___ ;
(PW Name) (Rank) (ISN)

a prisoner of war in custody of the United States of America on this date,

has a credit balance of _____ $ ___14,80___
(Words) (Amount in figures)

for pay, allowances and other moneys credited to his individual account

during the period of his internment.

Bescheinigung ueber Guthaben von Kriegsgefangenen

Ich bescheinige hiermit dass _____
(Name des Kriegsgefangenen) (Rang)

_____ , Kriegsgefangener im Gewahrsam der Vereinigten Staaten von
(ISN)

Amerika, ein persoenliches Guthaben im Betrage von _____
(in Worten)

$ _____ aus Sold, Zuschlaegen und sonstigen waehrend der Gefangen-
(in Zahlen)

schaft erhaltenen Geldsummen bestehend, besitzt.

LORENZ A. SULZENFUSS
1st Lt., C. M. P.
German Personnel Officer

_____
(Signature of Certifying Officer)
(Unterschrift des die Bescheinigung
ausstellenden Offiziers)

_____
(Rank and Title)
(Rang und Amt)

POWC, Camp Rucker, Alabama
(Station)
(Dienststelle)

The above statement includes all moneys due me from the United States

of America on this date.

Die obige Bescheinigund schliesst saemtliche Geldsummen ein, die mir

gegenwärtig von der Regierung der Vereinigten Staaten zustehen.

Alfred Klein
(Prisoner of War)
(Kriegsgefangener)

WD AGO FORM 19-70   Hq.4th SvC,Atlanta,   THIS FORM SUPERSEDES W.D., P.M.G. FORM NO. 133, REVISED.
1 Mar 45   11169,6-8-45-200,000   WHICH WILL NOT BE USED AFTER RECEIPT OF THIS REVISION.

Thrifty prisoners were allowed to establish savings accounts which were repaid them
prior to repatriation. *(Alfred Klein)*

ARMY SERVICE FORCES

NINTH SERVICE COMMAND
SCU 1983
PWC, RUPERT, IDAHO

ARBEITS-BESCHEINIGUNG	WORKING CERTIFICATE

Werner R I C H T E R Capt. 8 WG 13 333
NAME

Geboren am 28. November 1914	Born November 28, 1914
in Leipzig	in Leipzig
Arbeitete als Kriegsgefangener im K. G. Lager, Rupert, Idaho, U. S. A.	Worked as a Prisoner of War at PW Camp, Rupert, Idaho, U. S. A.
Vom 15. Nov. 45 Bis 20. Jan. 46	from Nov. 15, 45 to Jan. 20, 46
In K.G.-Kompanie	In POW Company
als Schreiber	as a Clerk
Seine Arbeit Umfasste:	His work included:
Schreiben aller Kompanie-Berichte und -Listen	Typed all company reports and rosters

Bewertung:	Rated:
Arbeitsausfuhrung: Befriedigend	Performance: Satisfactory
Betragen: Sehr gut	Conduct: Very good
Leistungsfahigkeit: Befriedigend	Efficiency: Satisfactory
Befahigung: Befriedigend	Aptitude: Satisfactory
Zusammenarbeit: Sehr Gut	Co-operation: Very good
Englischkenntnisse: Hervorragend	Knowledge of English: Excellent

Arthur T. Yates Awarded *Leonard W. Levy*

ARTHUR T. YATES	20 January	LEONARD W. LEVY
Captain CMP		Compound Administrative NCO
Compound Commander	1946	*Supervisor of Work Detail*

Repatriated POWs were presented with certification of their skills and cooperation for use in post-war Germany. *(Werner Richter)*

POW labor as a blow to organized civilian labor. The appearance of the labor union question was bound to arise, and the test case occurred at a New Jersey meat packing plant over POW payment of union dues. In December, 1943, Local 56 of the Amalgamated Meat Cutters and Butcher Workmen (AFL) demanded that 25 cents a week in dues had to be deducted from the wages of the 165 German POWs employed by the Seabrook Farms at Bridgeton, New Jersey. Meetings between the representatives of the union and the meatpacking plant quickly revealed that the real problem was not simply the union's loss of $41.25 a week. The basic issues, it became clear, concerned the very nature of the employee-employer-union relationship. The first question was simply that of who was responsible for decisions regarding the prisoners' wages: the POW who performs the work; the employer who pays his wages directly to the United States Treasury; or the War Department, which pays each working prisoner a standard 80 cents per day in canteen coupons? Since the prisoners had no control over their wages, of course, the problem was passed on to the employer, who in turn declared that the collection of union dues from the Nazi war prisoners working at Seabrook Farms was "strictly a matter between the union and the Army . . . and we don't know the Army's attitude." [45] The second and more basic question concerned the fundamental position of the labor union itself. In the words of the union representative:

> We have a closed shop with Seabrook and we feel that to maintain our contractual status there we should get the regular migratory worker's dues from the prisoners.
> Our real concern is that more prisoners may be brought in from time to time until our contract won't be worth the paper it's written on, because there will be more prisoners than union members.
> And what about the jobs of our members who are in the armed forces? What are we going to say to them?
> Consideration must also be given to our members who may lose their jobs because of seasonal work in other plants. Surely they should have the preference of filling jobs over war prisoners! [46]

In fact, these issues were never resolved. The War Manpower Commission, anxious to avoid an open war with the nation's powerful labor unions, embarked on a massive recruiting program during December of 1943 to induce farm workers, soldiers on temporary leave, women, and high school students to take jobs in the meat packing industry. By the spring of 1944, the industry's labor requirements were filled, and the several hundred POWs already at work in various meat packing plants were reassigned to different jobs.

The second major area of trouble with regard to POW labor was the railroad industry. In the early spring of 1943, in response to the growing labor shortage in the industry, J. J. Pelley, the president of the Association of American Railroads, cautiously suggested to the War Department that POW labor be used to temporarily fill the ranks. The Undersecretary of War, on June 28, dutifully responded that, indeed, the Geneva Convention permitted the use of POW labor on railroads, though they were limited to track maintenance.[47] In a series of rapid meetings between Mr. Pelley's Association, the Office of Defense Transportation, the Interstate Commerce Commission, and the War Department's chief of transportation (as well as with Paul V. McNutt, Chairman of the War Manpower Commission, and James F. Byrnes, Director of the Office of War Manpower Mobilization), a policy of POW utilization was worked out. When the arrangement was revealed to the public in mid-September, 1943, labor union reaction was instant and outraged. American railroads were, and still are, the most unionized industry in the nation, and the War Department found itself at loggerheads with the powerful Brotherhood of Railway Clerks and the entire Association of Railway Labor Executives. George Harrison, President of the union, carried on a vociferous campaign, at one point declaring of Secretary Stimson:

> My God, does he not know that Railroading is a most delicate operation. . . . We carry on night and day in split second schedules. I have not been able to get a reason for turning loose Nazi soldiers, skilled in demolition practices, so that they may run amuck on the railroads.[48]

By the following day, on October 15, railway union locals, representing more than 1 million railway workers, adopted resolutions declaring their refusal to work with prisoners of war "lest railroad traffic be adversely affected." Despite governmental assurances that "the safety of railroad movements would not be impaired and the safety of railroad workers would not be endangered by such use of prisoner labor," [49] the nation's railroad workers threatened a nationwide shutdown if POWs were assigned to work on the railroads. The unions did not hesitate to immediately challenge the government's policy in court in a test case concerning the Chicago, Burlington & Quincy Railroad's application for 250 POWs from Camp Clark, Missouri, to help construct a railroad switching yard in Lincoln, Nebraska. The legal challenge was, in fact, dismissed, as the War Department concluded that the union's fear of sabotage was unfounded. Victorious or not, the government was now wary of further labor unrest and consequently decided against detailing prisoners to heavily unionized segments of the industrial home front. Regarding the railroad industry, POW labor was used very rarely and only in emergencies and in isolated areas.

The final American industry which vehemently opposed the introduction of German war prisoners was that of forestry and pulpwood. Raw pulpwood is the basic material used in the manufacture of such essential items as blue print paper, carbon paper, chart and map paper, photographic and other sensitized paper, ordnance and shell wraps, and shipping boxes of every variety. Since these items, and a host of other paper products, were of significant importance to every segment of the war effort, the many companies which formed the pulpwood industry had no small amount of influence on the government. As the manpower drain began to make itself felt in the forestry industry, therefore, company spokesmen and politicians went on the offensive. Following a series of conferences with the representatives of the paper industry at the beginning of August, 1943, the Congressional Subcommittee on Brand Names and Newsprint unanimously agreed to recommend that the pulp and paper industry be classified as an area essential to the war effort.[50] Behind the scenes, on August 6, the Pulpwood Industry Advisory Committee pleaded with General Somervell to furlough 5,000 experienced pulpwood cutters and loggers from the Army or at least for the Army to organize 10,000 Negroes into labor battalions to cut pulpwood timber in the South.[51] While there is no record of the Army's response, the answer must have been less than satisfactory, for on August 19, the American Paper and Pulp Association took its case before the public. Reiterating the "drastic shortage of paper," the Association's executive secretary, E. W. Tinker, stressed the industry's immediate need for Army personnel—and prisoners of war.[52]

Requests for POW labor poured into the offices of the War Manpower Commission from small pulp companies throughout the Northeast,[53] and by February 17, 1944, a spokesman for the War Production Board could announce that 5,000 prisoners were already employed in cutting timber for pulpwood.[54] As with any other industry, the War Manpower Commission determined the need, and local rate of pay; and the contractor was responsible for providing housing, supervision, tools, and transportation. Moreover, the Timber Production War Project of the Forest Service provided a safety training program designed to offer the POWs the necessary instruction in the use of hand tools. The results, however, were not encouraging. The cost of using POWs proved extremely high due to the need for increased supervision, security considerations, housing, and the cost and maintenance of the tools which "free" labor generally provided for itself. Production, moreover, was considerably lower than that normally generated by free labor, averaging less than a cord per day per man, and was not significantly increased by the introduction of the PMG's incentive plan.[55] If the use of prisoner labor in this industry was a disappointment to pulpwood companies, it was a horror to the labor unions.

Within weeks of the War Production Board's decision to utilize prisoner labor in the paper and pulpwood industry, the International Woodworkers of America arose in anger. The union blamed the need for POW labor on the industry's failure to negotiate with the unions in good faith, thus allowing the continuation of substandard wages, and forcing workers to seek jobs in other industries. Hinting strongly that the government was in collusion with employers to break down the wage standards established by the union, especially in the South, the I.W.A. requested that the POW directive be rescinded and that proper wage levels for native Americans be considered.[56] An outcry from the Timber Workers Union, Local No. 29, Duluth, Minnesota, was not quite as understanding. "It astounds us to think that men would be brought in," raged union president, Ilmar Koivunen, "who have undoubtedly participated in the taking of American lives, and who would be housed according to International Law and the Geneva Agreement in camps that would have electric lights, adequate bathing facilities, clean sheets and bedding and other camp conditions that we lumberjacks have been struggling to obtain for seven years. All this would be given to the fascist criminals but nothing is being done to provide these conditions for the timber workers." [57] Despite the labor unrest, employer dissatisfaction, and, judging by the poor production figures, the recalcitrance of prisoners as well, the utilization of POWs in the pulpwood industry continued to limp along for the remainder of the war. It was best summarized, perhaps, by the closing words of an internal WPB report which concluded: "The use of prisoners of war in the production of pulpwood . . . is only justified because it enables the industry to obtain production which could not otherwise be secured. It is universally true throughout the country that operators would give up their prisoners of war today if they could be replaced by free labor." [58]

The Success of the Labor Program

Despite these difficulties with the unions and the overall, befuddling morass of governmental red tape with which the small employer found himself faced in obtaining prisoner laborers, the contract program appears to have been a solid success. The POWs performed a vital role in alleviating the acute domestic labor shortage. "I don't know whether people appreciate the value of prisoners to the war program," commented Major General Russel B. Reynolds, Commanding Officer of the Sixth Service Command. "Working in a variety of shops and in other occupations, they are conserving a vast quantity of manpower, doing jobs in which either soldiers or civilians otherwise would have to be used." [59] Their background of intense military training made them steady and uncomplaining workers. The War Department made periodic statements designed to calm anxious representatives of the civilian labor force: "Efficiency of prisoners-of-war labor, while not comparable to that of free labor, has been such as to justify its use." [60] But POW guards and work supervisors generally conceded that the healthy and "beautifully trained" German prisoners were easily manageable and highly efficient.[61] Employers agreed. Canners and food processors in nothern Illinois, for example, unanimously concurred: "Many area employers have been dependent almost entirely on the pool of prisoner labor in maintaining their businesses. During the summers of 1944 and 1945, it would have been virtually impossible to carry out the harvesting and processing of crops without their labor; while other smaller businesses would have closed their doors." [62] German prisoners were used on more than 300 farms in Maine, New Hampshire, and Massachusetts, and were credited with saving the entire Maine pea crop, the greater part of the Massachusetts cabbage harvest, and the entire New Hampshire apple crop.[63] In short, there is little question that while their productivity often fell short of that of prewar "free" labor, the prisoners of war were of substantial value to the economy. Moreover, the program not only kept the prisoners busy, while enabling them to earn 80 cents a day in canteen coupons, but produced a substantial amount of hard cash for the Federal Treasury. Since the War Department required the employer to pay the same rate per unit of work completed that he would have paid free civilian labor if such had been available, the difference between the prisoners' 80 cents (paid by the government), and the standard daily wage after deducting the employers' costs of transportation, housing, and security, was paid into the Treasury. In June, 1945, Brigadier General Bryan was able to announce to the House Committee of Military Affairs that to date, "contractors have paid into the United States Treasury $22,000,000 in cold cash." [64] An additional indication of the significance of the POW contract labor program may be drawn from the sharpness of protests by outraged and crestfallen employers when faced with losing their POW laborers when the repatriation schedule was finally announced at the end of the war. Even the POWs profited from contract labor, for those who chose to save their paltry 80 cent coupons were often able to return to Germany with several hundred dollars in savings by the end of the war.

The labor program produced a political dividend as well. As stipulated by the Geneva Convention, POW officers were not required to work except on a voluntary basis, nor could noncommissioned officers be forced to provide anything more than supervision over the remaining thousands of German enlisted prisoners. The ramifications of this stipulation were two-fold: First, the work force would consist almost entirely of German privates and corporals, whose separation from their officers generally provided a more docile and manageable labor force; and second, the leisure time afforded to the officers who chose not to work (and not many did) provided the fertile soil for a steady increase in Nazism. On the other hand, the general trend toward Nazism among idle officers was seldom acted upon; for without continual access to their enlisted men in the work force, their political resentment was effectively truncated. Ultimately, approximately 7.3 percent of the prisoner officers volunteered for employment, as did approximately 45 percent of the noncommissioned officers (including some thousands who claimed to be NCOs who were sent to work when they could not produce the required credentials regarding their rank).[65]

This is not to imply that the enlisted prisoners were particularly eager to work, for often they were not. There was plenty to do during the day without a new manual labor program. A reluctance to embark on a new program of manual labor was expected by both Washington and Berlin, and each provided part of the solution. Early in the work program, individual camp commanders, searching for a legal means of encouraging prisoners, arrived at the method of reducing reluctant prisoners' food rations, and by the summer of 1943, the "No Work–No Eat" dictum became standard War Department policy. Berlin was anxious to prevent trouble in the camps over this work policy since nothing was to be gained by mass resistance. More-over, if the German POWs successfully refused to work, Berlin reasoned, American POWs in German hands would quickly adopt the same policy. Sterner measures would be called for by both countries, which might lead to a dangerous escalation of POW strikes and administrative retaliation. Berlin therefore informed the German POWs to comply with the new work program. The moment in June, 1943, when the information was received is recalled by Warrant Officer Werner Baecker, then at Camp Roswell, New Mexico:

The Americans showed us the Directive from the *Oberkommando Wehrmacht* [Supreme Command of the Wehrmacht] which had been transmitted to us through the International Red Cross. It said: "In the interest of the prisoners . . . it is recommended that you put yourselves at the disposal of the American work program, according to rank, and do what is required." The *OKW* believed that it was preferable that we work to keep up our morale and to retain our physical fitness. But this Directive certainly raised a storm. The officers, non-commissioned officers, and even the enlisted soldiers of the *Afrika Korps* rampaged around the camp, saying that "This Directive is a fake—it's impossible that we are being asked to aid the enemy." The Americans watched us for several days, and then they announced a time limit beyond which those who refused to work would be classifed as "fanatical Nazis" and immediately transferred to a camp for hardened cases. That made a lot of us think—especially when they began transferring guys who refused to work, the very next night. So everything calmed down and we began to work.[66]

To a sizable minority of hardened Nazi prisoners, however, directives and transfers were not enough incentive to motivate them to work. For such prisoners, the War Department was forced to turn to other measures.

Prior to the massive influx of prisoners during the summer of 1943, the War Department prevented POW camp commanders from exercising little more pressure than a reprimand, an admonition, the withholding of privileges, and, in extreme cases, a court martial. With the arrival of thousands of new prisoners, however, these were useless gestures. How much influence could a simple admonition or reprimand have on combat-hardened enemy soldiers? And to expect that such minor pressure, administered not by their own leadership, but by American camp commanders and guards, would effectively make productive workers out of disruptive prisoners, would have been to expect too much even from the Geneva Convention.

Sometimes the Germans were made to complete their tasks by using humorous subterfuges. On one occasion at Camp Crossville, Tennessee, for example, the prisoners refused to clean up their kitchen and mess hall. It was, for the moment, a symbol of defiance. Nothing could move them, and day by day the situation became worse. The threat of disease was becoming as real as the impending escalation of force. The solution appeared spontaneously when two American camp authorities, while checking supplies in a storehouse, noticed the "everpresent eavesdropper" with his ear pressed against the knothole in the wall. The American officers winked and began their ruse:

> "Lieutenant, the prisoner who is coming is no ordinary one. He's a general officer, one of their really bigtimers. . . . Give him double—no, give him triple space."
> "Right, Sir. Will do."

The stoolie stole away. For the next few days, the American officers allowed themselves to be wheedled and cajoled into disclosing the name of the incoming POW celebrity. Finally, one American "gave in," swearing the German to secrecy, told him that " . . . It's Rommel."

GENERAL ROMMEL! THE DESERT FOX!

> The activity in the compound for several days was unbelievable. Even the kitchen was cleared of mounting debris and was made spotless. More cleaning up. But, company didn't come. Days passed. No company. Weeks passed. No fox, desert or any other kind.[67]

The prisoners had been outfoxed.

At the other extreme, there is but a single, unsubstantiated reference to the use of gross brutality as an instrument of motivation in an autobiographical novel by a Harvard-trained physician named Dr. Edward C. Malewitz. In the book, the central character, Dr. Tony Feldman, describes an incident at Camp Rupert, Idaho, where Malewitz was, in real life, assigned as the camp physician.

> Four POW's refused to obey a legitimate order by the colonel. He placed them in the middle of a flat, open field with the temperature down into the twenties. One blanket per prisoner, one roll of toilet paper. Four machine guns to prevent escape. The next morning, four Nazis dead, frozen solid. The grey clouds were so low they seemed almost within arms reach. Taps sounded by a bugle echoed across the desolate fields. Tony had never felt more miserable. He had to pronounce them dead and sign as a witness of correct punishment for gross disobedience. Then it was over and the earth returned to earth. How could he prove all this? He never saw their names. Nothing was ever printed.[68]

While it would be reasonable to assume that among 400,000 prisoners and guards, scattered over 511 camps, such incidents could have occurred, there are simply no other references to such actions in either the records or the personal recollections of the participants.

On the whole, however, experience had proven that the only consistently effective disciplinary measures were those which affected the POW's food and pay, and in October, 1943, the Provost Marshal General's Office reinterpreted Article 27 of the Geneva Convention to permit the detaining power to use reasonable pressure to encourage prisoners to comply with a work order. Called the policy of "Administrative Pressure," the reinterpretation authorized the camp commander to impose restricted diet and reduced privileges for any prisoner who refused to obey a lawful order, including a work order. This was not a punishment, the War Department reasoned, since the prisoner could terminate the pressure at any time simply by complying with the order; such "administrative pressure" was just an inducement to obey a proper command.

The need for such a "No Work, No Eat" policy was not born out of idle concern. From 1943 until the end of the war, there were hundreds of minor incidents of work slowdowns and stoppages at camps across the country and a number of inconsequential attempts at sabotage as well. The prisoners seldom accomplished anything more dangerous than what during peacetime would be termed malicious mischief or vandalism—the destruction of American mail, the cutting of telephone wires, the spoiling of food, and the damaging of machinery—and the camp authorities were quick to respond. An examination of the *Prisoner of War Punishment Records* for the first two months of 1944 at Camp Campbell, Kentucky, for example, provides a representative illustration of the average violations and punishments within the camps: [69]

1/21/44 (Names of 20 POWs)	Unsatisfactory work; slow, grouped up, then refused to work.	7 days confinement on bread and water.
1/20/44 (Names of 20 POWs)	Damaged trees and property; carved swastikas on trees and refused to remove them; poor workers; arrogant.	7 days confinement on bread and water.
1/21/44 (Name of 1 POW)	Poor worker; exceeded rest periods; poor attitude.	No beer for 1 mo. & deprived of shows for same time.
2/04/44 (Names of 3 POWs)	Scrap lumber detail; refused to work, refused to give names to guard, then gave false names.	7 days confinement on bread and water.

1/29/44 (Name of 1 POW)	Stole 1 file and 1 pr. pliers from Motor Pool; tried to smuggle tools in compound wrapped in rags.	1 month on "Ash and Trash"; no pay work; no shows for 3 months.
2/16/44 (Name of 1 POW)	Violation of 96th Article of War; Refused to obey order of 1/Sgt. to return to work; struck Sgt. Lang (POW) in face with fist.	Court-Martial. Found Guilty: To be confined at hard labor at such place as reviewing authority may direct, for 3 months....

While the offenses ranged from minor violations to an intention to do serious harm, no acts of vandalism occurred outside of the POW camps, and the military authorities were swift to segregate any visibly hardened cases from the main body of prisoners.

The only incidents which hit the newspapers, however, were those involving several major sit-down strikes by prisoners, and the public was always reassured by a description of the government's humane but firm reaction. On July 7, 1944, for example, 70 German POWs, transported to Utica from nearby Camp Pine, New York, to pick peas, went on strike when their ultimatum to the authorities for an extension of their bedtimes went unheeded. In a terse article of less than 20 lines, the public learned that the striking prisoners were instantly placed in solitary confinement for 30 days on a diet of bread and water for the first 14 days and that they were to be replaced by another labor force from Camp Pine.[70] On June 22, 1944, 94 Germans at Camp Worland, Wyoming, who called a strike to protest the lack of benches in the trucks which transported them to and from work, were immediately placed on a bread-and-water diet until work was resumed.[71] At Camp Perry, Ohio, on March 3, 1945, the entire POW community of 2,180 men were put on a diet of bread and water for two weeks following their decision to join in a sit-down strike by 180 of their fellow POWs.[72] Readers of *The New York Times* on July 16, 1944, were amused to see that 200 protesting German prisoners at the Letchworth Park (N.Y.) camp quickly scampered back to work following Colonel John M. McDowell's cryptic order: "Book of Genesis, Chapter II, verse 19."

Military police scanned their Bibles to interpret the order and found the reference to read: "In the sweat of thy face shalt thou eat bread till thou return unto the ground."

The 200 prisoners quickly got the idea and went back to work to eat.

A final example of the rash of POW sit-down strikes with which the War Department was faced, as well as of the countermeasures available to the Government, concerned a short-lived sit-down strike at the Benton Harbor, Michigan, POW camp. In a two-sentence announcement in *The New York Times* of August 11, 1944, the interested reader was simply informed that:

> A German prisoner of war was slightly wounded by a ricocheting bullet today when he and approximately fifty other Nazis refused to go into formation until two warning shots were fired. The other prisoners resumed their duties.

In summary, it must be noted that despite the alarming nature of these events, the small amount of news space devoted to such POW strikes was entirely realistic. POW protests and work-halts occurred very rarely in comparison with the total number of prisoners in camps across the country. The overwhelming majority of POW camps in the United States never experienced so much as a ripple of organized opposition. When difficulties did occur, the authorities responded swiftly with firm and generally well-directed disciplinary measures.

Thus far the prisoner of war program appeared to be a reasonable success—better than anyone had dared to expect. The POWs had been routinely processed and well cared for and were now adjusted to their daily schedules. Both the War Department and the POWs themselves were pleased with the relative efficiency of the operation and were beginning to relax. Local communities, initially apprehensive at the news that they would be hosting unknown numbers of enemy soldiers, were quickly growing used to the daily sight of groups of blue-denimed men marching crisply to and from their tasks. The work programs were also working smoothly, keeping the prisoners busy while at the same time providing the nation's industries with desperately needed labor. Despite a number of minor POW demonstrations by a faction of hardened cases and the public outcry of organized labor, by 1945, 95.6 out of every 100 prisoners of war who could be employed under the terms of the Geneva Convention were working for private employers or on various military establishments,[73] at an estimated cash value of over $100 million. The POW work program seemed, indeed, a success. With the attempt to occupy the time of the prisoners now completed, the question remained: Who or what would occupy their minds?

CHAPTER IV

Escapes

Without question, the central issue which most concerned the War Department with regard to prisoners of war was the very reasonable fear of mass escapes. From the moment that the first shiploads of hardened German captives arrived in November, 1942, the government was haunted by the specter of thousands of escaped Nazi prisoners sabotaging and raping their way across the United States while American military forces were locked in combat overseas. As a result, Washington intended to leave little to chance in the area of POW security. Elaborate precautions were taken in the location and construction of the camps, and all participating American military personnel were continually reminded by the steady flood of ASF regulations and memos that the prevention of escape was their highest priority concern. To that end, camp commanders were encouraged to find the most efficient balance of security measures from among such options as additional floodlights, patroling war dogs, the censoring of prisoner mail, sporadic bed checks, the creation of prisoner informants, shakedown inspections, and a general aura of firm military discipline. Since each camp had different characteristics and problems, the security measures adapted by one commander would seldom be applicable at another camp, and as a result, the procedures required to maintain control varied widely from camp to camp. Regardless of these differences, it quickly became apparent that these security measures were more than adequate to control the thousands of incoming enemy soldiers. Escapes, in fact, occurred infrequently, most large camps experiencing no more than three or four such events during the entire war. The War Department's fears gradually melted away.

The Factors and Statistics of Escape

In addition to a wide variety of security measures, the War Department was pleasantly surprised to find that three major factors worked in its favor. The incoming prisoners were still harnessed to the internal hierarchy of their army, despite their new surroundings. Washington was relieved to find that it was not faced with a chaos of hundreds of thousands of uncontrollable individuals but rather with a tightly obedient military unit in which each rank was responsible for its actions to its direct superior. The best way to handle the prisoners, therefore, was to turn their control over to themselves, and hope that the senior officers could be influenced to keep the lower ranks orderly. While this tactic led, unfortunately, to the inadvertent strengthening of German militarism and Nazism inside the camps, it proved very helpful in defusing the looming threat of random escapes.

The second unexpected ally in the War Department's security efforts was the comprehensive recreational and educational program and the immediate attraction of these opportunities to incoming prisoners. The dazzling array of artistic, musical, athletic, educational, and spiritual outlets provided by the War Prisoner's Aid Committee of the YMCA, the National Catholic Welfare Council, and International Committee of the Red Cross, as well as by the War Department and the prisoners themselves, produced a strenuous recreational program which occupied much free time which otherwise would have been spent in less desirable pursuits.

The third and final obstacle to escape was the realization by the incoming prisoners that there was simply no place to go. The most elemental grasp of geography indicated the very limited number of options: north or south would bring the escapee to the well-scrutinized borders of Canada or Mexico, and east or west would bring him only as far as the beaches of the Atlantic or Pacific oceans. Moreover, the long train rides which had transported the POWs across the country from the docks to their new camps showed the startled foreigners that, regardless of the direction in which they escaped, the distances involved would be substantial. Even if they did escape, they certainly could not rely upon many sympathetic American civilians for help.

Yet such logic did not prevent a number of enemy captives from attempting to escape, and while these constituted less than one percent of the 360,000 German prisoners in the United States, they were generally motivated by factors far less sinister than the compulsion to rape, pillage, or sabotage. The first such reason for escapes, in fact, was that it was legal to do so, a privilege guaranteed by the Geneva Convention of 1929. Simply put, it is the duty of captured soldiers to escape. Unlike a civilian criminal who is under a legal and moral obligation to serve out a sentence which society has deemed appropriate, a captive soldier is not a criminal—since he was acting as an instrument of his country's martial policies—and is under no legal obligation to remain incarcerated. More than that, the captured soldier, regardless of nationality, is charged by his oath of service to resist his captors and to escape at every opportunity. The German government did not neglect to inform its captive soldiers in American camps of these facts, both through the offices of the International Red Cross and the American War Department. In a "Memorandum Addressed to German Soldiers," which was provided to all POWs as guaranteed by their rights under the Geneva Convention, German captives were reminded to keep physically strong, to make themselves fully familiar with their rights, and to take every opportunity to escape.[1] Some prisoners, as a result, did exactly as ordered.

Another factor which often prompted POWs to escape was the temptation provided by the gradual reduction in the number and quality of their guards. As discussed earlier, the manpower requirements of the overseas conflict necessitated the decision by Generals Somervell and Bryan to adopt the policy of "calculated risk." By accepting a certain percentage of escapes in order to insure the shipment of more soldiers overseas, the War Department tacitly acknowledged the temptation which would appeal to a number of prisoners. Not only did the government reduce the number of camp guards, but the quality of those guards, already admittedly in question, deteriorated as each successive level of fitness was transferred to the front. Moreover, the War Department chose to fill the diminishing ranks with American soldiers who themselves had been prisoners of war in Germany—a questionable method of improving the emotional or psychological level of the camp guards, much less reducing the friction between the guards and their prisoners.[2]

The final factor which accounts for most of the attempted escapes was nothing more sinister than the availability of opportunity. Despite the comprehensive sports and educational programs, prisoners were often on agricultural work sites under minimal supervision with the lure of an unknown country only steps away. Some walked from their work parties to find female company; others wanted to shop in local stores or mingle with people; still others only wanted to be alone. Whatever their motivation, the many prisoners who escaped on impulse were almost always rounded up within hours or days of their disappearance with little more to show for their effort than a few hours of freedom and an increase in the War Department's statistics. In fact, most such escapes never even came to the public's attention.

Regardless of the motives which drove the prisoners to escape, they attempted to do so from the very moment of their arrival in the United States. The earliest recorded escape attempt occurred on November 5, 1942. Two German prisoners, Karl Kuft and Hans Jourat, jumped from the train carrying them from a transshipment point at Cincinnati, Ohio, to their new homes at Camp Forrest, Tennessee. They were apprehended two days later outside of Bowling Green, Kentucky.[3]

As the number of incoming German prisoners soared, the number of escapes continued to keep pace. By the following year, in November, 1943, there were 171,484 prisoners in the United States, and the number of escapes had risen to 81. A year later, with 360,455 enemy captives in American camps, attempted escapes had reached 1,028, and from the mid-summer of 1944 to the midsummer of 1945, German prisoners of war were escaping at the rate of about 100 per month or slightly more than three escapes per day. These figures may seem alarming at first glance, but considering that the United States held more than 360,000 German prisoners, the monthly rate of escape was approximately 3 escapees per 10,000 captives, a ratio which the War Department was to boast (justifiably) was better than that achieved by the penitentiary system. A June 30, 1944, comparison follows:

COMPARATIVE ESCAPE RATE FROM POW CAMPS
AND FEDERAL PENITENTIARIES

	Average Population	Escapes	Rate
Federal Prisoners:	15,691	69	.0044
Prisoners of War:	288,292	1,036	.0036

Moreover, boasted the government, most federal penitentiary prisoners were confined behind permanent walls, and their escapes retarded by the latest scientific devices; while POWs were held within barbed wire compounds and sent out from the camp daily on work projects. Finally, the large majority of escaped prisoners were apprehended and returned to military control within 24 hours of their escape, at which time they were routinely interrogated by the authorities, given a token punishment as directed by the Geneva Convention, and returned to the prisoner community.

Escape from the POW Camp

Like their American counterparts in Nazi POW camps, German prisoners preparing to escape were governed by an internal "Escape Committee." This powerful committee had to approve all plans and carefully study all preparations made by the prisoners. It determined if the men had the proper supplies, information, money, and other items before they were allowed to leave, and in case of failure, the committee made a thorough review of the entire effort.[4] The wide spectrum of specialists in the prison community enabled the committee to draw upon a variety of talents. Tailors manufactured such articles as civilian suits; carpenters built tunnel shoring and trap doors; and tinsmiths, chemists, cartographers, photographers, and linguists provided the many details required for a successful escape. Former architects and artists were responsible for counterfeiting the documents which would enable escaped prisoners to move easily in American society. Social Security cards, military orders, drivers' licenses, letters of identification were often ingeniously forged with little more than an engraved plate carved on a piece of linoleum, India ink, salvaged cardboard, and an intricate "rubber stamp" carved from a raw potato.[5] Yet, despite the apparent crudeness of these makeshift items, hundreds of escaped prisoners had little or no difficulty in crossing the United States on trains and buses or in applying for employment on farms or in large cities. In the final analysis, however, no matter how thorough the preparation, or how convincing the camp-made civilian clothing and identification papers, the first and foremost problem was the actual escape from the POW camp.

"It was not complicated to escape," recalls former *Afrika Korps* major Tilman Kiwe in reflecting on his many escape attempts from Camp Trinidad, Colorado, and Camp Alva, Oklahoma. About his third attempt, he recalled:

> The organization of the camp first obtained an American uniform for me that the guards must have traded for our military decorations or pretty wood sculptures. A tailor in the camp fashioned a very smart civilian raincoat. The problem was that it was grey-green, but we were not short of chemists in the camp. With boiled onions they obtained a marvelous shade of orange-yellow, and with tea they darkened it a bit to a perfect, inconspicuous color.
>
> Before leaving this time I worked to perfect myself in English, especially in American slang. There was a prisoner in the camp who had spent 23 years in America; he was an interpreter and he took me well in hand. I could soon pass absolutely for an American. . . . Preparations were making progress. The organization had furnished me with the necessary money—about a hundred dollars. . . . The day was set for the escape. . . . I slid under a barrack. They were all on blocks; though there wasn't much room, I changed clothes, and stepped out in the uniform of an American Lieutenant. I waited until around 10:30 and went to the guard post. The sentinel must have thought I was taking a walk. I gave him a little sign with my hand, said "Hello," threw him a vague salute, and hop! I was outside! [6]

Although the majority of escapees left merely by absenting themselves while the guard's attention was directed elsewhere, many times more ingenious methods were employed. The prisoners cut wire fences, passed through the camp gates in makeshift American uniforms, smuggled themselves out of camps aboard commercial delivery trucks, jumped over the compound fences from barrack rooftops, climbed out of hospital windows, and tunneled like moles. At Camp Mexia, Texas, a group of prisoners decided to break out by constructing dummies which their comrades stood up at the back of the line during morning inspection so that none of the guards would know that the men had gone. "It worked fine," said former POW Werner Richter, "until one of the dummies fell over." [7] At another Texas camp at Hearne, six German prisoners spent part of every day constructing a makeshift boat in a hidden area along the nearby Brazos River; it was a remarkable craft made of waterproof GI ponchos with umbrellas for sails. One night they escaped and sailed their improvisation down the Brazos, hoping to reach the Gulf Coast. It was an ambitious project, but they were apprehended less than five miles downriver from the camp.[8] At Camp Somerset, Maryland, one prisoner made several "practice escapes" during which he actually left the camp and returned before making his final escape.[9] A far more spectacular escape occurred on December 24, 1944, from Papago Park Camp not far from Phoenix, Arizona. While the guards were preoccupied with controlling a volatile POW demonstration with tear gas and clubs, 25 German prisoners, mostly submarine officers, escaped through a 200-foot tunnel which had been bored through rocky soil. "Construction of the tunnel must have taken many months," Colonel William A. Holden, camp commandant, confided to the press. "The tunnel started underneath an outdoor coal box and went from twelve to fifteen feet below the ground . . . we believe the prisoners may have had only coal-stove fire shovels for tools in cutting the rock." [10] The complete story of the Papago Park escape, published as a suspenseful narrative called *The Faust-ball Tunnel,* revealed some startling advance preparations. The three U-boat captains who led the mass escape, for example, had first made a trial run all the way from the POW camp, 130 miles, to the Mexican border. They were more than 40 miles into Mexico when they were finally captured by the authorities and returned to camp with all information required for the later mass escape. Moreover, when the 25 escapees were finally recaptured, some were carrying packs of nearly 100 pounds, containing spare clothing, cereals, canned goods, medical supplies, maps, and cigarettes.[11]

Similar tunnels were discovered at several other camps across the country. At Fort Ord, California, near Monterey, American authorities aborted an escape by some 500 German POWs when they stumbled upon a 120-foot tunnel running five feet underground from the edge of the compound toward the stockade limits. Working at night, the prisoners had dug through the sandy soil with garden tools, disposed of the excavated dirt by scattering it throughout the compound, and had shored the walls of the two and a half-foot wide tunnel with boards from fruit boxes, scrap lumber, and flattened tin cans. Much relieved at having frustrated the escape, the camp authorities called in the Army Engineers to dynamite the nearly-completed tunnel, and the prisoners were put to work filling in the excavation.[12] A far more sophisticated tunnel was found at Camp Trinidad, Colorado, with the accidental discovery of a hidden, electrically-lighted, 150-foot tunnel which extended a full 65 feet beyond the fence. "The entrance to the tunnel was located beneath a trapdoor in a closet of a barracks building in the German officers' compound," explained camp commandant Lieutenant Colonel William S. Hannan, "and the exit was covered with foliage growing in dirt-filled boxes which would be lifted out by the escaping men." [13] There was, in fact, no end to the variety of escape methods utilized by determined prisoners, and where ingenuity left off, persistence alone often succeeded. For Major Tilman Kiwe, however, now transferred to Camp Alva, Oklahoma—a site reserved for obdurate cases—success was still elusive:

> This time I prepared my escape more seriously. For three months I let my beard grow, and I completely transformed my appearance; I now had lacquered hair, parted in the middle, and glasses. And a real civilian suit this time. And, in order not to make the same mistake twice, I obtained a real American suitcase, so I would look less like a foreigner. . . .
>
> This time I almost made it into Mexico, but was arrested by the Border Patrol at the Rio Grande River. . . . And once again I found myself back in the prison camp, with my thirty days in jail as expected.[14]

Indeed, through the war the majority of escapes, 65 percent, occurred by getting through, under, or over the stockade fence. This included tunneling, slipping through the gates in trash containers, hanging beneath trucks and jeeps, and every imaginable scheme in between. The second category, comprising 30 percent of the escapes, occurred by leaving work sites, by diverting the guard's attention, hiding among the agricultural produce, or simply walking away. The remaining 5 percent were listed by the War Department as "Miscellaneous," and generally comprised those escapes which occurred without the knowledge of the camp commander and came to light only on the capture of the escaped prisoner.

The War Department also noted that with regard to the type of prison camp from which these escapes took place, 46 percent occurred at base

Closeup of the tunnel exit through which 25 German submariners at Papago Park, Arizona, nearly made good their escape to Mexico. *(National Archives)*

The rogue's gallery of the 19 remaining fugitives from the Papago Park escape. All were eventually caught and returned to camp. *(Department of Library, Archives, and Public Records, Phoenix)*

Four German prisoners, apprehended near Wichita, Kansas, pose happily with the two highway patrolmen who caught them. *(UPI)*

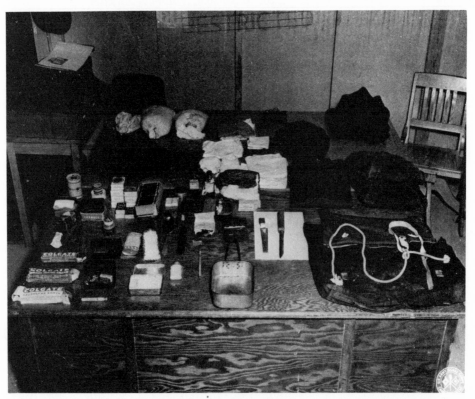

A display of the items carried by two escapees from Camp Indianola, Nebraska. Both Germans were recaptured within 24 hours of their break. *(National Archives)*

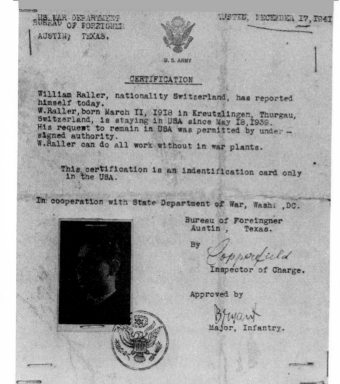

Homemade identification documents found on a recaptured POW indicate not only the detailed preparations involved in many such escapes, but also the incredible optimism. Note the hand-drawn seal on the otherwise legitimate Army stationery, the misspellings, and the "Bureau of Foreingner." *(National Archives)*

A far more sophisticated document which evidently required an examination by the FBI Laboratory in Washington to declare it a forgery. *(National Archives)*

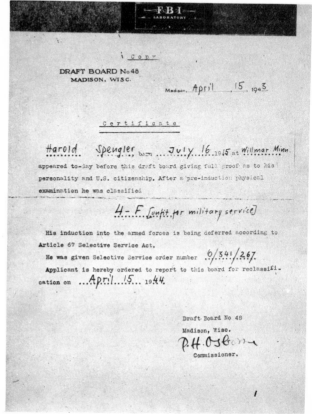

One of the snapshots found on the recaptured pair of German prisoners, which ultimately led to the arrest and conviction of several Japanese-American girls in a sensational trial. *(UPI)*

camps, 16 percent from branch camps, and as previously mentioned, 30 percent from work details. Finally, the War Department calculated the percentage of escapes which took place in each Service Command, which, for the month of May, 1944, were as follows:

Service Command	Percentage of All Escapes	Percentage of Total Number of Prisoners Held in United States
First	8.5	1.0
Second	0.0	2.0
Third	0.0	4.0
Fourth	8.5	18.0
Fifth	5.0	5.0
Sixth	7.0	5.5
Seventh	14.0	15.5
Eighth	43.0	40.0
Ninth	14.0	9.0
	100.0	100.0 [15]

Yet despite the dry, bureaucratic manner in which these statistics were noted by the government or the apparently cavalier manner in which Major Kiwe earlier described his many escape attempts, both groups were well aware that in each such escape the prisoner was taking his life in his hands.

The wide range of security procedures discussed previously—periodic searches, night patrols, guard dogs, and so forth—were primarily designed to deter potential escape attempts while still in the planning stage. The moment the plans were actuated, however, and the prisoners made a break to leave the camp, the guards were forced to consider their final option. Every large camp contained a so-called caution line which ran alongside the inner stockade fence or, in some cases, between the two stockade fences. The prisoner who crossed that caution line in an attempt to flee was liable to be fired upon. To prevent any misunderstanding on this point, the War Department took great pains to inform all American guards that they must wait until the last possible second before firing, that they must shout "Halt" at least three distinct times, and that they must remember, above all, that a prisoner's behavior and not his proximity to the fence was the critical factor. The decision was thus placed in the hands of the guards. The War Department further instructed the Camp Commandant to ensure that the POW community understood the significance of the guards' responsibility as well as the numerous variations of the word "Halt" which they might encounter.[16] Nonetheless, by the end of the war, 56 German prisoners had risked the odds in their attempt to escape and had been shot to death. This final and powerful option provided the real force behind the various other security measures and was no doubt responsible for preventing an untold number of prisoner escapes. In the main, it was a judiciously-used deterrent—though there were exceptions.

On October 15, 1943, at Camp Concordia, Kansas, for example, a German prisoner was shot to death while trying to retrieve a soccer ball. Witnesses to the shooting stated that the prisoners were engaged in a football match and had been warned several times against chasing the ball beyond the caution line. In this case, the caution line was a 2½ foot high guardrail with warning signs in both English and German some 18 feet from the main fence. One prisoner, Adolph Huebner, evidently defied the guard's warning and, according to the authorities, deliberately kicked the ball into the forbidden area. He then hopped over the rail and ran after the ball, looking back over his shoulder and taunting the sentinel. The guard fired once, shooting him through the head.[17] Another incident occurred at Fort Knox, Kentucky, in November, 1944, when two POWs were shot to death by an American guard who was otherwise "unsuccessful in persuading the prisoners to leave the fence." [18] In another case, under different circumstances, a mentally unbalanced German prisoner was shot as he was being transferred from Camp Robinson at Little Rock, Arkansas, to Mason General Hospital, a neuropsychiatric institution at Brentwood, Long Island. Traveling aboard a Pennsylvania Railroad passenger train and guarded by two military policemen, Herman Mattschutt evidently went berserk among the crowded civilian commuters and was shot as he fought to climb through a window of the speeding train.[19] During the last days of the war, at the branch camp at Ovid, Colorado, an American guard, newly returned from combat overseas, killed three German prisoners after "they had made threatening remarks and were acting as though they intended to attack him." [20] Similarly, at a branch camp near Parma, Ohio, an American guard shot and killed a prisoner after the German threatened him and advanced toward him "after being ordered to stop singing a song which ridiculed American servicemen." [21] Such occurrences, however, were rare and involved only a tiny fraction of the hundreds of thousands of prisoners and American personnel involved.

Equally rare, though highly publicized, were the several instances in which the prisoners escaped or remained at large with the help of American citizens. The first such case came to the public's attention almost as an afterthought to an otherwise sensational escape and capture. On April 16, 1942, Lieutenant Hans Peter Krug, a German *Luftwaffe* pilot, broke out of the large POW camp at Bowmanville, Ontario. As part of the British Commonwealth, Canada had long held German and Italian prisoners, transferred to their shores from the overcrowded camps in England. On a far smaller scale, Canada encountered many of the difficulties which plagued the American experience. One such problem was escapes, and while only a handful ever successfully crossed into the United States, one of them was Hans Peter Krug. After stealing a boat near Windsor and paddling to Belle Island in the Detroit River, Krug fled rapidly through Detroit, Chicago, and Dallas en route to Mexico. He was arrested in San Antonio on May 1 when a hotel clerk became suspicious and called the F.B.I., and within days, Krug was back in his Canadian POW camp. Case closed. But, nearly a month later, *The New York Times* announced that U.S. Attorney General Francis Biddle would bring the first treason indictment of the war against a Max Stephan of Detroit for supplying Krug with food, lodging, and money.[22] Max Stephan was found guilty and sentenced to death by hanging, though this sentence was later commuted to life imprisonment.

Nearly two years later, on February 19, 1944, an American army guard was arrested by the F.B.I. and charged with treason for helping two German prisoners escape from Camp Hale, Colorado. The Germans were apprehended by Mexican authorities three miles south of the Mexican border and returned to American officials. An investigation revealed that one of the prisoners was in fact their U.S. Army camp guard, 23-year-old Private Dale H. Maple, who had provided them with supplies and the opportunity to escape. The guard, it was learned, had a long history of pro-Nazi sympathy and had, in fact, been dismissed from Harvard University's R.O.T.C. program because of his rabid political views. Not one to be caught unaware, the ever-present J. Edgar Hoover announced that Maple's views were known to the F.B.I. as early as 1940, though one is forced to wonder how a man with such visible pro-Nazi sentiments was allowed to become a POW guard over the people he most admired. A month later, yet another revelation was made public: Maple had not been alone—five additional guards and three WACS were also involved in the escape. Within weeks, all nine, including Maple, were brought before a court-martial at Camp Hale, pleaded guilty to lesser charges, and except for Maple received sentences ranging from four to six months' confinement.[23] Private Maple was charged with desertion and aiding the enemy. He was quickly found guilty and sentenced to be hanged. President Roosevelt commuted the sentence to life, and in 1946 it was further reduced to ten years. Today he is a successful California insurance man.

In a less sinister case, two guards at Camp Ellis, Illinois, evidently anxious for the company of their new-found friend, provided a suit of civilian clothes to a German prisoner and took him along with them to a tavern for the evening. All three were arrested; the German was returned to camp, and the two guards were sentenced to a surprisingly harsh term of five years at hard labor.[24]

A rather unusual case of civilian aid to escaping German prisoners occurred the following month in Colorado. Two *Afrika Korps* corporals who had escaped from Camp Trinidad, Colorado, were captured by the F.B.I. several days later in Watrous, New Mexico. Among their possessions, the authorities found a photograph showing the two Nazis embracing three Japanese women who turned out to be Japanese-American sisters working on a farm near the camp. The sisters were Nisei who had been relocated from their homes in Inglewood, California, to the Granada Internment Center at Apache, Colorado, and who were, therefore, prisoners themselves. Whether their short relationship with the Germans was ideological or merely biological, the fact is that the Nisei girls aided their escape. At their well-publicized trial, in which the two Germans acted as witnesses against the girls, the jury returned a guilty verdict to the reduced charge of conspiracy to commit treason. The girls each received a two-year prison sentence and a $10,000 fine.[25]

The sensational publicity which surrounded these infrequent cases of American aid to escaping enemy POWs, and the wide range of sentences meted out revealed a major judicial problem. While there was a law prohibiting any aid to a civilian prisoner escaping from a penal or correctional institution, there was simply no comparable law against aiding fleeing prisoners of war. The escaped POWs, after all, were not classified as fugitives from justice, nor military deserters, nor wanted criminals. Thus, the courts were left to choose between the war-time law against treason (which, under certain rare circumstances, was indeed applicable) or the far less severe charges of obstructing justice or failing to notify the authorities about a military emergency.

The first step toward solving this problem was finally proposed by Attorney General Francis Biddle in May, 1944, but the Congress of the United States did not pass such legislation until April 30, 1945! On that date, Public Law 47 was approved, making it unlawful "for any person to procure the escape of any enemy prisoner of war or civilian internee, or to advise, connive at, aid, or assist in an escape, or to harbor, protect, or otherwise conceal an escaped prisoner of war." [26] In short, nearly anyone who knowingly dealt with an escaped POW was now liable under the law, and the maximum penalty was $10,000 fine or imprisonment for not more than ten years, or both. The new law was welcome, the more so since there had been several earlier cases in which this legislation would have been used to good advantage. But justice had already been served, however capriciously, and the courts were now to learn that with the war nearly over, the legislation was to be of little value in the few cases which were to occur. Moreover, with the end of the war, the very definition of "prisoner of war" came into question: If the war was over, were these men still prisoners of war? And if they were no longer prisoners of war, how could civilians be prosecuted for treason after aiding their escape? The government's solution to these vexing questions became one of compromise. The few remaining defendants in post-war America would indeed find themselves liable to the provisions of Public Law 47, but with the passage of the war years came a relaxation of the full weight of the statute's penalties. Two major cases at the end of 1945 illustrate the government's post-war position concerning aid to escaped prisoners.

On November 23, 1945, six months after the end of the war in Europe, the F.B.I. arrested Joseph Ottman, an Austrian-born American citizen, and charged him with treason. An investigation revealed that Ottman, a New York subway employee, had befriended two German prisoners who had escaped from Camp Hull, Canada, and had allowed them to use his lodging for a single night before they moved on. The two prisoners were apprehended 24 hours after leaving Ottman's home and disclosed his name. The 43-year-old Ottman was arraigned before the United States Commissioner on May 26, 1946, and charged under the new Public Law 47. Although liable to a penalty of ten years' imprisonment and $10,000 fine, Ottman was finally sentenced to serve one year and two days in the federal penitentiary. He ultimately served his year in prison and was placed on probation until 1950.[27]

The final case, rather bizarre in light of the public's hostility toward the enemy, involved a 45-year-old American woman—the proud mother of three GIs—who was arrested by the F.B.I. and Army intelligence officers for cohabiting with an escaped German prisoner of war. According to the F.B.I., Mrs. Fannie Welvaert was employed at Lovell General Hospital, Fort Devens, Massachusetts, where she became acquainted with 22-year-old Horst Becker, a German prisoner detailed to the hospital from the nearby camp. In a collaborative effort, Becker escaped from Fort Devens on September 13, 1945, after which the couple moved in with Mrs. Welvaert's parents. A month later, a quarrel with Mrs. Welvaert's mother drove them to a rooming house in Worcester where they were arrested on November 1. She was convicted under Public Law 47 and sentenced on November 10, 1945, to six months on each of two counts. Ultimately, the sentences were suspended, and she was placed on probation for two years running from January 22, 1946, to January 22, 1948.[28] As with the Ottman case, the stringent penalties were greatly tempered by the shift in public interest to bread-and-butter domestic issues as well as the obvious absence of treasonous motivation. Nonetheless, one point should be clearly established. Considering that a total of 1,073 German prisoners escaped between November, 1942, and February 1, 1945, the number of cases which involved aid from American citizens was insignificant: less than 20. Thus, between the many security obstacles, including the guards' option to shoot, and the rarity of civilian aid or sympathy, escape was far from a simple matter.

Escapees at Large

Once at large, most escaped prisoners resorted to virtually the same tactics. Often they slept in woods or fields by day and tramped the highways at night. They foraged for food in fields, orchards, and gardens. They attempted to get to the Canadian or Mexican borders or into the vast anonymity of large urban areas. Yet however sophisticated their plans or provisions, the escaped prisoner seldom got far. Some prisoners were tripped up by small details, others by a lack of English or knowledge of American customs, and still others by totally unforeseen circumstances. In mid-1944, for example, a German escaped from Camp Mexia, Texas, and was found a day and a half later huddling in a railroad box car, hungry and thirsty, on an unused rail spur line in the middle of the downtown area. He had been unaware that neither the car nor the spur line was in use. In another escape from the same camp, a prisoner who made a successful break from an agricultural work party had cut across a fenced-in pasture and had been run up a tree by an angry Brahman bull. When the guards who were searching for him along the highway were attracted by his cries for help and rescued him, he was enormously grateful to get safely back to camp.[29] At Camp Hearne, Texas, an escaped POW was found marching along the highway between Hearne and the nearby town of Franklin wearing civilian clothes over his camp uniform and heartily singing German army marching songs. He was gently returned to camp and for some reason could not understand how the local farmer who caught him had seen through his clever disguise.[30] At yet another Texas stockade, Camp Barkeley outside of Abilene, the few escape attempts invariably found the German prisoners sleeping in the bandstand in Abilene's central park.[31]

Camp West Ashley in Charleston, South Carolina, saw only two escapes of note, and both were almost vaudevillian in character. The first occurred on March 10, 1945, when Corporals Paul Preller and Conrad Teewan slipped away from camp to take up residence in a small cave some two miles away. With no loftier goal than to "get away from it all for awhile," Preller and Conrad had used their past six weeks of mosquito control detail to dig a two-man cave complete with board floors, shelves, and a month's supply of clothing, food, water, cigarettes, matches, and candles. For the next three days the two men camped out in their little home while the F.B.I. and camp guards searched all the way from Charleston to Savannah. The end came when they were spotted by a passing tenant farmer from nearby Maryville who, in turn, alerted Captain G. S. Vincent at the prisoner of war camp. Thirty minutes later, a posse found the two men sitting on the bank of the Ashley River, not far from the entrance to their cave, and swiftly herded them back to camp.[32] The second escape occurred within a week of the first when three 22-year-old German privates, Max Lauer, Willi Steuer, and Edward Gielen, slipped under the wire on a moonless night with the intention of returning to Germany. They hiked to the Charleston Army Air Corps base at nearby Ten Mile, stole an unattended jeep, and made for Savannah where they hoped to stow away on a neutral ship. What followed is best described by the *Charleston News and Courier:*

> They couldn't wear their khaki prison fatigues with the P.W. on the back. After all, what would people think? They couldn't wear civilian clothes, because if they were caught they would be accused of being spies—a hanging offense. That left only one thing—their German Army uniforms, what every well-dressed fugitive from a POW camp was wearing. So, Max, Willi, and Eddie, the pride of the Panzers, cooled it down Highway 17, in full uniform including combat ribbons.
>
> But the natives had sharp eyes and a woman near Beaufort thought it was mighty peculiar to see three men running around in German uniforms when she had been reading in the papers how the allies had been winning the war. She told the sheriff and within an hour, Max, Willi and Eddie were safely tucked away in the Beaufort sneezer.[33]

Incidentally, the plan would have failed even if the trio had made it to Savannah. There were only two neutral ports in the United States (New York and Philadelphia), and Savannah was not one of them.

In Arkansas, an escapee, after 24 hours' freedom, asked a farmer to drive him back to camp. He confessed that he had intended to make his way to Mexico but that after spending a day in the woods, harassed by mosquitoes, he decided that Hitler could get along without him.[34] A German prisoner who escaped from a camp in the state of Washington entered a Rainier, Oregon, cafe after a four-day trek through the wilderness and ordered a badly-needed cup of coffee. He could not make himself understood to the waitress, and after a number of attempts in feeble English, he reached for a paper napkin and pencil and overcome with frustration simply wrote: "I am an escaped German war prisoner!" [35]

In Wyoming, two German escapees succeeded in getting almost three miles from their camp and were already celebrating their new-found freedom when they ran headlong into a detachment of American troops on maneuvers. They were returned to camp at gunpoint and presented to the startled camp authorities who were not yet aware of their escape.[36] In another escape attempt, three Germans slipped away from a cannery worksite near Milton, Oregon, and were spotted near Walla Walla, Washington, by the pilot of a low flying small plane. After radioing the authorities, the pilot "flew low and shouted to them to stand up. They did. He circled over the spot until guards reached the field." [37]

There was, in fact, no such thing as a "standard apprehension" of an escaped POW. One German, for instance, was recaptured outside of Lisbon, New Hampshire, when he accepted an automobile ride from, of all people, the local police chief.[38] On another occasion, an escapee from Camp Atterbury, Indiana, was captured by an eight year old boy, who, playing with a toy pistol, ordered an imaginary adversary to come out of an abandoned shack near the boy's home in Columbus, Indiana. No one could have been more surprised than he when Franz Wilming stepped out to surrender.[39] On still another occasion, an escapee made it to Chicago in time to celebrate New Years Eve, 1946, in a local tavern. When the party moved to a private home for sandwiches, Paul Stachowiak went along, too. Everybody thought he was the guest of somebody else, but when he began to boast that he had just escaped from Camp Grant in nearby Rockford, Illinois, one of the more sober partygoers called the police.[40] Another prisoner was captured by a Pennsylvania Railroad detective in Oil City, Pennsylvania, when he failed to understand that his ticket did not entitle him to remain in the parlor car; [41] five others in a henhouse on a farm outside of Indianola, Nebraska, were captured by several country boys armed with shotguns; [42] and still another escapee from Camp Como, Mississippi, was tripped up as he sat down in the back of a southern bus directly beneath the strange sign that read: "Colored People Only." [43] One of the more ludicrous escape attempts concerned two German prisoners who were hitch-hiking their way south across the State of Texas. According to the news reports:

> One was more than 6 feet tall and of sturdy frame; the other short, broad-shouldered, big tummied. They wore khaki shirts and shorts. . . . they hailed a truck and climbed to the seat beside the driver.
>
> "Where you heading?" asked the driver.

"We're Boy Scouts," was the reply, "going to an international convention in Mexico."

The driver, suspicious of the men's accent and the hairy muscle-knotted legs extending from the shorts, halted at the nearest town, and turned the brawny "Scouts" over to the authorities.[44]

Equally ludicrous was the apprehension of 23-year-old Werner Schwanbeck, an escaped German paratrooper from Fort Knox, Kentucky. Shortly after 8 P.M. on February 19, 1945, Schwanbeck boarded the city bus in downtown Nashville, Tennessee, wearing his full German uniform with heavy paratrooper boots and the inverted chevron of a private, first class. Apparently none of the other passengers thought anything of it. In fact, the bus driver only began to get suspicious "because he didn't seem to know where he wanted to get off," though another passsenger later claimed to have known the German's identity all along "because I knew that his boots weren't American-made." Regardless of the suspicions present on that Nashville bus, the hungry, tired, and frightened Schwanbeck continued to ride unmolested until he told the driver in broken English that he wanted to return to Fort Knox.[45]

One last example—this with more serious consequences. Three German submariners escaped from Camp Crossville, Tennessee, and fled into the hills. Several days later, according to author John Hammond Moore, the trio came to a mountain cabin and started to get water from a pump. An irascible granny appeared in the doorway, aimed a gun in their direction, and told them to "git." Unschooled in the way of mountain folk, they scoffed and paid no attention. A few moments later she drew a bead and fired, killing one of the seamen almost instantly. When a deputy sheriff informed the old lady that she had killed an escaped German prisoner of war, she was horror-stricken, burst into tears and sobbed that she would never have fired if she had known the men were Germans. "Well, m'a'm," he asked, puzzled, "what in thunder did you think you were aiming at?" "Why," she replied, "I thought they wuz Yankees." [46]

The best description of the majority of the escaped POWs was made by Sheriff Harold Ellsworth of Lewiston, Illinois, near Camp Ellis. "Fact is," recalled the sheriff,

... they made us feel kind of sorry for them, these German escapees. We would find them there, in the streets, without a word of English, in Bloomington, in Peoria, in Galesburg; or else in the woods, completely lost like strayed sheep. Yes, I tell you, it was rather pitiful. Besides, local people weren't afraid of them. When they met up with one, they called us; we came, put a hand on their shoulder, and gently brought them back to camp.[47]

On the other hand, a minority of escaped German prisoners had a bit more luck and remained at large somewhat longer. Two German prisoners, Karl Tomola and Wolfgang Kurzer, who had escaped from their camp at Scotts Bluff, Nebraska, on July 11, 1944, successfully wandered at liberty across the United States and Canada for more than four months. Following their escape, the two crossed into Canada where they worked and traveled through the summer and fall, ultimately recrossing the border at Rouses Point, New York, in November. From Oneida, New York, they moved to New York City where they attempted to ship out as seamen but were turned down for lack of proper credentials. As a result, both stowed away on the Spanish merchant ship *Castilla Ampudia* at a South Philadelphia pier, where F.B.I. agents found them hiding in empty oil drums on the deck of the ship with two weeks' food supply and ten pounds of chocolate.[48]

An Illinois prisoner, 35-year-old Erich Gellert, slipped out of Camp Grant near Rockford by hiding under a pile of dirty clothes in a commercial laundry truck. Jumping off in Rockford, the former camp laundryman used the American currency which he had collected from the small change left in guards' pockets to purchase a bus ticket to nearby Chicago. From there, he traveled north by bus to Milwaukee, Wisconsin, where under the name of Richard Koll, he began looking for work. When the F.B.I. finally arrested Gellert several months later on April 4, 1946, he was a contented farm worker in Cedarburg, Wisconsin.[49]

An escapee from Camp Somerset, Maryland—a 21-year-old tank man named Karl Hermann Pospiech—apparently had little difficulty in walking away from camp in a U.S. Army uniform which had been used in a prisoner stage play. Within days after his October, 1945, escape, he moved into a rooming house in New York City and set about getting a new name, a Social Security card, a job, and an American discharge pin. For the next five months, until he was finally arrested in April 1946, "Henry Elmer Brown" was a $36-a-week shipping clerk at Roberta Roberts perfumery, who spent his evenings at Carnegie Hall concerts and at the Metropolitan Opera.[50]

In another case, a young veteran of Rommel's Panzer Corps went under the wire at Camp Forrest, Tennessee, because he "didn't like America." After his escape, Heinz Hoefer walked to Tullahoma, Tennessee, not far from the camp, washed off his camouflage, and caught the 9:25 morning train for Nashville. Eventually he intended to go on to New York, ship out as a seaman, and somehow get back to Germany. On his first afternoon as a free man, Hoefer went pub-crawling with an unsuspecting American GI home on leave, proving, if nothing else, that he had been successfully assimilated into American society. The very next day, however, he was stopped by the authorities in a routine check, asked to show his Selective Service card, and, unable to produce one, was promptly arrested.[51]

One prisoner who escaped from Camp Chaffee, Arkansas, in September of 1943, remained at large for several days in nearby Charleston despite the fact that he continued to walk around in his prison garb with the letters "PW" stenciled across his legs, seat, and back in bright yellow paint. Trudging around town, he finally found himself in a Catholic church where he was eventually recognized as an escapee by a woman in his pew. The priest, when informed, confronted the man, Michael Huebinger, who readily admitted his identity. "Then it's your duty to return," the priest said. Huebinger went home with one of his "captors," drank a cup of coffee, and was then driven back to camp.[52]

One prisoner who escaped from Camp Stark near Percy, New Hampshire, made his way to New York City and survived for more than three months despite a continued search by state and federal authorities. An artist of some ability, the young German successfully supported himself by selling his paintings to passers-by in Central Park. He was eventually arrested by agents of the F.B.I. as he purchased more art supplies to sustain his thriving business—he had simply become too successful and thus too visible.[53]

A final example of POW escapees who had successfully eluded early recapture ended with an unusual twist. When Nazi POW Emanuel Kalytka escaped from the Halloran General Hospital on Staten Island one Sunday morning "just to see the good old United States," he could not have imagined that he would trigger the most intensive manhunt ever conducted in the New York metropolitan area. As soon as his absence was confirmed, the F.B.I. broadcast a general alarm that swiftly encompassed nine states. Cordons of military and city police, as well as civilian volunteers with baseball bats, searched the Willow Brook Park section of Staten Island. Three police launches prowled the waters of the nearby inlets, and four Coast Guard cutters covered the southern and eastern shore line of the island. Machine gun units were set up at the Manhattan, New Jersey, and Brooklyn ferry slips and at all bridge crossings. Mounted military policemen rode at alert through the surrounding woods. Bloodhounds were brought in by the state troopers. Incredibly, the 29-year old Kalytka slept undisturbed all night in the woods and spent the following day peacefully strolling through Clove Lakes Park. He spent the next night asleep in the woods near Sea View Hospital. By Tuesday, the German was getting extremely hungry and decided to return to Halloran Hospital's POW barracks for some decent food. Early Wednesday morning, before dawn, he slipped past the guards and hid in the basement of the building in which the prisoners were kept until time for the noon meal to be served. Unobserved, he then joined the rest of the prisoners in the mess hall and was finally noticed and apprehended after finishing his cream of mushroom soup, roast veal, potatoes, carrots, lettuce salad, chocolate cake, and milk.[54]

Prisoner escapes, it is evident, were as varied as imagination and circumstances allowed. They did, however, have one thing in common: the overwhelming majority were recaptured within three days. The actual figures, based on the total of 1,073 Germans who escaped in the United States between November, 1942, and February 1, 1945, were as follows:

Length of time at large

One day or less	648
Two days	148
Three days	111
Four days	38
Five days	21
Six to fourteen days	86
Fourteen or more days	21 [55]

The War Department was also pleased to report that the majority of prisoners were captured by regular civilian authorities, which did not cause any unnecessary drain on military personnel who might have been required for the war effort elsewhere. Nearly 42 percent of the apprehensions, in fact, were made by federal authorities and members of the nation's city, county, and state police; of the remaining balance, 24 percent of the prisoners were captured by military authorities; 18.7 percent were captured by private citizens; 7.3 percent of the prisoners surrendered voluntarily; and 8.2 percent were captured by groups ranging from the Boy Scouts to the Forest Rangers.[56] So successful were these security agencies that the War Department's final tally announced on November 23, 1947, revealed that of a total of 2,222 German escapees, only 17 still remained at large.[57]

These 17 fugitives represented the only successful, long-term escapes from among the more than 360,000 German prisoners in the United States. They were no more clever than any of the other 2,205 escaped prisoners, nor were their plans any more sophisticated. Their success was based entirely on better luck and more favorable circumstances. Yet, the majority of even this handful ended in capture, and by 1951 only six remained at large.

The first of these last six fugitives was apprehended in March, 1953, and

Therefore, prisoners of war and soldiers were to be punished by exactly the same methods and with identical disciplinary actions and by the same courts. The prisoner, for instance, could not be deprived of his rank, nor tried twice for the same offense, nor made subject to collective punishment. Within the framework established by Article 45, these disciplinary procedures fell into two broad categories. The first category concerned the powers of the commanding officer. Specifically, the camp commander was empowered to discipline his prisoners by the following methods:

A. *Administration Pressure.* As authorized by both Army Regulations and the Geneva Convention (Article 104), the commanding officer was permitted to issue an admonition, reprimand, or other verbal reproof.

He could also choose to withhold a privilege, usually a diet restriction. According to Army Regulation 600–375, this pressure might be continued as long as the offense continued to exist.

The third option available to commanders was the discontinuance of pay and monetary allowances. The total allowance for enlisted prisoners was ten cents per day or three dollars per month. Since a special arrangement between the United States and Germany assured that tobacco and other necessities would not be negotiable items with either nation's prisoners, the American camp commander was restricted from withholding more than two of the prisoner's three dollars. Officer's pay did not fall under this category and could only be withheld by court-martial action.

As the number of prisoners increased and the demand for their employment grew, it quickly became evident that simple administrative pressure might not suffice. More prisoners meant the possibility of more incidents: sit-down strikes, direct disobedience of orders, the stealing of farm implements, and minor acts of vandalism. Camp commanders often found that a simple admonition or reprimand—or the restriction of diet known as the "No Work–No Eat Policy"—was not sufficient. Under the 104th Article of War and Articles 54–59 of the Geneva Convention, camp commanders were authorized to escalate their control over their prisoners by utilizing, when necessary, disciplinary rather than administrative controls.

B. *Disciplinary Measures.* In this area, the commander was authorized to punish recalcitrant prisoners by assigning extra fatigue (work during the prisoner's free time) for up to one week. "For best results," commanders were told by the War Department, "this extra fatigue should be performed in full view of his fellow prisoners . . . as a weapon of ridicule. On such extra fatigue, no loafing should be allowed, but you must be a hard task master to make such extra fatigue worthwhile."

The second disciplinary option was hard labor without confinement. At the commander's discretion, a prisoner could be made to do a full days' work without pay, a punishment which could continue for up to one week. Again, the War Department stressed that "hard labor be put on a task system—that is, the prisoner be given a certain task to do each day and make that task difficult. Remember, this is a punishment and must stand out as one." A third and final option to commanders, as authorized by the provisions of Article 59, allowed the prisoner to be placed in confinement for up to 30 days, 14 of which might be on a restricted diet. "With this grant of power," camp commanders were warned, "be cautious—be fair—be impartial. Above all, use it judiciously without animosity and hatred . . . to maintain the discipline within your camp. *A very appropriate use of this punishment is its application to escaped prisoners of war. On the first escape of a prisoner of war, we would certainly recommend 14 days without hesitation. On the second escape: 30 days.*[68]

The answer, then, was clear. The question of how to punish escaped prisoners of war was solved for more than 500 camp commanders across the country since the most stringent disciplinary measure in their arsenal of options was also the very method advised by the PMGO and the War Department. Consequently, after each of the more than 2,000 escaped prisoners was brought back to camp by the F.B.I. or military authorities and briefly interrogated about his method of escape (as required by military regulations), he was automatically marched to the camp stockade for 20 to 30 days. "It wasn't so bad," recalled the veteran escapee, Major Tilman Kiwe:

> I was received back in camp by the American second officer, a man named Fischer, who spoke German and often chatted with us prisoners. I knew him well. "Why did you do this to me?" he asked me. "To me—a friend—why did you do it?"
> The regimentary punishment for escapes [at Camp Trinidad] was

thirty days on bread and water. But the camp prison was not too unkind. Most of the time, the doors of the cells were left open; we walked around the interior of the prison and chatted. The guards were rather accommodating.

In all, I spent 111 days in jail. . . .[69]

In addition to administrative pressure and disciplinary punishment, camp commanders had a third means of maintaining control: the initiation of court-martial proceedings. Reserved for more serious offenses than those which could be dealt with through reprimands or restricted diets, the court-martial system was long acknowledged by the Articles of War, Army Regulations, and the Geneva Convention. Aside from the summary court-martial which was largely superceded by the increased powers granted to camp commanders in 1944, the Army had two types of procedures: the special court-martial composed of three to five officers and the general court-martial composed of five to eleven officers. The less serious of the two, a special court-martial, adjudicated over such offenses (committed by American soldiers or POW enlisted men) as the willful damage of government property or disrespectful behavior toward a superior officer. Sentences meted out by such special courts-martial averaged six months confinement at hard labor with forfeiture of pay. The general court-martial procedure, on the other hand, was reserved for more serious offenses—murder, sabotage, desertion, and so forth—and could, with the approval of the President of the United States, result in the death penalty.[70] A defendant before either a special or general court-martial had the right to an attorney of his choice and, in the case of prisoners of war, to an interpreter as well.[71] Additional protection for the rights of POWs charged with major offenses (as guaranteed by Article 60 of the Geneva Convention) also required that the Swiss Legation be notified prior to the trial. Such notification was important for several reasons. The Swiss forwarded all such information to the German War Office, thus preventing the news of such courts-martial from being used by the irresponsible German propaganda machine, but more importantly requiring identical notification from Berlin concerning similar trials of American prisoners. As always, the safety of Americans in enemy hands was of paramount concern to the War Department, though this concern never resulted in a compromise of justice. On the contrary, the War Department and the PMGO continued to emphasize that all prisoners were to be treated "fairly, but firmly. Don't enter into arguments—make a cold determination as to the punishment which befits the offense—award that punishment coldly, impartially, and fairly—and above all with dignity." [72]

Unlike the Canadian Government, which interpreted the Geneva Convention to read that all felonies committed during an escape were considered part of the escape and thus subject to standard disciplinary measures, the U.S. War Department separated the escape and the felonies (if any) into two categories. Any prisoner, therefore, who was found to have damaged government property, stolen or "borrowed" a civilian or military vehicle, or broken into a civilian home to steal clothing while at large became liable for court-martial upon his capture. The overwhelming majority of special and general courts-martial—in excess of 80 percent—were politically motivated and concerned such matters as the assault on one prisoner of war by another, a prisoner's refusal to obey an order from an American or German superior officer, or the willful vandalism of U.S. Army property. Nearly 20 percent were, indeed, escape-related. Among the 48 special courts-martial convened through August 31, 1945, several representative examples are as follows:

On August 8, 1944, POW Kurt Koch escaped from Camp Clarinda, Iowa; while fleeing south through Missouri toward the Mexican border, he first stole a civilian truck then abandoned it in favor of a stolen Ford sedan. In Orrick, Missouri, on August 10, 1944, Koch also stole a leather jacket and a slack suit. Following his capture, he was returned to Camp Clarinda to stand before a special court-martial, by which he was found guilty and sentenced to six months at hard labor in the camp stockade with the additional forfeiture of all pay.

On October 6, 1944, two submarine officers, Martin Boning and Josef Dunz, attempted to escape from Papago Park, Arizona (several months before the spectacular mass escape on December 24, 1944). In the process, they were charged with damaging U.S. property in the form of the stockade fence to the amount of $5.00. A special court-martial of both prisoners found them not guilty of the charge, and both were acquitted.

On October 5, 1944, after escaping from Fort Devens, Massachusetts, Leopold Paradeiser and Walter Wildner stole a civilian automobile to facilitate their flight. Their capture saw their return to Fort Devens where they stood trial before a special court-martial. Both were convicted and sentenced to six months at hard labor in the camp stockade.

General courts-martial, by definition, were concerned with more severe offenses. Among 119 such procedures concerning POWs through August 31, 1945, the following are examples which resulted during the commission of an escape:

On January 7, 1944, four obdurate Nazis escaped from Camp Phillips, Kansas. As they crossed the state, Enno Meyer, Hans Hass, Alfons Rutkiewitz, and Karl Schroeder stole and abandoned a number of civilian automobiles in Elmdale, Chase County, and Smolan, Kansas. Upon their capture, they were all tried by general court-martial, convicted of violating Article of War 96, and sentenced to five years hard labor at the U.S. Disciplinary Barracks, Fort Leavenworth, Kansas, plus the forfeiture of $2.00 per month. In an epilogue to this case, ten months later, on October 3, 1944, POW Enno Meyer broke out of Fort Leavenworth to be recaptured on February 5, 1945.

On July 8–9, 1944, an escapee from Camp Pine, New York, Victor Terberger, illegally entered a number of private homes in the cities of Diane and Carthage, New York, in search of food, clothing, and money. Court-martialed for violation of Article of War 93, he was sentenced to five years at hard labor in the Federal Reformatory at Chillicothe, Ohio.

In an escape attempt from Camp Gordon, Georgia, on April 20, 1944, Gerd Gutzat and Hermann Mueller stole an automobile in Augusta and were tried for violation of Article of War 96. Both received three years at hard labor at the Federal Correctional Institution, Milam, Michigan.

On May 23, 1945, two escapees from Camp Fannin, Texas, tried to facilitate their flight by stealing an unattended river skiff near Haslam, Texas. Josef Rondorf and Ignaz Luke were found guilty of violating Article of War 96 and sentenced to eight years at hard labor at the Southern Branch Disciplinary Barracks at Camp Hood, Texas.[74]

As with all other aspects of the prisoner of war experience in the United States, justice conformed to a strict interpretation of the Geneva Convention. Proceedings were governed by elaborate regulations, reviewed by military officials, and were often attended by representatives of the Swiss Legation. They were, by all accounts, far more fair and humane than the treatment meted out to escaped American or British prisoners of war in German hands.[74] Examining the American court-martial proceedings from a different angle—as a barometer of POW intentions—one point becomes quite clear: the POWs were only interested in escaping without complication. Despite J. Edgar Hoover's alarmist warnings, not a single case of military sabotage or assault on an American citizen by a fugitive prisoner is on record. Perhaps the most important fact is that of the more than 425,000 enemy prisoners of war which were maintained in the United States from 1942 through 1946, only an insignificant number ever managed to escape captivity: 2,222 Germans, 604 Italians, and 1 Japanese. And all but one lone German prisoner were eventually apprehended.

If there was an additional lesson to be learned from the issue of prisoner escapes, it was that the greatest danger did not lie with the few men who escaped but with the many thousands of hardened Nazis who remained behind.

CHAPTER V

Wrestling for the Tiller

The problem of prisoner escapes, though highly visible and potentially dangerous, never seriously materialized, much to the relief of the War Department, communities near the camps, and businesses which utilized POW labor. While potential escapes were generally defused by the natural geographical and cultural obstacles presented by the United States, the War Department could also congratulate itself on its vigilance and determination. Yet even as the nation was becoming confident in its role as the custodian of so many thousands of its captured enemies, a far more insidious problem loomed behind the scenes within the camps themselves: the growth and entrenchment of Nazism.

The Second World War, unlike the First, was a war of ideologies. Despite the untold numbers of books, articles, and movies on the subject, Fascism was not a great deal clearer to Americans in 1942 or 1943 than it had been in 1933. Fascism in general and Nazism—the German variety—in particular were viewed by the American people as a blur of swastikas, marching Prussian robots, violent racism, strutting leaders, brown-shirted hooligans, and a veritable sea of hysterical followers. Not that this was untrue, certainly, although most Americans would not have been familiar with references to the mystic nationalism of the post-Napoleonic Father Jahn or the romantic *Realpolitik* and racial myth of Fichte, Hegel, and Wagner. Nazism appeared simply a monstrous and evil political philosophy, the new religion of an apparently incorrigible German Nation. Above all, to Americans it was a philosophy of aggressive militarism.

With Nazism and militarism thus interchangeable, the War Department, as well as the American public at large, saw the incoming thousands of German prisoners of war as representative of the detested enemy philosophy of world enslavement. But the assumption that every German soldier was an obdurate Nazi was far from accurate.

The German Army and Nazism

The German Army, the *Wehrmacht,* had in fact remained rather aloof from the Nazi movement through the early 1930s. While many segments of

German society easily embraced National Socialism—industrial cartels, workers' organizations, universities, press, radio, musicians and artists, and church leaders—the aristocratic General Staff sought to avoid any political cooperation. From 1933 to 1938, the Army wavered between its desire to protect itself from National Socialist encroachment and its readiness to work with a regime so aggressively military-minded. For its part, the Nazi regime sought to push the expanding Army back into a more limited, purely military realm and exclude it from political decision making. As a result, the Army stood by as Hitler savagely crushed the SA on June 30, 1934, assassinating two of the Army's own generals. The Army accepted the order that the swastika had to be worn on all uniforms and, on August 2, acquiesced to the momentous act of swearing personal allegiance to the "Fuehrer and Chancellor, Adolf Hitler."

The relationship between the Army and the regime remained an uncomfortable truce. The General Staff greeted all additional efforts to Nazify the military with quiet resistance and a measure of ridicule.[1] Until the very beginning of the war, in fact, members of the German military were generally prohibited by their High Command from membership in the Nazi party, and those recruits who entered as party members were made to understand that their affiliation lapsed during military service.[2] The Nazification of the military was, nevertheless, inevitable. Until the Nazi seizure of power in 1933, lieutenants had constituted the most heavily-Nazified stratum of the officer corps; between 1933 and 1939, promotion and new recruitment had made the rank of major the most heavily indoctrinated; and during the war, the Nazi tide finally engulfed the highest levels of the military hierarchy.[3] It was the July 20, 1944, attempt on Hitler's life, however, with its deep involvement of the nation's military heroes, that led to the immediate and complete Nazification of the Army. The traditional military salute was replaced by the outstretched arm and "Heil Hitler" greeting; the Waffen SS (the military arm of Hitler's blackshirts) was given equal status with the regular military; and political indoctrination officers in the ranks were now men to be taken seriously. The German Army was completely under the government's control.

Problems in Dealing with POW Nazism

The average German soldier and, thus, the average German prisoner of war in the United States was not a fanatical ideologue. He was a nationalist, to be sure, and in large measure wholly captivated by the mystique and omnipotence of Hitler's leadership. But there were wide differences among them. Some prisoners were professional soldiers, while others were wartime conscripts. They represented different units and had fought in different campaigns. The circumstances surrounding their capture may have varied widely. In addition to the German prisoners, there were Austrians, Poles, Hungarians, Yugoslavs, and Russians. Some were Party members, but most were not. Estimates of the number of Nazis in American prisoner of war camps, in fact, range from a ridiculously low 6 percent to an equally ridiculous 90 percent. Unfortunately, it was not until late in the war—in an effort to belatedly segregate the prisoners for the reeducation program to follow—that several serious studies were undertaken to plumb the exact depth of Nazism within the camps. These studies confirmed that approximately 40 percent of the prisoners could be considered pro-Nazi (between 8-10 percent were judged to be fanatic, and about 30 percent were deeply sympathetic).[4] More importantly, these surveys indicated that confidence in Adolf Hitler was not synonymous with an attraction to National Socialism; nor did blind obedience to military orders and tradition indicate a sympathy for Nazism. A prisoner who was anti-American was not necessarily pro-fascist; nor was a German nationalist necessarily an advocate of racial atrocities. It was this mass of contradictions which, from the moment the prisoners of war arrived in the United States, confused the War Department and allowed the drastic increase of Nazi influence inside of the prisoner of war camps to occur.

An additional complication in the War Department's efforts to sort out the political problems occurring in the POW camps was the uneven quality of the American personnel. The guards were often drawn from those who were least skilled, and, as the war progressed, from among recently-returned American prisoners of war. As has been seen, there was at least one occasion when a camp guard despised the Germans to the point of firing into a group of unarmed prisoners or, at the other extreme, when a guard aided in their escape. In addition to this wide disparity of quality, camp personnel were generally unprepared to deal with the ideological chaos brewing on the other side of the fence for a number of other reasons.

First, a majority of the guards admired and respected the German combat veterans in their charge, especially the hardened (and more political) *Afrika Korps*. Almost without exception, the recollections and memoirs of American guards echo the sentiments of Sergeant Richard Staff, formerly attached to Camp Hearne, Texas, and Camp Robinson, Arkansas:

> Damn! They were a well-disciplined bunch of guys—physically healthy, well-trained, and excellent soldiers. They still maintained the dignity and

discipline that they had learned in the German Army, and I—we all—respected them.[5]

Secondly, the lack of German language abilities among the guards allowed the POWs substantial latitude. "What could we do?" shrugs Staff:

> Since they carried on their conversations in German, all we could do was to stand back, listen, and try to look intelligent as though we knew what they were talking about—just in case they were talking about us.[6]

Politically, this language problem became most evident in a particularly embarrassing incident at Camp Breckinridge, Kentucky. In late January, 1944, camp commander Colonel Payton Winlock personally led a parade of several hundred prisoners to church on Sunday morning, while the entire group heartily sang the Nazi Horst Wessel song. The incident quickly came to the public's attention through letters smuggled out of camp by anti-Nazi prisoners and eventually received a full airing in a stern broadcast by Walter Winchell. Understandably regretful at the adverse publicity, Colonel Winlock could only acknowledge that "he did not either recognize the Horst Wessel tune or understand the words of hate the prisoners sang, since he does not speak German." [7] Despite the language barriers experienced by Sergeant Staff and Colonel Winlock, and the strict regulations against it, fraternization between guards and English-speaking prisoners occurred with some regularity.[8]

In fact, reminiscences of former guards and prisoners often touch upon the warm relationships—however transitory—which formed between them. Most were based on the mutual disenchantment of people who did not wish to be where they were at that moment: far from civilian life, far from combat, or far from home. Sometimes it was simply the respect of one good soldier for another. Whatever the basis, most participants recall these fleeting friendships with fondness. "I became a guard at Fort Leonard Wood, Missouri, after I had been wounded in the South Pacific," recalls William Hahn. "I would have preferred to go to Germany with the 71st Infantry Division, but my malaria kept me from leaving. Still, it wasn't all bad. I had chums among the PWs, and several who worked in the kitchen often slipped me a 'fryer' [chicken] to take home. I also got hot loaves of bread from the prisoners in the camp bakery." [9] Dick Staff, a guard at Camp Robinson, Arkansas, recalls similar friendships with his prisoners. "One, I remember spoke perfect English; in fact, it was like talking to another guard. He had lived in the U.S. years before—worked at the Monsanto Chemical Company in St. Louis—and had gone to Germany to settle the estate of some deceased relatives. While there, he was drafted into the German army, was captured, and ended up here. We used to talk at length. . . .[10]

Nor were these friendships only prevalent among the disgruntled lower ranks. The former American commandant of Camp Trinidad, Colorado, Colonel Lambert B. Cain, for instance, corresponded with his former prisoner, Freiherr Rüdiger von Wechmar, years after the war was over. In one particular letter, saved with care by the recipient, Colonel Cain reminded his "dear friend" that "I shall always remember you and your brother officers with a great deal of admiration for your brave and gentlemanly conduct at a time when your minds were greatly disturbed over the situation of your loved ones at home." [11]

However, such fraternization, especially among the enlisted personnel, often contained the seeds of a new and particularly thorny problem: politics and ideology. The truth is that American personnel were simply unprepared to deal with the growing ideological struggle within the camps. When guard–prisoner conversations turned to politics—which they often quickly did—the Americans found themselves at a disadvantage. They were simply unable to adequately refute a strong argument from any politically-oriented German prisoner. Indeed, when the argument turned to America's discrimination of its Negroes, which the Germans were particularly fond of bringing up, what logical answers could the guards have offered? [12] "Sometimes," one guard sighed, "we feel that the Nazis have all the causes in the world to fight and we have none." [13]

That the War Department recognized the inability of its camp personnel to effectively counter the arguments put forward by German prisoners was evidenced by the appearance of a surprising publication. In order to give the American guards some ammunition for future political arguments, the Army in late 1944 published a 13-page pamphlet entitled *Fact vs. Fantasy*. The pamphlet listed seven standard Nazi "fantasies" such as "Germany did not lose the last war; she was stabbed in the back" and "America should appreciate Germany's problem with the Jews, for the United States has its own minority problems," and "There is no persecution of the Church in Germany." To answer each of these arguments the pamphlet provided short, fact-filled answers.[14] Considering that each rebuttal to the seven "typical German fantasies" was no more than two paragraphs in length, the pamphlet could not have been much help in a serious ideological confrontation. Thus, as a result of their general admiration for the prisoners, their inability to speak or understand German, and their difficulty in countering effective political arguments, the most immediate barrier to the successful growth and influence of Nazism within the camps—the guards—was of little ideological value in the face of German fanatics.

Two additional problems, not necessarily restricted to the guard–prisoner relationship, tended to complicate the government's initial efforts at ideological control and discrimination. The first revolved around the difficulty of the average American guard and camp or service commander to distinguish between prisoner incidents motivated by boredom or dissatisfaction and those motivated by genuine Nazism. The prisoners, for instance, delighted in mischievous pranks to confuse the guards or circumvent the rules, regaling in the silly humor of the situation. They were generally taken aback by the swift and disproportionate punishment which followed. POW Alfred Klein, then at Camp Foley, Alabama, vividly recalled such a prank and his surprise at the guard's reaction:

> During the construction of a U.S. Navy shooting range on a small island in the Gulf off Pensacola, we occasionally found big turtles which had crawled ashore. We decided to abuse one of the turtles politically! When the guard wasn't watching, we painted a large swastika in red paint on its shell and pushed the turtle back into the water. After a while, the turtle came ashore again, and as soon as we saw it, we alarmed our guard and drew his attention to this political phenomenon. His bewilderment was beyond belief—unfortunately not for very long! He became enraged, screamed at us "Nazis," and promised us several days on bread and water when we got back to camp. He was not lying. Anyway, we had our fun.[15]

Other prisoners, those at Camp Charleston, South Carolina, confounded the authorities during the harvesting of tomatoes in nearby St. Andrew's Parish. While packing the vegetables into crates, a group of prisoners secretly slit swastikas into the tomatoes with their thumbnails. No more than a prank, surely, to gleefully advertise to consumers their presence in the packing process, the prisoners were nonetheless startled at the ferocity with which the camp commander, Captain D. C. Williams, investigated the "sabotage" and isolated the culprits.[16] In another incident, prisoners assigned to repair the roofing at Billings General Hospital at Fort Benjamin Harrison, Indiana, learned first hand that their humor was not appreciated by the authorities. A group of six POWs mischievously arranged two-tone shingles to form a giant swastika on the roof of the hospital. Attracted by their laughter, the camp authorities ordered the six men to return to the roof and rearrange the shingles, after which, as noted by testimony before the Committee on Military Affairs, they were all placed on a diet of bread and water for a period of 14 days.[17]

On the other hand, incidents of serious Nazism were treated with the same severity. A group of German prisoners en route from Fort Reno,

Oklahoma to another camp, for example, threw hundreds of propaganda leaflets from the moving train. Crudely mimeographed with swastikas in the corners of the sheets, the leaflets read: "Americans, who is sitting behind the front line? The Jews! Who gets killed in action? The American soldier! ... Jews are the Americans' ruin, the Jews need the American people for their personal interest." [18] Prompted by the outrage of local citizens, the Army ultimately placed the culprits on bread and water for 14 days—the identical punishment meted out to pranksters. In another incident in June, 1944, the F.B.I. traced similar propaganda pamphlets (these cryptically signed by the "American-Soviet Committee," which had appeared in camps across central Texas) to a group of POWs using the camp commander's mimeograph machine at Camp Mexia, Texas.[19] Again, the punishment was identical to that which would be received by non-political mischief-makers.

The reason for the similarity in punishment did not lie in the lack of alternative options, for, as noted earlier, the catalogue of available administrative disciplinary actions was lengthy and varied. The real difficulty lay in the fact that camp and service commanders generally saw little difference between the pranks and real Nazi-inspired incidents. The Army deplored disturbances of any sort, regardless of motivation. The fact that most of the incidents used a swastika—the very symbol of Nazism—led American personnel to conclude until late in the war that the vast majority of prisoners were hopelessly political and generally unsalvageable. The best one could hope for was a quiet and orderly camp, in which discipline was ideally maintained by the prisoners themselves.

The last area which tended to complicate the government's efforts at political discrimination among the prisoners was the unwritten policy to make any concession which helped keep the camps quiet. As discussed frequently throughout this study, the United States was almost obsessed with adherence to a liberal interpretation of the Geneva Convention, often far in excess of any agreed-upon requirements. The reason, of course, was the government's concern for the safety of the more than 90,000 American prisoners in German hands [20] and the well-founded fear that any trespass against the rights of prisoners in American camps would bring swift and perhaps brutal retaliation in Europe. Since the obdurate Nazis in American camps were the most vocal and demanding, and since, in the final analysis, they most closely represented the political views of the regime which held so many Allied prisoners in its grasp, it was the Nazis who often extracted concessions from the War Department which helped solidify their hold over the large majority of nonpolitical or anti-Nazi prisoners.

For example, the Geneva Convention requires that prisoners salute in the manner accepted by their army. In the case of the German Army, a soldier whose head is covered lifts his hand in a conventional military salute.

If his head is uncovered, he stands with elbows back at attention. In short, there was no Hitler salute in the German Army until its introduction following the July 20, 1944, attempt on Hitler's life. Yet the Hitler salute, a blatant political gesture, was accepted by the War Department from the moment the first prisoner arrived.

In another example of such concessions, German prisoners who happened to die during their incarceration in the United States—and a total of 477 did [21]—were often carried to the camp cemetery in a coffin draped with a swastika flag. Article 76 of the Geneva Convention provides for the honorable and respectful burial of all prisoners who die in captivity. The War Department, however, went one step further. On September 23, 1943, the government agreed to allow the casket of the deceased prisoner to be draped by the national flag desired by his fellow prisoners. [22] If the same German soldier had died on the battlefied, he would not in all probability be buried under a swastika flag. Moreover, the War Department informed all camp commanders that it had "no objection to the display by prisoners, adjacent to their bunks or on lockers, of small pictures of their national leaders, national flags or emblems." [23]

A similar example of such unnecessary concessions may be seen in the government's decision to expand the Convention's requirement allowing the celebration of traditional national holidays to include camp-wide festivities every April 20, Hitler's birthday. A final example appeared in an officially-sanctioned article, "Our Nazi War-Prisoners," published in the mass-circulation *Pic Magazine*. In a lengthy discussion of prisoner activity in an unnamed camp, the author, an American officer, noted that on one occasion, "the captives started teasing and vexing some of our guards because of their Jewish descent." The author then admitted that:

> The guards were finally withdrawn, not as a concession to racial prejudice but in order to avoid any incident which could serve as a pretext for retaliation against American soldiers, Christian and Jewish, taken prisoner by the Nazis. [24]

Surely, such concessions as these could not have but clouded any effort to effectively reduce the growing influence of Nazism within America's prisoner of war camps.

Internal Nazi Control of POW Camps

While the government certainly was aware that the political ideology of the incoming prisoners ranged from anti-Nazi to rabid Nazi, even including

Comrades stand with arms raised in the official Hitler salute at the gravesite of a
fellow POW, at Jefferson Barracks, Missouri. *(UPI)*

Funerals were generally the occasion for the appearance of political trappings.
1) Funeral at Camp Robinson, Arkansas. *(U.S. Army Photo)*
2) Funeral at Camp Swift, Texas. *(U.S. Army Photo)*
3) Funeral for General Hans Schubert. *(National Archives)*

Since the POWs were permitted to display political symbols, such drawings as this of Hitler were not uncommon. Camp Evelyn, Michigan. *(U.S. Army Photo)*

Army censors monitored all POW mail in an effort to both gauge the level of political activity within each camp, and to isolate those who appeared potentially dangerous. This example of such political mail, written a week after the attempt on Hitler's life on 20 July, 1944, reads as follows: "My Führer! On the fortunate outcome of the criminal assault on your life, permit me to congratulate you from the depths of my heart. In honest joy and steadfast loyalty. . . ."

"Break it up, you Krauts! Ain't you got anything better to do than stand around planning the next war?"

(GRIN AND BEAR IT, by *George Lichty,* © *Field Enterprises, Inc., 1944. Courtesy of Field Newspaper Syndicate)*

a number of Communists, it was not immediately prepared to attempt to isolate the influences of these groups inside the camps. Considering the problems already present in running a prisoner of war program without any precedents or guidelines, and the continual need to maintain the camps with the smallest possible drain on the overseas war effort, priorities forced the authorities to place the internal control of the camp in the hands of the most disciplined prisoner group.

The normal procedure was to channel camp control through the prisoners' regular hierarchy of command with the key link between the American commander and the prisoner community being the camp spokesman. According to Article 43 of the Geneva Convention, the camp at large was obligated to appoint a representative to deal with camp administrators and inspection teams on its behalf, an opportunity seized most often by the more aggressive Nazis. Yet instead of disrupting the prisoner of war program, the Nazi-dominated camps, in fact, were usually models of efficiency. The Nazis realized that an orderly and well-run camp would give them the continued backing of the American authorities and, therefore, the continued control over the camp. As a result, they were given an almost free hand, and without an effective intelligence system and adequate guidelines, the War Department moved slowly to counter their influence.

In addition to the government's desire to insure tranquility and discipline within the camps by placing power in the hands of politically inspired spokesmen or the German military hierarchy, there was one further reason—perhaps the most significant—for the rapid increase in Nazi influence. The first large body of prisoners to arrive in the United States and, consequently, those to whom all later arrivals would be forced to submit, were the most thoroughly indoctrinated Nazis. "The first captives from North Africa," wrote the Harvard historian, Sidney Fay,

> . . . were a tough lot—the toughest of any group of German prisoners—partly because they had waged a remarkably heroic though unsuccessful campaign . . . and partly because they were captured at a time when Hitler's fortunes had not sunk so low as at present. . . .
>
> When captured probably 80-90 percent of them were still fanatically Nazi-minded. These were the ones who were reported to be incredulous when they saw the skyscrapers of New York still standing, and who assumed that the accounts in the American press of Allied successes were only propaganda lies. . . .
>
> They made the camp a hell for the anti-Nazis and the political moderates.[25]

Thus, the members of the *Afrika Korps,* rigidly disciplined and admired by their fellow prisoners (as well as American guards) as the cream of the German military, established the political patterns within the camps from the moment of their arrival. They elected the camp spokesmen from among themselves, and while appearing to be cooperative with the authorities by acting in an exemplary manner, often controlled the later, less Nazified, arrivals. "The first thing that struck me as I entered Camp Hood, Texas," recalled Private Carl Amery, a 21-year-old *Afrika Korps* veteran from Tunisia, "was that German discipline recreated itself right away, with its orders, its commands. The *Afrika Korps* was a disciplined force where everybody obeyed as one man; and since the Americans respected the Geneva Convention, they let us develop right away a parallel hierarchy which took the prisoners in hand. I had come home." [26]

Thousands of late arrivals to the United States were stunned and apprehensive to find that their new homes were already politicized. A typical reaction of those who appeared after the summer of 1944 is described by Corporal Hein Severloh:

> We had arrived at Camp McCain, near Jackson, Mississippi. We were a group of 250, all taken in Normandy. I have to say that the first thing that struck me was that those who were in the camp were all in light grey, the uniform of the *Afrika Korps,* and we, in the midst of them, were all in grey-green; that made a curious effect. We were the first grey-greens to arrive in this camp. We were already at the end of our nerves, but they, they made us feel right away that we were second-class men, a bunch of nothings, without manners, without courage, that if we were there it's really because we didn't fight. And in this camp everything was stupifying: the discipline, the guys from the Afrika Korps who posted each morning bulletins of victory, official German communiques; imagine the effect that had on us! We thought we would go crazy. It was necessary to stop a good number of men from going to throw themselves on the barbed wire to get shot by an American sentinel. . . ." [27]

Even hardened members of the *Afrika Korps* quickly learned to toe the political mark. Sergeant Werner Baecher, for example, was assigned the task of combing through the camp's daily newspapers and presenting a news review to the men assembled in the mess hall after each evening meal. He recalls:

One evening I announced that American troops had landed in Sicily. There followed a painful silence. A young officer cadet came towards me. I can still see the scene, as if it happened just an hour ago. He told me: "You know, certainly, that you are a traitor!" Flabbergasted, I asked him "Why?" "Because you are repeating enemy propaganda—giving news items that aren't true." Needless to say, I quickly stopped my news reviews. From then on, it was they who transmitted the news, and who knows what that may have been—the capture of Leningrad, invasion of England, etc.[28]

At most camps, however, the political pressure was more subtle. POW librarians, for example, often merely hid books which had been banned by Hitler; sometimes the prisoner in charge of the canteen sold cigarettes or magazines to those who were loyal to Hitler; on other occasions, an outwardly cooperative POW managed to get an administrative job at camp headquarters and conveniently lost records or altered routine forms. At Fort DuPont, Delaware, one self-appointed Nazi leader decided on the direct approach. Every Sunday morning, it was revealed,

the Nazi posted himself, pencil and paper in hand, outside the compound church, which has a congregation of some two hundred, and warned would-be churchgoers that if they entered he'd note their names and they would discover the consequences when they got back to Germany.[29]

In some camps where the Nazis were in strong control, even the chaplains were not exempt from such political influence. Lieutenant Dankwart von Arnim, a former member of the 1st Panzer Division, recalled an occasion when a military chaplain spoke to the assembled prisoners during Easter Mass and closed his sermon with the words: "Let us pray for our poor suffering Fatherland. May peace come quickly." He was immediately booed and even struck by the outraged men who were nearest to him. To the men, he was a defeatist and, consequently, a traitor. Fearful for his safety, the chaplain applied to the American authorities for a transfer to a different camp, which was quickly granted. "But just before his departure, since he was the chaplain, after all, a group of German officers came to salute him. And as a spokesman, one of them made a little speech: 'Mr. Chaplain, we regret your departure, but it is your own fault. Your transfer will be especially sad from your point of view, since this camp [Alva, Oklahoma] is a model camp, and the one that the Fuehrer will liberate first.' "[30]

Such harassment served to bring most recalcitrant prisoners into line or drive them to other camps, but when it did not, harsher methods were brought into play. One of the most effective holds over non-Nazi or anti-Nazi prisoners was the warning that reprisals would be taken against their relatives back home and against the prisoners themselves after their re-patriation to Germany. They were reminded that when sick or wounded POWs were exchanged, lists of names of "bad Nazis" would be smuggled out of the United States and presented to the dreaded leader of the SS, police, and Gestapo, Heinrich Himmler. Not only would their relatives be in immediate jeopardy, but when they themselves went back to Germany after the war, the non-Nazis were assured, they would be confronted with their records as prisoners of war.[31] *"Show that you are a Nazi,"* an official communique reminded them. "And if any of your comrades should suc-cumb to Jewish-Bolshevik influences," the communique noted ominously, "set him a good example." [32] These threats were not taken lightly by either the prisoners or the increasingly vocal critics of the War Department's *laissez-faire* policy toward the prisoners.

Journalists and news reporters were the first to publicly acknowledge the political struggle in the camps. James H. Powers, the well-known Foreign Editor of the Boston *Globe,* declared, "50 per cent of the German noncoms definitely support Hitler and his government. They are, in reality, a police force in the camp.... The effect of their rule is a little Germany, where persecution of the anti-Nazis is thorough and violent." [33] The widely syndicated columnist Dorothy Thompson concurred: "Men who put up provocative signs on the walls, bragging that they will win the war, and go around giving Nazi salutes are Nazis.... They will go home in excellent health, having been well fed and cared for. And meanwhile, on American soil, we shall have kept alive all the symbols of their party dictatorship." [34] The German-American press, which maintained sensitive links among the anti-Nazi prisoners, was especially outraged at the unrestricted growth of Nazism. Gerhart H. Seger, editor of the German-language newspaper *Neue Volkszeitung* published in New York, warned: "Already the Nazis are organized in the prisoner of war camps throughout America. Any German prisoner who shows any interest in democracy or America is punished by his fellow prisoners.... The Nazis in our prisoner camps even have organized Gestapo units." [35] Even the normally sedate *New York Times,* in an editorial entitled "The Gestapo in America," lashed out at the authorities who failed to realize "that we were capturing Nazi gangsters as well as run-of-the-mill soldiers." [36]

Similar sentiments were echoed by numerous anti-Nazi prisoners in letters to their families and in private conversations with trusted guards. By the Army's own admission, on numerous occasions prisoners rattled the gates and asked guards for protection ... [saying that] ... a court among the prisoners had sentenced them and they would be dead by morning if they were kept in the stockade." [37] One particularly poignant effort to alert the War Department to the growing danger concerned a letter written in November, 1944, from a Private Friedrich Schlitz to his American commander at Camp Campbell, Kentucky. Schlitz wrote:

> I take this unusual step of writing this letter, as it was impossible to see you.
> I am told that you don't like anti-Nazis, but I appeal to your fairness. . . .
> I acknowledge that a snappy behavior looks nice, machine-like. You feel it is like a good running motor, smooth and dependable. But it is all a facade. . . . Those who are your enemies are respected. Those who had to fight against you as they had no other choice, and who flocked to you for protection, who work for your victory, which means their victory, these are contempted! WHY? [38]

The answer to Schlitz's desperate question is best provided by another POW, Dankwart von Arnim, who spent the war years in Camps David, Maryland, and Ruston, Louisiana. "The Americans doubtlessly thought that it was simply better to have a well-disciplined Nazi camp commanded by an American corporal, than a camp of 10,000 very good German democrats, inevitably at odds with one another, which might require a company of Military Police to control." [39]

A final warning about the political struggle within the camps occurred as part of the public and governmental controversy surrounding the later reeducation program for the war prisoners. As the result of a November, 1944, Harvard University investigation of camp conditions, the group's highly respected leader, Professor Warren A. Seavey, implored the War Department to initiate immediate and radical changes. Citing the many mistakes made by the government, Seavey declared that "the Nazi element has succeeded in getting control and intimidating the other prisoners . . .[and that] . . . United States policy in prisoners' camps was strengthening Nazism among the war captives." [40]

To these, and a number of other charges that the United States was encouraging Nazism rather than eliminating it,[41] Secretary of War Henry L. Stimson, grudgingly admitted that while "occasionally, groups of Nazi prisoners have attempted to dominate their fellow prisoners," he concluded assuringly,

> there has been substantial success in curtailing the activities of such minorities and in preventing coercion of prisoners by Nazi extremists. . . . The War Department is cognizant of the problems created by Nazi elements in our camps, and every effort is being made. . . . I therefore feel that there is no necessity for an investigation. . . .[42]

It is ironic that only weeks before Stimson's rejection of Seavey's proposal the total population of 3,300 prisoners at Fort Lewis, Washington, held a massive demonstration in celebration of Hitler's birthday, including the appearance of the Nazi flag atop the stockade pole.[43] As if to further mock Secretary Stimson's unwarranted optimism, the German government informed the War Department via Switzerland that all German personnel were henceforth ordered to use the Nazi raised-arm salute as the official greeting.[44] It was, of course, a legal order by the head of state, and consequently, as guaranteed by the Geneva Convention, the War Department could do no less than dutifully authorize its introduction into the camps.[45]

To the anti-Nazi prisoners who were trying to swim against the rising tide of Nazism in the camps, however, the new salute appeared to be another indication of American concern with the outward appearances of POW control while allowing internal politics to seek their own level. One example of the ludicrous situation which the War Department had allowed to develop in the prisoner of war camps was recalled by POW Tilman Kiwe shortly after the introduction of the new salute. During one of his infrequent stays behind barbed wire, Kiwe had an occasion to see the American commander at Camp Alva, Oklahoma:

> I entered the camp commander's office, my hat under my arm. He started to howl: "Is that how you salute a superior officer in Germany? I demand that you salute me exactly as you would one of your German superior officers! Out!"
>
> "Fine," I thought, "I'll back out and come in again with my arm raised."
>
> But he started howling again: ". . . and the Heil Hitler!"
>
> So out I went again, to enter for the third time, this time raising my arm, clicking my heels, and yelling "Heil Hitler!" [46]

The War Department finally acknowledged the situation at the end of the war, though the subject of camp terrorism was made to appear as an expected and temporary occurrence which was easily brought under control. In an otherwise authoritative article on the German prisoner of war experience, the former Director of the Prisoner of War Division of the Provost Marshal General's Office, Colonel Martin Tollefson, stated that:

> Prisoner-of-war discipline was an exceedingly important but not particularly difficult problem. The German *Afrika Korps* prisoners were the first to come here in large numbers. Many of them came in victorious and arrogant moods, showing a desire to take the law into their own hands.... As an illustration, what appeared to be a wave of murder and forced suicides was abruptly started. Such crime and lawlessness, however, although apparently well and extensively planned, was stopped or eased virtually in its inception.
>
> This change in attitude ... might have been due to the fact that the prisoners were informed promptly that no "kangaroo courts" or substitutes would be tolerated and that Nazi laws, regulations, and indoctrinations would not control or regulate conduct in our camps....[47]

The Provost Marshal General since June, 1944, Archer L. Lerch, noted that "the War Department early became aware that Nazi elements would try to dominate camps, and early measures were adopted to cope with the situation.... One of the reasons for this success," reported General Lerch, "was that:

> Every camp has been notified that a notice should be posted on the prisoner of war bulletin board ... stating that any prisoner who fears for his own safety need only report that fear to the nearest American officer or enlisted man, and he will be given protection.[48]

Despite the apparent complacency of these statements, the War Department—privately—had long been aware of the problem and was deeply concerned. After an official three-month inspection of 32 separate POW camps, for example, the Office of War Information sadly reported that they had discovered a majority of Nazis in each.[49] Even more ominously, in March, 1945, General Lerch was informed that "from 5 to 10 per cent of personnel in practically every camp were fanatics who controlled the activities of all other prisoners."[50] Given the rather small sampling involved in these investigations, however, and the Army's admitted difficulty in distinguishing between the Nazi and anti-Nazi prisoners, there is some evidence of exaggeration—even hysteria—regarding the number of camps under Nazi "control." That is to say, the trend toward political control of the prisoner camps by a minority of Nazis was correctly diagnosed; how many of the camps were so controlled and to what degree is impossible to estimate. Several points are clear. The success obtained by the Nazis with the camps, however widespread, often created a totalitarian environment in the prisoner system. Secondly, the government was painfully aware of the politically-motivated terrorism wielded by the *Afrika Korps* captives and the Gestapo agents who roamed among the POW communities. And lastly, the Army's initial efforts to curb these activities had proven largely ineffective.

Realistically, in fact, there was little which could have been done to isolate and neutralize the clandestine and powerful groups in each camp. Had the War Department attempted to segregate the prisoners directly after their capture, in itself a questionable undertaking considering the lack of guidelines and qualified interrogators, there may have been an opportunity for substantial success. Once the POWs had settled into captivity, however, and circumstances had allowed the instruments of camp control to pass into the hands of the prisoners, the War Department could do little more than try to wrest power from the POWs themselves. It was to be an enormously difficult task. As late as March, 1944, in fact, a number of camp commanders at the Seventh Service Command conference in Omaha, Nebraska, could do little more than compare notes on the effects of political terrorism in their camps. After acknowledging that hardened Nazi prisoners continued to circumvent every American countermove to restrict their influence, an unnamed camp commander volunteered the following experience:

> I was advised that four prisoners were asking to be transferred to another camp. A secret tribunal had judged them traitors to the Nazi regime. I saw them before their departure, and they were happy enough to leave the camp. These four prisoners were veterans of the campaigns in France, Russia, and North Africa, and while they denied being traitors to Germany, they did admit to having criticized Hitler. Now they were desperately afraid of reprisals against their families. . . . One of them told me that he was sure he would be hanged the very minute he set foot on German soil. . . . .
>
> There are prisoners in the camps who are, in their hearts, violently anti-Nazi, but who are desperately afraid that their comrades will discover their true convictions. . . .[51]

All participants sadly agreed and moved on to the problems of obtaining badly needed guard replacements and supplies.

The Physical Dangers of Anti-Nazism

For the prisoners, however, the subject was far from closed. Nazi influence within the camps continued to grow as the minority of hardened politicals threatened the others into line. Those prisoners who were not intimidated by peer pressure or by threats of reprisals against their relatives living in Germany—and who were outspoken or simply unlucky—often found themselves in physical danger. Prisoners accused of "disloyalty," by whatever standards, were occasionally dragged from their sleep by roaming bands of Nazi "vigilantes" and beaten senseless. The victims quickly learned that very little provocation was required for such punishment. Arriving at Camp Ellis, Illinois, for example, a young aviator named Pips mistakenly confided to several earlier arrivals that the war was lost. What happened next was later recounted by his friend, Hans Werner Richter:

> An impression of menace emanated from the silent bloc. They quickened their pace as Pips, Buchwald, Guhler, and I walked on into the central compound.
> "Traitors! Deserter! Bandits!" The insults hissed.
> "They're nuts!" said Buchwald, who walked beside Guhler.
> "All from the *Afrika Korps,*" said Pips.
> "Where are you from?" somebody shouted.
> "Italy."
> "Deserters, in other words. You'll pay for it!"
> "Shut your trap!" Pips hurled back, furious. The somber wall closed around him, cold, hostile, sweating with hate.... The same evening we met up with what was called the "Lagergestapo," the camp gestapo.... Pips was seized in the barracks and badly beaten, then dragged by the legs out of the barrack, his poor bloody head bouncing over the ground....
> Pips was taken, what was left of him, that is, to a hospital. We never saw him again....[52]

At Camp Scottsbluff, Nebraska, a prisoner who wanted to write to his father, an American resident, was severely beaten by fellow-prisoners who declared the father was "not a good Nazi." He was warned that he had better not write the letter, but he insisted and found himself in the camp hospital. The

Seventh Service Command admitted that "no American officer or guard witnessed the incident." [53] In testifying before the Congressional Committee on Military Affairs in a routine examination of the POW project, the commander of Camp Ellis, Illinois, Lieutenant Colonel C. P. Evers, casually conceded that "The prisoners had considerable trouble among themselves.... On one occasion 15 Nazis so unmercifully assaulted a Polish prisoner that he required hospital treatment for several days." [54] The number of similar incidents were legion and occurred at nearly 200 camps. So helpless were the authorities in the face of such formless violence that one terrified anti-Nazi prisoner at Camp Breckinridge, Kentucky, was offered no more protection than "a bottle of gentian scent, which he was to hurl at his assailant, so that the latter might be identified by the scent in the morning." [55] When asked why he, or any other POWs, declined to notify the Red Cross representative or the camp authorities, Hans Werner Richter replied:

> It would have been absolutely impossible. I believe I saw a Red Cross representative once, but he was passing so far away.... And besides, if we had dared to tell him something, you can imagine what the consequences would have been . . . slaughtered in the night.
>
> And as far as the camp authorities are concerned, that would have served only to attract reprisals. For the Americans, it was very simple. Whatever happened among the prisoners was not to be interfered with, according to the Geneva Convention, except in the case of murder, of course.[56]

As it turned out, murder was soon to follow.

Where threats and beatings failed, the execution and forced suicides of random anti-Nazis succeeded. The War Department's initial lack of control over the internal events of the prisoner communities led to an eight-month reign of violence, carried out from September 1943 to April 1944, by the now substantially larger segment of fanatical Nazis. Many of the larger camps organized midnight tribunals and "kangaroo courts" which censured and condemned "traitors" and "deserters." Threats of impending execution took the form of premature obituary notices and chicken-bones in the anti-Nazis' bunks,[57] after which the victims waited in terror for the inevitable.

One of the earliest such executions occurred at Camp Concordia, Kansas, on October 18, 1943. Captain Felix Tropschuh, age 30, was suspected by the camp gestapo of having informed the authorities about an impending escape attempt, and his personal diary revealed "statements against Nazi ideology." On this evidence, he was brought before a "court of honor," found guilty, and "expelled from the German community of fellowship." He was placed in a room with a rope and a chair on the night of October 17, and a number of Nazis posted themselves outside of the door until morning. When Tropschuh failed to appear at early roll-call, a guard was sent to check his room and found him dead. The Army found the cause of death to be "suicide." [58]

The following month, on November 4, 1943, a Corporal Johann Kunze at Camp Tonkawa, Oklahoma, unwittingly attended a secret late-night meeting of some 200 POWs at the camp mess hall. The doors were barred, and he quickly learned that the assembled men had been called together by the spokesman to witness the exposure of a traitor in their midst. The traitor, he was shocked to learn, was himself. He was accused of having given information to the American authorities regarding secret installations in Hamburg, which would have been useful in future Allied bombing raids. He was found guilty by popular acclamation and beaten to death with clubs and broken milk bottles.[59] In this particular case, five of the guilty Nazis, including the camp spokesman—all older sergeants in the *Afrika Korps*—were apprehended, tried by an American court-martial at nearby Camp Gruber, and found guilty.[60] The State Department then carried out the procedures required by the Geneva Convention to inform Berlin via the Swiss Legation of the entire matter. On July 10, 1945, after every facet of the case had been properly examined (including the very real fear of reprisals against American prisoners in German hands), the five Germans became the first foreign war prisoners to be executed in the history of the United States.[61]

The next month, on December 23, 1943, a prisoner was beaten to death at Camp Hearne, Texas. Corporal Hugo Krauss, 24, was born in Germany but lived in New York from 1928 to 1939 with his parents who had become naturalized citizens. Enamoured with the Third Reich, he returned to Germany at the expense of the German-American Bund and later joined the German Army with which he served in Russia and North Africa. Captured and shipped to Texas, Krauss's fluency in English enabled him to become an interpreter for the camp commander, which, alone, made him suspect in the eyes of his fellow prisoners. His naturalized American parents in New York only implicated him further, and his criticism of the German Government and praise for all things American sealed his fate. "After the lights were put out at 9 P.M. on December 17, 1943, from six to ten men entered the compound through a hole they had cut in a wire fence . . . and invaded Krauss' barracks. He screamed for help but no one came to his aid. His barracks mates looked on while his skull was fractured, both arms were broken and his body was battered from head to foot." He died in the camp hospital six days later.[62] No perpetrators were discovered.

In January, Private Franz Kettner, 39, was ostracized from the "German community of fellowship" at Camp Concordia because he was an Austrian and because he refused a Nazi demand that he steal articles from the camp storeroom. He was booed in the mess hall, publicly threatened, and finally sentenced to death by the kangaroo court. Kettner was found dead in his bunk, his wrists slashed, on January 11, 1944.[63]

In March, at the Papago Park internment camp, outside Phoenix, a newly arrived enlisted prisoner from the German Navy, Werner Dreschler, was found hanged in a barrack washroom. His fellow prisoners suspected that he had supplied information about his U-boat to American interrogators, and his execution was reportedly ordered at a kangaroo court, which denounced him as a "dog who had broken his oath." Within six hours after he had arrived at the camp, he was beaten and strangled in his barracks by a group of men, who then carried his body to a washroom and hung it up by a rope from a rafter. The body was discovered early the following morning on March 13, 1944. An investigation by Colonel A. H. Means, camp commander, quickly led to the arrest of seven members of Dreschler's own U-boat crew. They were eventually court-martialed for the crime, to which they later proudly confessed, and on August 25, 1945, at the Disciplinary Barracks at Fort Leavenworth, Kansas, all seven were hanged by the U.S. Army.[64]

Later that month, at Camp Chaffe, Arkansas, yet another German prisoner was killed by his Nazi comrades. Hans Geller, a 21-year-old paratrooper, twice wounded, whose three brothers had been killed in action as German soldiers would certainly appear to have been above suspicion. However, Geller spoke and read English well and appeared to be cooperating too closely with his American work supervisor. When he requested that two new men assigned to his work detail be sent elsewhere, since their political activities were interfering with their work, the die was cast. A kangaroo court found him guilty of anti-Nazi activity, and that night, March 25, 1944, a prisoner officer appeared at Geller's door to mention that a new arrival from Sudern, Geller's home town, was anxious to meet him. Geller walked unsuspectingly out into the darkness to his death. An investigation led to the arrest and court-martial of POW Sergeant Edgar Menschner, who was sentenced to hang. Menschner's sentence was commuted by President Truman on July 6, 1945, to 20 years confinement at the United States Disciplinary Barracks, Fort Leavenworth, Kansas.[65]

The last of this series of political murders occurred on April 6, 1944, when Corporal Horst Gunther, 24, who had been denounced as a traitor by a fellow prisoner, was found dead near Camp Gordon, Georgia. His crimes appear to have been that several prisoners suspected that he might have alerted the authorities to a pending prisoner work-stoppage and that he liked jazz music.[66] On the basis of such obvious sentiments of anti-Nazism, Gunther was condemned by a midnight kangaroo court. He was lured to a tent at the Aiken Side Camp, South Carolina, where two German sergeants, Erick Gauss and Rudolf Straub, strangled him to death in the presence of five other prisoners. His body was then carried elsewhere and hanged from a telephone pole to make it appear that he had become "despondent" and committed suicide. Gauss and Straub were tried at Fort McPherson, Georgia, and sentenced to death. Then came the normal flurry of diplomatic activity with Germany, via Bern, to guarantee the rights of the condemned men, and, if necessary, to exchange the Germans for condemned Allied prisoners. In the midst of this routine, the war came to an end. Since there was no further threat to American prisoners in German hands, the Provost Marshal General's Office directed that the executions be carried out. President Truman concurred, and both men were hanged at Fort Leavenworth, Kansas, on July 14, 1945.[67]

In addition to these seven celebrated Nazi-inspired murders, there were dozens of other such incidents. Some prisoners rushed the fence, either under orders by the political fanatics or in fear of their lives, and were shot by the American guards as escapees. At least one prisoner threw himself, or was thrown, under a passenger train near Camp Hearne, Texas. No less than 72 others were simply listed by the Army as "suicides." [68] At Camp Grant, Illinois, a group of fanatical Nazis tried to kill 42 suspected anti-Nazis in a single blow by burning down their locked barrack in the middle of the night.[69]

In the end, there is no way of knowing with any certainty exactly how many prisoners died as a result of the struggle between Nazis and anti-Nazis within the camps. A recently-published French study of the POW experience in the United States, for example, authoritatively places the official number of clandestine executions at exactly 167.[70] On the other hand, John Mason Brown, former director of the Special War Problems Division, Department of State, stated equally authoritatively: "the general public appears to have a grossly exaggerated idea of the Nazi-criminal aspects of camp life; there have been a total of only 2 murders and not over 10 severe beatings due to political reasons." [71] General Archer L. Lerch, equally conservative, reported that "we have had only five murders and two forced suicides that could be attributed to Nazi methods," and, based on his figures, logically added that, "the murder and suicide rate among German prisoners of war from all causes is lower than the rate shown by insurance statistics for the general German public in time of peace." [72] However many of the German prisoners were assaulted, executed, or driven to suicide by the Nazi minorities in the POW communities, it is clear that the War Department had inadvertently allowed a portion of POW control to slip into the hands of a small fanatical element. While that minority was almost always made up of Nazis, it must be noted that when, on very rare occasions, strong Communist or otherwise anti-Nazi elements controlled a camp, they tended to be as ruthless and domineering as the Nazi extremists.[73] The War Department was painfully aware of the problem, as well as of mounting public criticism of the government's laxness, and several belated solutions—segregation and reeducation—were already in various stages of implementation. Whatever the reason for the fortuitous and unexplained end of the eight-month long reign of terror in the camps,[74] the War Department gratefully accepted the lull and rushed ahead with its campaign to segregate the Nazis from the anti-Nazis.

The Segregation of Nazis from Anti-Nazis

From the beginning, prisoners had been separated by rank—officers to one camp, and enlisted personnel to another—as required by the Geneva Convention.[75] Naval personnel were also separated from army and air force personnel. No concerted effort was made to distinguish between the various shades of their politics since it was assumed that they were all firm believers in National Socialism. At first, this view was reasonably accurate since the first prisoners to arrive were hardened veterans of the *Afrika Korps.* In any case, as long as there were only a relatively few prisoners in the United States—about 1,000 at the end of January, 1943—there were no real difficulties. Unfortunately, the War Department did not use this opportunity to consider the politics of the tens of thousands of additional prisoners who were soon to arrive, nor did it respond to several British invitations to coordinate political segregation policies. When the number of incoming POWs rose sharply to 150,000 and then to 200,000 and 250,000, the task of segregating the prisoners became almost too formidable. In fact, the War Department had hardly prepared any firm guidelines or even a clear definition of the problem, let alone a solution.

The first step came in a written directive on February 18, 1943, which ordered the separation of any anti-Nazi prisoners from among the incoming thousands. When such prisoners could be identified as anti-Nazi, they were to be sent to one of three designated camps reserved for anti-Nazis: Fort Devens, Massachusetts; Camp Campbell, Kentucky; and Camp McCain, Mississippi. There were two major problems, however. First, this initial effort to segregate POWs was based on the premise that it was somehow easier to identify an anti-Nazi than it was to identify a Nazi. The anti-Nazi, it was presumed, would volunteer himself to the authorities or would, perhaps, already be known to the War Department's Intelligence Division. The difficulty in identifying anti-Nazis quickly became apparent, especially when they were intimidated by their fellows, and only the most prominent anti-Nazis (usually intellectuals who had been imprisoned in Germany before their conscription into the Army) were generally found on the Intelligence Division's lists.

The fact that anti-Nazis were originally selected for isolation and transfer indicated that most Americans were convinced that the vast majority of the incoming POWs were obdurate Nazis and that the few dissenters among them could be readily removed and salvaged. As the government soon learned, however, there were fewer Nazis than anti-Nazis. Thus the War Department had chosen to isolate members of the rather shapeless majority from the fewer, more visible, and far more dangerous Nazi minority. The term "anti-Nazi" was a loose and "catch-all" label which encompassed nearly any political philosophy short of National Socialism. So long as the War Department was determined to isolate these types of prisoners, their job was difficult at best. During a conference of camp commanders of the Seventh Service Command, Major William F. Matschullart conceded:

> About the only way to distinguish a Nazi from an anti-Nazi is when you see a man being pursued by a crowd of fifty others who are howling for murder, you can be sure that the man who is running is an anti-Nazi.[76]

As a result, there were some notable errors. The most outstanding mistake, as reported with some chagrin by General B. M. Bryan, Assistant PMG, involved the newly designated anti-Nazi compound at Fort Devens and its 1,300 special prisoners. "After these men had been confined for approximately 2 months," Bryan noted, "four prisoners [came forward and] stated that they were Gestapo agents, and that they had secured all the information they desired about the anti-Nazis in that compound. . . . [Their task accomplished] they now wished to be transferred to a Nazi prisoner-of-war camp. These four men are still at Fort Devens and are well-subdued by the anti-Nazis." [77]

In addition to the inherent difficulties involved in isolating anti-Nazis rather than Nazis, the February directive contained a second major weakness. This revolved around the War Department's decision to place the initial segregation process in the hands of inexperienced service and camp commanders. Based on the seemingly logical premise that governmental guidelines would not be as valuable as on-site observations by American personnel, the directive, in effect, created different standards for prisoner segregation in each of the nine service commands and more than 500 base and branch camps. Not until July, 1944, in fact, did the Provost Marshal General's Office attempt to standardize the requirements for political segregation. With such a variety of standards, there was, naturally, a certain unevenness of policy. Among the more interesting results was the occasional effort by a few American officers to advise qualified prisoners *against* transferring to an anti-Nazi camp. Their logic, simply put, was that regular camps, with internal discipline firmly in the hands of the prisoners, were easier to control than the chaotic "democratic" camps. The more prisoners who could be retained in the regular camps, the fewer the problems in the three other camps. POW Dankwart von Arnim, for example, recalls such an occasion during a routine intelligence interrogation:

> First, they asked me about the situation of our troops at Aix-la-Chapelle, which was absurd since, at that moment, the city was already in the hands of the Americans. Still more absurd, they asked me about the situation of the Germans in Paris! At the end of the questioning, an American officer told me: "Good, now you have the choice between a normal camp or an anti-Nazi camp." I didn't hesitate. Yet, to my surprise, the American said to me: "You know, I don't advise you to. These are horrible guys; deserters, communists." I told him: "I'm going there anyhow." [78]

Another prisoner, Corporal Willibald Bergmann, remembers a similar attitude at Camp Sheridan, Illinois:

> Five or six prisoners went to see the commanding officer. They told him that they demanded to be transferred, that they didn't dare return to their barracks. The Americans did, in fact, send them to an anti-Nazi camp, but we could easily see that the Americans were not happy about it. They didn't like them. To them, the anti-Nazis were a special breed, who were always opposed to everything. Then the Americans turned to us and sighed: "In a Nazi camp, there is order and discipline—no problems. . . ." [79]

While such feelings on the part of American personnel were by no means universal, or even common, they do reflect the type of problems which occurred when the first undefined policies for segregating the prisoners were placed in the hands of inexperienced or unqualified personnel. Nevertheless, the February directive was the first halting step forward.

A small segment of anti-Nazi prisoners, incidentally, were not pleased with the segregation effort, despite the fact that it was designed, in part, to protect them from their hostile fellow prisoners. Some, like POW Franz Wischnewski, resented the better treatment shown to more important anti-Nazis. "After three weeks of interrogation at Norfolk, they sent me to an anti-Nazi camp at Ruston," recalls Wischnewski:

> Our train stopped once, at Washington, to let aboard some prisoners of note, such as the writer Alfred Andersch. He had been at Dachau, then drafted into the army and shipped to Italy, where he deserted. This was an intellectual, an interesting character for the Americans, who had much regard for him. He was allowed in the Dining Car, where he was served by Blacks. We, anti-Nazi small fry, they threw us a can of K-rations! [80]

Others began to develop "second thoughts" once they had settled into their new anti-Nazi camps. Some doubted the widsom of their decision: Their postwar careers might well be irrevocably tainted by the abandonment of their comrades and their open association with the enemy. Notes Dankwart von Arnim:

> After I found myself at the anti-Nazi Camp David, Maryland, one of my distant relatives, von Jago, also an officer and a POW, sent me the following letter from his camp. "Do all you can to get out your camp. For your career, as a German, and as a human being—the fact of having been in an American anti-Nazi camp will be impossible to admit."
>
> It was a horrible situation. I was a "non-person," a monster ... and, I believe, still in danger from hidden Nazi elements.[81]

Von Arnim was wrong—and right. Far from being ostracized in post-war Germany, former anti-Nazi prisoners found themselves vaulted into positions of power by the American occupation government as the only "certified" non-Nazis available. He was right, however, in questioning his safety. Genuine as well as self-appointed Gestapo agents occasionally gained entrance into anti-Nazi camps, as previously noted, and sometimes remained undetected long enough to terrorize important anti-Nazis and compile lists of names for "later judgment." Despite the War Department's painstaking precautions to protect its anti-Nazi prisoners, it was not impossible for groups of determined Nazis to penetrate the screen. For example, the PMGO purposely created anti-Nazi camps near enough to regular camps so that their mailing address would not attract undue attention and, perhaps, reprisals against their families in Germany. In this case, however, a group of Nazi NCOs simply infiltrated the central prisoner of war postal service, headquartered at Camp Hearne, Texas, which was responsible for the distribution of all mail to POWs in the United States. Working under the supervision of American personnel, the German postal workers secretly studied camp censorship and postal markings, gained access to restricted camp rosters, and even steamed open letters.[82] That this ring was ultimately discovered and the entire postal operation transferred to the relatively safe hands of Italian prisoners at Fort Meade was of little comfort to the small segment of German anti-Nazis who felt that the risks resulting from their decision were not worth the benefits.

Within six months of the War Department's first directive on the segregation of prisoners, the government came to the realization that it had approached the problem from the wrong angle. In a terse, single page letter to all service commanders on July 19, 1943, the War Department ordered that all "Nazi leaders, Gestapo agents, and extremists" were now to be isolated and transferred to a special camp at Alva, Oklahoma.[83] While the new directive signaled a logical shift of policy to the segregation of the more visible (and dangerous) Nazis, it also contained several weaknesses. The government, for example, had not defined the terms "Nazi leaders" or "extremists," which not only made their identification somewhat difficult but provided some camp commanders with the opportunity to use the directive to transfer troublesome POWs.[84] By the late spring of 1944, the practice had become widespread enough to prompt the War Department to consider the following reminder to camp and service commanders:

> ... certain symptoms of barbed-wire psychosis such as suspicion, distrust, bumptiousness, and irritability growing out of concern for friends, relatives, and conditions in Germany ... should not be mistaken for symptoms of Nazi convictions or affiliations and should not lead to the consigning to Alva of reclaimable material among the German prisoners.[85]

And finally at the end of September, 1944, at a Third Service Command POW Conference, Colonel Sherburne informed all the attending commanders that "the PMG [General Archer Lerch] has told us that we cannot get rid of any more of our trouble-making Germans. This may be your fault for recommending border-line cases—being too anxious to clean out all suspicious cases. . . ."[86]

To prevent any further misuse of the discretionary authority granted to them by the July directive, each service command was assigned a certain quota in October, 1943, which they could not exceed. The first quotas of Nazi prisoners to be sent to Alva were to be drawn from the heavily politicized camps in the Fourth through Eighth Service Commands and were as follows:

Service Command	POW Officers	POW Enlisted Men
Fourth	150	1025
Fifth	0	500
Sixth	0	522
Seventh	350	753
Eighth	250	1000 [87]

The quota system was not graciously accepted by many service and camp commanders. Some complained that it "hampered the entire segregation effort and tended to interfere with efforts of the individual commander to weed out effectively the Nazi elements"; others, that it "delayed the actual transfer of prisoners who have been designated for shipment to Alva." Most commanders resented the quota system because it implied that they were making excessive and perhaps unjustified use of the segregation policy. The most serious objection to the quota system came from Captain Walter Rapp of the Special Projects Division, who sharply criticized the entire segregation directive as well as its quota feature. The whole policy was hamstrung, Rapp argued convincingly, by the War Department's failure to adequately define the term "Nazi" and to distinguish the activities of a "Nazi" from those of a "pro-Nazi." Moreover, incoming prisoners should not be integrated with those already in camps, Rapp noted, and the future screening of all POWs should be left in the hands of the Assistant Executive Officer in cooperation with the camp Intelligence Officer. As far as the quota system was concerned, he declared that "there certainly must be something wrong with the way the segregation directives are carried out since the amount of enlisted men at Alva, Oklahoma is far below the actual amount of Nazi sympathizer enlisted men in the German Army at present in this country." While there were nearly 325,000 German prisoners in the United States as of September 8, 1944, only 3,392 enlisted men with Nazi sympathies were at Alva. Since American officials themselves believed there were at least 40–50,000 enlisted men with Nazi sympathies in POW camps, the tiny fraction at Alva could only be attributed, Rapp argued, to a poorly defined segregation policy and a quota system which only hampered segregation efficiency.[88] Whatever the merits of Captain Rapp's constructive criticism, and they appear to have been considerable, the War Department took no action.[89]

The segregation program reached a plateau which, despite its many inherent weaknesses, would have remained satisfactory were it not for the unexpected burst of political violence which erupted inside the number of camps. The beatings and murders between October, 1943, and February, 1944, and the public outrage which resulted galvanized the War Department into action. A comprehensive plan was immediately initiated, and the PMGO hierarchy hummed with requests for clarification on such subjects as the future screening of incoming POWs, the potential segregation of non-commissioned officers, and a final definition of "anti-Nazi" and "Nazi." While the War Department was hammering out its new plan, a number of emergency stopgap measures were implemented to provide relief in the violence-prone camps. A new area—Camp Campbell, Kentucky—was designated as an immediate haven for anti-Nazis whose lives appeared to be in danger, and a policy was adopted whereby POWs who feared physical harm could request the authorities to segregate them at once.

Finally, on July 17, 1944, the comprehensive directive appeared. Rescinding earlier policy statements, the directive contained what the War Department hoped were the ultimate requirements for a basic and successful segregation program. First, all German Army officer prisoners were to be separated from their non-commissioned officers and enlisted men. The only exceptions were to be prisoner chaplains, Protected Personnel,[90] and enlisted orderlies assigned to officers. Moreover, German officers were to be henceforth divided into two broad classifications: pro-Nazis, who were to be shipped to Alva, Oklahoma; and non-Nazis, who were to go to Camp Ruston, Louisiana. Secondly, German naval prisoners were to remain at the four camps in which they had already been isolated, Camps McCain, Mississippi; Papago Park, Arizona; Beale, California; and Blanding, Florida. Third, as German officers were being divided by their politics and transferred to either Alva or Ruston, all German NCOs were to be isolated at the following camps assigned for each service command:

First through Fourth Commands	Camp Aliceville, Alabama
Fifth through Seventh Commands	Camp Clark, Missouri
Ninth Command	Camp Indianola, Nebraska
	Camp Douglas, Wyoming
Eighth Command	Camp Brady, Texas
	Camp McLean, Texas
	Camp Tonkawa, Oklahoma
	Camp Lordsburg, New Mexico

Fourth, all German prisoners eligible for repatriation (the sick, wounded, and Protected Personnel in excess of those required by the Geneva Convention to minister to the prisoners) were to be transferred to Camp Atterbury, Indiana. Disabled POWs who were not eligible for repatriation were to be sent to Camp McAlester, Oklahoma. Finally the entire process of segregation and transfer was to occur with the least amount of interference to the continued maximum use of POW labor.[91] And there it was. With the exception of some minor alterations and policy adjustments, the July, 1944, directive remained the standard method for the political segregation of the more than 370,000 German prisoners incarcerated in the United States to the end of the war.

There were, of course, some problems. Camp commanders, though more experienced with the passage of time, were still largely responsible for the segregation of their prisoners. While decisions at the camp level did provide the advantage of speed, in that anti-Nazis could be more quickly transferred to "safe" camps than if they had to wait until the Provost Marshal General's Office made the proper adjudication, camp commanders still occasionally used the prerogative to rid their camps of troublemakers.

Camp commanders also continued in some measure to look upon their rag-tag anti-Nazi elements with disdain, while disciplined and obedient prisoners—often Nazis—were generally viewed with admiration. So common was this illogical situation that *Collier's* Magazine in August, 1944, felt compelled to carry a brutal exposé entitled, sarcastically, "Land of the Free." A fictional account of an unnamed POW camp in the United States, the short story described the futile efforts of an anti-Nazi prisoner, Gottfried Schlegel, to alert the American camp commander about the political activities in the compound while trying desperately to survive the persecution by his fellow prisoners. Each time he complained about being beaten or terrorized the commander became less tolerant, finally sighing that "I know one thing: Five companies of real Nazis don't make as much trouble as one anti-Nazi." During one such confrontation, the American lieutenant asked:

"Now tell me why they beat you up again, Schlegel. Any special reason this time? . . ."

"The old story, sir. They call me traitor, deserter, swine. So—they beat me. No special reason, no."

"Look here, Schlegel. I'm your friend and I'm getting worried about you. Do you have to provoke them?. . . . Sometimes I think you have a persecution complex," [Lieutenant] Coulter said, in exasperation. "You think there is a Gestapo agent in every corner."

"There is," Schlegel said. . . .

After each such confrontation, the prisoner was returned to the compound. Ultimately, the inevitable occurred, as it often did in real life, and the *Collier's* story closed on the following scene:

> Colonel Barnbridge picked up the report which [Sergeant] Walsh had dropped on his desk. . . . Prisoner of War Soldat Gottfried Schlegel: Suicide by slashing wrists with broken bottle. . . .
> "All right, Walsh," he called to his adjutant. "I suppose that covers the matter. Maybe now we'll have some order here again." [92]

In another unvarnished description of the realities of camp life, an article in the October, 1944, issue of *Collier's* frankly admitted: "Our officers don't like the anti-Nazis. I have heard them called Hitler's scum." [93]

In a few instances, the feelings of the American personnel went even deeper. During an Eighth Service Command Conference on Prisoners of War in 1944, the commander of Camp Alva candidly shared a raucous anecdote with his fellow commanders by which he plainly commiserated with the anti-Semitic feelings of his prisoners. Colonel Hall amusingly related that:

> A German spokesman asked me [if he could] . . . call a certain Jewish tailor to get him to come down and make them new uniforms. I said it would be unnecessary to talk to him himself. I told him that if that Jew heard a German voice over the telephone that he would run to Canada. (Laughter) [94]

While these feelings were hardly representative and undoubtedly reflected the opinions of a tiny minority of American personnel, the July directive nevertheless failed to provide the necessary segregation standards and guidelines to allow national policy to rise above personal hatreds.

Another weakness in the July directive concerned the government's failure to separate the Austrian prisoners, whose faith in Nazism was rapidly eroding, from the Germans. There had long been a segment of the informed public which advocated the separation of the "redeemable" Austrians from the "hopelessly unsalvageable" Germans, and they drew upon an impressive array of arguments to bolster their position. On July 27, 1942, for instance, Secretary of State Hull stated that the Government of the United States "has never taken the position that Austria was legally absorbed into the German Reich." Moreover, Hull, Eden, and Molotov, in their declaration issued jointly at Moscow on November 1, 1943, stated that the United States, Great Britain, and the Soviet Union "regard the annexation imposed on Austria by

Germany as null and void." The fact that the British initiated such a separation of its prisoners and advised the Canadians and Australians to take similar measures only made the argument more plausible. The issue was brought up before Congress in an impassioned speech by Representative Herman P. Eberharter of Pennsylvania; [95] a Committee for National Morale embraced the cause of "saving" the Austrian prisoners; and letters to the *New York Times* stressed the need for such separation as part of any reeducation program.[96] From within the camps themselves came a flood of petitions from Austrian POWs to the Provost Marshal General's Office attesting to their deep hatred of anything German and citing the numerous acts of discrimination and brutality they were receiving at the hands of their fellow prisoners. Fourteen Austrians at Camp Chaffee, Arkansas, in February, 1944, went so far as to appeal publicly to Archduke Otto von Hapsburg, the heir to the long-deposed Austrian monarchy, who was then living in exile in New York.[97] The final and most persuasive argument for the separation of Austrian prisoners was that provided by the Geneva Convention, Article 9, which states that "Belligerents shall, so far as possible, avoid assembling in a single camp prisoners of different races or nationalities."

To all of this commotion, the venerable Secretary of War Henry Stimson, when pressed for his position by the Secretary of State Cordell Hull, firmly replied:

It is the opinion of this Department that Article 9 of the Geneva Prisoner of War Convention does not have the effect of placing on the United States the obligation to segregate prisoners of war of Austrian origin or nationality.[98]

When continued publicity caused the Secretary of State to ask Stimson once again how he intended to solve the Austrian prisoner problem, the latter tersely responded that "the War Department is entirely willing to give further consideration to the possibility of such segregation should cogent reasons appear for holding it to be politically advantageous." [99]

There was, in fact, little political advantage to be gained by the separation of Austrian prisoners from the German majority at this late date in the war, and despite the obvious benefits to the belated reeducation program, the Prisoner of War Division of the PMGO, for different reasons, was forced to agree. "The segregation of Austrians from German prisoners of war will not be of special advantage to the Special Projects Program," advised the Assistant Director of the Prisoner of War Division, Major Edward Davison, in August of 1944:

Considerable numbers of born Austrians have lived and worked in Germany most of their lives, much as a native Scot may live and work in England. Will these be counted as Austrians or Germans? Many Austrians are rabid Nazis. . . . Others again may be communists. Expert personnel will be needed to accomplish a reliable segregation. It is doubtful whether such a segregation can be carried out by prisoner of war camp personnel.[100]

Thus, it was decided that because of the difficulties involved in separately screening each prisoner who claimed Austrian citizenship and the lack of trained personnel to undertake such a task, both nationalities would remain imprisoned together. The final weakness in the July, 1944, directive was really a problem which had plagued the segregation effort from the beginning: what constitutes a Nazi or an anti-Nazi? Before the War Department could separate the prisoners and ship them to different types of camps, there had to be workable guidelines and accurate definitions for the political categories into which the POWs would be divided. In February, 1943, the War Department had settled on two categories: "anti-Nazis" and "others." In July, 1943, the categories were reversed to become "Nazis" and "others." By July, 1944, the War Department realized that the term "Nazi" did not adequately distinguish between the estimated 8 to 12 percent obdurate Nazis and the additional 40 percent who were Nazi sympathizers. Moreover, the relative scarcity of genuine anti-Nazis, especially among the officers, led the War Department to assume that the best one could hope for might be "non-Nazis." Thus, the new political categories became "pro-Nazis" and "non-Nazis."

Prisoners, however, could be reclassified from one category to another, and, in fact, the political leanings of the prisoners vacillated wildly as war communiques brought news of major victories or disastrous defeats. The segregation of POWs was further complicated by the conflicting government projects. The War Department's G-2 (Intelligence) Division, was, in effect, working at odds with the State Department's project to screen and repatriate non-German nationals,[101] which was, in turn, working at cross-purposes with the reeducation program of the Special Projects Division. Moreover, each camp and service commander used a different screening standard and resented the interference of any project which disrupted the order of camp life or hindered the maximum employment of POW labor. In short, the screening and segregation program was in a shambles. In mid-August, 1944, Colonel Russell Sweet of G-2, when confronted with a problem involving the classification of some prisoners, threw up his hands and unknowingly summarized the state of the screening and segregation effort: "We don't care what you do with them. You can classify them any time you want if it is for the good of the order. We don't worry anymore about classification!" [102] In the main, his evaluation of the present was also the prophesy of the future.

While the War Department issued several later directives—one in September, 1944, another in October, and yet another in November—they did little to alter the basic framework. Protected Personnel, for example, were shifted to a central pool at Camp McAlester, Oklahoma, from their earlier collecting point at Camp Atterbury, Indiana; Camp Hearne, Texas, and Camp Opelika, Alabama, were added to the list of places reserved for the isolation of NCOs, and the quota systems for Alva were expanded.

Yet positive models for the proper screening and segregation of the prisoners continued to abound. The British, for instance, had long since divided their German prisoners into three groups: "whites" or non-Nazis; "grays" or those who were undecided; and "blacks" or hardened Nazis and sympathizers. While the motivation for the division was originally to provide reliable workers for Britain's POW employment program, the existence of white, gray, and black camps made later efforts at reeducation substantially easier.[103] The Canadians also provided an excellent model from which America might well have profited, though, indeed, they had far fewer prisoners to deal with. The Canadian Department of National Defense expanded the number of categories to five, and by July, 1945, had produced the following results:

	Ardent Nazis	Nazis	Dark Gray	Lt. Gray	White
Officers	286	466	759	643	181
Enlisted	—	50	1,071	1,667	383
Warrant Officers	4,171	2,806	11,164	7,996	2,249
Total	4,457	3,322	12,994	10,306	2,813 [104]

Even within the United States, there were numerous suggestions for a successful program. As the screening and segregation program lurched on, the War Department received detailed solicited proposals from some of the brightest individuals in and outside of the government.[105] They fell on deaf ears. A variety of journalists and political scientists also made valuable suggestions to the War Department with identical results.[106] Most importantly, there were two superb screening and segregation operations already in practice at the service command level. The First and Third Service Commands had independently created programs which utilized carefully selected and trained interrogation teams to interview each prisoner individually. Depending on their responses, the prisoners were classified into seven categories, including non-German nationals, and Communists.[107] Both programs were quite successful, but an investigation by the Special Projects Division ultimately rejected as impractical the creation of a similar, nationwide screening system. It would be too complicated, noted Edward Davison, head of the Special Projects Division; would require too many trained interrogators; and would take, perhaps, a year to construct. As a result, American policy remained relatively unchanged until the late spring of 1945 when, in May or June, the segregation of anti-Nazis and regular prisoners, respectively, was officially ended.[108]

It is difficult to assess the effect that the rise of Nazi influence within the camps had on the prisoner of war program. One is forced to wonder why the War Department had not considered the political variety of prisoners who were soon to come into its charge, and adequately prepare for their separation. Once circumstances had allowed such influence to take hold and to jeopardize the nonpolitical majority, why had the War Department not moved more ruthlessly and efficiently to control and root out undesirables? Why was the War Department reluctant to build upon its own successful models and those of its Allies? The answers to these and numerous other questions lie in the consideration of several factors. The first and most all-encompassing factor was simply the uniqueness of the whole POW experience. As has been noted so often in this book, the United States had no guidelines or precedents with which to face so unusual and formidable a task. Without guidelines, therefore, the government was forced to move cautiously and to rely in large measure on methods based on trial and error. When it became apparent for example that the initial decision to segregate anti-Nazis was proving unworkable, the War Department shifted its screening policies to isolate Nazi prisoners instead. That an opportunity for early success had passed was due to inexperience rather than ineptness. The second factor to consider was the War Department's absolute reliance upon the dictates of the Geneva Convention as the best means of protecting American personnel in enemy hands. Since the Geneva Convention required prisoners of war to disclose no more than their proverbial "name, rank, and serial number," the War Department was initially hesitant to probe too harshly into their political beliefs. As a matter of fact, the prisoners were not even required to answer such questions. Moreover, any blatant violation of the Convention such as the ruthless suppression of political activity in the camps, the War Department feared, might be quickly felt in *stalags* across Germany.

The third factor was that of war priorities. In the midst of the chaos produced by maintaining a two-ocean war, of planning and fighting battles of heroic proportions, and of constructing diplomatic alliances which might well shape the post-war world, the tiny POW program was not, certainly, among the highest priority programs in the war effort. The enemy soldiers involved, after all, had already been "neutralized" and removed from the field of battle. The fact that the POW program was not vital to the prosecution of war accounted, in large measure, for the lack of qualified personnel required to properly screen incoming prisoners and the War Department's periodic disinterest in such a task. Another factor to be considered was the decreasing level of Nazi indoctrination found in captured soldiers during the final year of the war. As prisoners poured into the United States following the Normandy invasion, the War Department was heartened by the appearance of a growing number of captives who were "plainly from the very bottom of the *Wehrmacht's* manpower barrel .... who eagerly made known that they were not Nazis, ... that in their opinion Heinrich Himmler was a 'Schweinhund'; that if it had not been for the SS the war would have been over soon after D-Day; and that the Reich was 'kaput.' " [109] This trend, in conjunction with the sudden end of political terrorism in the camps in April, 1944, convinced the War Department that despite its many imperfections the current screening and segregation policy would probably suffice.

According to Professor Edward Pluth, an astute analyst of this era, the final factor "that proved the main barrier to an effective segregation program ... was the granting of priorities to the work program." Pluth goes on to explain:

> Camp commanders were frequently reminded of the importance of achieving and maintaining full employment of their prisoners. In those instances where Nazi elements tended to obstruct this program, camp commanders made use of the existing directives in their attempt to segregate the recalcitrant prisoners; otherwise they were reluctant to take steps toward the in-depth screening and segregation program desired by the Special Projects Division. ... In the last analysis it was the conflict between these two programs, the reluctance of many camp commanders to challenge the status quo in the camps, and the hesitancy on the part of the War Department to force compliance that stood in the way of a stronger segregation program.[110]

A particularly pithy summary of the segregation issue was made by an anti-Nazi POW to journalist Daniel Lang of *The New Yorker* during a tour of Fort DuPont, Delaware. After a lengthy discussion about the ideological struggles which had occurred in the camp, the prisoner concluded, "You

Americans are too soft. You don't help us anti-Nazis as much as you could and you don't hinder the Nazis as much as you could. But," he sighed, "I suppose that is democracy. . . ." [111]

Democracy, in fact, was a subject which the prisoner at Fort DuPont and more than 300,000 other prisoners of war would soon hear a great deal more about. A rising tide of public concern, beginning as early as April, 1943, questioned the logic of returning the prisoners to Germany at the end of the war without at least "exposing them to democratic teachings. Shall they be returned to Germany just as we captured them . . . still convinced Nazis? Is this not an opportunity to send back a group to Germany which might become the core on which democracy could eventually be built?" [112] After many months of cautious planning and no small amount of debate, the War Department, in September, 1944, officially concurred. With that decision began one of the most unusual programs of the entire prisoner of war experience: a secret and highly controversial effort to influence the prisoners through a massive campaign of books, films, newspapers, lectures, and camp elections as well as an intensive indoctrination of approximately 25,000 selected prisoners at special experimental schools and training centers. If the prisoners were to be converted from Nazism, it was logically reasoned, there should be an alternative philosophy immediately available. With the end of the war in sight, the War Department took up the challenge with the selfless dedication of a crusader.

CHAPTER VI

Hearts and Minds—1945

As Americans began to sense the end of the war in Europe, there was growing concern about the political makeup of post-war Germany. What had begun as a war to support Britain had become, in the minds of most Americans by 1944, a war of ideologies. It was now obvious that the forces of Democracy would win, but the problem of Germany's future ideology still remained. Would fascism be supplanted by communism? By the return of monarchy? By democracy? After so great a struggle, it seemed unthinkable to most Americans that the enemy's Nazi ideology might remain unaltered and its population unrepentant.

A large segment of the American population feared the worst. A survey conducted by the *New York Times Magazine,* for example, disclosed such sentiments as "Let them know that they've been beaten; they only respect strength anyway" and "For my money you could flood the whole damn country for twenty-four hours, and then start from scratch."[1] Similar feelings could be found at every level of American society. The prestigious President of Columbia University, Dr. Nicholas Murray Butler, concluded: "it will take another generation—at least 25 years—before the German mind can be completely purged of the evil effects of the Nazi spirit." Another well-known academician, Harvard anthropologist Dr. Ernest A. Hooten, went one step further. "To convert or re-educate a Nazi is impossible," declared Dr. Hooten. "The only alternative," he argued, ironically in racial terms, "is to dilute the German stock, adulterate the Nazi strain and destroy the national framework by a process of out-breeding. . . . Under this method I would do this: Send into Germany the Czechs, Austrians and others who would settle and intermingle with the German people; keep out of Germany the German armies and put them to work rebuilding the lands which they have occupied. . . . Killing Hitler, Goebbels, Goering and other leaders is no solution to the German problem because their followers are just as culpable as the leaders themselves. . . . The distinction between 'good' Germans and 'bad' Germans is an erroneous one."[2] A substantial number of Americans— after more than three years of war news and personal sacrifice—tended to agree that there existed little distinction between "good" and "bad" Germans. Moreover, they saw little difference between the German military in Europe and the captive German soldiers in the United States.

The American public was in some cases so anti-German that a reader of the *New York Times* seriously suggested that the shortage of blood plasma to our soldiers overseas be filled by the "systematic bleeding" of the German POWs in our midst. The reaction, as one would expect, was instant and savage, but not, surprisingly, in defense of the POWs. "Please, anything but that!" a reader responded. "We women will hurry to the nearest station to donate all the blood that is needed. Good, pure blood, full of the clean corpuscles of love, charity and kindness, but never must we permit our menfolk to be injected with the fiendish and ruthless blood of the enemy. Spare them that humiliation." [3]

The growing number of news reports concerning kangaroo courts, camp terrorism, escapes, and POW work strikes only reinforced the general public's desire to lump all German soldiers together as incorrigible. Captain Joseph Lane of Camp Cascade, Iowa, declared to a reporter from *The New York Times:*

> I've seen more than 100,000 Germans pass through my cage, and I know these bastards. They're no good. They're treacherous; no morals, no scruples, no religion, no nothing. I've seen how they try to insinuate themselves into our big hearts by trying to be sugary sweet and pathetic. And I've seen them come in acting like we were scum under their feet.
>
> I hate them all and my men hate them. We want a peace that will knock them down on their knees and keep them there until they learn better. I don't know what in hell you're going to do about re-educating their officers. My private suggestion is that you just kill them all and save the world a lot of headaches for the next couple of generations. Most of them are just hopeless.[4]

Nor did any hope for a Christian renaissance among the prisoners appear to be a reality in the immediate future. In a widely-publicized statement by the American chaplain of the POW camp at Huntsville, Texas, the nation's religious leaders were assured that "The Nazis are treacherous, mad, and fanatical, often trying at night in their barracks to lynch comrades who are not Nazis. You might as well preach Christianity to a wall as to these Hitlerites." [5] Was there no hope, then, to salvage any of the POWs in America's camps? If not, what could the world possibly expect to accomplish in post-war Germany?

Public Frustration about POW Reeducation

A small segment of American society, however, believed that the answer lay in exposing the prisoners to another kind of religion: political democracy. Democracy had proven its superiority, after all, by having been the credo of the winning side. More than that, it was the traditional right of the victor to impose its philosophy upon the vanquished. Like true believers in any faith, Americans were convinced that the political heretics of Nazi Germany would themselves come to see the obvious benefits of democracy if only they were properly educated. In any case, post-war Germany would be a political vacuum, and if democracy were not to fill the void, the dreaded specter of communism might. By mid-1944, this logic would be clear to thousands of Americans, and by the end of the war, it grew into a tiny crusade.

The application of this logic on the prisoners of war in the United States began modestly enough. A letter to the editor of *The New York Times* by one H. Landsberg in April, 1943, first broached the subject of "stamping out the misshapen ideas of nazism" in post-war Germany by a program of reeducation. While there was no disagreement about the aims of such a program, Landsberg wrote, "no procedure in sight promised success." He suggested:

> . . . there exists the possibility of experimenting . . . with various methods that might help in the re-education process. Already a considerable number of enemy prisoners are in our hands, and in their camps introduction of certain educational methods may help in testing procedures to be followed later on in occupied territory.[6]

The suggestion sparked a number of similar proposals from random educators and clergymen, but all went unanswered by the government. Finally, one group decided to take the initiative.

In the late spring of 1944, a committee to seek the reeducation of Nazi war prisoners announced its formation. Headed by Gerhart Seger, editor of the German-American newspaper *Neue Volkszeitung*, the new committee contained a prestigious cross-section of Americans: Dr. Monroe Deutsch, vice-president of the University of California; Dr. Henry Smith Leiper, Federal Council of the Churches of Christ in America; Louis Lochner, former chief of the Associated Press Bureau in Berlin; Congressman Howard J. McMurray of Wisconsin; Dr. George H. Schuster, president of

Hunter College; Dorothy Thompson, whose syndicated column was read by millions of Americans; and Thomas Mann, world-famous German author living in exile in the United States. Prompted no doubt by the recent eruption of political violence in the POW camps, the Committee noted that "about 25 per cent of the German prisoners . . . are fanatical Nazis, about 60 percent are in between, and about 15 percent [are] anti-Nazi. Up until now," Seger declared, "the policy of the Government has been to separate the anti-Nazis from the others, which only results in the exposure of the major group to the violent Nazi propaganda." The aim of the Committee, therefore, was to impress upon the War Department the importance of segregating the Nazis so that the two remaining groups could be reeducated about the "ideals of democracy." [6]

Almost immediately the letters-to-the-editor columns in newspapers across the country heated up in debate. Within two days of the Committee's announcement, in fact, an outraged reader wrote *The New York Times* to challenge any program's ability to distinguish between Nazism and Germanism. "The German character . . . yields only to force. . . . Collectively he will respond favorably only to such a humiliating beating as is now on its way to him. Let's not waste our substance on his 'reeducation' now. Wait until he has absorbed the lesson our fighting sons are teaching him." [8] It did not take long—four days—for another letter to appear in the *Times*. Taking issue with the earlier writer's statement that the reeducation of POWs could not occur until after Germany's defeat, the editor of the *Austro-American Tribune* wrote, not unsurprisingly, that the only obstacle to the immediate reeducation of the prisoners was to remove the Austrians from among them. The remaining POWs, then, would be an amorphous mass, ready for exposure to democracy.[9] Four days later, almost like clockwork, another letter appeared in the *Times*. The writer made a long and lucid appeal to introduce democratic teaching at once and cited the rumors of similar education programs by the British and Russians.[10] As the public debate raged on, syndicated columnists chose sides and waded in.

Dorothy Thompson had long made her feelings known, and her membership on Seger's committee to reeducate prisoners of war culminated her many efforts to rally the War Department and the public to the POW problem. Another powerful advocate of an immediate reeducation program was Paul Winkler of the *Washington Post*. In a column written in the midst of the public debate, Winkler summarized the various arguments against reeducating the prisoners and then challenged them individually. However the task was to be accomplished, Winkler concluded, the important thing is:

> That as many Germans as possible should be won away from Nazi ideas and converted to those of democracy. The psychological and

ideological battle which totalitarianism has long waged against democracy is still going on, in the prison camps on American soil. Unfortunately, for the moment, only one side is fighting it.[11]

As interest in prisoner reeducation continued to mount through the autumn of 1944, it seemed obvious to the majority in support of such a program that their obstacle was the War Department itself. First (it seemed to critics), the War Department had failed to effectively segregate the proper prisoners into separate camps; and now the War Department evidently could not see the logic in initiating an immediate reeducation program to convert the POWs during the short period they would remain in American charge. Not only had the government failed to act on its own, but it consistently appeared to reject the sound proposals of others. The Seger Committee's efforts to influence the War Department toward a reeducation program fell on deaf ears. Syndicated columns and editorials went unanswered.

A direct appeal to the government fared no better. When Professor Warren A. Seavey of Harvard Law School tried to interest Secretary of War Henry L. Stimson in the results of a personal investigation of the segregation and reeducation of German prisoners, he ran into a wall of silence. Seavey submitted his comprehensive report on April 28, 1944, which was politely rejected by Stimson on May 11.[12] Apparently undaunted, Professor Seavey presented his recommendations to Stimson once again in a letter on May 17. Once again Stimson politely rejected the advice, this time concluding firmly:

> The War Department believes that any procedure such as you suggest would be met with suspicion, hostility, and resistance, and instead of being persuaded by the unwelcome teaching, the prisoners would only turn against it. . . . I cannot agree with you, therefore, that such a course of action would accomplish the objectives you have in mind or serve the best interests of the United States.[13]

For the next six months, through the summer and autumn of 1944, Professor Seavey and his team of Harvard researchers tried in vain to convince the War Department about the logic of POW reeducation. Finally, stymied in their direct approach, the Harvard group made public their entire correspondence with the War Department to *The New York Times*.[14] The resulting exposé frustrated many Americans who simply could not understand the government's narrow-minded stubbornness. How different public reaction would have been if the real truth had been known.

The Establishment of a Secret Reeducation Program

As early as March, 1943, in an effort to break the grip of Nazi groups in the camps, the government decided that, indeed, a reeducation program might be in order. That month a proposal was referred to General Frederick Osborn in the War Department to draft a plan by which "prisoners of war might be exposed to the facts of American history, the workings of democracy and the contributions made to America by peoples of all national origins." General Osborn passed the job on to Brigadier General S. L. A. Marshall, who vividly recalls the events which followed:

> I was distant from Washington on a very critical operation. So I knew nothing about it until, returning to the Pentagon on a Saturday night, I was told that the plan had to be on [George C.] Marshall's desk by 0800 Monday morning. At that point, I blew my top, went to Washington to take on a snootful, just to clear my head. I knew [the hasty job I submitted] was good enough to bank the fires until I could determine what the problem was all about.
>
> Then I wrote the *real* plan and substituted it for the dummied-up job. It called for screening the prisoners at once, separating the bad eggs from the amenable ones, ignoring the former and starting education courses for the latter with emphasis on democratic theory and practice . . .[15]

The plan was considered "inadvisable," however, by the Provost Marshal General, Major General Allen Gullion, and on June 24, 1943, it was shelved for what became a full year.

The next year passed in a storm of camp violence and public outrage. Stories of Nazi atrocities, murders, and forced suicides began to appear in the press, while the War Department moved ineffectually to segregate the most visible Nazis and anti-Nazis into different camps. The issue of reeducation became commonplace in letters-to-the-editor columns, as a possible solution for the current camp violence as well as for the potential rehabilitation of post-war Germany. The War Department remained silent. General S. L. A. Marshall's plan remained on the shelf.

By the early spring of 1944, Dorothy Bromley of the *New York Herald Tribune* and Dorothy Thompson became so frustrated with the government's lack of action that they decided to take the problem directly to Eleanor Roosevelt. Apparently shocked at the severity of Nazi violence in

American camps and dismayed at the lack of progress by the military authorities, Mrs. Roosevelt took the unusual step of inviting Major Maxwell McKnight, chief of the Administrative Section of POW Camp Operations, to dinner at the White House. "I've been hearing the most horrible stories ... about all the killings that are going on in our camps with these Nazi prisoners," Mrs. Roosevelt told her anxious guest midway through the meal. "I was told that you would be able to tell me whether there was truth to these stories. . . ." The startled McKnight begged the question ("After all, I was only a major") until he could clear the matter with his superior, Assistant Provost Marshal General Bryan. Told by his superior to hold nothing back, McKnight was invited to the White House for a repeat performance several evenings later where he and Mrs. Roosevelt held a frank discussion of the whole problem. She was appalled and assured McKnight that "I've got to talk to Franklin. Right in our backyard, to have these Nazis moved in and controlling the whole thought process!" [16]

Mrs. Roosevelt did, indeed, speak to the President. He in turn spoke to the Secretaries of War and State, Stimson and Stettinius, who, in turn, instructed the new Provost Marshal General, Archer L. Lerch, to pull General Marshall's year old plan down from the shelf. According to General Marshall: "The PMG dusted off the plan and said something like 'We anticipated the problem all along.' " [17]

Through the month of March, 1944, the War Department pondered the problems involved in initiating a reeducation plan. The two major obstacles, as always, concerned the limitations imposed by the Geneva Convention and the availability of qualified personnel. The problem of the Geneva Convention was especially complicated since to force propaganda upon the prisoners was not only patently illegal but might invite serious retaliation against American prisoners in enemy hands. Consequently, it was decided from the earliest moments of such discussion that even the consideration of a reeducation plan must be veiled in complete secrecy.

As the War Department examined and reexamined the Geneva Convention for a loophole, it finally settled on Article 17. That article states, simply, that, "So far as possible, belligerents shall encourage intellectual diversions and sports organized by prisoners of war." [18] There it was. The Geneva Convention encouraged intellectual diversion, and it was up to the War Department to select the proper subjects and media. Representatives of both the War Department and the State Department arrived at a tacit understanding "that if selected media for intellectual diversion were made available in the camps, the curiosity of the prisoners concerning the United States and its institutions would provide the means for their reeducation." [19] On March 30, 1944, prompted by President and Mrs. Roosevelt's continued personal interest, the Secretary of State wrote to the Secretary of War suggesting that a program be established under control of the military establishment for the reorientation of German prisoners of war.[20]

When Secretary Stimson replied in the affirmative on April 8, the program became official. In his secret letter, Stimson stated that the Assistant Chief of Staff, G-1, and the PMGO ("both of whom have been apprised of our correspondence") should meet with representatives of other concerned agencies "to arrive at mutually agreeable recommendations for such a program as we are discussing and for its early implementation." Stimson's significant letter closed on two additional points. The first was that "our objective should not be the improbable one of Americanizing the prisoners, but the feasible one of imbuing them with respect for the quality and potency of American institutions." The second point, of critical importance to the continued protection of American prisoners in German camps, was Stimson's admonition that "it is essential to the success of such a program that it shall be carried through without publicity." [21]

The public, consequently, knew nothing about the initiation of the reeducation program until the end of the war, and criticism of the War Department continued to rage. Meanwhile, behind the scenes the experimental project was taking shape. On May 22, the program was placed under the control of the PMGO, and on August 23, the PMGO created a subcommittee to establish policy and procedures. Finally, on September 6, 1944, the reeducation program was officially inaugurated—and the public knew nothing about it.[22] In fact, the severest criticism of the War Department appeared in November, 1944, with the publication of a two-part article in the *Atlantic Monthly* entitled "What To Do With German Prisoners," which summarized the government's stupidity in its handling of German prisoners.[23] Ironically, at the moment the article appeared, teams of reorientation specialists were already arriving at POW camps to set up the reeducation program.

The Staffing of the Program

After the general structure, procedures, and aims of the reeducation experiment were worked out during August and September, the Provost Marshal General created the Prisoner of War Special Projects Division and placed the entire program in the hands of the highly competent Lieutenant Colonel Edward Davison. An officer from the Morale Services Division and a veteran of earlier attempts to segregate the prisoners, the British-born Davison was a nationally-known poet, teacher, and author; had been a

Guggenheim Fellow in the 1930s; and had served on the faculties of the Universities of Colorado and Miami before the war.[24] With the able assistance of Maxwell McKnight, Davison assembled one of the most remarkable staffs of the war. He began by recruiting a German novelist who had fled Hitler, Walter Schönstedt, as an interpreter and advisor.[25] He next recruited Robert L. Kunzig, an attorney and instructor at General Osborn's Information and Education School at Washington and Lee University. Then came the eminent Harvard Dean and President of the American Academy of Arts and Sciences, Howard Mumford Jones; Robert Richard, an Air Corps officer and former professor at the University of Colorado; and Dr. Henry Lee Smith, Jr., a language and dialect expert.[26] Dr. William G. Moulton, the famous linguist, was selected because of previous work with military training programs and fluency in German; and Colonel T. V. Smith, a former congressman from Illinois and a professor at the University of Chicago, joined the project as a writer and lecturer. "Davison had collected a group of leaders and educators who would make any university proud." [27]

The objective of the program was crystallized by the PMGO as follows:

> The prisoners would be given facts, objectively presented but so selected and assembled as to correct misinformation and prejudices surviving Nazi conditioning. The facts, rather than being forced upon them, would be made available through such media as literature, motion pictures, newspapers, music, art, and educational courses. Two types of facts were needed; those which would convince them of the impracticality and viciousness of the Nazi position. If a large variety of facts could be presented convincingly, perhaps the German prisoners of war might understand and believe historical and ethical truth as generally conceived by Western civilization, might come to respect the American people and their ideological values, and upon repatriation to Germany might form the nucleus of a new German ideology which will reject militarism and totalitarian controls and will advocate a democratic system of government.[28]

The modest goal of teaching the German prisoners to "understand and believe historical and ethical truth as conceived by Western civilization" was to be achieved by providing them with:

- films to belie the Nazi charge that America is decadent, inefficient, and corrupt;
- books in the German language stressing the Christian ethic, and revealing the true history of Germany and America;

- a national German prisoner of war newspaper, plus individual camp newspapers, to give the anti-Nazi prisoners an opportunity to express their convictions and lead the others away from the Nazi faith; and
- opportunities for self-education in democracy, history, civics and the English language.

"The success of this type of re-education," concluded the PMGO idealistically, "is guaranteed by the essential truth of the materials presented. . . . Truth, unlike false propaganda, speaks for itself and is sustained by events." [29]

Once the administrative staff had been assembled and the program's goals established, the most pressing problem of the newly-formed Special Projects Division (as with every other facet of the prisoner of war program) became the location of qualified personnel. Nine field grade officers were immediately required to administer the program in each of the nine service commands, and while it was mandatory, of course, that they be sensitive and knowledgeable organizers, the real personnel difficulties lay elsewhere. Within each service command, company grade officers, designated as Assistant Executive Officers, were needed for each base POW camp. These AEOs (approximately 150 altogether) were destined to be the backbone of the program and, as such, were required to possess a variety of special talents and abilities. They had to be reasonably objective about the Germans they were going to instruct; they had to be patriotic but not irrationally so; they had to be fluent in German; they had to have a college education (preferably in liberal arts); and they had to have imagination and good judgment. Such talented officers would have been difficult to find in peacetime much less during the last year of the war. In fact, the first attempt to locate 150 officers with these qualifications failed when it was found that the Intelligence agencies and the Allied Military Government had absorbed the majority of available German-speaking personnel. As a result, the German language requirement was modified, and the three major service commands—Army Service Forces, Army Air Corps, and Army Ground Forces— were each ordered to supply a quota of potential candidates. As the names of candidates began to trickle in, the embryonic Special Projects Division moved to the next step: the screening and training of its future instructors.

The incoming prospects entered the project through a ten-day combination screening-orientation conference, a total of five of which were held at Fort Slocum, New York. Since the whole program was classified "Secret," the candidates chosen by their respective service commands had little idea what awaited them at the end of their eight-hour journey from New York City. After their arrival, however, "there was a feeling of excitement among the officers . . . as the full scope of the program was revealed to them." Then began ten days of hard work, recalls an individual familiar with the second of such conferences between November 16–29:

> There were preliminary tests and consultations with advisors who were officers of the Division. At the end of the conference, each student officer had to take a comprehensive examination and to submit a hypothetical staff study concerning re-orientation of prisoners of war. The advisors met, qualifications of each student were reviewed, and assignments to various camps made.
>
> Training at the conferences took the form of lectures and seminars conducted by officer and civilian specialists. Instruction ranged from outlining the program itself to analyzing phases of German history and psychology, especially the psychology of the prisoner of war. The instructors were men who had worked with Germans in Europe before the war as well as in the camps in this country. A larger share of the instruction was aimed at familiarizing the students with German propaganda, suggesting means of combatting it, and of introducing positive democratic propaganda through every feasible medium.[30]

As a result of these five conferences, a total of 262 officers and 111 enlisted men were finally accepted and trained by the PMGO's Prisoner of War Special Projects Division for assignment to service command headquarters, prisoner of war camps, and to its own staff. The entire process, from first authorization to final staffing, took only four months. The result, however, was not accomplished without problems.

For instance, lower level officers and enlisted men who were chosen by their service commands to attend Colonel Davison's conferences were usually located by the qualifications listed in their records. These records, it turned out, were often wholly inaccurate because "a large percentage of the officers had claimed that they spoke German, which in most cases was found to be grossly exaggerated when tested at Fort Slocum." [31] On the other hand, those officers with adequate fluency in German were not necessarily suitable in other areas. Many prospective candidates saw little future in the reeducation effort and disqualified themselves at the conferences by displaying a poor attitude; others dropped out as they became aware of the distance and isolation of their camp assignments or the reduced opportunities for promotion at such posts.

Sometimes, a qualified and enthusiastic officer who looked forward to a camp assignment found that his former commanding officer refused to release him to the new program. Ultimately, there was the problem of time. Davison had only three days, by military regulations, to screen and train the more than 100 officers who attended each conference and to decide whether the candidate was good material for reorientation work or whether he should be returned immediately to his last post. "It is an enormous job," sighed one government official, "with up to forty percent being screened out during any given Conference—an indication that the Branch is trying hard not to burden its progress with too many officers of questionable qualifications." [32]

Under such circumstances, and after only four months in existence, it would appear that Davison's project was progressing as well as could have been expected. Moreover, the Army was making every effort to maintain a smokescreen of secrecy around the program to prevent the creation of a corresponding "Nazification Program" against American prisoners in Germany. To throw the curious off the scent, for example, one of Colonel Davison's own superior officers, a Colonel Howard, stated publicly that the government's only job was "to feed, keep healthy, and confine prisoners for the duration of the war and, beyond that, to get from them as much productive labor as possible." [33] Another officer in a widely-read *Atlantic Monthly* article noted simply that "It is not our business to change these men's habits or beliefs or to reeducate them." [34] Even more to the point, the camp commander of Fort McClellan, Alabama, Lieutenant Colonel Laurence D. Smith, frankly decared that "it was a waste of time to attempt converting or re-educating German prisoners to the American way of thinking." Speaking before a local civic club, Colonel Smith stated that the prisoners "do not like anything they have seen in this country. That dislike, together with the knowledge that they must leave this country when the war ends, makes them invulnerable candidates for American re-education." [35] While there is no way to ascertain how many of these spokesmen were voicing their true feelings, the veil over the reeducation effort continued to remain intact, and the program moved quietly to its next stage of development.

One of the earliest decisions of the Special Projects Division was the creation of a special camp—a working headquarters—where the assembled staff could brainstorm new programs in complete secrecy and where selected prisoners could be brought to assist and participate. A former CCC camp in Van Etten, New York, with a capacity of 150 men was chosen as the first home for the experimental program; it became active on October 31, 1944. Five months later, a more accessible location was chosen, and the special camp—called the "Idea Factory" or simply "The Factory"—was shifted to Fort Philip Kearney, a former Coast Artillery Post in the middle of Rhode Island's Narragansett Bay. To protect the program and its future POW participants from enemy reprisals, The Factory utilized the mailing address of an ordinary camp at Fort Niagara, New York. With the additional help of Rhode Island's governor, J. Howard McGrath, The Factory continued its experimental reeducation program in complete secrecy for the duration of the war.

The staff then assembled a task force of specially qualified German prisoners, a shifting group of about 85 former professors, linguists, and writers who had been under observation for some time in their respective camps as dedicated anti-Nazis. The prisoners were volunteers, all were officers, and in an effort to practice the democratic ideals which they were about to teach others (as well as to reduce any conflicts between the ranks), the prisoners began by renouncing their *Wehrmacht* ranks. From then on, the POWs worked as equals in an atmosphere of creativity, enthusiasm, and high morale. Because of their special assignment and carefully verified backgrounds, the prisoners at Kearney enjoyed far more freedom than regular POWs. There were no armed guards or towers, and the prisoners would go by ferry to Jamestown in Army trucks to pick up their supplies, often socializing with the other passengers who, of course, had no idea they were talking to German prisoners of war. Once settled into their new routine, the staff and its POW assistants began the creation of the program itself.

The organization of The Factory was divided into the following sections;

FILM SECTIONS: The chief function was to review films and transcribe radio programs, translate synopses for films, recommend the use of films and radio, and to study postwar policies in regard to films and radio.

TRANSLATION BUREAU: As indicated, this section translated the many surveys taken among the POWs from German into English, and such items as pamphlets prepared by the Office of War Information and the Prisoner of War Special Projects Division from English into German.

CAMP ADMINISTRATION SECTION: This section, headed by a POW camp spokesman, was responsible for the general supervision and welfare of the prisoners, and for the normal maintenance of the camp facilities.

REVIEW SECTION: Analyzed, evaluated, and made recommendations concerning all material submitted by interested government agencies and the branches of the Prisoner of War Special Projects Division.

CAMP NEWSPAPER SECTION: This section was charged with the continuous review of all camp newspapers (65 as of October, 1945), recommendations about their content and editorial policies, and the gathering of material of interest to the S–2 (Intelligence) sections in the various prisoner of war camps.

A NATIONAL MAGAZINE: a periodical for the German POW community, prepared entirely by the Kearney prisoners.[36]

Of all the diverse undertakings encompassed by these six sections, the most immediate and optimistic project became the creation of a national prisoner of war newspaper.

Der Ruf and Camp Newspapers

Commissioned within two weeks of The Factory's creation, the periodical was named *Der Ruf* (The Call) and placed in the hands of the Kearney prisoners. Under the joint editorship of Dr. Gustav René Hocke, a prizewinning German novelist, and Curt Vinz, a former publisher in Germany (with editorial guidance supplied by Schönstedt and a Captain Pestalozzi), *Der Ruf* was established as a bimonthly newspaper-magazine handsomely made up on high-grade paper and liberally illustrated. Designed to give "the German Prisoner ... realistic news of all important military and political events, a true picture of the German homefront, ... entertainment and a true understanding of the American way of life," [37] *Der Ruf* was an enormously sophisticated German-language publication. Members of the Special Project team themselves joked that it was "a newspaper which even Thomas Mann would find difficult to understand." Indeed, its initial success, the team agreed, was "because it seems the Germans believe that anything they can't understand must be pretty hot stuff." [38] *Der Ruf* was designed, indeed, to appeal to the most literate among the prisoners in the hope that they might, in turn, influence their less literate comrades. Starting at the intellectual end of the POW spectrum, it was agreed, was more logical than trying to appeal directly to the fanatical Nazis at the opposite end. Moreover, the intellectuals might someday rise to positions of political influence in post-war Germany, whereas former Nazis would surely not be easily reintegrated. The newspaper's keys to success, therefore, would have to be academic sophistication in intellectual matters and scrupulous honesty in reporting war news and POW problems.

The first issue appeared in camp canteens on March 6, 1945, priced at a modest five cents. The Division had, in fact, debated the question of giving the paper rather than selling it but decided that the prisoners would probably be less suspicious of something they had to purchase. The first issue was an intellectual blockbuster. The front page contained a lengthy article entitled "The Inner Power" *("Die Inneren Mächte"),* which discussed the human soul through the eyes of Schiller, Goethe, and Schopenhauer.

The rest of the paper contained articles on the Yalta and Teheran conferences; current battlefield news from Europe; Field Marshal Gerd von Rundstedt's winning of the Ritter Cross; and a discussion of the Allied bombing raids over Germany. A music section covered the Metropolitan Opera season in New York; a literary section discussed the most recent Nobel Prize for Literature; a lengthy section aired the sensitive issue of American racism and reviewed the history and geography of the South and the roots of slavery. Then came a column of letters-to-the-editor from prisoners of war with comments on the value of attending church services; trends in camp sports; the making of a violin; and interesting reading. Finally, a frank and optimistic editorial was addressed to "German Prisoners of War and Internees in America":

> This is the latest and best news for all of us who for months, perhaps years, have lived in a state of uncertainty. . . .
>
> DER RUF will reach every one of us. It is the call from Camp to Camp throughout the United States, from Michigan to the Gulf of Mexico, from the Atlantic Ocean to the Pacific. It is the call of all Germans who are sharing the same tragic fate. It is the call from home, unreachable and darkened by somber clouds, our home which is living and strong within us. . . .
>
> Administration, editing and composition of this newspaper will be done by German prisoners of war, who, like you, live in barracks behind barbed wire, and like you, have their daily annoyances: regulations, K.P., work detail, count. And, Brother! How often we have been counted!!. . . .
>
> We want you to help us, write to us. American authorities have authorized direct correspondence between you and the editors of DER RUF (Directions for writing are on another page). . . . Send us contributions covering every interest. This is your paper. We ask only one thing of you: think and be aware . . . have a sense of responsibility. . . . Our work is hard and arduous. Our work is for Germany and the German people.[39]

The first issue was out, and the men at The Factory held their breaths.

The reaction to the first several issues was mixed. The prisoners were natually suspicious. At Camp Trinidad, Colorado, seven POW officers were apprehended in the act of burning a batch of copies. At Bradley Field, Connecticut, the first issue was received with "overwhelming enthusiasm" and at Farragut, Idaho, the prisoners were "impressed." At Camp Hulen, Texas, the first issues of *Der Ruf* were characterized as "Jewish propaganda" and "not fit for the men"; while the prisoners at Monticello, Arkansas, and at Clarinda, Iowa, were merely "skeptical." The Army carefully monitored outgoing POW mail for any references to *Der Ruf* through the first five issues and obtained sentiments ranging from "We await each issue of *Der Ruf* with much impatience. . ." (Camp Carson, Colorado) to "*Der Ruf* is an outburst of 'dull despair' " (Camp McCain, Mississippi).[40] The monitoring revealed two important trends. The first was that the controversy surrounding the appearance of the newspaper caused the prisoners to take sides and, more importantly, to identify their positions to the authorities. Committed Nazis, for example, openly boycotted *Der Ruf* and tried to convince others to do the same, while those who had democratic leanings often rose up to advertise and protect the paper. The large body of "neutrals" were often driven by curiosity to purchase the paper, and while they may not have chosen to actively join either extreme, their carefully monitored correspondence unwittingly revealed their ideological status. The prisoners, in effect, were helping the authorities to segregate them.

The second trend disclosed by POW correspondence—that *Der Ruf* was becoming increasingly popular with the prisoners—showed indications that the reeducation program was, indeed, on the path to success. For instance, only 11,000 copies of the first issue (March 1, 1945) were printed, but by the publication of the sixth issue on June 1, 1945, the number required reached 26,000 copies. In July, sales topped 33,000; by mid-August, 48,000; and by October 15, 1945, each issue of *Der Ruf* sold more than 73,000 copies! [41] The Special Projects Division had reason to be proud of its first effort.

It should be noted that the Special Projects Division monitored POW reaction for yet another reason. In a cooperative effort with the Office of Censorship, the hundreds of thousands of incoming and outgoing letters were examined for evidences of virulent Nazism—not to isolate potential troublemakers in the camps, although such information was always welcome, but to identify unrepentant Nazis among the civilians in occupied Germany. The names and addresses of suspects were then forwarded to the proper authorities in the War Department for transmission to SHAEF, and then to the Allied Military Government in Germany.[42]

In addition to the publication of *Der Ruf,* the Special Projects Division and its educational experts at The Factory took a special interest in existing camp newspapers. Such publications, of course, had been permitted and encouraged by the authorities from the beginning of the POW experience as both an acceptable intellectual diversion [43] and a visible barometer of political activities among the prisoners. As part of the new reeducation program, the Division now requested that all camp publications be forwarded to its offices. Copies of more than 50 bimonthly and monthly camp papers were carefully analyzed at The Factory to determine the existing levels of Nazism and measure the effects of the appearance of *Der Ruf* as well as the general reeducation program. This first investigation of camp newspapers, in March, 1945, indicated that: approximately 3 were anti-Nazi; approximately 7 were neutral, with straight entertainment value only; 1 was religious (Christian) only; approximately 25 were Nazi; approximately 8 were violently Nazi.[44]

Once each paper was properly categorized, the men of the Camp Newspaper Section at The Factory monitored each issue in search of hopeful trends. And indeed, a gradual transformation in the editorial policies of many papers took place. In fact, as early as July and August, 1945, the Special Projects Division began to note the following examples of change:

Lagerzeitung (Camp Algona, Iowa): In April 1945 this newspaper was completely nonpolitical. It printed stories about sports and camp life and poems. A report on this paper of August 9 showed that the paper was printing articles which fitted the purpose of the re-education program. . . . A leading article in this issue, called *What We Have to Learn* by Prisoner of War Rolf Bernegau said: "We must learn to understand other people and think internationally. Only in this way can we return to the community of nations."

Die Brücke (Camp Breckinridge, Kentucky): In April this paper contained Nazi propaganda, such as the symbol of the werewolf and sentences like "the eyes of the Fuehrer are stern and severe." The August edition of this paper, with new editors, had an article on the revival of labor unions in German, and an open letter to the camp commander from the editorial staff which requested permission to have American lecturers visit the camp and present talks about the land and people of the United States.

Deutsche Woche (Fort Lewis, Washington): In April this paper contained hidden Nazi propaganda. The July 28th issue, under new editors, contained the following article: *The Faults of National Socialism* by Prisoner of War Zwiauer which stated: "We should make sure that there is no militaristic or violent solution of any questions or problems. Never again should wars decide questions; they will only create new difficulties."

Der Querschnitt (Camp Opelika, Alabama): This paper contained undesirable propaganda in April. The June issue reprinted the entire

Constitution of the United States, and an article called *America, the Land of Freedom and Hope* which dealt with the Declaration of Independence and the appeal, "Take Part in the Lectures on Democracy," which were to take place shortly.[45]

So significant was the change in the political attitude of the nation's POW newspapers—whether brought about by the influence of *Der Ruf,* the end of the war, or, more logically, the involuntary replacement of editorial personnel—that the Special Projects Division soon had a new set of figures. A survey of 80 camp newspapers, including a number which did not exist when the first report was undertaken in March, 1945, indicated that by the fall of 1945 the attitudes of the camp papers had changed to: 24 democratic tendency; 18 strongly anti-Nazi; 32 nonpolitical; 3 religious (Christian); 1 camouflaged Nazi; 2 militaristic.[46]

There may have been yet another reason for the changes in attitude: the long-term effects of the Division's general educational programs.

General Education Programs

Classroom activities had been organized by the prisoners from the earliest days of the POW camps, and, as in the case of camp newspapers, had been encouraged by the authorities as a welcome diversion. With the creation of the reeducation program, however, the PMGO recognized that this extensive classroom structure presented a perfect opportunity for democratic indoctrination. In short, the PMGO made careful plans to assume control over these camp classrooms.

The first step concerned the gradual control and censorship of all POW books and reading material which came from abroad. From the beginning, the prisoners had relied on books produced in Germany, and sent to them by the War Prisoners' Aid Committee of the International YMCA and the International Red Cross. In addition, the German government had provided the POWs with *Soldatenbriefe,* elementary textbooks prepared for the German Armed Forces. Nearly every camp had a small library of books secured in this way, and a PMGO investigation disclosed that much of the reading material available to the prisoners contained some Nazi propaganda. Consequently, in December, 1944, while plans for *Der Ruf* were already underway, the Special Projects Division moved to correct the situation in two ways. The first method involved the general censoring of all available camp books. American commanding officers were instructed to send lists of their library books to the Division where members of The Factory's Review Section would then judge their political content. Books arriving from Germany were examined directly in the customs warehouses in New York before being released for shipment to the camps. By June, 1945, the Division had compiled a large catalogue of approved and disapproved books, and long lists of such books were sent to Assistant Executive Officers at each camp to aid in the reorganization of their libraries. As undesirable books were being weeded out, the Division initiated its second effort: to develop large quantities of anti-fascist reading material to fill the growing gaps.

The Factory began by commissioning a series of purchasable paper-bound books eventually totaling 24 titles known collectively as the *Bücher-reihe Neue Welt* (New World Bookshelf). Since the wary prisoners would have instinctively reacted against a blatant frontal assault on their political beliefs, the Special Projects Division played upon the normal prisoners' hunger for reading matter by providing them with reprints of "good litera-ture by authors whose integrity and righthandedness were beyond doubt." [47] The Factory started with the works of German authors which had been banned under the Nazi government such as Thomas Mann's *Achtung Europe* (Attention Europe), *Der Zauber Berg* (The Magic Mountain), and *Lotte in Weimar* (Lotte in Weimar); Carl Zuckmayer's *Der Hauptmann von Koepenick* (The Captain from Koepenick); Franz Werfel's *Das Lied von Bernadette* (Song of Bernadette); and Heinrich Heine's *Meisterwerke in Vers and Prosa* (Masterworks in Verse and Prose). These were quickly followed by German translations of Stephen Vincent Benét's *America,* Wendell Willkie's *One World,* and books by Joseph Conrad, Ernest Hemingway, and William Saroyan. The first of these modestly-priced books (25 cents) ap-peared in POW camp canteens at the beginning of May, 1945, and the reaction was immediate and gratifying. Favorable reports and reorders poured in from camps across the country:

This is to advise you that your last shipment of 105 books was sold about an hour after arrival ... [Halloran General Hospital, Staten Island].

... This station could use at least 250 of any new books shipped in addition to the original quota ... [Camp Bowie, Texas].

The response at our two Branch camps of Grady and Altheimer, Arkansas, was beyond our fondest expectations. Canteens were sold out within an hour after books went on sale. Grady expressed a desire for almost 600 more and Altheimer for about 400 more ... [Camp Mon-ticello, Arkansas].[48]

Bolstered by this success, the Provost Marshal General concluded that while "There is no absolute measure of the influence upon the minds of the Prisoners of War of the good books made available to them. . . . surely these books have exerted some influence, and perhaps, a great one." [49]

In addition to the republication of approved literary classics, the Division undertook to write a selection of its own books and pamphlets. The first of these was a booklet originally conceived as a handout for POWs arriving in the United States during the early days of the war. The idea had been abandoned in the initial chaos but was now revived by the men at The Factory. The result was the mass publication of the *Kleiner Führer durch Amerika* (A Brief Guide Through America), which described the geography, natural resources, history, and institutions of the United States. It became immediately popular as a souvenir and text for study, and was one of the standard items to be found in the baggage of nearly every POW upon repatriation to Germany after the war.

During the summer of 1945, three additional pamphlets appeared in POW canteens: *Eine Einführung in das Amerikanische Schulwesen* (An Introduction to American Schools), *Eine Einführung in die Amerikanische Verfassung und Verwaltung* (An Introduction to American Government), and *Kurze Geschichte der Vereinigten Staaten* (A Brief History of the United States). Written for the Project by Dr. Howard Mumford Jones with both German and English texts, these booklets served the dual purpose of providing information to a growing body of interested POWs while at the same time improving their use of the English language.

The bilingual structure of the Jones pamphlets was far from accidental since the PMGO believed that a prisoner's knowledge of English dramatically increased his opportunities to learn more about America and democracy. Consequently, it became a matter of policy—especially after V-E Day— to use the English language whenever possible in dealings with the POWs and to teach as many as possible to read and speak with fluency. To that end, Dr. Henry Smith of the Division prepared a series of technical manuals (TM 30–1506, A–E) entitled *Englisch wie Man Spricht* (English as One Speaks It), which were generously distributed throughout the POW community. As their mastery of English improved, the prisoners were encouraged to subscribe to approved American newspapers and periodicals. Qualified POWs were also allowed to enroll in correspondence courses arranged through the American Council on Education with cooperating universities and at the United States Armed Forces Institute. As with all other facets of the reeducation program, the teaching of English—whether through educational pamphlets or intensive classroom activity—was designed to produce "a much broader and, in the long run, a more important objective: . . . to strengthen these anti-Nazis' understanding of democracy." [50]

Movies and Other Programs

The reeducation program did not restrict itself, however, to reprinting books or providing English lessons. Recognizing the power of the motion picture as an informational medium, the Special Projects Division lost no time in establishing a regular film circuit covering all the prisoner of war camps in the country. Until the inauguration of the so-called "Intellectual Diversion Program," the American movies which had been shown in POW camps had been generally chosen by the Nazi minorities to embarrass the United States. Since the POWs were permitted to rent 16-millimeter films from various commercial distributors, the camp spokesmen often selected films to persuade their followers of the truth of Nazi allegations which pointed out rampant gangsterism, corruption of morals, and the debilitating effects of American democratic life. A preliminary investigation by the PMGO disclosed that the motion pictures most often requested by camp spokesmen were: *Lady Scarface, Millionaire Playboy, Seven Miles from Alcatraz, Parole, Dead End, Boy Slaves, Legion of the Lawless, Wolf Man, Too Many Blondes, Swing It, Soldier,* and *Highways by Night.*[51]

To counteract this situation, the Special Projects Division set up an elaborate film program in May and June, 1945, that "reflected the American scene without distortion and which fostered respect for our democratic institutions." [52] Consequently, a carefully balanced diet was prepared using various documentary films from the Army Signal Corps and the Office of War Information together with many of Hollywood's best offerings. From the OWI came such exciting documentaries as *Cow Boy, Steel Town, T.V.A., Swedes in America, Rockefeller Center, Aircraft Carrier, The Autobiography of a Jeep, Arctic Passage, Medicine on Guard,* and *The Battle of Supply.* Hollywood, naturally, offered a more entertaining bill of fare, though the government was careful about what the POWs were allowed to see. "Films glorifying gangsterism or . . . prison escapes; ridiculing any member of the United Nations; . . . depression or slum pictures; films containing racial slurs; depictions of strife between capital and labor; and the so-called 'blood and thunder' cowboy pictures, were to be disapproved." [53] What resulted was a list of 115 motion pictures designed to impress the prisoners with respect for American statesmen, inventors, military strength, and technical achievements. The list included such films as: *Abe Lincoln in Illinois,*

Adventures of Tom Sawyer, Back to Bataan, God is My Co-Pilot, Burma, Song of Bernadette, Story of Alexander Graham Bell, The Human Comedy, and *Thirty Seconds Over Tokyo.*

Initially, attendance at these movies was voluntary, and no strong propaganda was used. However, with the fall of Germany, combat bulletins, Army indoctrination films, atrocity newsreels, and movies with a strong anti-Nazi sentiment were rapidly introduced. By the late summer of 1945, the POWs were watching the *Why We Fight* series, *Confessions of a Nazi Spy, The Moon is Down, Tomorrow the World, The Seventh Cross, Watch on the Rhine, The Hitler Gang,* and *Hitler's Children.* Prisoners were charged 15 cents admission, and Assistant Executive Officers were required to submit reports to the PMGO on the attendance and audience reaction to each showing.[54]

The War Department placed particular emphasis on the showing of atrocity films both as a lesson in "collective guilt" and as a tool in the reeducation effort. Attendance for all prisoners was mandatory, and in many camps they were required to sign a register afterward. The prisoners' reactions were carefully monitored and, as expected, varied widely. During a showing to 150 POWs at Halloran General Hospital, for example, "a few men held handkerchiefs over their eyes, and one sat with bowed head and with hands tightly covering his ears for most of the film. . . . The majority, however, remained outwardly unmoved." [55] At Fort DuPont, Delaware, the POW projector operator confided to an interested reporter that "Some of the men think the bodies in the movie are Germans whom the Russians tortured." [56] On the other hand, after viewing a 25-minute atrocity film, a thousand prisoners at Camp Butner, North Carolina, dramatically burned their German uniforms, and at numerous camps across the country, groups of prisoners voluntarily took up collections for the survivors of the Nazi concentration camps.[57] The overall influence of these films on prisoners' attitudes was disappointing, however. A sophisticated PMGO survey of more than 20,000 POWs about to be repatriated home indicated that only 36 percent of those interviewed accepted the facts of the camps as true.[58]

With the exception of the atrocity newsreels, the results of the film programs were excellent. The prisoners were deeply impressed by the scope and technical achievements which typified the Hollywood motion picture. In fact, the PMGO tested the prisoners' preference by including two German-made films among the available choices, *Ein Prinz Verleibt Sich* (A Prince in Love With Himself) and Schubert's *Frühlingstraum* (Spring Dream), and without exception the prisoners bypassed them for the American films. So popular was the film program that between June 15, 1945, and January 31, 1946, a total of 8,243,035 admissions were recorded by the PMGO, an average of 30 feature films seen by each POW in the United States. The program, moreover, was wholly self-sufficient, generating a total of $1,236,-455.20 for the Central Prisoner of War Fund.[59]

The men at the Fort Kearney Factory were just getting started. Programs of every variety sprang from their late-night brainstorming sessions. For instance, the Division initiated a program to use the already established POW glee clubs, bands, and large orchestras to aid in reeducation. Most camps had musical instruments but had little sheet music. Consequently, The Factory produced a substantial volume of sheet music designed to stimulate interest in the United States through an appreciation of its music: Sousa marches, cowboy songs, Gershwin tunes, and such popular radio hits as "Pistol Packin' Mama" and "Mairzy Doats." American music quickly became enormously popular with the prisoners, and while there is no way of knowing, it may perhaps have had a positive influence in the reeducation effort.

Similar methods were used for stimulating interest through drama. Lists of acceptable plays were sent to the AEOs by the Division, which also helped in organizing drama clubs, obtaining material for sets and costumes, and even coaching the actors.

The Factory devised methods to use other recreational activities as well. Equipment was provided for both German and American games, and as time passed, the program leaned toward all-American games like baseball, basketball, and horseshoe pitching.

Nor was religion neglected as a means to reorient the prisoners. American chaplains, supplemented by auxiliary prisoner clergymen, were mobilized to prove to the prisoners that "Religious tolerance, freedom of worship, and freedom of expression—all these are part and parcel of the American way of life." [60] The Office of the Chief of Chaplains immediately cooperated by providing the POWs with Bibles, religious books, and pamphlets and by encouraging their camp chaplains to assist the prisoners in organizing secular education and in securing libraries and musical instruments. As a result of these efforts, as well as the gradual segregation of ardent Nazis and the approaching collapse of the German war machine, church attendance rose dramatically, an average of 30 percent between October, 1944, and February, 1945.[61]

The Effect of the Reeducation Program

This entire effort, startlingly, continued to remain a closely guarded secret. The War Department was not taking any chances. Any premature unveiling of the reeducation program would not only jeopardize the safety of Americans in Germany but, more immediately, would certainly cause the German prisoners to react badly, especially at a moment when Nazi elements in the camps still had sufficient power to sabotage the War Department's efforts. Yet several times the secrecy of the Intellectual Diversion Program was nearly uncovered, causing the War Department to scramble in an effort to cover its tracks. "The closest call the program's secrecy ever had," writes one investigator of the period, Judith Gansberg, "occurred in Waco, Texas." She goes on to explain:

> In February 1945, an officer from Camp Mexia made a speech to the Waco Kiwanis Club. The next day the *Waco News Tribune* headlined "Courses in American Life Taught POWs." It went on to explain that "this orientation program is encouraged with a view toward the United States after their repatriation to Germany following the war."
>
> The Eighth Service Command immediately ordered the story killed before it could be released by the wire services, but they never picked it up, anyway. In a comment to the Waco paper, the army called the story "fanciful." [62]

That the reeducation program continued to remain an air-tight secret was proven by an incident which occurred in April, 1945, less than a month before V-E Day and more than five months after the arrival of the AEOs to the prison camps. Representative Richard F. Harless of Arizona, an outspoken critic of the War Department's POW policy, made an unexpected and well-publicized inspection of Camp Papago Park to substantiate his charges of "soft treatment of German prisoners of war." [63] Although the reeducation program was in full swing, Representative Harless did not apparently notice. The War Department could only breathe a sigh of relief as Harless loudly declared to the press and to Congress that he not only found "pampered, well-fed German prisoners as fat as hogs" but that "the United States had not done a single thing to educate German prisoners in the American way of life." Furthermore, he was joined by Representative Robert Sikes of Florida, who thundered that the "German war prisoners should be thoroughly indoctrinated into the workings of democracy. . . . by force, if necessary." [64] The secret of the reeducation program was safe for the last month of the war.

On May 28, 1945, 20 days after V-E Day, the existence of a reeducation program for POWs was finally announced to the public. A seven-page statement was released by General Bryan, in which he explained that "We are taking some 350,000 German prisoners of war—men meandering in a

Several members of the editorial staff examine the latest issue of their 12-page mimeographed news bulletin *Die Kameradenpost*. Camp Polk, Louisiana *(U.S. Army Photo)*

The key to the reeducation program was a basic understanding of English. Here, an American Special Projects Officer (seated) conducts such a class, aided by a POW at the board, at Indiantown Gap Military Reservation, Pennsylvania. *(National Archives)*

The POWs at Halloran General Hospital's movie theater watch the official atrocity films in silent discomfort. 26 June 1945. *(UPI)*

A newly-arrived German POW is shown a display of atrocity pictures. *(Imperial War Museum)*

In an effort to provide an
additional avenue of reeducation,
numerous humanitarian and
religious organizations—
such as the National Catholic
Welfare Council—donated
a wide selection of
books and church supplies.
(National Archives)

An indication that the reeducational program may have had some influence on the
POWs was this particular campaign at Ft. Devens, Massachusetts, to "Save the
Children of Europe; without consideration of race, religion, and nationality."
(National Archives)

Here a POW points out the results of the "Save the Children of Europe" campaign: $16,465.80! *(National Archives)*

Former Special Prisoners are back in uniform, now as "reliable" rural and city policemen. Here they are shown getting instructions in the use of the German Army carbine at the Police School in Strobl, Austria. *(National Archives)*

morass of myths—and conducting a well-calculated, thorough and pointed program of exposition." Following a lengthy general description of the program (during which no reference was made to the first six months of secret reeducation), Bryan concluded humbly, "I do not say that our way is the only way to conduct this program. . . . Ours is a good way, though—the results show that. It is an American way." [65] Surprisingly, considering the earlier furor to reeducate the POWs, the public and the press were now relatively disinterested. On June 15, a blurb appeared in *The New York Times,* followed by a comprehensive description in the Education Section of the same issue.[66] Another appeared in the same newspaper on July 8; and then came articles in the *Chicago Tribune* and *Publishers Weekly,* followed by a few others.[67] An eight-column review of the reeducation program appeared in the *Fort Smith* [Arkansas] *Times Record.*[68] And that, in large measure, comprised the public's immediate response.

If the public was not moved by the program, the prisoners were. The results of the first six months' reeducation, combined with the collapse of Nazi Germany, were already causing groups of prisoners to come forward. At Fort Devens, Massachusetts, for example, 1,391 out of 3,102 German prisoners imprisoned there, voluntarily signed a petition calling on Germany to surrender.[69] Prisoners at the previously pro-Nazi camp at Florence, Arizona, sent a heartfelt letter of condolence to the Army on the death of President Franklin D. Roosevelt; and at Camp Indianola, Nebraska, prisoners publicly condemned the horrors of Nazi concentration camps and the "hopelessness, fear, hunger and sickness" left as Hitler's legacy.[70] From Branch Camp #7, Brush, Colorado, to PMGO Lerch came a lengthy petition signed by 125 German NCOs, reaffirming their lifelong dedication to the principles contained in the Four Freedoms of the Atlantic Charter.[71] In fact, in camps across the country, groups of prisoners renounced their allegiance to National Socialism; subscribed portions of their canteen funds to the American or German Red Cross; and pledged their support toward the creation of a democratic new Germany.

Several thousand prisoners went one step further. They volunteered to enlist in the American Army, unbelievably, to fight against the Japanese! The idea of using German POWs in the Pacific Theater had, in fact, occurred to the men in The Factory months earlier, though nothing came of the plan. Intrigued by the possibilities suggested by Italian POWs at an Arizona camp who volunteered to fight the Nazis in October, 1943,[72] and by the more successful effort of POWs holding citizenship with Allied nations to be returned to their respective armies,[73] the Special Projects Division proposed a secret plan to interest German prisoners in joining the war against Japan. In an astonishing four-page proposal to create anti-Japanese sentiment among the POWs, the Division suggested that the POWs be reminded that it was their own Kaiser Wilhelm II who first coined the phrase "Yellow Peril" and that Japan had fought against Germany during the First World War. In a bizarre appeal to Nazi racism, the German POWs were to be reminded that:

> Japan is not only waging a war against the Anglo-Saxon powers but *against the white race.* . . . [and that] the Nazi policy of a common battle with the "yellow race" against the Anglo-Saxon powers . . . stands definitely in opposition to all racial doctrines advanced by the Nazi party.[74]

Not only would the creation of such a German Volunteer Corps against Japan benefit the American war effort, argued the Division's secret proposal, but such an effort would benefit the prisoners themselves. The German Volunteer Corps could lead to:

a. The utilization of numerous German officers and enlisted men whose rehabilitation and return to Germany is not desired by us while partisan warfare conducted by the Nazis goes on.

b. The prevention of a complete moral breakdown amongst German prisoners of war by creating a positive task for the sake of a right cause.

c. Possible resettlement. In case it should ever be desired to colonize and resettle parts of the Western Hemisphere (Alaska and West Canada), islands in the southwest Pacific and other parts. . . . It might become possible that as an exchange for their service against Japan, German prisoners of war could be given the promise of such resettlement.[75]

Attracted less by these arguments than by the obvious saving of American lives, the Division's plan was taken under serious consideration by a top secret committee at the highest military level. After protracted discussion, representatives of the Offices of Plans and Operations, the Judge Advocate General, Military Intelligence, and the Provost Marshal General concluded that if the POWs were utilized against Japan, it could be in only one of two capacities: regular enlisted men in the U.S. Army or mercenaries. Neither category was acceptable since:

> Use as enlisted men would entitle them to all the rights and privileges of an American soldier, to include dependent and pension benefits, the provisions of the GI Bill of Rights, and probably the right to attain American citizenship. Use as mercenaries—which would require legislative action by Congress—would establish for the first time a precedent which is unsound from the democratic point of view.[76]

General Somervell concurred,[77] and the subject was closed though newly "democratized" German POWs continued vainly to offer their combat services on behalf of the United States.[78]

What now concerned the War Department, however, was not the creation of a German Volunteer Corps but the looming problem of administering the United States Zone in occupied Germany. It was obvious that there would be an urgent need for reliable, English-speaking Germans as administrators and policemen under the new Military Government, and the Special Projects Division was instructed to consider the possibility of using "acceptable" prisoners of war. Meetings were held between the Civil Affairs Division, War Department Special Staff, and the Provost Marshal General's Office through April and May, 1945, and resulted in two experimental programs.

Under the direction of Drs. Howard Mumford Jones, Henry Smith, Edward A. Kennard, William Moulton, and a POW named Henry Ehrmann, two installations were made available in the Second Command. Fort Getty, Rhode Island, was designated as an Administration School (referred to cryptically as Project II), while Fort Wetherill, Rhode Island, became the Police School (or Project III). Together they constituted the "United States Army School Center," which was directed from nearby Fort Kearney. To obtain potential students, the Intelligence Officers and Assistant Executive Officers at each POW camp were requested to submit the names of their most promising and cooperative anti-Nazis, resulting in a list of 17,000 candidates.[79] By checking the names and records of the men on this list against the official German records which were now available to the occupation forces, the men at The Factory pared the final number of students down to 3,700 men.

The curricula of the Police School and the Administration School, while different in its specialized training, were based on a foundation of English language, American and German history, and the structure of civil and military government. The daily schedule was fairly demanding, recalls Howard Mumford Jones. "They were taught English for three hours each weekday morning—divided into groups of eleven—by an American GI of the most common sort. This way they learned colloquial English as well as a sense of democracy. In the afternoon I met them for an hour in American history; the next hour Ehrmann taught them German history; and the third hour was devoted to military law. (This last subject was, in my judgment, a sheer waste of time.)" [80] As each class of several hundred POWs passed through the 60-day cycle (May–June; June–July; July–August; August–September; September–October, 1945), a graduation ceremony complete with speeches and certificates acknowledged their achievement. Ultimately, a total of 1,166 prisoners graduated from the Getty-Wetherill program and repatriated directly to Germany. They were now, the Provost Marshal General's Office proudly proclaimed, "deeply imbued with the magnificence of the democratic way of life." [81]

As each class was graduated, it was held until repatriation arrangements could be completed. At the beginning of October, 1945, however, all plans shifted into high gear. "When General Eisenhower let us know he needed our students for minor German government posts, as the only ones who could be depended upon," recalls Dr. Jones, "we shipped the entire class to Europe, armed with the proper books and cigarettes. Convincing the captain of marines on that ship that we were acting under orders was one of the most difficult diplomatic tasks of my career. Once in Europe, to continue the saga, the POWs were immediately put into barbed wire enclosures, since the Army is marvelous in its snafus, but by and by the PMGO's men got them out. Only then were they put to work." [82]

As it turned out, however, few of these graduates were used as hoped. While each POW returned to Germany with a special certificate and a recommendation to the Military Government, a 1948 follow-up study indicated that most were ignored by an occupation government which did not have a clear understanding of the project or was simply too busy. On the other hand, the same study indicated that these Getty-Wetherill graduates showed "a far greater willingness to participate in public affairs than the average German. . . . Their criticism of the attitudes of fellow Germans was clear, incisive and surprisingly non-nationalistic." [83] Those Getty-Wetherill graduates who were used by the Military Government, however, became important figures in post-war Germany. Some examples are:

Karl Oswald, Property Control Custodian, Office of the Military Government of Württemberg-Baden, Stuttgart;

Dr. Hans Friedemann, Civilian Property Control Board, Office of the Military Government of Land Greater Hesse, Weisbaden;

Hans Bott, Ministry of Culture and Education, Württemberg-Baden Civilian Government, Stuttgart;

Freimut Springle, Ministry of Economics, Bavarian Civilian Government, Munich;

Dr. Oscar Goldschmidt, Arbitration, Industrial Relations Commission, Austrian Civilian Government, Salzburg; and

Egon Altdorf, Assistant Editor of the Wiesbaden *Kurier*.[84]

Perhaps the most prominent graduate of this program was Dr. Walter Hallstein, who was to become the rector of the University of Frankfurt several years after the war and the President of the European Economic Community in the 1960s.[85]

The immediate success of the Police and Administration program, however, led Colonel Davison and the Special Projects Division to consider applying the lessons learned at Getty and Wetherill to a general mass-education effort. Such idle speculation was jolted into reality when the War Department suddenly announced in the summer of 1945 an agreement with France to turn over to that country all the German POWs in the United States for use in construction. Faced with the prospect of losing many thousands of potentially "rehabilitatable" German prisoners to hard and embittering labor in French mines, The Factory buzzed with alternative plans. When the War Department then announced its intention to see all German POWs returned to Europe by March 31, 1946, the Division decided to wait no longer. The last weeks of October, 1945, saw the men at The Factory working at a frenzied pace to develop a plan to select, process, and, in 6-day cycles, reeducate "perhaps 20,000 cooperative German prisoners of war." [86] With the time already running short, the completed plan was rushed to the Pentagon for the approval of the many departments involved, and after badgering uninterested listeners and banging on desks, Davison finally got the project approved on November 20, 1945. The site chosen was Fort Eustis, Virginia, and the project was known thereafter as the Eustis Project.

Because there was no time to send interview teams to the many camps, the Division once again requested the nine service commands to submit the names of their most cooperative anti-Nazi POWs, a total of 25,000 in all. Prisoners so selected by their camp and service commanders were then asked to fill out a lengthy questionnaire, a *Fragebogen*, designed to reveal those who knew the most about Germany's liberal traditions. The POWs were asked to write short essays on such questions as:

> The German philosopher Fichte was the exponent of what ideas?. . . . Name some of the important reforms in the school system under the Weimar Republic. . . . Who was the first president of the Weimar Republic?. . . . Name a character from the *Magic Flute*. . . .[87]

The completed questionnaires were screened by POW members of The Factory at Fort Kearney working on a crash 24-hour schedule, and their results were rushed to Fort Eustis by special messenger even as the truckloads of potential candidates were arriving. On the basis of these reports, followed by a personal interview and a polygraph test, the prisoners were divided into three categories: black (obdurate Nazi), gray (undecided), and white (confirmed anti-Nazi). The blacks (13 percent of the total) were transferred to the regular POW camp at Fort Eustis; the grays (fully three-quarters of the incoming men) were reevaluated and eventually divided into either blacks or whites. The remaining men were classified as whites and enrolled in what became known as "The Six-Day Bicycle Race.'

The first cycle began on January 4, and the last one ended on April 5, 1946. During those three months, more than 20,000 German prisoners went through a total of 12 training cycles at the Fort Eustis Special Project Center, 2,000 men at a time. The six-day schedules were marvels in logistics. First came a disarmingly honest opening address by Colonel Alpheus Smith, commandant of the school. "He didn't pull his punches," recalls one impressed prisoner. "He admitted, much to our shocked surprise, that American democracy wasn't perfect. But he said that the trouble wasn't with democracy; the trouble was with some Americans. Then he told us about the great benefits that Americans have, and he told us that a few bad Americans, a few bad things in the U.S. haven't spoiled democracy . . . and that democracy was the best thing there is in human society." [88] With the completion of this speech the prisoners climbed aboard a treadmill which remained in motion for ten hours each day for six days. William G. Moulton, today the Chairman of Linguistics at Princeton University, still vividly recalls his duties at Eustis. "On Day 1 of the six-day cycle, I gave Lecture I to a thousand POWs at 8:00 A.M., and then repeated it to a second thousand at 9:00 A.M.; then I gave Lecture 2 to a thousand POWs at 1:00 P.M., and repeated it to the second thousand at 2:00 P.M. On Day 2 I gave Lecture 3 at 8:00 A.M., and repeated it at 9:00 A.M.—and then my assignment was done until the next six-day cycle began." [89] The program revolved around 12 major topics:

1. The Democratic Way of Life
2. The Constitution of the United States
3. Political Parties, Elections, and Parliamentary Procedures
4. Education in the United States
5. American Family Life
6. The American Economic Scene
7. American Military Government
8. Democratic Traditions in Germany
9. Why the Weimar Republic Failed–I
10. Why the Weimar Republic Failed–II
11. The World of Today and Germany
12. New Democratic Trends in the World Today.[90]

Lectures in both German and English were followed by open discussion among the prisoners, then films, then more round-table forums, filmstrips, and finally English lessons. Church services were offered every evening. The POWs were also encouraged to take advantage of the Center's carefully-stocked library, as well as a gymnasium with facilities for basketball, volleyball, boxing, and ping pong. The Center even maintained a staff of Personal Counselors to help individuals with problems concerning their families in occupied Germany: addresses, communication, money, and anxieties over their safety.[91]

Writer Quentin Reynolds spent several days at Eustis as a guest speaker and made an effort to talk and listen to the prisoners. It was difficult at first because he remembered the hostility of the many prisoners he had met in Europe only months before, as well as the horrible recollections of the concentration camp scenes. "But gradually," he wrote, "I noticed something different about these Germans at Fort Eustis. Their eyes were clear—not sullen; they laughed at one another's jokes; there was nothing furtive about them. They ... they ... well, damn it, they were different." [92]

Reynolds was no less impressed by the Center's staff. "Each night," Reynolds recalled, "usually far into the night, the staff gathers at Colonel Alpheus Smith's house to discuss individual cases. . . . They live this educational project 24 hours a day." [93] An American staff member, Robert Kunzig, today a Judge of the United States Court of Claims, recalls that "the working conditions among the men in The Factory and at Eustis were excellent. They were extremely amiable. The POW staff members and the editors were, of course, prisoners, but the close working relationship resulted in their being almost colleagues." [94]

Each cycle culminated in a formal ceremony with addresses by the Commanding Officer of the Center and guest speakers, a speech by a POW "valedictorian," and the reading of Stephen Vincent Benét's "Prayer for United Nations." Since the war had long ended and the veil of secrecy had been removed, news correspondents were invited to attend the ceremony. They were, as planned, much impressed by what they saw:

> A German prisoner of war, shapeless in his blue-black uniform and without name or rank as far as the United States Army was concerned, stood on the stage of the assembly hall ... and pledged himself and a thousand of his listening comrades to return to the Reich to support democracy as "a conscious way of living as practical, decent and successful people." [95]

Colonel Edward Davison, Director of the Special Projects Division, sat in the front row, as did Colonel Alpheus Smith, Commanding Officer of the Center; General B. M. Bryan, Assistant Provost Marshal General; and the 40 members of the teaching staff. "When, in a voice that rose and fell like that of a skilled orator, he had concluded," noted the correspondent from the *New York Times,* "there was thunderous applause as there was for the brief speeches by General Bryan and Colonels Davison and Smith." The new graduates were about to be repatriated home to Germany for hopeful inclusion in the occupation government, and as the applause began to die down, a new detachment of prisoners was already arriving.[96] Ultimately, 23,147 men went through the Eustis Center and, as would be expected, many rose to prominence in post-war Germany. One of the graduates of the Eustis program to reach a very high position is Baron Rüdiger von Wechmar, today the Permanent Ambassador of the Federal Republic of Germany to the United Nations.

As each completed cycle led to the beginning of the next, the reeducation program moved closer to termination. The Factory at Fort Kearney had closed as the Eustis school began its operations. By March, 1946, the Getty and Wetherill schools completed their work, and the remaining prisoner-teachers were either shifted to Eustis or repatriated to Germany. A few teachers were eventually assigned to a similar reorientation school at Querqueville, France, which had been hastily established by Davison and Schönstedt the previous November. On April 1, 1946, four days before the last cycle graduated at Eustis, *Der Ruf* ceased publication with issue 26. Finally, the Eustis school closed down on April 8, 1946, signaling the end of the reeducation effort in the United States. As Kunzig, Moulton, Kennard, Henry Smith, and others went to see the last group off on the train, "a prisoner spotted Smith, waved, and called, 'Let's face it, Major. There's no future in the PW business!' "[97]

It is difficult to determine the success of the reeducation effort. From the beginning, the PMGO had realized that very little could be done in such a short period of time. In any case, only those prisoners who already leaned toward a democratic ideology were even considered. If one is to judge by the responses of departing prisoners, an official PMGO poll of 22,153 POWs indicated that:

- Approximately 74 percent of the German prisoners of war who were interned in this country left with an appreciation of the value of democracy and a friendly attitude toward their captors;
- about 33 percent of these prisoners were definitely anti-Nazi and pro-democratic;
- about 10 percent were still militantly Nazi;
- approximately 15 percent, while not strictly Nazi, still were not favorably disposed toward America or democracy.[98]

Based on the government's loose assumption that prior to the inception of the reeducation effort, 13 percent of the prisoners were devout Nazis, 13 percent anti-Nazi, and 74 percent neutral,[99] it appears that the program was effective in changing 23 percent to a strong anti-Nazi position and 61 percent from a neutral to a positive appreciation of democracy. Nazi strength was reduced, however, by only three percent.

Overall, the reactions and results of the novel reeducation programs vary as widely as the personalities and motives of those involved. "The reeducation experiment," recalls former POW Alfred Klein, "was one of the biggest mistakes made by the U.S.A. Such a democratization could not be carried out by a program, rather it had to result from within the prisoner himself—from numerous experiences during the imprisonment." [100] Heinrich Matthias, a prisoner at McAlester, Oklahoma, and later Mexia, Texas, states that "in my opinion re-education should have started in 1943 as we had a good life in the United States and suffering was nil; even the worst Nazis admitted—although sometimes secretly—that there was something quite good about the American way of life. But it all began too late, and a good chance was missed." [101] Yet another former POW recalls that "Ft. Eustis is the greatest thing that ever happened to me. Even though it was only a short course, it was an experience that you remember for a lifetime. Eustis restored my faith in God and man." [102]

Nor were members of the American effort in complete agreement. In October, 1947, a former colonel of Intelligence candidly remarked: "There in the Pentagon, we thought it was just window-dressing to shut up a bunch of Leftist writers, such as Dorothy Thompson, whose demands got too hot on the necks of the War Department." [103] Others, like the noted historian Professor Harold Deutsch, a former high ranking officer in the O.S.S., believe that while the reeducation program was justified and morally pure, it was run by incompetents. "We made mistake after mistake: the Nazis weren't segregated until after the damage had been done; the best men were wasted in the wrong areas; and so on. In retrospect, it was only common sense and our basic humanity which saved us." [104]

Yet the majority of American participants are convinced that despite the shortcomings caused by secrecy and haste, the reeducation program was a reasonable success. If only one prisoner, it was argued, could be "democratized" and then placed in a position of political influence in post-war Germany, the project would have entirely justified itself. Moreover, the entire reeducation effort hardly cost the taxpayers a nickel since the books, newspapers, and film admissions were paid for by the POWs, and the purchases made at the school canteens largely supported the maintenance of each project. For those involved, it was a noble commitment by intellectuals and educators who saw in the dismantling of an evil philosophy a positive contribution to the war effort. As Dr. Moulton commented: "This was, we felt, the most positive, constructive thing that was done.... It was a *con*structive thing to do in something as *de*structive as a war." [105] Colonel Alpheus Smith summed up the reeducation effort by declaring: "Maybe this is doing some good ... it certainly isn't doing any harm.... Twenty-five years from now maybe we'll know whether we have failed or succeeded." [106]

Unfortunately, only three brief and inconclusive surveys have been made among prisoners who went through the special schools. One was conducted by the Office of Information Control, Office of Military Government (US) in Württemberg-Baden among 150 former students. The object was to reassess the effects of the reeducation program on a random group. In this particular case, the results were disappointing. The interviewers found that "the principles and attitudes which sustain a democracy were only partly absorbed by the former POWs, and remained superficial and brittle enough to be easily forgotten." [107]

The second survey was made by Dr. William Moulton for the Office of Military Government in May and June, 1947, and sought to examine the new occupations of the men. Of the 106 men interviewed, all graduates of Eustis, 25 worked in the German civil administration; 19 in private business; 17 in military government; 12 in education; 8 as students; and 7 in radio or press. All had experienced considerable difficulty in adjusting to post-war German social structure,[108] due mainly to their frustrated hope of immediate service to a new democratic German government. They had undergone a thorough, if rapid, "democratization" process, in some instances in defiance of violence at the hands of their Nazi fellow-prisoners, only to find themselves completely ignored by the Military Government they were trained to serve.

The final survey, a general investigation entitled " 'The Cream of the Crop' Two Years Later" was conducted among 78 former project students during the spring of 1947. Encouragingly, nearly a fourth (23 percent) were members of one of Germany's political parties as opposed to only 5 percent of the general population. On the other hand, less than half of the total claimed to be sufficiently well-informed on current events. Significantly, 64 percent of the group was employed in some sort of government work, though all complained that they had been repatriated to Germany "with no special provision having been made for their future." Moreover, their reeducation certificate proved to be helpful to only four out of ten, and a fifth of those interviewed had never even made use of the certificate.[109]

On May 8, 1945, the war in Europe had officially come to an end. As the most "salvageable" 25,000 prisoners began their reeducation at Getty,

Wetherhill, and Eustis—leading to their immediate repatriation home—the remaining 350,000 POWs entered into limbo. With mixed emotions the prisoners awaited each new rumor regarding their future. Would they be returned directly to Germany? Soon? Was Germany devastated? Was it true that they might be used as slave labor by Britain, France, or even Russia? Might they be allowed to remain in the United States? And so it went for an entire, anxious year.

The government spent the same year equally unsettled about the prisoners' future. The War Department was extremely reluctant to allow the mass return of so many thousands of former enemy soldiers to newly-occupied Central Europe. At the same time, however, they could not maintain them indefinitely in the United States. Did the government have an obligation to offer the prisoners to its Allies for use as laborers in post-war reconstruction? Would labor-starved American farmers be able to continue without access to the prisoners, regardless of their ultimate destination? How would the War Department go about shipping more than a quarter of a million prisoners overseas?

In short, from the spring of 1945 to the spring of 1946, the United States Government, no less than its farmers, labor unions, allies, Military Government overseas, and, of course, the prisoners of war themselves, were caught up together in the final chapter of the POW experience: Repatriation.

CHAPTER VII

"Thank God It's Over!"

As with every other facet of the POW experience, the issue of repatriation led the United States to turn first for guidance to the provisions of the Geneva Convention. In this case, however, the Convention offered little real help. Based originally on the experiences of World War I, the 1929 Accords provided for the repatriation of war prisoners only as part of an armistice, which did not occur at the conclusion of the next war. No special provisions were made for the contingency of "unconditional surrender." In fact, the only guidance offered by the Geneva Convention was the broad admonition in Article 75 that "repatriation of prisoners shall be effected with the least possible delay after the conclusion of peace." Moreover, since one of the three principal Allies involved in handling German POWs—the Soviet Union—was not a signatory to the Convention, no legal cooperative policy could be expected.

Nor did the War Department derive any substantial guidance from the terms of the Instrument of Unconditional Surrender for Germany. Drawn up by the Governments of the United States, Great Britain, and the Soviet Union, the Unconditional Surrender agreement merely suggested that the repatriation of POWs be delayed until:

1. The termination of the war with Japan; or until
2. The conclusion of a treaty of peace with Germany, and as much longer as may be provided in such a treaty; or
3. During such time as the labor of these personnel is desired for the rebuilding and restoration of devastated areas; or
4. During such time as is required by security considerations.[1]

The individual policies of America's Allies offered little additional guidance. Russia's views toward repatriation were completely shrouded in mystery, though it was clear that her no-nonsense treatment of German prisoners and the ruthless exploitation of their labor would continue long after the end of the war. Great Britain, on the other hand, was as undecided about the repatriation of her POWs as the United States, though the continued absence of cooperation from Washington would have made any British plan unsharable.[2] Consequently, the War Department was forced to fall back on its own initiative.

There were several meager precedents. Throughout the war, Germany and the United States had arranged several exchanges of sick and Protected Personnel—a total of 1,166 such German prisoners being returned in five separate exchanges.[3] The War Department had also combed its German POWs for nationals of Allied nations to be returned as replacement troops, despite the occasional frustration when the identical men were recaptured in German uniforms.[4] The United States had also considered, however briefly, participating in a mid-war British-German scheme to exchange a total of 25,000 able-bodied prisoners from each side.[5] As a result of these and several additional minor experiences, the War Department had at least considered some of the problems involved in repatriating prisoners of war, though the major policy decisions still loomed ahead.

Stemming the Flow of Prisoners to America

The first such policy decision, the War Department quickly realized, was to somehow halt the flow of prisoners which continued to pour into the United States from European battlefields. Any effort at repatriation was futile if, as American-based POWs left for Germany, their places were filled by thousands of new prisoners. Since mid-1944, such a revolving door problem was a real threat. The Normandy invasion on June 6, 1944, initiating the final, year-long assault on Germany, was netting German prisoners by the hundreds of thousands. During August and September, as Allied troops swept across France, the sheer numbers of new captives forced the shipment of 58,000 POWs to the United States. An additional 58,000 arrived between October and November. Following the Battle of the Bulge in December and January, more prisoners poured in: 4,740 in March; 33,776 in April; 25,763 in May; and so forth.[6] It was a situation not easily reversed.

The European Theater was crowded with large temporary and central compounds where hundreds of thousands of exhausted, frightened, and often malnourished *Wehrmacht* soldiers awaited the end of the war. By the end of December, 1944, the number of Germans held in such compounds exceeded half a million men, and a top secret Army report predicted, near-hysterically, that even "after deductions for expected evacuations under present policy, for repatriations to Allied nations, and for transfers to the French and British, it is estimated that the number of prisoners remaining in

US custody in this theater ... by the end of August, 1945, ... will be 2,200,000." [7] In fact, the number of POWs outstripped even the ability to keep daily count. The feeding of so many captives exerted such a strain on the Army's overburdened supply lines, that General Omar Bradley recalls having to instruct all commanders not to accept additional prisoners until more supplies became available. Indeed, when the Army received word on May 1, 1945, that the entire 11th Panzer Division wished to surrender, Bradley invited them to come in, "but only if you bring your own kitchens and can take care of yourselves." [8]*It was obvious to the War Department that unless this tidal wave of German prisoners from overseas was halted, no possible plan could be arranged for the repatriation of the POWs already on American soil.

Consequently, on October 27, 1944, Chief of Staff George C. Marshall moved decisively and ordered General Eisenhower to cease the shipment of German POWs from Europe to the United States except for confirmed Nazis and other troublemakers who might pose a security problem and those with sufficient military information to be interrogated by authorities in the United States.[9] An identical message was sent to General McNarney in the Mediterranean Theater where an additional 100,000 German prisoners were being held in compounds scattered across North Africa. Predictably, both Eisenhower and McNarney loudly protested the War Department's decision, pointing out the folly of maintaining the ever-increasing numbers of POWs in their theaters. But the Chief of Staff remained unmoved. Thus the War Department had stopped the flow of incoming POWs, if only temporarily, and now was free to take the first step toward planning for repatriation.

From November, 1944, through V-E Day, memos passed from one section of the War Department to another and between General Eisenhower's European headquarters and Washington in an effort to hammer out a firm plan of action. Could the United States act independently of its Allies, for example, or should all POW policy be coordinated? Could the POWs now be utilized for labor previously proscribed by the Geneva Convention? In fact, since the war was over, could the Geneva Convention still be considered in force? In an effort to more fully exploit their labor without continued reference to the Convention, might not the prisoners be reclassified as "military detainees"? As military detainees, however, were they to be treated and fed on a par with American personnel? If the prisoners received less food than their captors, could they still be expected to perform a full day's labor? Yet, if they received equal rations, which were generally better than those provided to the soldiers of America's allies, would it not strain relations between the United States and the other victor nations? Such discussions continued to rage for months prior to the end of

* There were no incidents of mass deaths among the prisoners, as recently charged, and certainly no official plan to starve or deny them available medical aid.

the war. One lengthy memo went so far as to examine the possibilities of having to provide any injured German POW laborers with benefits under the Federal Employees Compensation Act! [10] Ultimately, the War Department arrived at the following conclusions:

- German prisoners in the continental United States at the time of the German collapse should be returned to the European continent as soon as it is feasible under the pertinent conditions, to be retained in custody, paroled, or repatriated and released . . . by the Commander-in-Chief of the U.S. Zone.
- German noncommissioned officers and incorrigible Nazis will be the last to be released from a prisoner of war status.
- Employable U.S.-owned German prisoners should be utilized to the extent possible on the European continent to meet labor requirements incidental to our redeployment and occupation.
- Surplus U.S.-owned German prisoners should be made available for transfer to the custody of other European United Nations.[11]

With these four statements, the War Department finally established the barest framework of its future repatriation policy. Its very ambiguity, in fact, became its advantage. No dates were mentioned, no deadlines set. The framework was thus entirely flexible. Equally significant, the framework contained no reference to the large numbers of German POWs collecting in the European Theater, which all but ended the voluminous correspondence to the War Department from General Eisenhower demanding the immediate evacuation to the United States of 400,000 prisoners. Thus, when V-E Day arrived, the War Department simply announced that all prisoners in the United States would be returned "as rapidly as possible consistent with the need for their labor on essential military and contract work, and the military situation abroad." [12] As additional plans were formulated during later months, the American public had an opportunity to react to the impending departure of its prisoners.

The Repatriation Issue

The issue of repatriation was no less controversial than any earlier facet of the POW experience. As always, there suddenly appeared a division of opinion. Newspaper columnists and powerful political figures chose sides, and public debate, having barely subsided from the reeducation issue, began anew.

One broad segment of the American public demanded the immediate return of the prisoners to Europe. Labor leaders who had opposed POW labor throughout the war were now adamant. They were joined by veterans organizations, patriotic groups, unemployed war production workers, and a variety of bellicose congressmen. "I say that the time has come when they should be sent back to Europe," demanded Representative George Bender of Ohio, "to rebuild the lands they have devastated. This procedure would not violate the principles of international law and would remove from idleness a group of dangerous, arrogant men who might otherwise one day form the nucleus of a new menace to the world." [13] Congressman Bender's suggestion that the POWs be used to rebuild war-torn Europe would, indeed, become an eventual reality; but it was certainly not the most vigorous argument advanced for the immediate return of the prisoners.

Senator Burnet Maybank of South Carolina put it succinctly: "The prisoners of war in this country should be returned to their native lands," he thundered to his fellow senators, "so that our boys who made possible the great victory in Europe, our gallant soldiers, will not find them here...." Maybank continued that he did not want to feel that the prisoners would in any way have the opportunity to "cost one American soldier or sailor his full wages, his just pay, and his full employment. Let Americans run America, and let the heroes of our armed forces return to the America they knew." [14] The argument of potential unemployment for returning American soldiers immediately struck a sensitive nerve in many of the nation's legislators. Soon thereafter Senator McMahon of Connecticut announced that not only should the prisoners be repatriated as rapidly as possible but that he personally had taken the question up with the Department of Justice to prevent their competition with American citizens. [15] Similar sentiments were echoed by the Wisconsin Legislature which rose as a body to demand prompt deportation of "imported war prisoners, foreign labor battalions, and refugees" for fear that the "gainful employment of our citizenry will be seriously jeopardized." [16] While it may be doubtful that the employment of a comparatively small number of prisoners in jobs which the average returning GI would most surely consider unacceptable "stoop-labor" could be viewed as a serious threat,[17] the government decided to take no chances with such an emotion-packed issue.

Brigadier General B. M. Bryan, Assistant Provost Marshal General, was instructed to issue an immediate statement to defuse the situation. Said General Bryan about the future of POW labor: "We'll get them all out of here just the minute any labor becomes surplus, and we won't let any grass grow under our feet doing it. We are not going to prevent any American from getting a job because of a prisoner.... If there's a civilian for the job, he gets it." [18] Union leaders and politicians were much relieved. To neutralize any remaining skepticism, Undersecretary of War Robert Patterson announced his directive to the chairman of the War Manpower Commission, Paul McNutt, to "urge upon all employers of prisoner-of-war labor the necessity of immediate action on their part toward replacing prisoners of war with free labor." [19] Patterson underscored his efforts by pointing out that, indeed, the War Department had already announced the imminent return of the first group of POWs, alternately listed as either 2,800, 10,400, 50,000, or 1,482 Germans.[20] Thus, it seemed that the repatriation issue had been easily resolved.

Such, however, was not the case. Another segment of American society—equally powerful and with equally persuasive arguments—was *against* returning the prisoners. The American Military Government in Germany, for example, was particularly appalled about the prospect of several hundred thousand German combat veterans arriving in the newly-occupied enemy nation. The situation was already unstable without the appearance of a new threat. "Not only would they probably be the only large group of Germans who are well fed and who are still strongly Nazi," lamented an American Military Government official, "but they would reach Germany at a time when food and supplies will be running low." The officer also pointed out that the sight of devastated German cities and towns would "undoubtedly inflame" the returning prisoners. Together with the food and fuel shortages, this "would probably result in their joining the malcontents already demonstrating against the Allies' rule." [21]

As in the case of the argument to deport the prisoners at the earliest opportunity, the most vocal critics against their early return also trumpeted the cause of labor and employment. While one group of the population—mainly patriotic organizations, labor union officials, and some politicians—voiced their resentment against POWs working in the United States, another substantial portion of the population claimed that they could not survive without it. Laborers were still in critically short supply, particularly in the South, and employers and farmers argued that their prisoners had been contracted for and their removal now would cause tremendous financial hardships for the employers. Poor Patterson was now buffeted by farm groups and politicians from agricultural areas, demanding that plans for repatriation be halted. First came a delegation of Arkansas congressmen led by Senator John L. McClellan to describe the desperate situation in their state and plead for the retention of POW labor. In fact, declared West Memphis Congressman E. C. Gathings, the State of Arkansas is "absolutely dependent upon the relief that can be obtained from prisoner-of-war labor." [22] Not long afterward came a delegation of angry Utah sugar beet growers.[23] Then followed representatives of the lumber and pulpwood industries. Ironically, several of the very congressmen who had earlier demanded the swift return of the German prisoners (such as Senator Maybank of South Carolina) did a complete turnabout in response to their constituencies and joined in the general appeal to the War Department for special consideration in retaining POW labor in their states.[24]

Not only did these delegations argue for the retention of POWs in the United States after the end of the war, but a majority went one step further. They wanted more prisoners shipped from the holding pens in Europe. During the meeting between Senator McClellan's Arkansas delegation and Undersecretary Patterson, the Senator declared that he and other Arkansans "strongly urged that thousands of Germans in U.S. custody abroad be brought to the United States as the only possible means to secure more labor for our farmers." [25] These sentiments were echoed by representatives of most labor-hungry petitioners. Privately, the government was forced to agree. In an urgent assessment of the situation, the War Food Administration declared that "the supply of farm labor at the start of this new production year [1945] is so acute that we appeal for assistance in getting full employment on agriculture ... a minimum of 100,000 prisoners of war." [26] A hasty government spot-check revealed that "the need will be for almost three times as many war prisoner laborers as were used last year." [27] Since, at the same moment, the European Theater was indeed jammed with German prisoners, as General Eisenhower had so often reminded the War Department, it seemed reasonable to Patterson and General Archer Lerch, Provost Marshal General, to solve both problems with one directive. Consequently, after a hurried but highly detailed analysis of the logistics, shipping, housing, and personnel required, the War Department revised its initial decision. A much-relieved Eisenhower was now authorized on February 22, 1945, to begin the immediate shipment of 150,000 POWs to the United States. The only stipulation noted in General Marshall's authorization cable to Eisenhower was that "if civilian occupation is known, include 5,000 machinists and 200 opticians, 200 medical officers and 100 dental officers." [28] The majority of the POWs, transported whenever shipping space became available, arrived in the United States by midsummer of 1945.[29]

If the various public pressures and arguments regarding the repatriation of German prisoners appeared to be working at cross-purposes (which was certainly true), it must also be noted that they were of little real consequence. Despite the political delegations and the concessions they extracted from the War Department, the fact is that the government had no real alternative but to return the prisoners at the earliest feasible opportunity, even if temporary agricultural needs demanded that a large batch of prisoners be brought into the country at the same moment. That the War Department had long made up its mind is clear. Within weeks after V-E Day, in fact, on May 25, 1945, the War Department issued a five-page, detailed memorandum to the entire military hierarchy which, in effect, committed itself to eventual repatriation. The directive contained instructions for the preparation of all POWs under Army control: the completion of required military records; the issuance of clothing and travel paraphernalia; and the arrangement for attending medical and guard units to accompany the prisoners when shipped. Although no deadlines were included, it was clear that the POWs were to be processed and held in readiness for ultimate repatriation home.[30]

The Repatriation Process

If there was no deadline, there was also no rigid pattern to the planned repatriation. Aside from the sick and wounded who are traditionally given first priority in any exchange, the remaining prisoners were repatriated according to several flexible requirements designed to minimize the hardships caused to either the military or industry. The factors which governed the repatriation process were: the need for continued labor in agriculture, the lumber and pulpwood industry, and in certain military hospitals; the availability of shipping facilities to Europe; the shifting of selected prisoners to and from special reeducation projects; and finally, the ability of the European Theater to receive the prisoners.[31] The resulting program, while satisfactory to all concerned, was often a halting effort which hinged as much on shifting politics as on railroad scheduling.[32] Moreover, it was not without periodic volatile issues.

Just such an issue appeared at the very beginning of the repatriation process and concerned the disposition of what the War Department referred to as "useless" prisoners. About 50,000 men fell into this category, divided into those who were sick or insane; those officers and NCOs who were not required to work; and Nazis. The sick, of course, were repatriated at the first opportunity. But uncooperative or obdurate Nazis, admittedly useless to the United States, presented a problem. When the Army first announced its intention to repatriate the German prisoners on May 19, 1945, it spoke only in terms of these 50,000 "useless" men.[33] The War Department was startled when the public responded with outrage. "Genuine Nazis are being rewarded for their convictions with a speedy reunion with their families," declared one writer to the editor of *The New York Times,* "whereas German prisoners who cooperate by relieving the labor shortage are kept from their homes for an indeterminate period of time." [34] Similar sentiments appeared in numerous other newspapers. "To send these German prisoners home at the cessation of hostilities seems highly impractical and even dangerous," declared the editor of the *Washington Post*. The reason for this danger, noted the editorial, was that "Germany today is in a far more anarchic and chaotic condition than in 1918. Returning prisoners might soon band themselves into *Freikorps* which could subsequently be united into a private army by another political or military adventurer." [35] A writer to the the *New York Times* agreed. At the very moment when the Allies were trying to cleanse Germany of Nazi influence, he wrote, and when that nation was groping for a new direction in its moral-political life, could America be blind enough to introduce thousands of Nazis? [36] The answer, assured the War Department hastily, was "certainly not," though it clearly did not have an alternative plan.

The largest single source of disappointment and outrage was, understandably, the 300,000 "useful" prisoners. They had spent their years of incarceration productively employed; they had skirted the daily political pressure of their Nazi comrades; and many had even found themselves attracted to the democratic ideals of their captors. While never enthusiastic in captivity, the majority of POWs had done as well as possible under the circumstances. Now that the war was over, they learned that it was to be the Nazis who were to return first. To salve their bitter disappointment, General Lerch himself was forced to explain the government's decision. In a "Proclamation to POWs" in the July issue of *Der Ruf,* Lerch conceded that "the American government might send back to Europe those who do not deserve our confidence and who show they are unwilling to learn from disaster. . . . But those men will not go back to Europe as free citizens. They will have no privileges. They will be prisoners still. . . ." [37] Such words were of small consolation to the thousands of average prisoners who did, indeed, watch many of their hardened Nazi comrades return to Europe before them.

Returning to Europe did not necessarily mean returning to Germany or returning as free men. The War Department was keenly aware of the dangers involved in returning such POWs to Germany. Yet, at the same time, the majority of the 50,000 men under discussion were certainly useless and would only cause additional difficulties if allowed to remain in the United States. The solution was obvious: ship them out of the country but not back into the mainstream of German society.

The solution appeared from an unexpected source. The destruction wrought by the war, combined with predictions of an unusually severe winter in 1945–46, led to the anticipation of a massive fuel shortage in Europe. Men were desperately needed in French and German coal mines.

In mid-July 1945, Secretary of Interior Harold Ickes, in his capacity as Solid Fuels Administrator, appealed for the release of 30,000 American GIs with mining experience to help alleviate the problem. The War Department politely argued against such a use of American soldiers, especially in light of their imminent demobilization. They countered with an alternative proposal, however: Use the prisoners. A cursory search of all POW records indicated that some 2,605 German prisoners in United States camps were previously experienced coal miners. Their return would not only aid the European fuel situation but would also reduce the burden of maintaining that many unwanted prisoners in America. Within weeks of Secretary Ickes' original suggestion, the problem was solved, and the Army announced the impending departure of the 2,605 POWs to German coal mines.[38] Many thousands of other German prisoners would eventually find themselves shipped to other destinations, but as of the spring of 1945, those programs were still in the planning stage.

Meanwhile, the repatriation of German prisoners lurched onward. Because of the demands for summer and fall agricultural labor, it was a slow and halting process. They left in small groups as they could be relieved from their employment or, in some cases, from the camp stockades. On September 15, 1945, for example, a rag-tag group of 715 "undesirables" (together with the American Nazi and former leader of the German-American Bund, Fritz Kuhn) sailed from New York aboard the American transports *Winchester Victory* and *Frederick Victory*.[39] Additional groups left the United States as rail transport from their camps and space aboard ocean-going vessels became available.[40] Despite periodic announcements that the repatriation of prisoners would be speeded up and that, in fact, the entire population of 362,170 German, 49,784 Italian, and 5,080 Japanese prisoners would be gone by the spring of 1946, progress was very slow.[41] As of November 20, 1945, only 73,178 German prisoners had been repatriated.

Evidently dismayed by its lack of progress, the War Department shifted into high gear. That November the government announced that all remaining prisoners in the United States "will be entirely out of private contract work, including agriculture, by the end of February, and will be withdrawn from military work by the end of March, 1946." Moreover, repatriation would no longer be concerned with small groups dependent on haphazard train schedules and available shipping space. From now on, the German prisoners would be shipped from the United States according to the following schedule:

December	1945	60,000
January	1946	70,000

February	1946	70,000
March	1946	83,000
April	1946	43,000 [42]

There it was—a firm commitment! The War Department had not only made clear its policy regarding the ultimate withdrawal of prisoners from domestic labor but also provided the public with the schedules and final date of departure.

The American agricultural community, as expected, received the government's decision without enthusiasm. Farmers bemoaned the nation's agricultural future without continued access to prisoner labor. Angry protests poured into the offices of state agricultural extension services, which swiftly echoed up the political chain. Senators Willis, Kilgore, Millikin, Wheeler, and Maybank, for example, rose in Congress to protest the predicament in which the government had placed their constituents. Representative Mendel Rivers of South Carolina publicly demanded that General Bryan, the Provost Marshal General, personally explain to South Carolinians the logic of the Army's decision.[43] Ultimately, President Truman himself was forced to reexamine the effects of the War Department's policy on the nation's agricultural productivity. Bowing to a combination of political pressure and legitimate concern, on January 25, 1946, he announced a 60-day delay in the repatriation of POWs involved in critical segments of the economy. Even this concession was not sufficient for many of the politicians now caught up in the fervor of their cause, and most demanded that the prisoners be retained beyond this 60-day period. President Truman, noting that free labor would soon become available in abundance, firmly refused to comply. The prisoners would continue to return as scheduled.

The day following the War Department's November 20 announcement was the occasion for a second policy decision. After protracted behind-the-scenes negotiations, the United States declared its approval of a joint Allied plan to transfer 1.3 million of the more than 2 million "American-owned" prisoners in Europe to French control. They were simply "to be used in labor battalions to help rebuild that country." [44] This decision involved a particularly thorny series of problems. While the use of conscript prisoner of war labor was certainly nothing new, the Geneva Convention, America's only guideline, neither sanctioned nor forbade it. Could the POWs be pressed into service even though the war was over? Moreover, could they be passed from one victor nation to another like war booty? The issues were considered by Allied diplomats at several war-time conferences, and after some soul-searching, the War Department reached its decision. On November 4, 1944, Washington privately informed General Eisenhower:

> In order to preserve American and British manpower for combat use and at the same time to make PW labor available for essential work, SHAEF is authorized to turn over as many as possible of the PWs in Europe to the French de facto authority as can be used by them in agriculture and rehabilitation work.[45]

As soon as this secret decision was made to supply prisoner labor to Britain and France (as well as Holland, Belgium, Luxembourg, Yugoslavia, and Greece), the haggling began. France quickly proved to be the biggest stumbling block, demanding at least 1.75 million prisoners, while the representative for SHAEF, Assistant Chief of Staff (G-1) Major General Barker, held firm at 1.3 million. After six months of heated negotiation, the figure of 1.3 million was finally accepted by Paris on June 25, 1945, and the first group of 375,000 Germans was transferred to French control from American holding pens in Europe. The POWs in the United States, of course, were unaware that many of them were slated for the mines and construction sites of Western Europe.

The entire plan almost collapsed, however. The War Department was startled to learn from the International Red Cross that the first contingent of prisoners assigned to France was not being maintained according to the standards of the Geneva Convention. In fact, the Red Cross revealed that starvation conditions existed in the French POW depots. The French admitted that their POWs were in poor health but claimed that it was really due to an American conspiracy to provide them with the worst physical specimens available. General Eisenhower was unconvinced and directed on September 27 that all further transfers be halted. During the following weeks, the French offered various guarantees for the improvement of prisoner conditions, including monitoring by the International Red Cross. Eisenhower was finally satisfied in November, 1945, and the War Department's announcement of November 21 thus signaled the resumption of prisoner shipments to France. Ultimately, 700,000 German POWs were transferred to France, 40,000 to Belgium, 10,000 to Holland, and 7,000 to Luxembourg, though the number which came from camps in the United States is unknown. Despite the logic of the decision to share its POWs with fellow members of the victorious United Nations—to help rebuild Europe,[46] to relieve the burden on both the American and European camps, and to express the public's outrage at recently unveiled Nazi atrocities [47]—it was to be a policy with distasteful ramifications. The most immediate impact of this policy was felt, naturally, in the prisoner of war camps in the United States.

The year 1945 had already been a difficult one for German prisoners in the United States. It began with a government decision to drastically reduce their menus, both to counter the increasingly frequent charges that the Army was "coddling" the POWs and, more realistically, because "the meat supply and other food reserves now on hand are rapidly being exhausted by the increased demands of our armed forces." Civilians, schools, and other institutions were urged to conserve food in order to build up the nation's reserves, and the POW camps were among the first to feel the pinch. According to the government's logic, Article 11 of the Geneva Convention only required that prisoners receive rations equal in *nutritional value* to those furnished to regular base troops; it did not mean that identical items had to be provided. Consequently, rations were immediately cut to a maximum of four ounces of meat per man per day, and items which were in short supply such as fats, canned fruits and vegetables, jams, and sugar were substantially reduced. Camp commanders were instructed to implement the following meat substitutions:

a. Meat from swine will be limited to feet, hearts, livers, kidneys, tails, neck bones . . . and oily pork not acceptable under existing specifications for Army feeding.
b. Meat from veal will be limited to utility grade carcasses. . . .
c. Meat from beef will be limited to shanks, flanks, skirts, livers, hearts, kidneys, ox tails, tripe, brains, and green bones. . . .
d. Fish will be limited to the cheaper grades of salted or round dressed fish. . . .
The caloric value of the ration has been established at a maximum of 3400 calories. . . .
The above changes will be put into effect immediately in all German prisoner of war messes.[48]

Within weeks after V-E Day, beef was served only twice a month, and margarine replaced butter at all times. Eggs became a rarity. More vegetables were added to replace the rationed items, and the camp menus relied heavily on the seasonal change of local produce.

Whatever the merits of the food conservation program to the war effort, most of the interested public clearly believed that the new policy was the War Department's response to revelations of Germany's poor treatment of its American prisoners. As the Allied forces swept across France and Germany, scores of enemy POW camps were liberated. While conditions among the camps varied widely, the American public was shocked to learn that its kindness toward German prisoners in the United States was seldom reciprocated by the other side. Newly-liberated American POWs grimly revealed random episodes of sick comrades who were forced to march 500 miles through snow and rain; of eating cats and fighting over potato peelings; and of German officers who had left starving American prisoners to die by the roadside.[49] The horrors of Auschwitz, Dachau, Buchenwald and Belsen-Bergen were now common knowledge, and the American people were enraged at the barbarism of the German nation. Then came the first fragmentary reports of the notorious massacre of more than 100 American prisoners at Malmedy, Belgium, by an SS unit on December 17, 1944, and many Americans could not help but look at the German POWs with new hostility.[50] Most, therefore, greeted the War Department's food policy with smug satisfaction.[51]

To the prisoners, however, the new diet appeared to be nothing less than childish revenge against members of the enemy armed forces. Since the policy coincided with the end of the war in Europe and the liberation of the American prisoners in German camps, the POWs reasoned that the War Department finally felt safe to do what it had long wanted: to punish the prisoners. Whatever the motivation, the prisoners felt the effects of their new diets very quickly. John Hasslacher, a former prisoner at Camp Trinidad, Colorado, remembered that the food at his camp was never ideal, but that there was enough meat and variety until V-E Day. "The moment the war was over," he recalled, "the daily rations consisted of: porridge with a bit of milk in the mornings, pea soup with lettuce salad and a slice of soft bread (of little nutritious value) at noon and in the evening. I believe coffee or tea was also served." [52] Heinrich Matthias remembers that after the first concentration camps were found in Germany in 1945, his rations were cut down to one third. "But," he emphasizes, "it was still better than what the people in Germany received!" [53] Depending on the availability of local produce at various camps, as well as the length of time until they were repatriated, most prisoners experienced a loss of weight as well as morale. On the average, the men lost about 10 to 12 pounds, although most today concede that it was "lazy fat" which they had put on during their captivity. In fact, the prisoners regarded the new diet as an annoyance more than as a serious problem. Former POW John Schroer recalls:

> For me, at Camp Rucker, it was less the change in diet which upset me, than the hostile treatment we received from the guards. We had always eaten in the same mess hall with the American personnel—their only privilege being able to go directly to the head of the line. After May,

that all changed; and we now ate different diets at two different times. Moreover, we could no longer buy cigarettes at the PX, and there were several surprise inspections to confiscate our earlier tobacco purchases. Fortunately we outsmarted these inspections by hiding our 10 or 15 cartons of cigarettes in the double walls of our barracks; but we knew that our relationship to our guards had certainly changed.[54]

From the American side, the only real objection, interestingly, came from an American agriculturalist in the wheat belt of Kansas. In a public letter to Representative Frank Carlson of Kansas, the superintendent of Fort Hays experimental station, L. C. Aicher, noted somewhat callously that "any farmer knows an underfed horse cannot turn out a good day's work, and humans react the same way." Lending credence to the myth that vengeance had been the motivating force behind the new food policy, Aicher went on to state:

If the Army desires to punish German prisoners for what happened in Germany, that, of course, is the Army's business. However, I do say that such treatment is very unfair to all of us who hire them as laborers and pay good wages for their use. . . .[55]

Aside from the annoyance of a few employers and most POWs (and the unknown damage which such prisoner resentment might have had on success of the reeducation program then underway in the POW camps), the new food policy was accepted by the 370,000 Germans as another unalterable nuisance of their confinement. Besides, the war was finally over, and their attention was riveted on their ultimate repatriation home.

Speculation and rumors consumed the POW communities through the summer of 1945, and the prisoners watched, transfixed, as their future was debated in the newspapers. None was particularly surprised to learn that they would be used to fill the domestic labor ranks until after the Japanese were defeated and the American armed forces demobilized. In any case, conditions in Germany were known to be chaotic: The economic structure had nearly collapsed, the countryside and urban areas were devastated and the Allied powers were still jockeying to solidify their respective zones. In short, the prisoners were content to remain in the relative comfort of their camps, work in agriculture, and wait until their camp commander saw fit to relieve them of their tasks and begin shipping them toward the nearest Port of Embarkation. The War Department's announcement on November 21 that the United States intended to ship prisoners to form labor battalions in France, however, burst among them like a bombshell. "This was nothing more than modern slave trading," Alfred Klein still fumes today. "We all deeply resented such treatment, and I am even today of the opinion that the U.S. foolishly nullified its long effort to instill in us the precious seeds of democracy." [56] Other prisoners expressed the sentiment that if the United States planned to "sell them down the river as slaves," there was little choice between Germany's Nazism and America's Democracy. A substantial number of other prisoners were unconvinced that France deserved rebuilding since "it was France which had declared war on Germany but was beaten." In any case, the prisoners agreed, "the American Air Forces had destroyed France and not the Germans." [57]

If the earlier food restrictions had weakened the delicate foundation of the prisoners' newly acquired democracy, the announcement that many would be sent to France caused the Special Projects Division to lament that the news "almost shot the bottom out of our re-education program." [58] Prisoner despair was compounded by the anxiety of not knowing who would be repatriated directly to Germany and who, by sheer chance, would end up in a labor battalion in Britain or France. In fact, the prisoners would not know their destinations until the very moment they arrived in Europe. But as of December, 1945, these problems were still many months in the future. Indeed, at that moment, there were still 313,234 German prisoners in the United States.

The Trip to Europe

That, however, was about to change. Since the War Department's November announcement, a frenzied effort was underway to ready the remaining POWs for imminent repatriation. At hundreds of branch and base camps across the nation, camp commanders resurrected their original five-page instructions from the previous May and began processing their prisoners. Each man, for example, was provided with a barracks bag, several woolen blankets, a first aid kit, and eating utensils, though the War Department memo itself acknowledged that the real task was not that of providing them with the bare necessities of life but of preventing them from taking too many of their unnecessary belongings. All radios were to be left behind, as well as "cameras, field glasses, binoculars, knives or tools, cigarette lighters, electric razors, foot lockers, suitcases, or other items in short supply." [59] One former POW, Corporal Alfons Heilmann, remembers that:

> I had bought a radio in America. I had lots of things when I was getting ready to leave, but they told us that we couldn't bring all that. I put all

of it in a trunk and shipped it to Nuremberg via the Red Cross. (The trunk arrived in 1950.) [60]

Prisoner luggage was limited, in fact, to a maximum of 30 pounds for enlisted men and 175 pounds for officers.[61] That the authorities were not always successful in curtailing the weight and commodities with which the prisoners left, may be concluded from one representative incident. When a relatively small group of 2,250 repatriated POWs were given a random shakedown upon their arrival in Liverpool, England, they were found to be carrying four million cigarettes in their baggage! [62]

Among the items which the prisoners were restricted from taking with them was American currency. As each camp prepared its prisoners for shipment, canteen coupons were redeemed, canteen profits were distributed, and the prisoners' trust-savings accounts were liquidated. The prisoners were issued government checks, with which they boarded the ships for Europe. The men generally left with about $50.00, though some officers left with several hundred dollars. "We called that $50 the economic miracle of West Germany in post-war days," recalls Wilhelm Sauerbrei, somewhat unrealistically. "It helped save the country, all that money brought home by POW's!" [63] Equipped, processed, and paid, the POWs were now at the mercy of the train and shipping schedules.

As the day of repatriation approached nearer, most prisoners confessed a reluctance to leave the United States. Motivated by a combination of genuine admiration for the American people and their material advantages, and the understandable hesitation to return to the hunger and chaos of post-war Germany, many POWs inquired of the camp authorities about remaining in the country or returning after repatriation. "To tell the truth," writes a former Naval Ensign, Gunter Wedekind, then held in Camp Mexia, Texas, "no one wanted to leave. If I could have, I wouldn't have hesitated. I would have stayed—and even tried to do so, unsuccessfully." [64] As various POW communities were alerted for travel, groups of men—especially those whose homes were now in the Soviet zone of Germany—pleaded to remain behind. Indeed, despite heavy security at the Port of Embarkation at Camp Shanks, New York, three prisoners became hysterical, broke away, and were caught almost immediately, and two others committed suicide. At least one additional prisoner escaped after arriving in England when, on June 20, 1946, POW Joachim Obier broke out of a British transit camp and made for the American Embassy in London to plead to be returned to Texas.[65] The War Department and the State Department, however, held firm: the POWs were leaving, one and all.[66]

Nor were their American guards and nearby neighbors entirely pleased to see them leave. Said one GI at Camp Grant, Illinois:

> Boy, those PWs set a table like it was gonna be for royalty—every knife, fork and spoon is exactly in place. And they're sure good workers. Yessir. I'll sure hate to see 'em go.[67]

In the small community of Kaufman in east Texas, the local women's clubs marked the departure of the prisoners and American personnel from nearby Camp Kaufman with a farewell dance in the camp recreation hall. A full description of the "gala affair"—complete with the fashions worn by the attending chaperons and the varieties of donated sandwiches and soft drinks—duly appeared in the newspaper's Society Notes.[68] Farmers, too, were sometimes personally sorry to see the Germans leave. Despite frequent references to the prisoners as "arrogant individuals" (and an occasional spasm of random violence such as the hushed-up affair in 1944 when two shotgun blasts were fired into a POW camp near West Helena, Arkansas),[69] many farmers viewed repatriation as the parting of friends.

The prisoners continued to depart aboard every available ship en route to Europe. By the end of March, 1946, only 140,606 prisoners remained; by the end of April the number had dropped to 84,209; and by the end of May, only 37,491 German prisoners were still in the United States.[71]

As the men collected at the main Port of Embarkation at Camp Shanks, New York, preparing to board the waiting ships, the scene was nearly always the same. The prisoners shuffled silently past a dock-side processing desk where several American officers checked their names against their rosters; past a few bored guards and curious news reporters; and finally up the gangplank. Hans Werner Richter remembers: "I walked in a giant column of prisoners of war, bent under the weight of my purchases from the camp—a sailor bag on my back, two heavy bags in my hands—my nose pointed toward the asphalt, under the smiles of passersby. That evening, how I detested this America that I had come to so admire. . . ." [72] Most of the men wore their German field caps, though the rest of their attire was a non-descript collection of woolen overcoats, outmoded Class X American uniforms, and random parts of the German uniform. Litter cases, walking wounded, and convalescents, of course, were carried aboard or guided by Red Cross or Army personnel. As if to make use of even the last moment, the Army distributed to each boarding prisoner the latest issue of Der Ruf— which the men silently stuffed into their pockets without reading.[73]

The sea voyage to Europe was generally uneventful. Each returning vessel carried about 3,000 prisoners who spent the nine-day trip to Le Havre doing what they had done throughout their imprisonment. They played soccer, handball, and basketball. Often the ship's stores contained an assortment of musical instruments which the men quickly used to organize jazz or polka groups. Others spent their time engrossed in politics. Hans Werner Richter recalls sourly that "on one side there were the Germans who were still completely infected by Nazism, who didn't accept defeat or considered it only an interim event before the next war. On the other side, those who accepted the conquerors' politics of collective guilt and of false and even dangerous re-education. . . . While we were, of course, all 'anti-Nazis,' I again saw the anti-Semitic demonstrations, the threats and fear and terror. But I kept quiet." [74]

Captain Robert Kunzig of the Special Projects Division remembers it differently. Escorting several thousand graduates from his Fort Getty and Fort Eustis schools, Kunzig recalls waking up one morning to a "horrible banging" directly over his head and went on deck to find the source of the noise. He was pleasantly surprised to find that:

> . . . the mate had passed out chipping hammers to prisoners who had volunteered for extra-gratuitous labor, and they were hard at work chipping the old paint off the *Eufaula.* Captain [Max A.] Rancord was beaming all over; and well he might, for during the nine-days' voyage he was to get virtually all his deck chipped and repainted. The other prisoners were hard at work in the mess halls, in the holds, in fact anywhere where there was a job to be done.[75]

As far as shipboard politics were concerned Kunzig recalls an equally idyllic scene. While strolling across the deck one evening, his curiosity was aroused by the sight of a large group of prisoners engaged in some sort of debate. "I walked back to investigate," Kunzig states, "and stopped short as scraps of conversation reached my ears. I couldn't believe I was hearing correctly, as 'Bill of Rights.' and 'Fourteenth Amendment' floated my way. It was a group of PW's and Americans in a friendly, hot, free-for-all political discussion. Both sides made sense; both knew what they were talking about." [76]

The experience of former German sergeant Karl Schindler, today an American citizen in Cleveland, Ohio, was much more mundane. "God, I was as sick as a dog for nine solid days," he recalls. "I didn't even have the strength to climb to an upper deck for the evening movies." [77]

Alfred Klein heartily concurs. "During the ten days at sea, from New

York to Le Havre, we had storms for eight solid days. The result was many 'offerings' to the sea god, Neptune. Even the ship's company were no exception: on the second day, as the Captain ordered us out of the 'offering places' (the toilets) and into the fresh air—at that very moment, even he reached his critical point and docilely joined us prisoners in line! Maybe he already wanted to show solidarity wth his future NATO allies?!" [78] John Schroer's central memory of that return trip, which he did not share with his fellow passengers, was the fear that the ship might be sunk. "As soon as I learned that our destination was Cherbourg Harbor, I began to worry. (You see, my last assignment in the *Kriegsmarine* before I was captured was to mine that very harbor.) When our ship finally steamed into Cherbourg, I can tell you that I was glued to the porthole, with a very strange feeling in the pit of my stomach. Fortunately, the Allies must have cleared a path through our mine field." [79]

When the ships arrived at Southampton or Le Havre and the prisoners unloaded into waiting truck convoys, Germany seemed tantalizingly close. A three-day train ride, perhaps, would have put them back in their old homes. Then came the disillusionment as random thousands of prisoners were shunted into labor battalions to work in Great Britain or France. Alfred Klein found himself in one of these groups, recalling that "Upon my arrival at Le Havre on May 5, 1946, our worst fears came true. We were not placed on a train to Germany, but were taken ten miles away to a camp at Bolbec. Every POW under forty years of age who was capable of working, had to put in three months for the Frenchmen. I, myself, was lucky and could return to Germany after barely two months, but in many other cases, this time stretched into years." [80] Even anti-Nazi prisoners were not exempt from such treatment, as Karl Schindler was astonished to learn firsthand. "I, who spent my entire 16 months at the anti-Nazi Camp Campbell, Kentucky, and at the branch camp at Maysville, found myself transferred to the huge depot at Reims, France. They took away all of my belongings. Even though I was in French hands only several weeks, it was very unpleasant." [81] Heinrich Matthias found himself escorted off the ship at Liverpool and handed over to the British authorities. "Naturally I was not very happy—the more so since we were not wanted by British labor unions who saw us taking jobs from their unemployed. Even worse, we were used to replace Italian prisoners. To be honest, I was treated more than correctly in England, although the food and accommodations were inferior to those in the U.S., but the British were very badly off themselves at that time. Luckily, it was felt that I would be more useful in helping democracy in Germany and I was sent home after 6 months." [82]

The total distribution of "American-owned" prisoners of war to Allied nations—either directly from camps in the United States, or from the bulging enclosures in Europe—was as follows:

> France received 700,000 German prisoners—of which 200,000 worked on farms, 55,000 in mines, 40,000 in construction, and 30,000 in forestry. The British obtained 175,000 prisoners under an earlier agreement, which, added to their own captives, totaled 385,000 men. Of this total, 85,000 were used to clear rubble, 35,000 mined coal, 20,000 were employed by the Air Ministry for unnamed tasks, and the rest worked in agriculture. Belgium received approximately 50,000 prisoners.
>
> An additional 50,000 were divided between the Netherlands, Scandinavia, Czechoslovakia, Yugoslavia, and Greece.[83]

Depending on the requirements of each country, the majority of POWs generally served in labor battalions for about four to six months, though many thousands were held substantially longer.

The Europeans were not the only ones to utilize prisoner labor. The American Military Government in Germany drew freely from the vast numbers of incarcerated or newly-repatriated prisoners, becoming the largest such employer in the entire Theater. Unlike its Allies, the United States proclaimed the men "Disarmed Enemy Personnel" directly after the war, which on one hand stripped them of any rights under the Geneva Accords, while on the other, enabled them to receive a higher level of treatment than could be offered to the same men as prisoners. The essence of the new designation, of course, was to allow them to be used for any job, however hazardous or distasteful, though the War Department insisted on paying them at the prevailing civilian wage level. Ultimately, more than one million former German captives were used in positions ranging from hospital technicians, civil servants and interpreters, to longshoremen, crane operators, and day laborers. Thousands were put to work as critically-needed coal miners, farmers, and truck drivers. Still others replaced American troops in the daily maintenance of army bases, depots, post exchanges, vehicle repair centers, and railroad terminals. Since the wartime prohibitions established by the Geneva Convention no longer applied, many hundreds of Germans were even pressed into service to clear enemy mine fields.[84] So important were all of these German workers to the American Military Government that the official history of the U.S. Quartermaster Corps declared that "without the . . . prisoners of war, it would have been impossible for the Quartermaster to carry out its mission." [85]

Despite this glowing endorsement, the War Department soon found itself forced to reconsider the continued use of prisoner labor. Back home, there was a rising tide of moral indignation from a growing segment of the American population against the labor program. The most bitter criticism came from the influential *Christian Century*. Referring to the use of prisoner labor in Britain and France as "slave labor," the magazine charged that the "United States cannot escape responsibility for helping to revive and perpetuate a primitive form of slavery. . . . of which every nation concerned has cause to be ashamed of itself." [86] To head off further criticism, and conscious of the need to speed the demobilization of the American forces in Europe, the War Department, during the spring of 1946, began to extricate itself from the POW-labor program in Europe.

Once the decision was reached, American withdrawal moved swiftly. With the exceptions of essential labor, certain high-ranking officers, members of the Waffen-SS, and suspected war criminals, the remaining hundreds of thousands of Germans were offered the standard options of immediate repatriation or being rehired as voluntary civilian workers. While there are no records to indicate the number who chose each option, the captives were released in wholesale lots, with only 31,000 prisoners remaining in American custody by December 31, 1946. The discharge of prisoners proceeded rapidly through the spring of 1947, and on June 30, 1947, the last American-held prisoner of war was officially released, making the United States the first major Allied nation to free its European war prisoners.[87]

France, utilizing the second largest number of German prisoners, held their POWs the longest. Motivated as much by vengeance as by the genuine labor needs of a country which had suffered enormous war damage, the French were extremely reluctant to return the prisoners to Germany. Moreover, the French government could point, with some justification, to the absence of any recognized German government and to the vague provisions of Article 75 of the Geneva Convention which authorized that prisoners of war who were guilty of a "crime or an offense of municipal law . . . may be detained until . . . the expiration of the punishment." The French had little difficulty in viewing the destruction brought to its nation by members of the German military as "a crime" and "an offense of municipal law."

As late as April, 1947, the French government still retained in excess of 440,000 German prisoners,[88] and one can only speculate on the date of ultimate return were it not for American intercession. Beginning no later than April, 1947, the French government was instructed to offer all German prisoners under its control, with special exceptions, a choice between repatriation to war-torn Germany as freed prisoners or remaining in France as salaried, voluntary workers. The men had three months to decide, after which those who opted to leave were shipped out in groups of 20,000 per month. The vast majority chose to be repatriated immediately, though nearly 10,000 remained to work well into mid-1948.[89]

The prisoners who returned home to Germany, either as repatriated POWs or as former voluntary workers, recount similar experiences: First, a memory of the long line of boxcars which carried the men from France to Germany; next, the daydreams of home as the train sped eastward; and finally, the moment when they entered Germany. "As the train approached the border, in the Saar region," recalls a former POW, "I was immediately conscious of a tenseness in the men. I could see it in their eyes. They crowded to the doors for that first glimpse. Then they saw. They saw, and they'll remember for all time. Ruin, desolation, and destruction were framed in that open door. The only sound was the lonely shriek of the engine far ahead." [90] As the trains wound their way through village after village en route to one of the major POW Discharge Centers, local townspeople crowded into the doorway of each boxcar, searching for sons, fathers, brothers. Many brought ersatz coffee or dry bread for the prisoners, though the situation quickly became reversed as the prisoners found themselves passing out chocolate and cigarettes from their camp purchases. When their supplies ran out, Alfred Klein remembers at least one occasion when the prisoners restocked by bilking their American guards. The Americans had brought along a prodigious amount of chocolate and cigarettes to trade on the black market, and the mischievous Klein "provided the young GIs with their first lesson in black marketeering" by purchasing the majority of their goods with worthless German occupation scrip.[91]

Arriving at POW Discharge Center #26 at Bad Aibling near Munich, for example, the prisoners spent between three and four days being processed for the last time. They filled out questionnaires, were fingerprinted, and, moving through a large *Luftwaffe* hangar, completed numerous forms required for their personnel files. Somewhere in the process, their belongings were searched for contraband items, and Alfred Klein, at POW Center #15 at Marburg/Hessen, sourly recalls that justice finally caught up with him. "When I wasn't paying attention, the U.S. guards and the Germans who worked for them, looted my baggage of many of the things I had saved from camp or had 'purchased' on the train home." Finally, at the end of a procedure lasting several days, the prisoners were handed their discharge certificates and 40 marks ($4) in cash. They were free!

A round-robin train of boxcars circulated through the American Zone several times a week, stopping at each Discharge Center, and the newly released German prisoners got free passage to the station nearest their homes. "I was released at Ingolstadt, north of Munich, in February, 1946," recalls Karl Schindler, "and I was too anxious to wait for the Army train. So

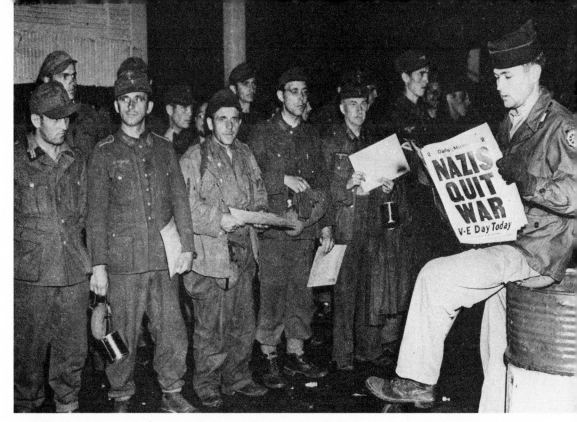

A large group of newly arrived German POWs await processing in New York even as their guard reads about Germany's surrender. *(Wide World Photos)*

German POWs board the U.S. hospital ship *Francis Y. Slanger,* at Camp Shanks, New York, bound for home. *(UPI)*

One of the major POW discharge centers in Germany: Prisoner of War Enclosure #26 at Bad Aibling, Bavaria. From here, special trains took them to all the main railway points in the U.S. Zone, from which they could begin life anew. *(National Archives)*

At each POW Discharge Center, the prisoners were checked for any tattoo marks indicating their membership in the heinous SS. . . . *(National Archives)*

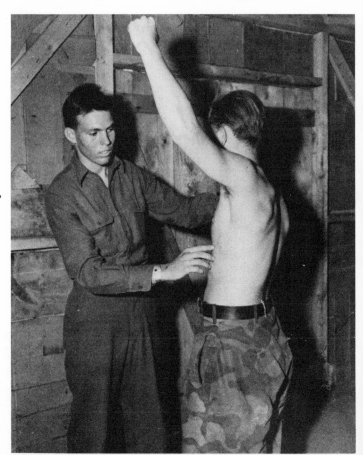

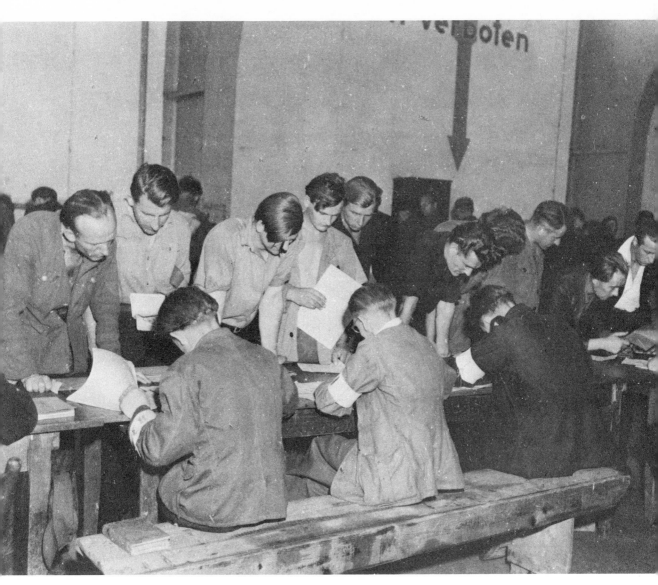

Their records were completed. . . . *(National Archives)*

Each man received 40 marks discharge pay and three days' food ration tickets, and officially became a free man. *(National Archives)*

The members of the Provost Marshal General's Office had every reason to congratulate one another. The POW program had been a success. From left to right: General Omar Bradley; Major General Allen W. Gullion (Ret.); Major General Archer L. Lerch, the Provost Marshal General; Brigadier General B.M. Bryan, Jr., the Assistant Provost Marshal General; and Colonal A.B. Johnson, executive. *(U.S. Army Photo)*

I bribed a train engineer with two cigarettes to sneak me aboard a regular train, and rode all the way to Nuremberg in the locomotive. Unfortunately, my wife had moved in with her parents in a different city and I had to hike 150 km. to finally see her." [92]

In the United States, the remaining prisoners were being funneled into the large base camps from the sprawling network of small branch outposts. Prisoners in Kansas, for instance, poured into Fort Riley from Big Springs, Eskridge, El Dorado, Hutchinson, Lawrence, Ottawa, Peabody, and Topeka; in Pennsylvania, the POWs arrived at Olmsted Field and Tobyhanna Military Reservation from camps in Gettysburg, Indiantown Gap, New Cumberland, Sheffield, and Valley Forge General Hospital; and so it went across the country through the spring of 1946. From the major camps in each Service Command the last trainloads of prisoners moved in to the Port of Embarkation at Camp Shanks, New York.

On July 23, 1946, the Army announced the departure of the last German prisoners in the United States. Through the entire morning of July 22, the 1,388 German officers and enlisted men trudged up the gangplank to begin their final voyage home. The last to leave American soil—a 22-year-old former electrician from Heidelberg—ultimately made seven "last trips" up the ramp at the request of insistent newsmen: three in continuous motion for the newsreel cameras and four with stops at fixed points to satisfy the still photographers. The lines were finally cast off at 3:00 P.M., and the harbor boat *General Yates* slowly steamed down to the Brooklyn Army Base and the waiting transport ship. As the Germans lined the rails of the departing *Texarkana* to take one last look at the receding shoreline of New York, "waving an indifferent farewell," a significant chapter in American history came to a close.[93]

As the last shipload of German prisoners pulled away from shore, Colonel Harry W. Maas, commanding officer of Camp Shanks, turned to a news reporter and sighed, "Thank God, that is over!" And, with the exception of 141 men who were serving prison terms, 134 who were in hospitals or psychiatric wards, and 25 escapees, America's first experience in maintaining nearly 400,000 foreign prisoners of war on its soil was, indeed, over.[94]

CHAPTER VIII

Conclusion

On July 23, 1946, the internment of the 375,000 German prisoners of war, plus the additional 60,000 Italian and Japanese POWs in the United States, was officially over. However unprepared the War Department had originally been, and despite the occasional major problems, there is little question that America's first prisoner of war experience had been a reasonable success. The POW program had not only successfully fed, clothed, housed, entertained, and, in many cases, even reeducated the hundreds of thousands of men in its care; it had also affected events far beyond its immediate responsibility. The severe domestic labor shortage, for instance, had been substantially alleviated by the use of prisoner labor; and the parallel use of the prisoners on nonstrategic military tasks freed large numbers of American troops for shipment overseas.

As the Allied forces fought their way across France and Germany, American commanders found that most German soldiers were aware of Washington's adherence to the Geneva Convention. The knowledge that they would be treated fairly after capture, in spite of what their officers had told them, became a great factor in breaking down the morale of German troops and making them willing, even eager, to surrender. So pronounced was this effect, General Eisenhower declared in a report to Congress, that he was able to drop safe-conduct passes by the millions over enemy lines, promising treatment in accordance with the Geneva Convention, "causing a considerable number to surrender." [1] Had these promises not been true, and believed, victory would have been slower and harder, and a far greater number of Americans would have been killed.

However, one major issue in the prisoner of war program—perhaps the central issue—is mired in controversy. How successful was America's humane treatment of the German prisoners in assuring reciprocal treatment of American prisoners in German hands? From the moment the first enemy POWs arrived in the United States, the War Department acted as though the continued safety and comfort of all American prisoners depended on the level of treatment shown the Germans in American camps. By November,

256

1944, the Committee on Military Affairs of the House of Representatives confidently reported to the American public that, while the general level of care available in Germany was lower than that provided in the United States, Berlin was maintaining its end of the relationship.[2] The public was reassured.

Yet, behind the scenes, the War Department was troubled by reports that the differences in levels of treatment were far wider than originally thought. Red Cross representatives and returning American prisoners brought back stories of badly overcrowded German camps; windows boarded up for lack of window-pane glass; less than one hot shower per month; a severe shortage of drugs and medical supplies; a general lack of food; overwork, often in excess of 12 hours per day, with the low compensation of only 70 pfennigs (28 cents); and, occasionally, cases of brutality by the German guards.[3] As additional American wounded and Protected Personnel were periodically repatriated, and the conditions in the German camps became public knowledge, the War Department was forced to acknowledge that a wide imbalance in POW treatment did, indeed, exist. "Yet, for us to treat with undue harshness the Germans in our hands," declared the Assistant Provost Marshal before Congress, "would be to adopt the Nazi principle of hostages. The particular men held by us are not necessarily the ones who ill-treated our men in German prison camps. To punish one man for what another has done is not an American principle." [4] Whether the War Department's decision to drastically cut the rations and luxuries of its German POWs that very month was, as the prisoners believed, an attempt to do just that is open to conjecture.

Far more ominous, however, were the occasional chilling reports to the War Department concerning actual atrocities against American prisoners, particularly bomber personnel and paratroopers. As early as December 23, 1943, the German government had tried to curtail the early bombing raids over Germany by threatening the Allied governments with reprisals against captured airmen. This threat brought a strongly-worded reply from President Roosevelt that "if these threats are carried out, the governments of the United States and Great Britain will adopt the most drastic measures. . . ." [5] The German government did not follow through with its threat. While there were a number of isolated atrocities committed against American prisoners throughout the war, they were usually the acts of fanatical SS troops. Though it was apparent that the War Department could do little to prevent such random acts of violence, Secretary of War Stimson and the Joint Chiefs of Staff periodically debated the wisdom of issuing some sort of ultimatum. The problems were obvious. Too stern a warning, for example, might be misinterpreted to include all of the German population, thereby stiffening resistance in their war effort; or, such a warning might be used as an effective enemy propaganda weapon as an indication of an Allied effort to enslave the German nation. Most importantly, if such a warning was issued, and greeted with widespread disregard, was the War Department prepared to abandon the dictates of the Geneva Convention? It was not. Secretary Stimson eventually settled on the following course of action:

1. A warning to [enemy] military commanders . . . that they will be held accountable for atrocities committed against prisoners of war in areas under their command;
2. An appeal to the honor code of the German *Wehrmacht* by high-ranking officers of the German Army now in this country;
3. Full publication of incidents and of the names of individuals and units involved . . . with detailed statements as to any punishment meted out to such of them as are captured. . . ;
4. Vigorous protests to the Protecting Power on all atrocities. . . .[6]

The fact that stronger measures were not adopted clearly indicates that the War Department was convinced that the random acts of savagery against American prisoners were not sanctioned by Berlin or the German High Command. But, true to its word, the War Department faithfully catalogued the details of every reported execution of an American prisoner, and where the perpetrators could be identified—by name or military unit—they were eventually hunted down and arrested by the American Military Government.

The War Department was also convinced that the conditions experienced by the 90,000 Americans in German camps, atrocious as those conditions may have been, were often the best that could have been expected in a country which was losing the war. Food, medical supplies, fuel, material for camp construction, all were in desperately short supply. In many areas, the prisoners genuinely fared no worse than the local civilian population. Moreover, the German guards, much like their American counterparts in the United States, were often the least qualified men available. As a result of these difficulties, the conditions in Germany's POW camps were certainly far below those maintained in the United States.

On the other hand, conditions could have been worse. Not only could the German government have consistently withheld what little food and fuel was available, but it could have prevented the distribution of the massive supplies of supplemental food and medical aid provided by the International Red Cross Committee, the American Red Cross, and the British Red

Cross.[7] Without question, these supplies enabled countless thousands of American POWs to survive the hardships of their imprisonment. Part of the reason for Germany's approval of such supplemental supplies was, of course, that it cost them nothing and allowed them to provide as little food as necessary. At the same time, however, evidence indicates that the German government was moderately concerned about unduly upsetting the Allies' commitment to the Geneva Convention, and thereby jeopardizing the safety of their own prisoners in Britain and the United States. Ultimately, the Germans grew to realize the value of the Geneva Convention, and although they periodically exploited America's commitment to the limit, they carefully avoided precipitating a rupture. Consequently, American POWs in German camps, however uncomfortable and harsh the conditions those captive GIs were required to endure, were reasonably assured of their most basic rights. At the end of the war, the American Red Cross could report with justifiable pride that "the fact that over 99% of our American prisoners captured by Germany are now returning home and that the American Red Cross has been able to get a large volume of relief supplies to American and other Allied Prisoners of War are due in great part to the correct observance by the American Army of the Geneva Convention."[8] If for no other reason—and there were many—the protection of the thousands of American prisoners in German hands fully vindicated the POW program. Moreover, the American experience showed that prisoners can be well treated and still be used to the advantage of the capturing power. As such it was strikingly successful.

With the end of the war, the American POW experience receded, unlamented, into the past. At its most visible, the prisoner of war program had been only a minor part of the war effort and had only risen to prominence when the public became concerned with such issues as escapes, coddling, and the continued availability of agricultural labor. That it should have been so quickly forgotten by the government at the end of the war is perfectly understandable; Washington had long since turned its attention to such weighty matters as the conflicts in Greece, Turkey, Palestine, China, and the rising hysteria of the Cold War. In fact, with the exception of an occasional reference to the POW program in the many military analyses of the war, the government has forgotten this significant chapter in America's wartime experience. One unusual reference appeared in a recently-declassified report of 1951, in which the German POW program was reexamined in preparation for the "handling of [Soviet] prisoners of war and defectors in the event of war with the USSR."[9]

Communities which once hosted large numbers of German prisoners have also forgotten those years, as nearby camps gradually disappeared. One by one, the branch camps were shut down during the post-war months and their meager facilities sold at auction. In accordance with the Surplus Property Act of 1944, the War Assets Administration disposed of all camp material, on a bid basis, in order of four priorities: United States Government agencies had first choice; then came the Reconstruction Finance Corporation (for resale to small businesses); then state and local governments; and finally nonprofit institutions. In Alabama, for example, on February 20, 1947, the *Birmingham Age-Herald* carried a large advertisement describing the sale of thousands of feet of water pipe, electrical equipment, and a telephone communications system which were no longer needed at the deactivated camp at Aliceville. Subsequently, the camp land itself was broken into parcels and sold to the City of Aliceville and to private citizens.[10]

At Milwaukee's Billy Mitchell Field, where more than 3,000 German prisoners worked to assemble batteries for the Army Transport Command, the barracks were turned over to the county to house the overflow from the House of Corrections farm in nearby Franklin, Wisconsin, and patients from the Asylum for the Chronic Insane in Wauwatosa. One mess hall was moved to Oak Creek to serve as an American Legion Memorial Hall; another was acquired by a Bayview Amvet Post for a clubhouse. One huge barrack building was sold to St. James Catholic Congregation in Franklin for use as a classroom.[11]

Camp Swift, seven miles north of Bastrop, Texas, was one of the largest army training and transshipment camps in Texas and at its wartime peak, held nearly 90,000 GIs and 10,000 POWs. Like dozens of other camps in Texas (Camps Bowie, Russell, Fannin, and Mexia), Camp Swift was deactivated directly after the war and sold back to the original landowners. Today, the former camp site contains scattered housing developments and ranches, a University of Texas cancer research center, and a unit of the Texas National Guard. A new government structure is about to be built on the old site after nearly two years of dogged public protest; ironically, considering the earlier use of the area, the $11 million structure will be a minimum security prison, a Federal Youth Center for youthful first offenders.[12]

In Arkansas, the three main camps were gradually phased out during the summer of 1946. Camps Chaffee and Robinson were located on permanent military reservations and their facilities were dismantled or used for other purposes over the years. Camp Dermott has all but disappeared, the land sold and divided into private plots, the huge city of barracks auctioned off for a pittance and hauled away, building by building. Not even a highway sign or historical plaque marks the desolate site.[13]

At Fort McClellan, Alabama, the sprawling headquarters of the army's Military Police training center, where several thousand German prisoners spent the war years, a few interesting items still remain. For instance, the ornate carved wooden bar in the Officer's Club is intact, though very few of the countless cheery Americans who have celebrated "happy hour" there are aware of its origins. Also intact is the POW-carved stonework located throughout the base. Of particular interest at McClellan is the German Memorial Service which is held on the third Sunday of each November, at a distant corner of the base cemetery. Each year, the dozen or so German POWs buried there are honored in a bilingual ceremony, presided over by a German liaison officer from Redstone Arsenal, with music supplied by the 14th WAC Army Band, and with decorations provided by both the German Embassy in New Orleans, and the dependent wives who make up the German Club of nearby Anneston, Alabama. The American chaplain recites prayers in English and German, and the WAC Army Band strikes up the national anthems of both countries. "It is," according to Betty J. Kelley, Public Relations Officer at Fort McClellan, "a short but very impressive ceremony." With these exceptions, however, any knowledge that German prisoners had once spent nearly four years at this base is almost unknown.

Papago Park, Arizona, the scene of the notorious mass escape in December, 1944, today includes two golf courses, the Phoenix Zoo, picnic areas, lakes, bicycle trails, headquarters of the Arizona National Guard, a blood bank, a trap-and-skeet club, the Hy-View Community Subdivision, and the Scottsdale Elks Club Lodge #2148.[14]

So it went across the country. Camps were sold back to the communities, turned into farmland or real estate developments, and all but forgotten. The only building remaining at the site of Camp Hearne, Texas, once bustling with activity, is the headquarters of the former commanding officers, which was purchased by the local post of the American Legion. Otherwise, all that remains are the crumbling foundations of the barracks that housed the POWs, a disused cemetery, and a waist-high concrete model of a medieval German castle, built by the prisoners and now almost completely overgrown with weeds. Only the persistently curious chronicler or the accidentally lucky tourist may stumble across an old camp site or happen to chat with a local resident who might dimly recall the appearance of the prisoners of war in his community. In the main, however, those days have slipped by, unrecorded, except as they added a few more varicolored threads to the rich tapestry of local American history.

If the local communities have forgotten about those days, the prisoners have not. Following their discharge, the newly-released men returned home to look for whatever remained of their earlier lives. The first moments in their home towns, after so many months or years of isolated captivity, were almost surrealistic.

"When a group of us arrived at the Munich station," explains former Captain Fritz Lempp, "people just stared at us. We were still wearing our army uniforms and medals—and we felt that they were looking at us with hostility. Someone finally approached me, and touching my uniform whispered 'It's no longer the time to wear that!' " [15]

Some found their families in good health and their homes intact, while others were not so fortunate. And then began the gradual process of rejoining German society with all the problems experienced by demobilized soldiers of any army after any war. Conditions in postwar Germany were frightful with severe shortages of both food and fuel. The POWs who spent the war years in the United States, however, were better prepared than the average German to make the best of the situation. An adequate diet, plenty of recreation, and perhaps several years of heavy farm work produced thousands of men who were returning home healthier and stronger than when they left. For those prisoners who returned to find themselves in the Russian Zone, the situation was far less optimistic. In fact, their very survival during the early postwar years often hinged on the arrival of food packages from concerned friends in the United States, almost always from the farm families who employed them. Such a relationship existed between the John E. Lane family of Kaufman, Texas, and their former farm-helper, POW Heinz Koppius. "Without your latest food parcel," wrote Koppius from the town of Altenburg in the Soviet Zone as late as January 25, 1949, "I would not, perhaps, remain alive. I always think of the happy time I spent in the Land of Plenty, the U.S.A., and of the kindness of your family. Here I feel like a stranger, and would be blessed if once more I could be one of your hands on your Texas farm." [16] Thousands of such relationships deteriorated with the passage of the years, and most of the former prisoners in the Eastern sector, including Heinz Koppius, were seldom heard from again.

A large portion of those situated in the American and British Zones fared much better. Since many had learned English while in captivity, they were readily employed by either the U.S. Army or the American Military Government and became part of the voluntary work force discussed earlier. Others joined the civilian municipal government as interpreters, clerks, civil servants, and liaison personnel to the American forces. As conditions improved, and civilian jobs more to their liking became available, the prisoners drifted into other fields. Today, Willibald Bergmann manufactures hand towels in Nuremberg; Hein Severloh sells insurance; Fritz Lempp is a bookseller; Von Arnim is the director of a medical clinic; Hans Werner Richter became a well-known writer, as did Carl Amery. Werner Baecker became the New York representative for a German television network.[17] Karl Janisch rose to become a justice on the Austrian Supreme Court; Walter Horst Littmann is a senior chemist in the German Department of Defense in Koblenz. Heinrich Matthias is today a high official in the Import-Export Department of Germany's second largest financial institution, the Dresden Bank. Alfred Klein went back into the military when the *Bundeswehr* was authorized in 1956, and today is a Lieutenant Colonel in the German Air Force and head of the Air Warfare Department at the German Air Force Academy at Fürstenfeldbruck. Eberhard Scheel is a co-partner of the well-known manufacturer of printing inks, Dr. Carl Milchsack Company, Frankfurt am Main. Reinhold Pabel, as noted earlier, is a contented bookseller in Hamburg. Scratch many an influential German today, in fact, and you will find an ex-POW who learned his basic English in Texas, Virginia, Oklahoma, or Tennessee. It is not unusual for former American officers traveling in Germany to be recognized and approached by their former prisoners, as U.S. Army General George Honnen learned when he was suddenly embraced by the manager of his hotel in Berlin in November, 1963.[18]

Indeed, if one were to visit the two most important German officials in the United States—Baron Rüdiger von Wechman, President of the General Assembly of the United Nations, and Brigadier General Hans A. Link, German Military Representative to the United States and Canada—one might be startled to hear that their years in the *Afrika Korps* were finished in Camps Carson and Trinidad, Colorado.

Predictably, a large number of former prisoners wanted to emigrate to the United States. A survey of more than 20,000 departing POWs at Camp Shanks, New York, indicated that "approximately 74 percent of the German prisoners of war who were interned in this country left with an appreciation and a friendly attitude toward their captors." [19] These attitudes, combined with the poor conditions in Germany, prompted many to begin the long and complicated process leading to a quota immigration visa. A few enterprising applicants, tired of waiting after only several years, searched blindly for American sponsors by writing to random government and municipal officials and by direct appeals through community newspapers near their former camps. In a letter to the *Columbia* [South Carolina] *Record*, for example, a former POW at nearby Fort Jackson, Julius Huhnke of Frankfurt, appealed to anyone who might remember him. "I want to go back to the U.S.A., and must have a sponsor for affidavit of support," he implored.[20] A letter to the *Dallas Morning News* from Hans-Jochen Sembach, living in the north German province of Schleswig-Holstein, was a bit more dramatic. "My finest period of war imprisonment was spent near you at Camp White

One of the few remaining traces of the POW experience in the United States is this yearly ceremony at the German War Memorial Cemetery, Fort McClellan, Alabama, in which officials from both armies commemorate those prisoners buried there. *(U.S. Army Photo)*

Rock. . . . Those were good times. . . . For me, Texas is unforgettable, with her great forests and plains, and her bold yet honorable young men. . . . I want back in old Texas, and I can work." [21]

There is no way of determing the number of former prisoners who were ultimately successful in emigrating to the United States. Although the United States admitted about 30,000 immigrants from West Germany per year from 1948 through 1960, the government did not maintain any figures as to the possibility of their wartime imprisonment in the United States.[22] One former prisoner who now lives in Los Angeles, John Schroer, has made an informal study over the years and suggests that approximately 5,000 such men now live in America.[23]

Occasionally, one may stumble onto a former German prisoner. As a composite, he has long since become a naturalized citizen, is generally successful in business, and, like any of the tens of millions of immigrants to the United States over the past century, has gratefully embraced the American dream. John Schroer is a good example. A former ensign in the German Navy who spent a year at Camp Montgomery, Alabama, Schroer was determined to return to the United States from the moment he was repatriated to Germany. "I was twenty-one years old, and had grown to like the American style of living," he laughs. "I suppose I was looking for adventure. My father had died in my absence, everything had been destroyed. It was up to me to take care of my mother and sister. So I began to work toward immigration." His jobs with the American Military Government—first as an economics expert, then as a liaison officer to German industry, and ultimately as an administrator of Marshall Plan funds—provided him with plenty of sponsors when the quota finally opened in 1951. A routine background check delayed his final visa for another year, but in 1952 Schroer finally arrived in the United States. He got a job as a company auditor, excelled at his work, and began climbing the corporate ladder. Today, John Schroer is the successful vice-president of the huge insurance conglomerate, the Swett & Crawford Group in Los Angeles, a subsidiary of Continental Corporation.[24]

Other former POWs have been located across the country. Guenter Mellage is a master carpenter in High Point, North Carolina; Karl Schindler is an industrial engineer in Cleveland; Henry Kemper is a gardener-handyman in Portland, Oregon. Others have been randomly found employed as a mechanic, a portrait painter, a well-known opera singer, and a chemist.

Even those thousands of former prisoners who chose to remain in Germany have not forgotten about their wartime experiences in America. Because the Germans saw their incarceration as an extension of their military service, the men often meet for periodic reunions in both Germany and the United States. More than 300 prisoners from Camp Mexia, Texas, for example, gathered for a reunion at Heidelberg in June, 1983, and crammed their signatures on several 6″ × 8″ photo postcards, which they mailed to favorite guards and townspeople. Periodically, announcements appear in the German newspapers and in military journals to remind former prisoners from a particular camp about an upcoming reunion or a social function. There is even an organization, the *Forschtungstelle für Deutsche Kriegsgefangenen*, in Munich, which loosely acts as a clearinghouse for all such POW-related matters.[25]

The veterans of the elitist *Afrika Korps (Verband Deutsches Afrika Korps)* are particularly active—banquets, charter flights, lapel insignias, and all the rest—maintaining no less than two periodicals: *Die Oase* and *Deutsch-Tunisische Rundschau*. Through these bulletins former POWs among them keep in touch, exchange birthday greetings, and even draw upon one another's professional services. So popular are such reunions that the *Verband* publishes directories of those held in various American camps, with their former ranks, birthdates, current occupations, and addresses.

A number of former prisoners, now affluent German and Austrian citizens, return to their old camp sites periodically to stroll through the "old neighborhood," noting changes and reminiscing. Alfred Klein made three such pilgrimages to Foley, Alabama: Christmas, 1959; May, 1961; and October, 1972. On each occasion, Klein and his wife were courted like visiting dignitaries. A similar reception awaited Heinrich Matthias, now a wealthy German banker, when he returned to Kaufman, Texas, in 1966. As his bus pulled into the downtown terminal, after an absence of 20 years, he was deeply moved to see nearly half the town's population eagerly awaiting his arrival. The same scene took place at McAlester, Oklahoma; Concordia, Kansas; Houlton, Maine; Douglas, Wyoming; Crossville, Tennessee; and literally dozens of other former camp sites. In what must be one of the more ironic epilogues of the POW experience in the United States, three former prisoners, Werner Richter, Walter Littmann, and Karl Janisch, were honored by Mexia, Texas, Mayor Billy Pollard in October, 1971, with certificates of honorary citizenship of Mexia and the Keys to the City.[26]

It was during one of these reunions, this one at Hearne, Texas, with a former POW named Wilhelm Sauerbrei, that the experience of the prisoners was best summarized. While driving up from Houston in a car full of community dignitaries and reporters, the former *Afrika Korps* corporal regaled the occupants with stories and recollections about his camp days.

"You must have had it pretty easy," the Houston reporter commented.

"I'll tell you, pal," Sauerbrei said confidently, "if there is ever another war, get on the side that America isn't, then get captured by the Americans— you'll have it made!" [27]

Appendix

Major German Prisoner of War Internment Camps in the United States

Camp Algoma, Idaho
Camp Aliceville, Alabama
Camp Alva, Oklahoma
Camp Angel Island, California
Camp Ashby, Virginia
Camp Ashford, West Virginia
Camp Atlanta, Nebraska
Camp Atterbury, Indiana
Camp Barkeley, Texas
Camp Beale, California
Camp Blanding, Florida
Camp Bowie, Texas
Camp Brady, Texas
Camp Breckinridge, Kentucky
Camp Butner, North Carolina
Camp Campbell, Kentucky
Camp Carson, Colorado
Camp Chaffee, Arkansas
Camp Claiborne, Louisiana
Camp Clarinda, Iowa
Camp Clark, Missouri
Camp Clinton, Mississippi
Camp Como, Mississippi
Camp Concordia, Kansas
Camp Cooke, California
Camp Croft, South Carolina
Camp Crossville, Tennessee
Camp Crowder, Missouri
Camp David, Maryland
Camp Dermott, Arkansas

Camp Douglas, Wyoming
Camp Edwards, Massachusetts
Camp Ellis, Illinois
Camp Evelyn, Michigan
Camp Fannin, Texas
Camp Farragut, Idaho
Camp Florence, Arizona
Camp Forrest, Tennessee
Camp Gordon Johnston, Florida
Camp Grant, Illinois
Camp Gruber, Oklahoma
Camp Hale, Colorado
Camp Hearne, Texas
Camp Hood, Texas
Camp Houlton, Maine
Camp Howze, Texas
Camp Hulen, Texas
Camp Huntsville, Texas
Camp Indianola, Nebraska
Camp Jerome, Arkansas
Camp Lee, Virginia
Camp Livingston, Louisiana
Camp Lordsburg, New Mexico
Camp McAlester, Oklahoma
Camp McCain, Mississippi
Camp McCoy, Wisconsin
Camp McLean, Texas
Camp Mackall, North Carolina
Camp Maxey, Texas
Camp Mexia, Texas

Camp Monticello, Arkansas
Camp New Cumberland, Pennsylvania
Camp Ogden, Utah
Camp Opelika, Alabama
Camp Papago Park, Arizona
Camp Peary, Virginia
Camp Perry, Ohio
Camp Phillips, Kansas
Camp Pickett, Virginia
Camp Pima, Arizona
Camp Polk, Lousiana
Camp Popolopen, New York
Camp Pryor, Oklahoma
Camp Reynolds, Pennsylvania
Camp Jos. T. Robinson, Arkansas
Camp Roswell, New Mexico
Camp Rucker, Alabama
Camp Rupert, Idaho
Camp Ruston, Louisiana
Camp Scottsbluff, Nebraska
Camp Shelby, Mississippi
Camp Sibert, Alabama
Camp Somerset, Maryland
Camp Stewart, Georgia
Camp Stockton, California
Camp Sutton, North Carolina
Camp Swift, Texas
Camp Tonkawa, Oklahoma
Camp Trinidad, Colorado
Camp Van Dorn, Mississippi
Camp Wallace, Texas
Camp Wheeler, Georgia
Camp White, Oregon
Camp Wolters, Texas

Fort Benjamin Harrison, Indiana
Fort Benning, Georgia
Fort Bliss, Texas
Fort Bragg, North Carolina
Fort Crockett, Texas

Fort Curtis, Virginia
Fort Custer, Michigan
Fort Devens, Massachusetts
Fort Dix, New Jersey
Fort DuPont, Delaware
Fort Eustis, Virginia
Fort Gordon, Georgia
Fort Greely, Colorado
Fort Jackson, South Carolina
Fort Kearny, Rhode Island
Fort Knox, Kentucky
Fort Leavenworth, Kansas
Fort Leonard Wood, Missouri
Fort Lewis, Washington
Fort McClellan, Alabama
Fort Meade, Maryland
Fort Niagara, New York
Fort Oglethorpe, Georgia
Fort Ord, California
Fort Patrick Henry, Virginia
Fort Reno, Oklahoma
Fort Riley, Kansas
Fort Robinson, Nebraska
Fort D. A. Russell, Texas
Fort Sam Houston, Texas
Fort Sheridan, Illinois
Fort Sill, Oklahoma
Fort F. E. Warren, Wyoming

Edgewood Arsenal, Maryland
Eglin Army Air Field, Florida
Glennan General Hospital, Oklahoma
Halloran General Hospital, New York
Hampton Roads Port of Embarkation, Virginia
Indiantown Gap Military Reservation, Pennsylvania
Holabird Signal Depot, Maryland
McCloskey General Hospital, Texas

Memphis General Depot, Tennessee

New Orleans Port of Embarkation, Louisiana

Olmsted Field, Pennsylvania

Pine Bluff Arsenal, Arkansas

Richmond ASF Depot, Virginia

Tobyhanna Military Reservation, Pennsylvania

Westover Field, Massachusetts

Monthly Census of Prisoners of War
Interned in the Continental United States

End of Month	Total	German	Italian	Japanese
1942:				
May	32	31	—	1
June	33	32	—	1
July	49	39	—	10
August	65	55	—	10
September	177	130	—	47
October	183	130	—	53
November	431	380	—	51
December	1,881	512	1,317	52
1943:				
January	2,365	990	1,313	62
February	2,444	1,026	1,356	62
March	2,755	1,334	1,359	62
April	5,007	2,146	2,799	62
May	36,083	22,110	13,911	62
June	53,435	34,161	19,212	62
July	80,558	54,502	25,969	87
August	130,299	94,220	35,986	93
September	163,706	115,358	48,253	95
October	167,748	119,401	48,252	95
November	171,484	122,350	49,039	95
December	172,879	123,440	49,323	116
1944:				
January	174,822	124,880	49,826	116
February	177,387	127,252	49,993	142
March	183,618	133,135	50,136	347
April	184,502	133,967	50,168	367
May	186,368	135,796	50,164	408
June	196,948	146,101	50,278	569
July	224,863	173,980	50,276	607
August	243,870	192,868	50,272	730
September	300,382	248,205	51,034	1,143
October	338,055	248,781	51,032	1,242
November	360,455	306,856	51,156	2,443
December	360,281	306,581	51,071	2,629

End of Month	Total	German	Italian	Japanese
1945:				
January	359,687	306,306	50,561	2,820
February	360,996	307,404	50,571	3,021
March	365,954	312,144	50,550	3,260
April	399,518	345,920	50,304	3,294
May	425,871	371,683	50,273	3,915
June	425,806	371,505	50,052	4,249
July	422,130	367,513	49,789	4,828
August	415,919	361,322	49,184	5,413
September	403,311	355,458	42,915	4,938
October	391,145	351,150	35,065	4,930
November	358,419	324,623	29,539	4,257
December	341,016	313,234	25,696	2,086
1946:				
January	286,611	275,078	11,532	1
February	208,965	208,403	561	1
March	140,606	140,572	33	1
April	84,209	84,177	31	1
May	37,491	37,460	30	1
June	162	141	20	1

SOURCE: ASF WD Monthly Progress Reports, sec. 11, Administration. Copy in Lewis, *Prisoner of War Utilization*, pp. 90-91.

Notes

Chapter I

1. For an excellent insight into these difficulties, see Anthony Cave Brown, *Bodyguard of Lies* (New York: Harper & Row, 1975), pp. 62–91, 247–48, 270; and Viscount Alanbrooke, *Diaries,* ed. Sir Arthur Bryant, 2 vols. (London: Collins, 1957), 1:357.

2. Quoted in J. Lawton Collins, *War in Peacetime: The History and Lessons of Korea* (Boston: Houghton-Mifflin, 1969), p. 35.

3. War Office secret telegram, Field Marshal Sir John Dill, London, to Viscount Halifax, Washington. June 7, 1943, WO 32/10714, No. 68A. Public Records Office, London.

4. Shunning the recommendations of its planning department to accept only 50,000 of the 175,000 POWs offered by London, the U.S. Joint Chiefs of Staff ultimately consented to accept the entire lot. There were two conditions, however: London had to agree to give Washington prior notice before each shipment, and she had to pledge to provide the necessary facilities to retrieve them when the war was over. *See* Memo, Major General George Grunert, Ch. Adm. Svc., SOS to CF, SOS, September 15, 1942. Subject: Plan for Acceptance of Custody of Prisoners of War Taken by the United Nations, cited in George Lewis and John Mewha, *History of Prisoner of War Utilization by the United States Army: 1776-1945* (Pamphlet No. 20–213, Washington: Department of the Army, 1955), p. 87.

5. The only estimates available to the officer in the field were contained in a single paragraph on prisoners of war:

> Knowing the approximate strength of the enemy's forces and the daily loss rates for gunshot injuries and gas injuries, the approximate number of prisoners of war can be estimated. For an enemy force in a major war, if the average daily loss rate per 1,000 is estimated to be .53 for gunshot and .24 for gas injuries, the average daily rate for captured and missing will be 10% of the gunshot and gas injuries or approximately .08 per 1,000. Hence, for an enemy force of 1,000,000, the average daily number of prisoners captured will be 80. As prisoners are not received at a uniform rate, special preparations must be made for the reception of unusual numbers when important engagements are anticipated. As a factor of safety, facilities for three or four times the estimated numbers per month should be available.

FM 101–110, War Department, *Staff Officers' Field Manual,* June 15,

1941, Section III, subsection 169. Subject: Estimate of Prisoners of War, p. 236.

6. "Office of the Provost Marshal General; World War I. A Brief History," File, Office of the Chief of Military History, Department of the Army, Washington, D.C., January 15, 1946, pp. 390–391; also Major General J. A. Ulio, The Adjutant General, to Commanding Generals, All Service Commands, War Department Memorandum, W580-1–43, June 15, 1943, AG 383.6. Stephan M. Farrand Collection, Hoover Institution of War, Revolution, and Peace, Stanford University, California.

7. "Provost Marshal General: A Brief History," p. 391.

8. If time permitted, the prisoners filled out the standard basic personnel record (W.D., A.G.O., Form No. 19–2), although a shorter form (W.D., A.G.O., Form No. 19–3) was available during harried conditions.

9. Prisoners had been encouraged to keep the original tags to this point by a firm notice printed on the back in several languages: "NO TAG = NO FOOD. DO NOT LOSE OR MUTILATE."

10. "Not so," argued Colonel Peter Rordam, a retired career Army intelligence officer, now living in Brownsville, Texas. "Not when I was there, anyway." Reminiscing about his years as an intelligence officer in North Africa, Colonel Rordam recalled:

> There were at least two or three German linguists in every front-line unit and plenty available back at the 'repo-depo' [replacement depot] in Casablanca. We even had university professors on tap. There was

nothing haphazard about our interrogation of the PWs—they were interrogated with great care by intelligence officers who knew as much about the subjects under discussion as the prisoners. Information taken from one prisoner was always compared with information taken from another. We used every psychological gimmick allowed.

Interview with Peter Rordam, February 10–13, 1976. Colonel Rordam's experiences, unfortunately, do not appear to typify the overall registration-interrogation picture, especially during 1943.

11. Reinhold Pabel, *Enemies Are Human* (Philadelphia: The John C. Winston Company, 1955), pp. 131–132, 141.

12. Interview with Henry Kemper, April 16, 1978. For an interesting description of the volume and variety of war souvenirs—from hand grenades to airplane parts—see Harold V. Boyle, "Odd Souvenirs Pass the Censors," *Kansas City Star,* July 2, 1943.

13. These British "Special Methods" troubled Washington and served as a continued obstacle to Allied cooperation. Moreover, a number of these practices backfired on the British. Following the disastrous British amphibious raid on Dieppe, on August 19, 1942, for example, the Germans captured the Operational Orders which stated that "Wherever it is possible, the hands of prisoners will be bound, so they cannot destroy their papers." In retaliation, the German High Command ordered *all* British prisoners to be shackled, as of 14.00, September 3d, causing: a British and Canadian counter-retaliation; a POW riot in Camp Bowmanville, On-

tario, on October 10; protests and coun-
ter-protests through the Swiss Legations
and the IRCC; discussions in Parlia-
ment; and a final, public threat by
Prime Minister Churchill that: "... a
careful record will be kept of the total
number of man-days on which British
and Canadian prisoners are chained,
and that double this number will be
served in chains by the Officer Corps of
the German Army after the defeat and
surrender of Germany has been
achieved." The German authorities
ceased the practice of shackling British/
Canadian POWs on November 22, 1943.
All relevant documents are available in
the British War Office Records, 32/
10719, Public Records Office. Also see
The Times (London), October 8, 9, 10,
12, 1942.

14. *See:* Air Ministry, Confidential
Orders, Series A, A.22–A.27/43, February 25, 1943, WO 32/11121. Public Records Office.

15. Priority Telegram, Major Gen-
eral E. C. Gepp, Director, Prisoners of
War, to Viscount Halifax, July 28, 1943,
No. 4977, WO 32/10723. Public Records
Office.

16. *See:* Prisoner of War Information Bureau Memos, WO 32/11121.
Public Records Office.

17. The importance of quickly re-
moving the POWs from the war zone
was best illustrated by the fact that when
Prime Minister Churchill was en route
to Washington in June, 1943, for a series
of war strategy conferences with President Roosevelt, his ship was not exempt
from POW duty, and he found himself
traveling with several thousand German
prisoners. See *The New York Times,*
June 8, 1943, p. 1.

18. Yvonne E. Humphrey, "On
Shipboard with German Prisoners,"
American Journal of Nursing, XLIII, No.
9 (September 1943), pp. 821–22.

19. Ibid.

20. For a detailed analysis of the
efforts by the various agencies to establish jurisdiction, see Edward Pluth's outstanding work, "The Administration
and Operation of German Prisoner of
War Camps in the United States During
World War II" (Ph.D. diss., Ball State
University, 1970), pp. 90–93.

21. Colonel A. P. Scotland, *The
London Cage* (London: Evans Brothers,
1957), p. 70.

22. Pabel, *Enemies Are Human,* pp.
147–8.

23. A large collection of censored
POW mail may be found in the Stephen
M. Farrand Collection, Hoover Institu-
tion of War, Revolution, and Peace. *See
also:* Memo, Swiss Legation to the U.S.
Department of State, July 9, 1943, De-
partment of State Records. For the State
Department's conciliatory response,
See: Memo, Department of State to
Swiss Legation, September 20, 1943, File
Number 711.62114 RG, 59, Department
of State Records. National Archives.

24. Henry Kemper interview, April
18, 1978.

25. *See: New York Herald Tribune,*
December 3, 1944.

26. Ibid.

27. *See: The New York Times,* September 27, 1943. p. 21.

28. Ibid., February 20, and March
10, 1944.

29. Lewis and Mewha, *Prisoner of
War Utilization,* pp. 84, 86.

30. United States Congress. House
of Representatives. Committee on Military Affairs. "Investigation of the National War Effort." House Report 1992,
78th Congress, 2nd sess. November 30,
1944, p. 11.

31. Maxwell S. McKnight, "The Employment of Prisoners of War in the United States," *International Labour Review,* 50, no. 1 (July, 1944), p. 49.

32. Arthur M. Kruse, "Custody of Prisoners of War in the United States," *The Military Engineer,* 38 (February, 1946), p. 71.

33. "The Employment of Prisoners of War in Great Britain," *International Labour Review,* 49, no. 2 (February, 1944): pp. 191–96.

34. Memorandum, John Mason Brown, Special War Problems Division, Department of State, "German Generals in the United States Custody," August 8, 1944. Farrand Collection, Hoover Institution.

35. Memorandum on visit to POW Camp Clinton, Mississippi, July 12–13, 1944. Farrand Collection, Hoover Institution.

36. *See, for example:* "Captives May Use U.S. Housing Units," *New York Times,* March 17, 1944, p. 19.

37. Third Service Command, "Proceedings of Prisoner of War Conference," September 29, 1944, pp. 9–10. Farrand Collection, Hoover Institution.

38. Pluth, "Administration and Operation of German Prisoner of War Camps," pp. 135–39.

39. General Bryan, "Prisoners of War," Conference of Service Commands, Fort Leonard Wood, Missouri, July, 1944, pp. 14–15. Farrand Collection, Hoover Institution. For a fascinating description of General Somervell, see Charles J. V. Murphy, "Somervell of the S.O.S.," *Life,* March 9, 1943, pp. 83–84.

40. Seventh Service Command, "Conference of PW Commanders," March 24, 1944, p. 33. Farrand Collection, Hoover Institution.

41. United States Congress. House of Representatives. Committee on Military Affairs. House Report 728, "Investigations of the National War Effort," 79th Congress, 1st Sess., June 12, 1945, Washington, D.C., p. 10.

42. "Fraternization and Low Morale of U.S. Guards," PMGO, *Reference Manual on Prisoner of War Administration,* Fort Sam Houston, Texas. 4–4.3, AA, Vol. 4, C–1, tab 117. Office of the Chief of Military History.

43. "Eight Germans Slain, 20 shot by Guard at Prisoner Camp," *New York Times,* July 9, 1945, pp. 1, 20. Bertucci's widowed mother blamed her son's actions on the appendectomy he received some five years earlier. "Something must have happened to him as a result of the spinal injection," reasoned Mrs. Bertucci, "otherwise he would never have shot those men in Utah."

44. John D. Millett, *The Army Service Forces: The Organization and Role of the Army in World War II* (Washington, D.C.: Office of the Chief of Military History, Department of the Army, 1954), p. 371.

45. James H. Powers, "What to Do With German Prisoners," *Atlantic Monthly,* November, 1944, p. 46.

46. Bernard Gufler, "Indoctrination of German Prisoners of War," Reorientation File, Provost Marshal General Operations.

47. War Office Directive, U.M. 1297, A.G.1.B. 19.7.41, Appendix A, B, C, WO 199/405. Public Records Office.

48. War Office Directive to All Commands, Reference 0103/2839. 16.11.40. WO 199/404. Public Records Office.

Chapter II

1. Terry Paul Wilson, *"Afrika*

Korps in Oklahoma: Fort Reno's Prisoner of War Compound," *The Chronicles of Oklahoma,* 52, no. 3 (Fall 1974), p. 361.

2. Van Horn interview, March 10, 1976.

3. Beverly Smith, "The *Afrika Korps* Comes to America," *American Magazine,* August, 1943, p. 28; "State Gets Three War Projects," *The* [Nashville] *Tennessean,* June 30, 1942.

4. William Arthur Ward interview, March 23, 1978.

5. Robert Devore, "Our 'Pampered' War Prisoners," *Collier's,* October 14, 1944, p. 58.

6. Smith, *"Afrika Korps,"* pp. 28–29.

7. *See:* R. A. Radford, "The Economic Organization of a POW Camp," *Economica,* 11 (November 1945): pp. 189–201.

8. The more humorous POWs quickly dubbed the "PW" designation as meaning *"Pensionierte Wehrmacht"* or German Army Pensioner.

Periodically, the Army had difficulties with local high school pranksters who painted "PW" on their clothing as a joke. The incidents became so numerous that on April 25, 1945, the Army publicly warned that such pranksters could be mistaken for escaped prisoners and possibly shot "if an order to halt is disregarded." " 'PW' Signs No Joke," *New York Times,* April 26, 1945, p. 25.

9. In contrast to the American reception of prisoners which depended largely on the disposition of the individual camp commander and his personal philosophy regarding the treatment of his prisoners, the British authorities were governed by a standardized, if inflexible, rule book. The official War Office booklet, *Orders for Prisoner of War Camps in the United Kingdom* (February, 1941), covered in 51 pages every imaginable situation, regulation, and required speech.

10. Within hours of their arrival at the POW camp on Angel Island, in San Francisco Bay, the prisoners had adapted to their new homes. "Barrack walls were plastered with leggy pictures of Rita Hayworth, Paulette Goddard, Greer Garson, Janet Blair, Ann Miller, Diana Barrymore. They even had a demure shot of Brenda Frazier and a 'Petty girl' from *Esquire,* making the 'V' sign with her fingers." Roger A. Johnson, "Nazi Prisoners Like It at West Coast Camp," *The Washington Daily News,* June 12, 1943.

11. Major General Archer L. Lerch, Provost Marshal General, "The Army Reports on Prisoners of War," *The American Mercury,* May, 1945, pp. 541–42; also *The Washington Post,* June 8, 1943.

12. Report to Mr. Weingaertner, Swiss Legation, From Johannes Oertel, M/Sgt. and POW Spokesman, Camp Clinton, Mississippi, July 12, 1944, p. 6. Farrand Collection, Hoover Institution.

13. McKnight, "Employment of Prisoners of War," p. 52. The POWs were entitled to purchase beer, even when their camps were located in "dry counties" where the sale of alcoholic beverages was prohibited. *See,* for example: *Fort Worth* [Texas] *Star-Telegram,* June 20, 1945.

14. Martin Tollefson, "Enemy Prisoners of War," *Iowa Law Review,* 32 (November, 1946), p. 57. The British did not find themselves similarly moved regarding their prisoners' eating habits and offered a much more spartan diet: a POW's weekly rations contained 14 oz, meat, 4 oz. margarine, 126 oz. bread, 9 oz. flour, 13 oz. oatmeal, 10 oz. sausage, 56 oz. fresh vegetables, 2 oz. cheese, 6

oz. tea or coffee, 7 oz. sugar, etc. *See:* A. J. Fisher, "394,000 German Prisoners of War," *The Central European Observer,* October 25, 1946, pp. 342–343.

15. U.S. Congress, "Investigations of the National War Effort," June 12, 1945, p. 8.

16. For detailed menus, as directed by the War Department, *See:* Memo to Commanding Generals of All Service Commands from Quartermaster General, "Guide for Use in Prisoner of War Messes," SPQSS 430.2, May 25,1944, 8 pp.; War Department Supply Bulletin SB10-232, "Italian Service Unit Menu Guide," August 24, 1945, 15 pp. Farrand Collection, Hoover Institution.

17. John Mason Brown, "German Prisoners of War in the United States," *The American Journal of International Law,* 38 (April, 1945), p. 204.

18. *See, for example:* T. W. Salmon, "A Preventable Type of Mental Disease in the Allied Expeditionary Force," Memo to the U.S. Surgeon-General, 1918; A.T.M. Wilson, "Report to the War Office on Psychological Aspects of the Rehabilitation of Repatriated Prisoners of War," Directorate of Army Psychiatry, 11/02/2, London, May 1944; Alexander Janta, "The German Ego in Defeat," *Plain Talk,* April, 1947, pp. 10–13; and finally, Dr. Johann Gottschick, "Neuropsychiatrische Erkrankungen bei deutschen Kriegsgefangenen in USA im Lichte Statistischer Betrachtungen," *Archiv für Psychiatrie und Zeitschrift Neurologie,* 185 (1950): pp. 491–510.

19. Letter from Alfred Klein, Munich, Germany, April 22, 1976.

20. "Nazi Officers Keep Busy in Colorado Prison Camp," *Kansas City Star,* June 11, 1944.

21. When the camps and their libraries were first constructed, little thought was given to the type of material on the shelves. Indeed, the new American administrators most probably did not read German, and if they did, they certainly had more important duties than the careful culling of hundreds of books for evidence of pro-German sentiment. In any case, what would have constituted such a sentiment? Statements against the United States? What about our then-ally the Soviet Union? Would a book, for example, which dwelled on a facet of American life or history of which we are not proud, perhaps *Uncle Tom's Cabin,* be grounds for the book's removal? On the other hand, wouldn't the removal of such a book from the shelves constitute an indictment of the very democratic process which the authorities were trying so hard to show to the prisoners? The Special War Problems Division of the State Department would ponder these issues for nearly a year before releasing a confidential five-page list of 225 German authors whose books were not approved for POW reading. Memo, Brigadier General Edward F. Witsell, Acting Adjutant General, to Commanding Officers, Prisoner of War Camps. Subject: German Authors Not Approved for Prisoner of War Camps, November 26, 1944. CONFIDENTIAL. SPX 383.6 (17 Nov. 1944) OB-S-SPMGA-M, MNE/gc 2B-939 Pentagon. Farrand Collection, Hoover Institution. This directive would be part of the massive reeducation program, discussed later. *See also:* A. C. Breycha-Vauthier, "Reading for Prisoners of War as Seen From Geneva," *Library Quarterly,* 11 (October, 1941), pp. 442–47.

22. "We went to the movies quite often," recalls Friedrich Hohman, a former POW at Fort Custer, Michigan. "We saw a lot of films in color, which in Germany was a rarity. I saw . . . Charles

Vidor's *Gilda* with Rita Hayworth and Glenn Ford; Hawks's *To Have and Have Not* with Humphrey Bogart and Lauren Bacall; Wyler's *Mrs. Miniver* with Greer Garson, etc." Daniel Costelle, *Les Prisonniers* (Paris: Flammarion, 1975), p. 136.

23. Memo, HQ ASF to all Service Commanders. Subject: Suggested List of Approved Motion Picture Programs for POW Camps. November 2, 1944, SPX 383.6, EVH/gc 2B-939 Pentagon. Farrand Collection, Hoover Institution.

24. For a complete list of every POW newspaper, see John Arndt (ed.), *Microfilm Guide and Index to the Library of Congress Collection of German Prisoner of War Newspapers Published in the United States from 1943-1946* (Worcester, Massachusetts: Clark University, 1965). For a review of similar camp newspapers published by American POWs in Germany, see Marion Hale Britten, "Newspapers in European Prison Camps," *American National Red Cross, Prisoners of War Bulletin,* 1, no. 4 (September, 1943), p. 4; and " 'Barbs and Gripes' at Stalag IIB," Ibid., 2, no. 10 (October, 1944), p. 10.

25. *Camp Report,* Camp Shelby, Mississippi, "Educational and Social Activities," p. 2. Farrand Collection, Hoover Institution.

26. *Inventory:* Special Service Stock Room, XO Recreation Room, Recordings, Prisoner of War Camp, Camp Campbell, Kentucky, no date. Farrand Collection, Hoover Institution.

27. In addition to such donations and canteen fund purchases, the POWs were able to draw upon a small annual Christmas gift from the Third Reich and His Holiness Pope Pius XII. For the Christmas of 1944, the 380,000 German captives in the United States collectively received the sum of $3,561.81. Farrand

Collection, Hoover Institution.

28. *Camp Report,* Camp Clinton, Mississippi, Johannes Oertel, PW Spokesman to Swiss Representative, July 12, 1944. Farrand Collection, Hoover Institution.

29. *Camp Report,* Camp Campbell, Kentucky, Georg Rupprecht, PW Spokesman to Swiss Representative, September 10, 1944. Farrand Collection, Hoover Institution.

30. Pabel, *Enemies Are Human,* p. 159.

31. For an official translation of the complete text, see *Letter of the German Red Cross,* May 13, 1944, to the Spokesman of Fort McClellan, SWP:EC. Farrand Collection, Hoover Institution.

32. An original copy of this *Studiennachweis für Kriegsgefangene* (gem. Verfuegung OKW 2f24.30c Kriegsgef. Allg. [IIIO Ns. 4407-42 vorn 30.6.1942]) may be found in the Farrand Collection, Hoover Institution.

33. HQ ASF, PMGO, "Universities Sponsoring Prisoner of War Camps," Tab 23, 4 pp. Office of Military History. *Also see:* John Hammond Moore, "Hitler's *Afrika Korps* in New England," *Yankee,* June, 1976, pp. 85-86. For a description of the recreational programs available to American POWs, see "Studies and Sports in German Prison Camps," *American National Red Cross, Prisoners of War Bulletin,* 1, no. 4 (September, 1943), pp. 1, 5; and "A First Contact Across Barbed Wire," Ibid., 2, no. 5 (May, 1944), p. 5.

34. Letter from Baron Rüdiger von Wechmar, May 16, 1978.

35. *Kaufman* [Texas] *Herald,* May 6, 1976; Letter from Alfred Klein, April 22, 1976.

36. "Western Prison Camp Revives Old Germany," *New York Times,* November 7, 1943, p. 14.

37. "War Prisoners Garden," *New York Times,* June 28, 1945, p. 16.

38. *Kansas City Star,* June 11, 1944.

39. Norman L. McCarver and Norman L. McCarver, Jr., *Hearne on the Brazos* (San Antonio: San Antonio Century Press of Texas, 1958), p. 79.

40. Interviews with Val Horn and J. Fort Smith, Mexia, Texas, March 10, 1976.

41. "Nazi Prisoners Aid Red Cross," *New York Times,* February 17, 1945, p. 10.

42. "Prisoners Give $2,371 to Charity," *New York Times,* October 6, 1945, p. 15.

43. *The Dermott* [Arkansas] *News,* April 22, 1945.

44. TM19–500, Chapter 2, Section X, para. 65, 2.43; John Hammond Moore, *The Faustball Tunnel* (New York: Random House, 1978), pp. 108–109.

45. Pabel, *Enemies Are Human,* pp. 156–57.

In at least one camp community, the acquisition of currency was organized and aggressive. Former *Oberleutnant* Klaus Michaelson recalls that at Camp Ruston, Louisiana:

We had already made a good amount of money with our whiskey we sold to the Americans; then we turned to other things. Our sentinels had to guard six hours at a stretch, and one day a group of our boys succeeded in infiltrating the first line of barbed wire entanglements, then climbed the ladder which led to the observation post, and opened the door of the lookout post without making a sound. ... The sentinel was sleeping, and we took his machine gun, the belts of ammunition, and slipped back to the camp. We then threw pebbles against the windows of the tower. The American woke up bewildered. Before he could sound the alarm, we shouted to him, "If you want your gun, that will be 10,000 cigarettes."

Half an hour later we had the cigarettes. There were no consequences.

So there you are; we now had a well-stocked treasury, permitting us to buy sporting goods and finance the escapes.

Costelle, *Les Prisonniers,* p. 143.

46. For an excellent investigation into a little-known subject, *See:* Radford, "Organization of a P.O.W. Camp," also "The Points System in Prison Camps," *American National Red Cross, Prisoners of War Bulletin,* 1, no. 3 (August, 1943), p. 9.

47. John Schroer interview, March 18, 1978.

48. Chaplain John Dvorovy, "Religion in Prisoner of War Camps," *The Army and Navy Chaplain,* July–August 1945, p. 17.

49. Ibid.

50. "Swedish Chaplains Here," *The New York Times,* March 24, 1945, p. 9.

51. Memorandum from Army Chaplain's School to All Graduates. Subject: Hints for Chaplains Assigned to PW Camps, September 1943, p. 1. Farrand Collection, Hoover Institution.

52. Dvorovy, "Prisoner of War Camps," p. 17.

53. Letter from Karl-Heinz Theiler, Kiel, Germany, January 5, 1976.

54. Letter from Alfred Klein, Munich, Germany, April 22, 1976.

55. John Schroer interview, March 18, 1978.

56. Pabel, *Enemies Are Human,* p. 148.

57. Camp Praise by German POWs in Camp Trinidad, Colorado. Farrand Collection, Hoover Institution.

58. Powers, "German Prisoners," p. 47.

59. Costelle, *Les Prisonniers,* p. 28.

60. A representative letter appeared in "Prison Camp Menus Criticized," *New York Times,* December 24, 1943, p. 12.

Chapter III

1. David Hinshaw, *The Home Front* (New York: G. P. Putnam's Sons, 1943), p. 245.

2. Charles I. Bevans, comp., *Treaties and Other International Agreements of the United States of America, 1776-1949,* 12 Vols. vol. 2: Multilateral, 1918-1930 (Department of State, Washington, D.C.: Government Printing Office, 1969), p. 944.

3. Lewis and Mewha, *Prisoner of War Utilization,* p. 89.

4. *List of Prisoner of War Labor,* Camp Shelby, Mississippi, September 14, 1944. Farrand Collection, Hoover Institution.

5. Powers, "German Prisoners," p. 46.

6. For a complete description of the POW savings and trust system, together with illustrative charts, graphs, and sample forms, *see:* War Department, *Circular No. 10,* January 5, 1943, 47 pages.

7. Major Maxwell S. McKnight, "The Employment of Prisoners of War in the United States," *International Labour Review,* Volume L (July 1944), p. 62; Walter Rundell, Jr., "Paying the POW in World War II," *Military Affairs,* 22, (1958), pp. 123-24.

8. Letter from John Schroer, May 20, 1976.

9. HQ, ASF, *Army Service Forces Manual, M-811, Handbook for Work Supervisors of Prisoner of War Labor,* July, 1945, pp. 7, 15.

10. *Minutes,* Conference held in General Styer's Office, October 1, 1945. Subject: Conference on Employment of Prisoners of War. Military Police Command, AFWESPAC, 383.6 Prisoners of War, Book 3, DPRB, TAG, as quoted in Lewis and Mewha, *Prisoner of War Utilization,* pp. 254-255.

11. U.S. Congress, "Investigation of the National War Effort," June 12, 1945, p. 8; *also* Lewis and Mewha, *Prisoner of War Utilization,* p. 254.

12. *Memorandum,* Robert R. Nathan, Planning Committee, War Production Board, to Donald M. Nelson, Chairman, War Production Board. Subject: Manpower, November 7, 1942, SECRET. Policy Documentation File: Log No. 1891, Class No. 241 C, RG 179, Modern Military Branch, National Archives (MMB-NA).

However critical the nation's manpower shortage, however, it was evidently not enough to offset employers' racial prejudices. Interned Japanese-Americans who were shipped from their camps in California and Arizona to relieve the labor shortage in the Midwest, for example, were refused employment and driven out by angry townspeople. *See:* the *Chicago Sun* and the *Chicago Tribune,* April 26, 1943.

13. Joseph T. Butler, Jr., "Prisoner of War Labor in the Sugar Cane Fields of Lafourche Parish, Louisiana: 1943-1944," *Louisiana History,* 14, no. 3 (Summer 1973), p. 286.

14. United States War Department, Technical Manual, TM 19-500, *Enemy Prisoners of War,* October, 1944, p. 5.1;

"Priorities in Allocation of Services of Prisoners of War," *Monthly Labor Review,* 58 (June, 1944), p. 1189.

15. War Manpower Commission, Region X, Regional Bulletin No. 337. "Utilization of the Services of Prisoners of War Labor," April 13, 1944, p. 5, War Manpower Commission Records. RG 179, MMB-NA.

16. "Rivers Protests Rule on Use of War Prisoners," *Charleston* [South Carolina] *News and Courier,* May 9, 1944.

17. The safety records of both the military and those industries which used POW labor were remarkably good. Taking as an example the most dangerous type of work—the shipment and storage of high explosives—the following statistics were prepared by the Safety Branch, Industrial Security Division of the Provost Marshal General's Office. The composite injury rate for the month of April, 1944, for instance, at ten major arsenals and ordnance depots was 5.7 per million man-hours of work. The relative safety of this operation is demonstrated by comparison with 9.2 for all Army Service Forces Depots during the same month and the national rate of 18.2 for all industries. No POW deaths were reported. "Reclamation of Explosive and Inert Ordnance Material," Safety Branch, Industrial Security Division, PMG, May 1945, Employment of German POWs, RG 160, MMB-NA.

Far more dangerous to the POW laborers were the possibilities of traffic accidents en route between camp and work site. *See:* "15 Nazi Prisoners Killed, 9 Others Hurt When Train Hits Truck in Michigan," *New York Times,* November 1, 1945, p. 6.

18. Merrill R. Pritchett and William L. Shea, "The *Afrika Korps* in Arkansas, 1943–1946," *The Arkansas Historical Quarterly,* 37, no. 1 (Spring 1978), p. 15. In New York and New Jersey where little space existed for branch camps, the WMC, the National Housing Agency, and the Federal Public Housing Authority planned to turn vacant housing units over to the POWs. *See:* "Captives May Use U.S. Housing Units," *New York Times,* March 17, 1944, p. 19.

19. Butler, "Prisoner of War Labor," p. 284.

20. Lewis and Mewha, *Prisoner of War Utilization,* pp. 128–129; "47,000 War Prisoners Pick Crops," *New York Times,* November 21, 1943, p. 35; "Farmers Ask for Germans," *New York Times,* March 30, 1944, p. 24; "War Prisoners Working on Southwest's Farms," *New York Times,* October 10, 1943, p. 8; "War Prisoners for Big Spinach Harvest," *Kansas City Star,* November 24, 1943.

21. Walter W. Wilcox, *The Farmer in the Second World War* (Ames, Iowa: Iowa State College Press, 1947), pp. 93–95.

22. "Prisoner Earnings Rise," *New York Times,* November 23, 1944, p. 14.

23. Wilcox, *The Farmer in the Second World War,* p. 95.

24. Interview, Wilma Wiley, Bastrop County Commissioner, September 10, 1976.

25. Quoted in Robert Warren Tissing, "Stalag-Texas, 1943–1945, The Detention and Use of Prisoners of War in Texas during World War II," *Military History of Texas and the Southwest,* 13 no. 1 (Fall 1976), p. 28.

26. There was only a wisp of union opposition to the appearance of war captives in southern cotton fields. In November, 1944, members of the Southern Tenant Farmers Union were called

on by their national convention meeting in Little Rock, Arkansas, to picket all cotton plants employing POW labor. Their influence on the program was negligible. "War Prisoner Labor Fought," *New York Times,* November 16, 1944, p. 8.

27. Lewis and Mewha, *Prisoner of War Utilization,* pp. 128–129.

28. "War Prisoners Are Solving the Feed Harvest Problem," *The Weekly Kansas City Star,* September 27, 1944.

29. Tissing, "Stalag-Texas," p. 29.

30. Butler, "Prisoner of War Labor," p. 293, note 30.

31. Ibid., p. 294.

32. Moore, "Hitler's *Afrika Korps,*" p. 86.

33. Quoted in Tissing, "Stalag-Texas," p. 29.

34. *Weekly Kansas City Star,* September 27, 1944.

35. "Nazis Hoe Cotton," *Business Week,* June 19, 1943, p. 18.

36. Letter from Alfred Klein, April 22, 1976.

37. Costelle, *Les Prisonniers,* pp. 113–114.

38. Ibid., p. 116.

39. Ibid.

40. Ibid., pp. 116–117.

41. Interestingly, the prisoners' concern for American Negroes did not go entirely unreciprocated. There evidently was fairly strong pro-Axis sentiment among a portion of American Negroes, who recognized some truth in the comments noted above. [*See:* Richard M. Dalfiume, "The 'Forgotten Years' of the Negro Revolution," *Journal of American History,* 55 (June, 1968): pp. 90–106; and Mary Penick Motley, comp. and ed., *The Invisible Soldier: The Experience of the Black Soldier, World War II* (Detroit: Wayne State University Press,

1975).] On the other hand, American blacks had no hesitation in striking back when such ideology led to racial slurs: "Negro Troops Beat Italian Prisoners," *New York Times,* August 16, 1944, p. 7.

42. "Camp Dix POWs in Kosher Meatpacking," *New York Times,* January 19, 1945, p. 14. *Also see:* "PWs Collect Newspaper on Square," *Huntsville* (Texas) *Item,* March 9, 1944; "Nazi Prisoners Make Jam," *New York Times,* October 5, 1943, p. 7; Rockford, Illinois, *Register Republic,* March 21, May 19, May 21, 1945, to name a small sampling.

43. A major difficulty which did not directly concern POW labor arose with the fall of fascist Italy on September 8, 1943, and its subsequent shift to the Allied side. In order to remedy the embarrassment of imprisoning the now Allied troops, the United States declared all Italian POWs, 53,607 in number, as "cobelligerents," a definition which stipulated that although the Italian captives could not be released, the United States could continue custodial care without the restrictions of the Geneva Convention. Henceforth, Italian prisoners would be given relative freedom and utilized for jobs which were otherwise prohibited to German and Japanese prisoners.

44. It was, indeed, true that the disease rate (colds, flu, minor infections) was much higher among prisoners of war than among civilian labor due to overcrowded conditions, drafty barracks, and the psychological trauma of recent capture and displacement. For a detailed description of every facet of the POWs' health and nutrition, see Stanhope Bayne-Jones, M.D., "Enemy Prisoners of War," *Preventive Medicine in World War II,* vol. IX: Special Fields,

ed. Ebbe Curtis Hoff, Ph.D., M.D., Office of the Surgeon General, Department of the Army (Washington, D.C.: 1969), pp. 394–400, 411–18.

45. "War Prisoner Pay is Held Inviolate," *New York Times,* February 12, 1944, p. 15.

46. Ibid.

47. Letter, Secretary of War Stimson to J. J. Pelley, President Association of American Railroads, June 28, 1943, quoted in Lewis and Mewha, *Prisoner of War Utilization,* p. 140.

48. "Rail Unions Angry, Harrison Asserts" *New York Times,* October 15, 1943, p. 13.

49. "Rail Unions Refuse to Have War Captives for Fellow Workers as Army Arranged," *New York Times,* October 15, 1943, p. 9.

50. "Wants Paper Field Classed Essential," *New York Times,* August 13, 1943, p. 23.

51. Memorandum, J. H. Ward, Operations Vice Chairman, War Production Board, to H. G. Batcheller, War Production Board, August 6, 1943, Log No. 1853, Class No. 551.244 C. RG 179, MMB–NA.

52. "Offers Plan to Bar Paper Shortages," *New York Times,* August 19, 1943, p. 23. No mention was made in the final program that the Army's labor battalions were to be composed only of Negroes.

53. *See:* "War Prisoners to Cut Pulpwood," *New York Times,* November 24, 1943, p. 11; "Says Prisoners Will Cut Wood," *New York Times,* December 7, 1943; "War Prisoners to Cut Pulpwood," *New York Times,* February 1, 1944, p. 29; "Nazis to Camp Upstate," *New York Times,* April 30, 1944, p. 3; and War Department, Prisoner of War Circular No. 1 (1944 Series), Subject: "Policies Governing Uses of Prisoner of War Labor in Pulpwood, Logging, and Lumbering Industries," January 1, 1944. For a complete investigation of the use of prisoners in the logging industry of one state, *see* Edward J. Pluth, "Prisoner of War Employment in Minnesota During World War II," *Minnesota History* (Winter 1975): pp. 290–303.

54. "Tighter Control of Paper Forecast," *New York Times,* February 17, 1944, p. 23. By June, 1944, the number had reached 11,000 prisoners.

55. The records of the War Production Board contain a number of field reports which itemize the high cost and low productivity of POW utilization. *See:* The Statement of Costs of Typical Prisoner of War Detail, Canal Wood Corporation, Conway, South Carolina, June 28, 1944; and Letter, Vice President of West Virginia Pulp and Paper Company, to Curtis M. Hutchins, Chief, Pulpwood Production Branch, Paper Division, War Production Board, April 3, 1945. Log No. 2384, Class No. 551.244, RG 179, MMB–NA.

56. Letter, Claude Ballard, International Vice President, International Woodworkers of America, to Donald Nelson, War Production Board, November 10, 1943. Log No. 1853, Class No. 430.44, RG 179, MMB–NA.

57. Letter, Ilmar Koivunen, President, Timber Workers Union, Local No. 29, Duluth, Minnesota, to Dreng Bjornaara, Director, War Manpower Commission, St. Paul, Minnesota, November 15, 1943, Class No. 430.44, RG 179, MMB–NA.

58. Report, Rex W. Hovey, Director, Paper Division, to Lawrence W. Lombard, Assistant General Counsel, War Production Board. Subject: Prisoners of War Pulpwood Program, June 2, 1944, Log No. 2364, Class No. 551.244, RG 179, MMB–NA.

59. *Rockford* [Illinois] *Morning Star,* March 15, 1945.

60. "Captives Aiding Farmers," *New York Times,* August 8, 1943, p. 15.

61. "*Afrika Korps* Men Build Dam in U.S.," *New York Times,* May 31, 1943, p. 19.

62. *Rockford Morning Star,* November 29, 1945.

63. "German Farm Labor in New England," *New York Times,* October 22, 1944, p. 6.

64. U.S. Congress, "Investigation of the National War Effort," June 12, 1945, p. 8.

65. "Captives Forced to Work," *New York Times,* May 21, 1945. p. 21.

66. Costelle, *Les Prisonniers,* pp. 112–113.

67. Herston Cooper, *Crossville,* (Chicago: Adams Press, 1965), pp. 92–93.

68. Edward C. Malewitz, M.D., *Thanks, Miss O'Brien* (New York: Vantage Press, 1977), p. 131. Dr. Malewitz is today a staff physician at the Student Infirmary, Southwest Texas State University, San Marcos, Texas.

69. Farrand Collection, Hoover Institution.

70. "German Prisoners Strike," *New York Times,* July 7, 1944, p. 17.

71. "Striking Prisoners Penalized," *New York Times,* June 22, 1944, p. 5.

72. "Nazis Push Camp 'Strike,'" *New York Times,* March 3, 1945, p. 7.

73. Lewis and Mewha, *Prisoner of War Utilization,* p. 171.

Chapter IV

1. "Memorandum addressed to German Soldiers," *German Forces Handbook* (1944), 383.6 POW Rights, Office of Chief of Military History. In an effort to protect the identical rights of American prisoners in German camps, the War Department dutifully adhered to these requirements. *See, for example:* German translation of the Articles of War *(Militaerstrafgerichtsordnung),* made available to all German captives (War Department, 1944, Reference ASF Circular No. 296) and the German-published *Verhalten in Kriegsgefangenschaft (How to Behave as a Prisoner of War),* Fuehrungsstab Ic., Berlin, August, 1944, 16 pp.

2. U.S. Congress, "Investigations of the National War Effort," June 12, 1945, p. 10; *Washington Post,* April 29, 1945; and *New York Times,* April 29, 1945, p. 16.

3. "Office of the Provost Marshal General: A Brief History," p. 479.

4. With Teutonic thoroughness, the Committee often prepared a written report analyzing each aspect of the abortive attempt and assigning blame or praise to the individuals involved. For an example of such a report, see the Farrand Collection, Hoover Institution.

5. William E. Kirwan, "German Prisoners of War," *Bulletin of the Bureau of Criminal Investigation, New York State Police,* 9, no. 8 (August, 1944), pp. 1–4.

6. Costelle, *Les Prisonniers,* pp. 153–57.

7. "POW Camp was Mexia Attraction," *Mexia* [Texas] *Daily News,* June 30, 1971; "World War II POWs Come Back to Texas," *Dallas Morning News,* October 10, 1971. The best sources of information regarding prisoner escapes, often are not camp reports or PMGO records but newspaper articles. In contrast to the spartan terseness of military reports, the media tried to investigate

and describe every facet of the escape including interviews with camp personnel and a follow-up after the inevitable recapture.

8. "Stalag Hearne—A Reminder of the Home Effort," *Bryan* [Texas] *Eagle,* October 14, 1973; interview with Norman L. McCarver, Jr., Hearne, Texas, October 15, 1975; and McCarver and McCarver, Jr., *Hearne on the Brazos,* p. 83.

9. "German PW Escapes and Holds Job Here," *New York Times,* April 5, 1946, p. 8.

10. "Nazis Dug 200-Foot Tunnel Through Rock to Flee From Arizona Camp, Colonel Says," *New York Times,* December 27, 1944, p. 10.

11. "25 Nazi Prisoners Escape; 6 Caught in Arizona Manhunt," *New York Times,* December 26, 1944, pp. 1, 11.

12. "Foil War Prison 'Break,' " *New York Times,* August 9, 1944, p. 19.

13. "Nazis Made A Tunnel," *New York Times,* November 9, 1943, p. 13.

14. Costelle, *Les Prisonniers,* p. 163.

15. War Department, *Prisoner of War Commanders Regional Conference,* 1944, Army Service Circular 161, pp. 33–35. Farrand Collection, Hoover Institution.

16. War Department, "Preventing Escapes," PW Circular No. 4, January 7, 1944, Section II. Farrand Collection, Hoover Institution. The War Department's position concerning sentries who injured or killed prisoners of war was transmitted to all service commanders in a "Restricted" directive as follows: "... Where a thorough investigation into the death of a prisoner of war fully discloses that the sentry involved was beyond any doubt justified in his action ... he should not be tried by court-martial ... It is considered unlikely that a sentry would be brought to trial by a Federal or State court for the killing of an enemy prisoner of war where a high official of the United States, such as the commanding general of a division or of a service command, has determined that no *prima facie* case existed." Service Commanders were admonished not to disclose the government's position "lest it be misunderstood by the public, by other governments, or by sentries as implied consent to careless or irresponsible use of firearms." AFS Circular No. 203, June 4, 1945 (PMGO, Prisoner of War Operations).

17. "Nazi Scorn in Kansas," *Kansas City Star,* January 16, 1944.

18. "Kills 2 War Prisoners," *New York Times,* November 6, 1944, p. 21.

19. "Nazi Shot Twice Trying To Escape," *New York Times,* July 29, 1944, p. 15.

20. "Guard, a Veteran, Kills 3 War Prisoners, Declares They Seemed Ready to Rush Him," *New York Times,* August 2, 1945, p. 9.

21. "Cleared in Shooting of Nazi," *New York Times,* February 12, 1945, p. 13.

22. "Canada Gets Back Nazi Flier," *New York Times,* May 8, 1942, p. 3; "Curbs at Border Opposed in Canada," *New York Times,* May 10, 1942, p. 25; "Treason Writ Asked; First In This War," *New York Times,* May 23, 1942, p. 7.

23. Moore, *The Faustball Tunnel,* pp. 71–73.

24. "Freed Nazi Captive Gets 5 Years," *New York Times,* July 21, 1944, p. 6.

25. "Embraces in Treason Trial"; "Guilty Only of a Plot," *Kansas City Star,* August 6, 11, 1944.

26. U.S. Congress. House of Representatives. 79th Congress. 1st Sess., Re-

port No. 59, "Relating to Escapes of Prisoners of War and Interned Enemy Aliens," February 7, 1945. Ibid., Senate 79th Congress, 1st Sess., Report No. 180, "Relating to Escapes of Prisoners of War and Interned Enemy Aliens," April 10, 1945.

27. "Aided Captive Germans," *New York Times,* November 24, 1945, p. 23; interview with Special Agent Michael Griffin, Federal Bureau of Investigation, Washington, D.C., April 15, 1977.

28. "Mother of 3 G.I.'s Held as Having Aided Nazi," *New York Times,* November 11, 1945, p. 7; interview with Michael Griffin, Federal Bureau of Investigation.

While American aid to escaped POWs was hardly a frequent occurrence, neither was it entirely restricted to German escapees.

A well-publicized case in point concerned an Italian family in Brooklyn which had offered safety to escaped Italian POWs from nearby Camp Shanks, not once but twice. The first time, POW Giuseppe Cimino was arrested in the Terranova's Brooklyn apartment in April, 1945. The family claimed that the POW had entered the apartment in their absence, and no arrest was made. When Cimino escaped again four months later, this time with a friend, Pietro Salpa, and both were later found in a furnished room obtained for them by Mrs. Terranova, the family was arrested by the F.B.I. and brought to trial. For details, see "3 Held as Aiding 2 Escaped PW's," *New York Times,* January 16, 1947, p. 11. For other cases regarding Italian POWs, see "20 Italians AWOL At Camp Kilmer," *New York Times,* October 30, 1944, p. 21; "Italians Back in Camp," *New York Times,* October 31, 1944, p. 21; and "Italian Fugitives Held," *New York Times,* November 24, 1946, p. 48.

29. Interview with J. Fort Smith, Mexia, Texas, August 7, September 9, 1975. Arnold Krammer, "When the *Afrika Korps* Came to Texas," *Southwestern Historical Quarterly,* 80, no. 3 (January, 1977): pp. 247–82.

30. *The Bryan* [Texas] *Eagle,* October 14, 1973; interview with Norman McCarver, October 15, 1975.

31. "Visiting Germans Take Look at Abilene Store," *The Abilene* [Texas] *Reporter-News,* October 3, 1971.

32. "German Prisoners Who Escaped Are Recaptured Here," *The Charleston* [South Carolina] *News and Courier,* March 13, 1945.

33. Jack Glawson, "P.O.W.," *Charleston News and Courier,* September 8, 1963.

While awaiting disciplinary punishment and a possible court-martial for stealing a jeep, two of the prisoners escaped once again. On April 10, 1945, Max Lauer and Willi Steuer bolted from their new home at the Charleston Army Air Base, walked 12 miles into Charleston, crossed the Ashley River bridge, and continued south. Armed with a roadmap of South Carolina, a raincoat, shaving gear, and 15 bags of peanuts apiece, the two *Afrika Korps* veterans spent the next five days walking more than 30 miles along the Rockville road to Ashepoo, S.C. Exhausted and very hungry, the men abandoned their plan to get to Germany via South America and presented themselves to an Ashepoo shopkeeper and asked to use his telephone to call the prisoner of war camp. See the *Charleston News and Courier,* April 11, 14, 16, 1945.

34. "Jim Citizen Helps FBI Catch Runaway Prisoners of War," *Kansas City Star,* September 3, 1944.

35. Ibid.

36. Ibid.

37. "Flier Spots War Prisoners," *New York Times,* July 28, 1944, p. 15.

38. "Auto Ride Traps Nazi Fugitive," *New York Times,* August 29, 1944, p. 8.

39. "Jim Citizen Helps FBI Catch Runaway Prisoners of War," *Kansas City Star,* September 3, 1944.

40. "Nazi Boasts, Spoils New Year," *New York Times,* January 2, 1946, p. 40.

41. "Those Italian Prisoners," *New York Times,* July 26, 1944, p. 18.

42. "Boys Cow Escaped Germans," *New York Times,* January 31, 1944, p. 3.

43. Costelle, *Les Prisonniers,* p. 148.

44. *Kansas City Star,* September 3, 1944.

45. "Nazi P.W. Is Captured On City Bus," *The* [Nashville] *Tennessean,* February 20, 1945.

46. Moore, *The Faustball Tunnel,* p. 65.

47. Costelle, *Les Prisonniers,* p. 145.

48. "Fleeing Nazis Caught on Philadelphia Ship," *New York Times,* November 13, 1944, p. 19.

49. "Find Escaped PW on Farm in Wisconsin," *Rockford Morning Star,* April 5, 1946.

50. "German PW Escapes and Holds Job Here," *New York Times,* April 5, 1946, p. 8.

51. J. Edgar Hoover, "Enemies At Large," *The American Magazine,* April, 1944, p. 97.

52. Ibid., p. 99. "Escaped Nazi Seized at Prayer," *New York Times,* September 18, 1943, p. 19.

53. "Escaped War Captive Lived On Art Here," *New York Times,* October 15, 1944, p. 11.

54. "Troops Search City for Nazi Prisoner," *New York Times,* June 12, 1944, pp. 1, 34; "Nazi Who Broke Out of Captivity Steals Back In; 'Caught' at Lunch," *New York Times,* June 14, 1944, pp. 1, 12.

55. War Department, "Prisoner of War Fact Sheet: Press Conference of Major General Archer L. Lerch, The Provost Marshal General," February 13, 1945, PMGO Prisoners of War File, Miscellaneous. MMB–NA.

56. "19 War Captives At Large," *New York Times,* November 24, 1947, p. 32.

57. Ibid.

58. Pabel, *Enemies Are Human,* p. 164; Hoover, "Enemies At Large," pp. 17, 97, 99, 100.

59. Reinhold Pabel, "It's Easy to Bluff Americans," *Collier's,* May 16, 1953, pp. 2–23. Obviously written to fan the fears of frightened Americans, the article began with the following: "Let us suppose for a moment that you are an ardent Communist living behind the Iron Curtain. You have been thoroughly trained in espionage and sabotage. You have learned to speak English with only a slight accent. . . . If you were that hypothetical agent, do you think you could live in Chicago . . . for the next 10 or 20 years without being caught? . . . On the basis of my own experience. . . ."

60. Quoted in Moore, *The Faustball Tunnel,* p. 244.

61. *Charleston News and Courier,* May 9, 1953.

62. "P.O.W.; Free Here 7 Years, Trapped As Fiancee's Mother Sees a Photo," *New York Times,* May 9, 1953, pp. 1, 6; "Love Helps Free Former P.O.W. to Marry and Honeymoon Abroad," *New York Times,* May 16, 1964, p. 21; Michael Griffin, F.B.I., interview.

63. Interview with Special Agent Thomas Coll, Federal Bureau of Investigation, March 31, 1977, Washington D.C.

64. *Charleston News and Courier,* May 12, 1959; and the *Charleston [South Carolina] Evening Post,* June 17, 1959. Michael Griffin, interview.

65. *See:* Robert Jackson, *A Taste of Freedom: Stories of the German and Italian Prisoners of War Who Escaped from Camps in Britain During World War II* (London: Arthur Barker, Ltd., 1964); Fritz Wentzel, *Single or Return? The Story of a German P.O.W. in British Camps and the Escape of Lieutenant Franz von Werra,* trans. Edward Fitzgerald (London: William Kimber, 1954); and Leo Dalderup and John Murdoch, *The Other Side; the Story of Leo Dalderup* (London: Hodder and Stoughton, 1954).

66. Hoover, "Enemies at Large," p. 97. "Hoover of FBI Urges Public Stay Alert, Warns of Sabotage in Final Lap of War," *New York Times,* May 21, 1945, p. 21.

67. "Investigation of the National War Effort," June 12, 1945, p. 10. While on the subject of sabotage, General Bryan went on to note that there had been, in fact, only three cases of sabotage committed by any POWs within the camps. The first case concerned two POWs who threw sand into the journal box of a railroad coal car; they were tried and sentenced to 10 and 15 years imprisonment at hard labor. The second case concerned a POW at Camp Chaffee, Arkansas, who drove nails into the tires of an Army jeep; his case was pending as of the end of the war. The last case, also under consideration, concerned several prisoners who ruined a large batch of paint at the factory to which they were assigned. While General Bryan's statement regarding the lack of sabotage by escaped prisoners is entirely correct, his citation of only three cases of minor "sabotage" within the camp structure appears grossly understated.

68. Prisoner of War Camp Commanders Regional Conference, 1944, pp. 54–59. Italics mine. See also TM 19–500, Chapter 2, Section X, paragraphs 58–60.

69. Costelle, *Les Prisonniers,* p. 163.

70. During the course of the war, four such murder trials were conducted, involving 15 prisoners. Since all were motivated by Nazism within the camps, the cases will be discussed later in that context.

71. All POW defendants were provided with a list of competent defense counsels from which the protecting power, acting on behalf of the prisoner, might choose. In a few cases, the accused prisoner requested that another POW serve as defense counsel though, due to a lack of knowledge regarding the American court-martial system, he could only serve as an assistant to an American counsel. *See:* War Department Circular No. 156, April 20, 1944, Sction IV.

72. *Regional Conference,* 1944, p. 63.

73. PMGO, "Descriptions of All P.O.W. Special and General Courts-Martial through 31 August 1945," *Prisoner of War Operations,* 4–4.3, A.A., v. 3.

Since the court-martial transcripts are not readily available, there is no way to ascertain the circumstances which might account for the wide differences. Even the official history of the PMGO's Prisoner of War Operations concedes that "There was no general uniformity in the length of sentences for comparable offenses, as, for example, the theft of automobiles during or after escapes. Sentences for this crime ranged from one to five years, throughout the various service commands." (p. 467.)

The 119 general and 48 special

courts-martial conducted through August 31, 1945, involved a total of 326 individual defendants. Of these, 277 were German and 49 Italian. Ibid., p. 466.

74. There are numerous accounts of the treatment received by Americans in German camps. Among the most informative are: Alfred Toppe, *German Methods of Interrogating Prisoners of War in World War II*, Koenigstein, Historical Division European Command, 1949; John A. Victor, *Time Out: American Airmen at Stalag Luft I* (New York: R. R. Smith, 1951); B. M. Cohen and M. Z. Cooper, *A Follow-Up Study of World War II Prisoners of War: Veterans Administration Medical Monograph* (Washington, D.C.: Government Printing Office, 1954); and the *New York Times*, May 14, 1945, p. C–3.

Chapter V

1. For an exceptional view of the military, and all other segments of the Third Reich at the grass roots, *see* Richard Grunberger, *The 12-Year Reich: A Social History of Nazi Germany, 1933-1945* (New York: Ballantine Books, 1971), pp. 149-66. *See also:* Alan Bullock, *Hitler: A Study in Tyranny* (New York: Bantam Books, 1967), pp. 599-600, 676-78; and Herman Mau, "Die zweite Revolution," *Vierteljahrshefte für Zeitgeschichte*, 1 (1953), p. 136.

2. Helen Peak, "Some Psychological Problems in the Re-Education of Germany," *Journal of Social Issues* (August, 1946): pp. 26-38.

3. Grunberger, *The 12-Year Reich*, p. 152.

4. Among the surveys which will be discussed later are Heinz Ansbacher, "Attitudes of German Prisoners of War: A Study of the Dynamics of National Socialistic Fellowship." *Psychological Monographs,* 62 (1948): pp. 1-42; Edward A. Shils and Morris Janowitz, "Cohesion and Disintegration in the Wehrmacht in World War II," *Public Opinion Quarterly* (Summer 1948): pp. 280-315; Helen Peak, "Some Observations on the Characteristics and Distribution of German Nazis," *Psychological Monographs* 59 (1947): pp. 1-44; and *United States Strategic Bombing Survey, Morale Division,* "The Effects of Strategic Bombing on German Morale," 2 vols. (Washington, D.C., December, 1946, May, 1947).

5. Interview with Richard Staff, September 15, 1976.

6. Ibid.

7. Dorothy Dunbar Bromley, "War Prisoners Include Nazis and Anti-Nazis," *New York Herald Tribune,* April 12, 1944.

8. "Fraternization," the War Department declared ineffectively, "is unauthorized, improper, objectionable, and contrary to good order and discipline. It will not be tolerated." (War Department, Prisoner of War Circular No. 3, January 4, 1944.) Nevertheless, fraternization was so commonplace that the Army was forced to acknowledge that "the guards feel that the prisoners are their buddies." Eighth Service Command, *Report of Conference on Prisoners of War and Prisoner of War Camps,* January 8, 1944, p. 4. RG 389, PMGO, Prisoner of War Operations Division, Operations Branch, Unclassified Decimal File, 1942-1945, Box No. 1308. MMB-NA.

9. Interview with William Hahn, April 22,1978.

10. Interview with Richard Staff, November 12, 1976.

11. Letter from Lambert B. Cain, U.S. Army Colonel (ret.), to Freiherr Rüdiger von Wechmar, February 2, 1959.

12. Perhaps the ultimate humiliation by America toward its blacks, in relation to the German POWs, occurred to a group of Negro GIs during the war, as they attempted to get served at a lunchroom in Salina, Kansas:

> As we entered, the counterman hurried to the rear to get the owner, who hurried out front to tell us with urgent politeness: "You boys know we don't serve colored here."
>
> Of course we knew it. They didn't serve "colored" anywhere in town. . . . The best movie house did not admit Negroes. . . . There was no room at the inn for any black visitor, and there was no place . . . where he could get a cup of coffee.
>
> "You know we don't serve colored here," the man repeated . . .
>
> We ignored him, and just stood there inside the door, staring at what we had come to see—the German prisoners of war who were having lunch at the counter. . . .
>
> We continued to stare. This was really happening. . . . The people of Salina would serve these enemy soldiers and turn away black American GIs. . . .
>
> If we were *untermenschen* in Nazi Germany, they would break our bones. As "colored" men in Salina, they could only break our hearts. . . .

Lloyd B. Brown, *"Brown* vs. *Salina, Kansas,"* New York Times, February 26, 1973, p. 31. Also see the excellent study by John Morton Blum, *V Was for Victory: Politics and American Culture During World War II* (New York: Harcourt, Brace, and Jovanovich, 1976), Chapter 6.

13. Quoted in Pluth, "Administration and Operation of German Prisoners of War Camps," p. 176.

14. War Department, *Facts vs. Fantasy,* Pamphlet No. 19-2, November 1944.

15. Letter from Alfred Klein, April 22, 1976.

16. "Prisoners of War Request They Be Returned to Work," *Charleston News and Courier,* July 7, 1944.

17. U.S. Congress, "Investigations of the National War Effort," November 30, 1944, p. 14.

18. *El Reno* [Oklahoma] *American,* May 3, 1945.

19. "FBI Traces Mysterious Propaganda Pamphlets to Mexia War Prisoners," *Mexia Daily News,* June 18, 1944.

20. A total of 92,965 American prisoners were held by Germany during the Second World War and were divided as follows:

Air Force 32,730 (50 percent officers)

Ground Forces 60,235 (10 percent officers)

A surprisingly lower figure of American prisoners in Germany (73,-759) is contained in another official report: Office of the U.S. Army, *Army Battle Casualties and Nonbattle Deaths in World War II, Final Report, 7 December 1941–31 December 1946,* CSCAP (OT) 87 (Office of the Adjutant General, June 1, 1953), p. 5.

Consistent with the requirements of the Geneva Convention, Germany segregated its prisoners of war by rank and placed them in the following types of camps: *OFLAG* (Contraction of *Offizier Lager,* or officers' camp); *STALAG*

(Stamm Lager or main camp for enlisted ranks only); *DULAG (Durchgangs Lager,* or transit camp and interrogation center). Air Corps personnel were separated from Army personnel and were maintained in an identical system of camps designated *LUFT* (air or air force), i.e., *STALAG LUFT III.* For the location of each camp and hospital containing American prisoners in Germany, Austria, Czechoslovakia, and Poland, see The American National Red Cross, *Prisoners of War Bulletin* 3, No. 2 (February, 1945), pp. 6–7. Also War Department, Military Intelligence Service, "American Prisoners of War in Germany," November 1, 1945, mimeographed, 108 pp. MMB–NA.

21. According to the Office of the Provost Marshal General, the 477 German prisoner deaths are tabulated in the following manner:

1. Deaths from Violent or
   Accidental Causes:
   - (a) Suicides   72
   - (b) Murders   4
   - (c) Homicides   3
   - (d) Shootings   40
   - (e) Accidental Deaths:
     - (1) Falling trees   12
     - (2) Motor vehicles   43
     - (3) Drowning   17
     - (4) Misc. industrial/
             agricultural
             accidents   21
2. Deaths from natural causes
   (including wounds sustained
   in battle prior to capture)   265
3. TOTAL DEATHS (through
   August 31, 1945)   477

PMGO, "A Brief History," p. 514. The number of German dead is disputed by Edward C. Corbett, Reserve, Louisiana, who has undertaken an apparently life-long investigation of each cause of death and place of burial. His early findings are available in his Masters Thesis: "Interned for the Duration: Axis Prisoners of War in Oklahoma, 1942–1946," Oklahoma City University, 1965.

22. PMGO, "A Brief History," p. 513; War Department, Prisoner of War Circular No. 1, September 23, 1943, para. 173(a).

23. War Department, Prisoner of War Circular No. 2, October 30, 1943, sec. IV (1); TM 19–500, Ch. 2, Sec. XII, p. 72.

The British Government made few such concessions to their 175,000 German prisoners. With regard to the display of swastika emblems and flags and portraits of Adolf Hitler, all willingly endured by American authorities, the Directorate of Prisoners of War of the British War Office came to the following conclusion as early as November 4, 1942:

> There is no record of the display in a Camp in Germany or Italy of portraits of His Majesty the King or the Prime Minister. In the absence of evidence that Imperial prisoners of war are allowed to display such photographs. ... the display of enemy flags, etc. in prisoner of war camps [in the United Kingdom, the Dominions, and India] cannot be permitted. This prohibition is not confined to the hoisting of flags in prisoner of war camps, but applies also to their display in any part of the camp.

Memo, War Office (Directorate of Prisoners of War), to Foreign Office (Prisoners of War Department). Subject: Display of National Flags by Prisoners of War. November 4, 1942, January 13, 1943. Serial No. 1048, 0103/3262. W.O. 32, 9887, ERD/1029. Public Record Office.

24. George W. Herald, "Our Nazi War-Prisoners," *Pic Magazine,* June 6, 1944, pp. 13, 45. Ironically, the subtitle of the article read: "Our experience with German war prisoners shows we must make them respect us. We must prove to them we are crusaders, not milktoasts."

25. Sidney B. Fay, "German Prisoners of War," *Current History,* 8, No. 43 (March 1945), pp. 193–95.

26. Costelle, *Les Prisonniers,* pp. 29–30.

27. Ibid., pp. 48–49. See also the excellent study by Hermann Jung, *Die deutschen Kriegsgefangenen in Amerikanischer Hand,* Band X/1 of Erich Maschke's series *Zur Geschichte der deutschen Kriegsgefangenen des Zweiten Weltkrieges* (Bielefield, Munich: Verlag Ernest und Werner Gieseking, 1972), pp. 127–33.

28. Ibid., p. 30.

29. Daniel Lang, "A Reporter at Large: Dopes and Simple Joes," *The New Yorker,* November 10, 21, 1945.

30. Costelle, *Les Prisonniers,* p. 187.

31. "Germany to Punish Families of Soldiers Who Surrender," *Washington Times Herald,* May 4, 1943.

32. Berlin, "How to Behave as a Prisoner of War," p. 3.

33. Powers, "What to Do with German Prisoners," p. 49.

34. Dorothy Thompson, "On the Record: Nazis Plot and Train in U.S. Prison Camps," April 24, 1944, Bell Syndicate.

35. "Editor Says Nazis Kill Captives Here," *New York Times,* February 24, 1944, p. 9.

36. Editorial, "The Gestapo in America," *New York Times,* January 18, 1945, p. 18.

37. "A Nazi Hold in Prison," *Kansas City Star,* January 13, 1944.

38. Memo, PW Friedrich W. Schlitz (8WG–25509), WV Compound, Company #5, to Major Mims, Executive Officer, Camp Campbell, Kentucky, November 29, 1944, 4pp. Farrand Collection, Hoover Institution.

39. Costelle, *Les Prisonniers,* pp. 75–76.

40. "Stimson Rejects Plan to Teach Nazi War Prisoners Democracy," *New York Times,* November 30, 1944, p. 5.

41. *See:* William L. Shirer's scathing article in the *Washington Post,* August 20, 1944; also "Nazi Prisoners are Nazis Still," *New York Times Magazine,* November 21, 1943; and Pabel, "It's Easy to Bluff Americans," *Collier's.*

42. Letter from Secretary of War Henry L. Stimson to Professor Warren A. Seavey, Harvard Law School, May 11, 1944, WDGAP, 383.6. MMB–NA.

43. "Nazi War Prisoners Heil Hitler's Birthday; Get Bread and Water as Army Takes Cakes," *New York Times,* April 23, 1944, p. 3.

44. The new salute was prompted by the July 20, 1944, attempt on Hitler's life, in which the military leaders of the *Wehrmacht* figured so prominently; it represented the final Nazification of the German Army. The decision was in no way connected with the political issues growing either inside or outside of the American camps.

45. While the War Department had little option regarding the introduction of the new salute, it did little to explain its reluctance to an anxious body of anti-

Nazis. Instead, the War Department took pains to explain the situation to camp commanders and pointed out the possible benefits:

> The new salute has, of course, distinct Nazi implications but so have the Swastikas on German uniforms and decorations which the prisoners of war are allowed to display. . . .
>
> The Nazi salute should not be made fun of or commented on by American guard personnel within hearing of the prisoners of war. The best way of treating it would seem to be the old-fashioned American poker-faced method. In the course of time many prisoners will tend to get tired of it. . . .
>
> We might be able to gain some advantages: personnel can endeavor to keep careful track of the prisoners who seem enthusiastic about the Nazi salute. . . . Observations should also be made on whether the Nazi salute is given in the strictly prescribed form (stiffly extended right arm) or whether it is given in a lackadaisical or sloppy fashion . . . A count of Nazi noses could thus become possible. . . .

Memorandum, John Mason Brown, Special War Problems Division, "Memorandum of the Swiss Legation on the Introduction of the Nazi Salute in Prisoner of War Camps as the New German Military Salute," August 11, 1944. Farrand Collection, Hoover Institution.

The introduction of the Hitler salute as well as all other political concessions was tolerated by the War Department as additional protection for the safety of American POWs in German hands. The moment the war in Europe was concluded (even before the official announcement of V-E Day) and all 92,000 American prisoners liberated, the War Department immediately declared that any further appearance of the fascist salute was forbidden. Moreover, stated Major General C. H. Danielson, "all German flags on which the swastika appears will be confiscated and prisoners will be prohibited from having in their possession or displaying Nazi emblems, insignia, or pictures." *New York Times,* April 28, 1945, p. 9.

46. Costelle, *Les Prisonniers,* pp. 88–89.

47. Tollefson, "Enemy Prisoners of War," p. 58.

48. Lerch, "The Army Report on Prisoners of War," pp. 546–47.

49. "Report on Prisoners of War Trip, November 27, 1944 to January 18, 1945," OWI, RG 207, NC–148, Box 2192. National Records Center, Suitland, Maryland.

50. Memo, Lieutenant Colonel John S. Myers, CMP, Special Assistant to the PMG, to Major General Archer L. Lerch, PMG, March 9, 1945. Subject: Public Relations Problems of PW Special Projects Division, RG 389, PMGO, Prisoner of War Operations, Administrative Branch, Decimal File, 1943–46, 383.6, General. MMB–NA.

51. ASF, Seventh Service Command, *Conference of POW Camp Commanders,* Omaha, Nebraska, March 24, 1944, pp. 51–52, RC, 389, PMGO, Prisoner of War Operations Division, Operations Branch, Unclassified Decimal File 1942–1945, Box No. 1308. MMB–NA.

52. Hans Werner Richter, *Die*

Geschlagenen (The Conquered) (Munich: K. Desch, 1949), pp. 145–46. *See also:* French edition, *Les Vaincus,* trans. Henri and M. Thres (Paris: Editions de Flore, 1950).

53. "Nazis Beat U.S. Captive," *New York Times,* August 15, 1944, p. 10.

54. U.S. Congress, "Investigations of the National War Effort," November 30, 1944, p. 10.

55. *New York Herald Tribune,* April 12, 1944.

56. Costelle, *Les Prisonniers,* pp. 39–40. Werner's assessment of American intentions was patently in error. While it is correct to state that the authorities were often helpless in the face of such random violence, they were far from unconcerned. At an Eighth Service Command Conference on prisoners of war in January of 1944, the commanders received a no-nonsense lecture by Lieutenant Colonel Leon Jaworski and Colonel Hyer in which they were ordered to respond instantly to any acts of camp violence. "Make an immediate search for the perpetrators," the commanders were told, "and look for fingerprints on suspected clubs and weapons. Turn them out in the middle of the night if that's when it happens and SPARE NOTHING IN THE INVESTIGATION!" ASF, Eighth Service Command, *Report of Conference,* p. 18. See also Leon Jaworski, *After Fifteen Years* (Houston: Gulf Publishing Company, 1961).

57. Dorothy Dunbar Bromley, "War Prisoners Include Nazis and Anti-Nazis," *New York Herald Tribune,* April 12, 1944.

58. "A Nazi Hold in Prison," *Kansas City Star,* January 13, 1944; "Nazi Scorn in Kansas," *Kansas City Star,* January 16, 1944.

59. Fay, "German Prisoners of War," pp. 196–197; Russell Porter, "Ex-Yorkville Man Slain as Prisoner," *New York Times,* January 17, 1945, p. 11.

60. This was clearly a politically-motivated murder, not a questionable case of suicide as before, and the Army moved instantly and aggressively to apprehend Kunze's killers. "We are using this Tonkawa case as a test case," stated the Eighth Service Commander. "We laid the case of these five men at Tonkawa before the War Department, and were told to go all out on this trial." ASF, Eighth Service Command, *Report of Conference,* p. 20.

61. PMGO, "A Brief History," pp. 466–71; Robert Otey, "Five Nazis Hanged," *Tulsa* [Oklahoma] *World,* July 12, 1945.

62. Ibid.

63. "Nazi Scorn in Kansas," *Kansas City Star,* January 16, 1944; Fay, "German Prisoners of War," p. 197.

64. For a thorough and highly engrossing narrative of the murder, the trial, and executions of the culprits, and the personalities of all involved, see Richard Whittingham, *Martial Justice: The Last Mass Execution in the United States* (Chicago: Henry Regnery Company, 1971).

65. Ibid., pp. 260–61.

66. Costelle, *Les Prisonniers,* pp. 66–68.

67. PMGO, "A Brief History," pp. 468–71; "Ex-Yorkville Man Slain as Prisoner," *New York Times,* January 17, 1945, p. 11; Fay, "German Prisoners of War," p. 197; "German Slayers Hanged," *New York Times,* July 15, 1945, p. 9; Costelle, *Les Prisonniers,* pp. 66–68.

68. PMGO, "A Brief History," p. 512.

69. "Suspect Nazis Tried to Burn Camp Building," *Rockford* [Illinois] *Morning Star,* December 1, 1944; U.S. Congress, "Investigations of the National War Effort," November 30, 1944, p. 9.

A graphic indication of the ferocity of these internal struggles can be seen from a display of confiscated weapons at Camp Maxey, Texas. "Here on the wall of one of the buildings," noted one visitor, "is a fearsome collection of crude, handmade knives and daggers found on Germans during their 'shakedown' search. . . . The weapons were fashioned from odd bits of metal. Some have ill-fitting wooden handles in which the blades are held by wire or string . . . One was found imbedded in the sole of a prisoner's shoe." Robert E. Hicks, "They Are Nazis to Core," *Kansas City Star,* December 5, 1943.

70. Costelle, *Les Prisonniers,* pp. 64–65.

Politically-motivated terrorism was not restricted to prisoner camps in the United States. Britain, despite her well-planned preparations, fewer prisoners, and longer experience at prisoner control, experienced a number of sporadic incidents of camp terror. *(See:* "Correspondence: German Prisoners," *New Statesman and Nation,* 27, February 12, 1944, p. 108; and "P.W. Camp 168," *New Statesman and Nation* 30, July 21, 1945, p. 38.) Canada, with less than 40,000 prisoners, was particularly hard-hit: Camp Medicine Hat, Alberta, for example, was a battleground of political mayhem, and at Camp Ozada, near Banff, the camp gestapo was confident enough to take their Canadian commander hostage in an effort to extract additional privileges! (George A. Yackulic, "Prisoners of War in Can-

ada," *Canadian Business* [Montreal], 17, no. 11 [November, 1944], pp. 48–51, 124–27; and Douglas Sagi, "My Fuehrer, I Follow Thee," *The Canadian Magazine, Winnipeg Tribune,* January 4, 1975, pp. 3–6). The Russians, apparently, had no such problem with their million and a half (as near as can be established) German prisoners.

71. John Mason Brown, "German Prisoners of War in the United States," *The American Journal of International Law,* XXXIX (1945), p. 213 n. 37.

72. Lerch, "The Army Reports on Prisoners of War," p. 547.

73. Pluth, "Administration and Operation of German Prisoner of War Camps," p. 316; "Report on Prisoners of War Trip, November 27, 1944, to January 18, 1945," OWI, RG 207, NC–148, Box 2192. National Records Center, Suitland, Maryland.

Author John Moore relates an episode when a group of German submarine officers, late of the U–162, were transferred to the anti-Nazi camp at Blanding, Florida, some 40 miles west of Jacksonville. As they approached the naval compound at their new home, containing about 250 naval POWs, they were stunned by their reception. The camp, anti-Nazi all right, was overflowing with Communists. " 'I had a terrible time there,' one POW recalls, 'The camp was full of Reds, criminals and traitors. I slept each night with a large stick by my bed, fearing for my life. We adamantly refused to go into the main compound and eventually persuaded the commanding officer to erect a 'dead line' separating us from the 'anti-Nazis' so called.' " *The Faustball Tunnel,* p. 109.

74. The government did not feel safe to announce that the camp violence

had ended until another nine months had passed. *See:* Russell Porter, "Prison Camps Rid of Nazi Terrorism," *New York Times,* January 16, 1945, pp. 1, 13; and Russell Porter, "Violence is Ended in Prisoner Camps," *New York Times,* January 18, 1945, p. 5.

75. The separation of prisoners by rank depended, of course, on establishing each man's true rank. Yet the task was not nearly as simple as it would appear. For example, the German Army had a number of ranks which did not correspond to American ranks. (An *Unterarzt* [Junior Physician] and an *Unterveterinär* [Junior Veterinarian], for example, received the pay of a 1st Sergeant but all the privileges of an officer. American forces had no equivalent rank.) Also, the prisoners were composed of many quasi-military organizations such as the German State Railways, Border Patrol, Customs Service, Merchant Marine, Waffen SS, and Allgemeine SS. Moreover, it was also discovered that German commanding officers, a few days before the surrender of Axis forces in North Africa, attempted to create noncommissioned officers in "wholesale" lots in order to prevent the capturing powers from utilizing the labor of many thousands of POW privates. Since the Geneva Convention was silent on the subject, the PMGO tightened its policy in this area and refused to accept as genuine any rank not substantiated by the prisoners' paybook *(Soldbuch)* or other authenticating documents. War Department, Prisoner of War Circular No. 11, 20 December 1943; Prisoner of War Circular No. 7, 20 January 1945; PMGO, "A Brief History," pp. 515-16.

76. Costelle, *Les Prisonniers,* p. 69.
77. U.S. Congress, "Investigations

of the National War Effort," June 12, 1944, p. 10.
78. Costelle, *Les Prisonniers,* pp. 74-76.
79. Ibid., p. 83.
80. Ibid., pp. 78-79.
81. Ibid., p. 74.
82. "Hearne Prisoner of War Camp Selected Distributing Point for Prisoner Mail in the U.S.," *Hearne Democrat,* March 24, 1944; Lewis and Mewha, *Prisoner of War Utilization,* p. 161; Tissing, "Stalag-Texas," pp. 27-28.
83. Memo, Major Ulio to Commanding Generals, 1st to 9th Service Commands, July 19, 1943. Subject: Nazi Activities in Internment Camps, RG 389, PMGO, Prisoner of War Operations Division, Classified Decimal File, Box No. 1637, General #1. MMB-NA.
84. Following a visit to Camp Alva in May, 1944, representatives of the Special War Problems Division reported that some prisoners had been transferred there as the result of personality clashes with their fellow prisoners or with American officers. "Report on Alva, Oklahoma." Visit by Lieutenant Colonel M. C. Bernays and Bernard Gufler, May 8-9, 1944, RG 389, PMGO, Prisoner of War Operations Division, General. MMB-NA.
85. Comments for the Chief of Staff, Army Service Commands, on Reorientation of German Prisoners of War, Secret, n.d., typewritten copy. Farrand Collection, Hoover Institution.
86. ASF, Third Service Command, *Proceedings of Prisoner of War Conference,* Baltimore, Maryland, September 29, 1944, p. 6. RG 389, PMGO, Prisoner of War Operations Division, Unclassified Decimal File, 1942-1945, Box No. 1308. MMB-NA.
87. Memo, J. A. Ulio, Major Gen-

eral, AJ, to Commanding Generals, Fourth to Eighth Service Commands, October 31, 1943, SPX 383.6. Subject: Nazi Activities in Prisoner of War Camps, RG 389, PMGO, Prisoner of War Operations Division, Operations Branch, Unclassified Decimal File, General, Box No. 1637. MMB–NA.

88. Memo, Captain Walter H. Rapp, Cav., to Chief, Special Projects Branch, n.d. Subject: Segregation of German Prisoners of War, Ibid.

89. Aware of the additional responsibilities which the segregation program placed on the shoulders of the already-overburdened camp and service commanders, the War Department did act on Rapp's advice by appointing an Intelligence Officer to each camp, whose responsibility involved the identification of ardent Nazis among the prisoners.

90. Protected Personnel encompassed three groups of prisoners considered neutral by the Geneva Convention's Articles 9, 10, 11, 12, 13, and 21: (1) Physicians, Dentists, and Sanitation personnel; (2) members of Volunteer Aid Societies; and (3) Chaplains. While members of all three categories may have been captured in the battle zone, they were not considered prisoners of war. If they could substantiate their Protected Personnel status, they were allowed to continue their humanitarian functions among the prisoners in the following ratios: 2 doctors, 1 dentist, 1 chaplain, and 6 enlisted medical men per 1,000 prisoners. Excess Protected Personnel were shifted to other camps or assigned to hospitals where they could minister to German sick and wounded. They received the same pay as POW employees of the same rank. Periodically, the United States accumulated more Protected Personnel than could be adequately utilized, and the excess personnel were repatriated to Germany. PMGO, "A Brief History," pp. 121–126; RG 389, PMGO, Prisoners of War Operations Division, Protected Personnel, 383.6, Unclassified Decimal File, General #3, Box No. 1319. MMB–NA.

91. Memo, J. A. Ulio, the Adjutant General to Commanding Generals, 1st through 9th Service Commands, July 19, 1944. Subject: Segregation of German Prisoners of War, RG 389, PMGO, Prisoner of War Operations Division, Special Projects Division, General #1, Box 1637. MMB–NA.

92. Vicki Baum, "Land of the Free," *Collier's,* August 19, 1944, pp. 11–12, 40–42.

93. Devore, "Our 'Pampered' War Prisoners," p. 14.

94. ASF, Eighth Service Command, Report of Conference, p. 42.

95. U.S. House of Representatives, *Congressional Record,* Vol. 90, Part 8, 78th Congress, 2d Sess., pp. A1245–A1247.

96. *See:* "Prisoner Separation Urged," *New York Times,* June 14, 1944, p. 18; "Austrian Prisoners Harmed," *New York Times,* July 20, 1944, p. 15.

97. Petition to His Apostolic Majesty, Otto v. Hapsburg, from (Pvt.) Johann Pammer, Co. D, Camp Chaffee, Arkansas, February 5, 1944. RG 389, PMGO, Prisoner of War Operations Division, Operations Branch, Unclassified Decimal File, General #5, Box No. 1312. MMB–NA.

98. Letter from Henry L. Stimson, Secretary of War, to Cordell Hull, Secretary of State, April 29, 1944, SPMGA 383.6, RG 389, PMGO, Prisoner of War Operations Division, General, Box No. 1637. MMB–NA.

99. Letter from Henry L. Stimson,

Secretary of War, to Cordell Hull, Secretary of State, July 24, 1944, WDGAP 383.6. Ibid.

100. Memo, Edward Davison, Major CMP, Assistant Director, Prisoner of War Division, to Chief, Camp Operations Branch. Subject: Segregation of Austrian Prisoners of War, August 22, 1944. RG 389, PMGO, Prisoner of War Operations Division, Operations Branch, Unclassified Decimal File, General #6, Box No. 1312, MMB-NA.

101. After it was realized by the PMGO that the German prisoners contained citizens of Allied nations—French, Dutch, Russian, Yugoslavs, Belgians, etc.—the War Department embarked on a screening program to segregate these prisoners and make them available to their respective nations as replacement troops. In cooperation with the various military attachés of the embassies of the Allied nations, more than 300 such POWs were delivered to their respective embassies and repatriated as replacements prior to V-E Day. Following the defeat of Germany, the War Department took steps to segregate all German prisoners who claimed citizenship other than German as of March 1, 1938, and a total of 4,942 prisoners were repatriated to their respective nations in a program separate from the routine repatriation of regular German prisoners. U.S. Prisoner of War Operations Division, Historical Monograph: Prisoner of War Operations Division, Office of the Provost Marshal General, 1946, 4-4.3, AA, Vol. 1, p. 251, OCMH; and ASF Circular No. 259, July 5, 1945, Part Two, TAB 49.

102. Memo, Edwards to Bryan, August 28, 1944, RG 389, PMGO, Segregation File, Screening and Segregation, Prisoner of War Operations Division,

383.6 General, Box No. 1637. MMB-NA.

103. A. J. Fisher, "394,000 German Prisoners of War," *The Central European Observer,* October 25, 1946, p. 342.

104. Department of National Defense, Army, Ottawa, Canada. Secret. "Estimated Classifications of German Prisoners of War in Canadian Custody as of Today's Date, 5 July 1945," WO 32/11132. Public Records Office.

105. *See:* Memo, Lieutenant Colonel Edward Davison, Director, Special Projects Division, to General B. M. Bryan, January 24, 1945. Subject: Intelligence Screening of PWs in the 3rd SC, 383.6 Screening, RG 389, PMGO, Prisoner of War Operations Division, Special Projects Division, Box No. 1637. MMB-NA. Memo, Major Frank Brown to Chief, Labor and Liaison Branch, April 27, 1945. Subject: PW Intelligence Screening and Records Segregation File: Screening and Segregation, Ibid. Memo, Captain Walter H. Rapp to Chief, Special Projects Branch, n.d. Subject: Segregation of German PWs, General #1, Ibid. Memo, Lieutenant Walter Schoenstedt, C.A.C., Hq. ASF, to John Mason Brown, Special Problems Branch, October 23, 1944, SPMGA (95). Subject: Draft of War Department Pamphlet "What About the German Prisoners?" Farrand Collection, Hoover Institution.

106. *See:* Philipp H. Lohman, "400,000 Germans," *New Europe,* April–May, 1945, pp. 12–14; Eugene Shays, "German Prisoners of War in the United States: Observations of a Soldier," *Fourth International,* December, 1945, pp. 366–71; and "Writes William L. Shirer in the New York Herald Tribune," *Reader's Digest,* January, 1945, p. 44.

107. Report: Intelligence Screening of PWs, Third Service Command, 383.6 Screening, RG 389, PMGO, Prisoner of War Operations Division, General, Box No. 1637. MMB–NA.

108. Memo, AG 383.6, May 25, 1945. Subject: Segregation of Prisoners of War. Memo, AG 383.6, June 16, 1945. Subject: Segregation of Prisoners of War, AGO Decimal File. MMB–NA.

109. "Arrival of Two War Prisoner Groups Provides Vivid Contrast," *New York Times,* May 14, 1945, p. 3.

As the war drew to a close, some incoming prisoners were often no more than 13 years of age, while others were past middle-age. A journalist touring Fort DuPont, Delaware, was introduced to three elderly POWs, close friends who had been captured together at Strasbourg. All three were grandfathers whose job was now to tend the greens on a nearby public golf course. "[My guide] spoke to the men, who stopped and tried to straighten up to attention, but he told them to relax. 'How goes it?' I asked. 'About the same as the last war,' [he] replied, 'except that this time I'm in America. The last time, the British captured me. Altogether I've been a captured man five years. I'm an experienced prisoner of war.' " (Lang, "A Reporter at Large," p. 73.)

Despite the poor quality of the incoming captives, the War Department was still apprehensive about a final eruption of Nazi violence including so-called "suicide clubs" following the eventual announcement of the war's end or Hitler's death. A variety of such predictions had been made by both American and POW authorities. *(See:* Memo, John Mason Brown, to Edward Davison, Chief, Special War Projects Branch, September 19, 1944. Subject: Observa-tion of PWs when told of Germany's Collapse. Farrand Collection, Hoover Institution. Memo, Alexander Lakes, PMGO, to General B. Bryan, April 13, 1945. Subject: V-E Day and Security in Prisoner of War Camps, 383.6 General, RG 389. MMB–NA; Gottschick, "Neu-ropsychiatrische Erkrankungen.") When the moment did arrive, however, there was no outburst of violence. One POW, Hans Werner Richter, vividly recalls the sentiments of his fellow prisoners at that instant. "The scene was red sweaters and black shorts; several of us soccer players were walking back on to the playing field. 'Our left three-quarter is a duffer,' somebody said. 'We'll never be able to win with him!' Gühler then crossed our path. 'Did you hear that Hitler died?' 'Where did you get that?' asked Gühler. 'The camp spokesman just announced it. . . .' 'Look, my friend, all the same we can't upset the whole team just before the match.' " (Costelle, *Les Prisonniers,* p. 192.)

110. Pluth, "The Administration of German Prisoner of War Camps," p. 383.

111. Lang, "A Reporter at Large," p. 70.

112. H. Landsberg, Letter to the Editor: "Education Against Fascism," *New York Times,* April 17, 1943, p. 16; Cummins E. Speakman, Jr., "Re-Education of German Prisoners of War in the United States During World War II" (M.A. Thesis, University of Virginia, 1948), p. 3.

Chapter VI

1. "What Kind of Peace?" *New York Times Magazine,* March 11, 1945, p. 44.

2. "What Shall Be Done With Germany?" *SEE,* April, 1945, pp. 36–37.

3. Anita De Mars, Letter to the Editor, "Use for German Prisoners Suggested," *New York Times,* December 28, 1944, p. 18; Marjorie Dugdale Ashe, Letter to the Editor, "No German Blood Wanted," *New York Times,* January 2, 1945, p. 18; and David Marshall Billikopf, Letter to the Editor, "German Blood Plasma Approved," *New York Times,* January 5, 1945, p. 14.

4. "What Kind of Peace?" *New York Times Magazine,* March 11, 1945, p. 44.

5. "Nazis Termed Treacherous by Chaplain," *Duluth Herald,* November 11, 1943; Hicks, "They Are Nazis to Core," *Kansas City Star.*

On numerous occasions, national and local church groups visited the camps, and the reports filed by such a team in Alabama are particularly illuminating. See "Reports on Visits to Prisoner of War Camps," quoted in W. Stanley Hoole, "Alabama's World War II Prisoner of War Camps," *The Alabama Review,* 20, no. 1 (January, 1967), pp. 105–109.

6. H. Landsberg, Letter to the Editor, *New York Times,* April 17, 1943, p. 16.

7. "Group Seeks to Re-Educate Nazi Prisoners; Only 25% of Those Here Called Fanatic," *New York Times,* June 8, 1944, p. 6.

8. L. J. Rubenstein, Letter to the Editor, "Plan for Germans Opposed," *New York Times,* June 10, 1944, p. 14.

9. Ernest Epler, Letter to the Editor, "Prisoner Separation Urged," *New York Times,* June 14, 1944, p. 18.

10. Lady Dorothy Moulton Mayer. Letter to the Editor, "Educate War Prisoners," *New York Times,* June 18, 1944, p. 8E.

At that moment, however, there was little substance to any rumors regarding Britain's reeducation program. As late as the spring of 1944, London proclaimed that "it would not countenance any campaign to re-educate and convert the Nazi prisoners." This attitude changed as governmental concern shifted to the political structure of postwar Germany, and during the summer of 1944, London cautiously and surreptitiously considered altering its earlier position. On September 18, 1944, the War Cabinet instructed the Political Warfare Executive of the Political Intelligence Division (of the Foreign Office) to begin the secret task of segregating and reeducating its German prisoners. As with nearly every other facet of the POW experience in Britain, there existed only the barest cooperation with Washington. During the next 15 months the British P.I.D.:

Organized 65 German-language lecture tours;

Produced and distributed 13,000 German and 15,000 English books;

Published a weekly camp newspaper similar to *Der Ruf,* called *Die Wochenpost,* and a 128-page, well-illustrated monthly digest called *Ausblick;*

Organized a staff of special Training Advisors who regularly visited each camp;

Successfully segregated a large number of the prisoners into political categories: "black" (Nazi), "gray" (undecided), and "white" (victims of fascism);

Established a special Training Center for selected prisoners at Wilton Park, Beaconsfield, where groups of 300 POWs were "democratized" in eight-week cycles.

For a complete evaluation of the British program, see Henry Faulk, *Group Captives: The Re-education of German Prisoners of War in Britain, 1945–1948* (London: Chatto & Windus, 1977). For additional information, see the excellent booklet prepared by the P.I.D., "The Re-education of German Prisoners of War" (December, 1945), 25 pages, Institute of Contemporary History, London; and a host of recently declassified letters, minutes, and position papers on the subject, located in War Office file 32, 11121, ERD/1918. Public Records Office.

The Russian reeducation program, however, is largely unfathomable. According to Red Army Colonel Osipenko, head of the Political Education Department: "There is no better educator than work—hard, physical work. It purifies a man's body and mind, renders him susceptible to new thoughts and new ways of living." (Philipp H. Lohmann, "400,-000 Germans," *New Europe* (New York), April/May, 1945, p. 14.) The "proof" of this philosophy of "hard, physical work" was offered by the Soviets themselves in a propaganda article entitled "Captured into Freedom." There was no political terror in Russian camps, they declared, because "the prisoner has learned how to see. Under the Nazi uniform a beast has slowly evolved back into a human being. In Russia he begins to realize that he is not something 'higher,' and so he exclaims suddenly: 'I love the Russians.' His icy heart begins to thaw. . . ." (Ferdinand Bruckner, "Captured into Freedom," *Soviet Russia Today,* May, 1942, p. 20.) Few of the prisoners ever returned to explain this educational phenomenon.

One insight into the general Russian attitude toward German prisoners of war occurred when a Soviet delegation toured the Allied sectors of liberated France during the summer of 1944:

> During their first visit the Soviets had asked to see a German PW cage. As they strayed through the camp, one of the Soviets stopped to interrogate a tall hard-muscled German captain wearing the wings of a parachutist.
>
> "And what do you think will happen to Germany after *we* win the war?" the Russian spoke fluent German.
>
> The paratrooper faltered then stiffened. Germany, he assumed, would probably be broken up into little pieces.
>
> "Not Germany," the Soviet officer spoke slowly, "not Germany, *Herr Hauptmann*—but Germans."

(Omar N. Bradley, *A Soldier's Story* (New York: Henry Holt and Company, 1951), pp. 334-35.

Several descriptions are available in Bruckner, "Captured into Freedom"; Henry C. Cassidy, "What To Do With German Prisoners: The Russian Solution," *Atlantic Monthly,* November 1944, pp 43–45; and Dorothy Thompson, "On the Record: Russia Leads the Way in Prisoner Propaganda," *Kansas City Star,* November 29,1944, p. 26.

11. Paul Winkler, "Reeducating Germans," *The Washington Post,* July 10, 1944.

12. Letter, Henry L. Stimson, Secretary of War to Warren A. Seavey, May 11, 1944. WDGAP 383.6. Farrand Collection, Hoover Institution.

13. Letter, Henry L. Stimson, Secretary of War, to Warren A. Seavey, May

26, 1944. WDGAP 383.6. Farrand Collection, Hoover Institution.

14. "Stimson Rejects Plan to Teach Nazi War Prisoners Democracy," *New York Times,* November 30, 1944, p. 5.

15. Quoted in the excellent study by Judith M. Gansberg, *Stalag: U.S.A.* (New York: Crowell, 1977), pp. 59–60.

16. Gansberg, *Stalag: U.S.A.,* pp. 61–62.

17. Ibid.

18. *Treaties, Conventions, International Acts, Protocols, and Agreements between the United States of America and Other Powers, 1923–37.* Vol. IV. Senate Document 134, 75th Congress, 3d sess. (Department of State, Washington, D.C.: United States Government Printing Office, 1938), p. 5232.

19. PMGO, "A Brief History," p. 544. On March 2, 1944, the Special War Problems Division of the Department of State drew up a comprehensive plan for the future reorientation of German POWs, which accurately predicted the problems and potential successes of the later reeducation program. *See:* Department of State, Special War Problems Division, "Indoctrination of German Prisoners of War," March 2, 1944, 8 pp., RG 389, 383.6 General. MMB–NA.

20. Letter, Secretary of State to Secretary of War, March 30, 1944, SWP, cited in PMGO, "A Brief History," p. 544.

21. Letter, Secretary of War to Secretary of State, April 8, 1944. "Secret" WDGAP 383.6. Farrand Collection, Hoover Institution.

22. Memo, Brigadier General Joseph F. Battley, Deputy Chief of Staff for Service Commands, to Commanding Generals, All Service Commands. Subject: Creation of PW Reorientation Program, September 2, 1944, SPMGA (37)

383.6, Secret. RG 389, 383.6 General. MMB–NA.

23. James H. Powers and Henry C. Cassidy, "What to Do With German Prisoners." Divided into two sections, subtitled "The Russian Solution" and "The American Muddle," the article was a scathing indictment of the War Department's policies and was considered important enough to warrant its republication in the December, 1944, issue of *Reader's Digest.*

24. Davison ultimately received the Legion of Merit for his leadership in directing the reeducation program and after the war went on to become the Dean of Hunter College's School of General Studies. Obituary: "Edward Davison, Poet and Teacher," *New York Times,* February 9, 1970, p. 39-L.

25. A man of mystery, Schönstedt was a former Communist, author, and mountain-climber, who simply disappeared in 1949. His belongings—manuscripts, correspondence, and scrapbooks—were ultimately donated to the Department of Special Collections, University of California, Davis.

26. Obituary: "Dr. Henry Smith, Jr., A Language Expert," *New York Times,* December 15, 1972, p. 50-L.

27. Gansberg, *Stalag: U.S.A.,* p. 66.

28. PMGO, "A Brief History," p. 545.

29. PMGO, "Story of the PW Reeducation Program," March 5, 1946, p. 3. Office of the Chief of Military History, Washington. Interestingly, the Special Projects Division cautioned its new staff in a secret memorandum that the reeducation plan was not to be "overdone." The POWs were to be "democratized" but not "Americanized," for while "the prisoners are to be sent home to live in Germany as favorably inclined

to the United States as may be possible, they are not to be so encouraged as to try to remain in the United States, or to return to the United States as immigrants." Memorandum on Reorientation of German Prisoners of War, Secret, typewritten, n.d., p. 4. Farrand Collection, Hoover Institution.

30. Speakman, "Re-education of German Prisoners of War," p. 25.

31. Memo, John Mason Brown to Bernard Gufler. Subject: "Concerning the Special Projects Branch of the Office of the Provost Marshal General," December 16, 1944, p. 8. Farrand Collection, Hoover Institution.

32. Ibid.

33. Speakman, "Re-education of German Prisoners of War," p. 4.

34. Powers, "What to do with German Prisoners," p. 49.

35. "Can't Convert the Nazis," *Kansas City Star,* September 20, 1944.

36. Gansberg, *Stalag: U.S.A.,* p. 68.

37. PMGO, "A Brief History," pp. 550–51.

38. Gansberg, *Stalag: U.S.A.,* p. 73.

39. Editorial, *Der Ruf,* Issue No. 1, March 1, 1945. *See:* PMGO, Special Projects Division, "Re-Education of Enemy Prisoners of War," unpublished manuscript, November, 1945, File 4–4.1, BA 1, TAB 12. Office of the Chief of Military History.

40. Ibid., "Reactions to *Der Ruf,*" 20 pp.

41. Ibid., "Distribution Statistics: *Der Ruf,*" TAB 16.

42. Memo for Director, Prisoner of War Special Projects Division, from Paul Neuland, Major, CMP, Chief Field Service Branch. Subject: Nazi Sympathizers in Germany, June, 1945, 383.6 General. MMB–NA.

Unfortunately, there is no remaining record of the number of dangerous individuals whose political views were brought to the government's attention by the examination of their mail. Some indication may be drawn from a brief description of the volume of mail handled during only two months, April–May, 1945. During that period, a total of 458,118 pieces of outgoing mail was read. Of these, 307,952 were passed; 105,208 pieces were passed with deletions; 42,979 pieces were condemned; and 1,979 pieces were returned to the senders. Incoming mail to the POWs during that same period amounted to 25,067 pieces, of which 21,409 were passed by the censors; 3,134 were passed with deletions; and 524 were condemned. References to military matters and suspected codes accounted for the majority of pieces thrown away or condemned. See Censors' Comments, RG 165 (WD General Staff), Intelligence Division, Captured Personnel and Material Branch, Box 435. MMB–NA.

43. For a fascinating investigation into the significant literature produced by POW authors, see Volker Christian Wehdeking, *Der Nullpunkt: über die Konstituierung der deutschen Nachkriegsliteratur (1945–1948) in den Amerikanischen Kriegsgefangenenlagern* (Stuttgart: J. B. Metzlersche Verlag, 1971).

44. PMGO, "A Brief History," p. 554.

45. PMGO, "A Brief History," p. 556.

46. Ibid., p. 557.

47. Ibid., p. 564. For the many difficulties involved in choosing the proper literature or in writing new material with values which would appeal to German prisoners, see the interesting analysis by Howard Mumford Jones, "Writers

and American Values," *New York Times Book Review,* August 5, 1945, p. 12.

48. PMGO, "Reactions to Buecher-reihe Neue Welt," "Re-Education of Enemy Prisoners of War," 5 pp.

49. Ibid., p. 5.

50. William G. Moulton, "Our Profession in Reverse: Teaching English to German Prisoners of War," *The Modern Language Journal,* 32 (October 6, 1948), p. 421.

51. PMGO, "A Brief History," p. 568.

52. Ibid.

53. Ibid., p. 569.

54. War Department, Prisoner of War Circular No. 10, February 14, 1945, "Motion Pictures for Prisoners of War."

55. "Germans Are Unmoved by Atrocity Film: Prisoners Lay War Crimes to 'Higher-Ups,'" *New York Times,* June 27, 1945, p. 5.

At most such showings, the American guards were far more impressed by the films than the prisoners, often taking out their hostility on their charges.

56. Lang, "A Reporter at Large," p. 72.

57. Gansberg, *Stalag: U.S.A.,* p. 103.

58. PMGO, "Poll of Prisoner of War Opinion," "Re-Education of Enemy Prisoners of War," p. 15.

59. PMGO, "A Brief History," p. 581.

60. Press Release, Brigadier General B. M. Bryan, Jr., Assistant PMG, "Re-Education Program for German Prisoners," May 28, 1945, typewritten, p. 6. Farrand Collection, Hoover Institution.

61. PMGO, "A Brief History," p. 587.

62. Gansberg, *Stalag: U.S.A.,* pp. 115–116.

63. The issue of pampering or coddling of the POWs was a familiar though generally unsubstantiated topic which grew in intensity as the war progressed. Beginning with a November 21, 1943, article in the *New York Times Magazine* which stated that the prisoners received all the food they wanted, including "piles of juicy hams, plenty of butter, steaks and sausages," (Cook, "Nazi Prisoners Are Nazis Still," p. 38), charges continued to crop up. During the next year and a half, the public was treated to recurring accusations concerning swimming pools, free cigarettes, country club conditions, turkey dinners at Christmas, five meals per day, pineapple fritters and marble cake, free hearing aids, pajamas, and transportation in Pullman cars. *See, for example:* "Axis Prisoners Find Ease in Tennessee," *New York Times,* June 20, 1943, p. 6; "House Group Sifts Prisoner 'Coddling,'" *New York Times,* August 20, 1944, p. 15; "Jersey Legion Head Urges Ban on War Captive Fetes," *New York Times,* October 20, 1944, p. 5; Drew Pearson, "Parents Irked at Food Nazis Get," *Washington Post,* February 4, 1945; "Time to Call a Halt," *St. Louis Globe-Democrat,* February 19, 1945; "Walter Winchell in New York," *New York Daily Mirror,* February 19, 1945; "What Would They Say?" *Huntington* [West Virginia] *Herald-Dispatch,* February 19, 1945; "Are We Coddling Nazi Prisoners?" *Fort Smith* [Arkansas] *Times Record,* May 3, 1945; "White Rock Camp Called Country Club by Dallasite Freed from Nazi Prison," *Dallas Daily Times Herald,* April 27, 1945; and "War Is Hell Dept.," *New York Times,* May 10, 1945, p. 25. Even America's Allies, France and Russia, could not resist the opportunity of joining the public outcry

against pampering: "Captives 'Coddled' in U.S., Russia Says," *New York Times,* May 26, 1944, p. 3; "Care of Prisoners Still Irks French," *New York Times,* December 3, 1944, p. 6. The majority of these charges proved false or, at most, grossly exaggerated.

The villain was neither the War Department nor an outraged public, nor certainly the prisoners: it was the aura of secrecy in which the government enveloped the entire POW program. Aside from frequent but routine press releases, the War Department and the Bureau of Public Relations made little or no effort to inform the general public or to clear up inaccuracies and misconceptions. For those occasions when the PMGO did rise to defend its treatment of POWs, *see:* Sidney Shalett, "Prisoner Coddling is Denied by Army," *New York Times,* May 7, 1944, p. 14; "Deny 'Coddling' of War Prisoners," *New York Times,* October 8, 1944, p. 14; John W. Colt, " 'Treat 'Em Well, Work 'Em Hard' is Army Policy," *Kansas City Star,* October 8, 1944; "Coddling of War Prisoners is Denied by Gen. Lerch at a Legion Meeting Here," *New York Times,* April 17, 1945, p. 40; Frederick C. Othman, "Nazis Smell Pretty and General's Glad," *Washington Daily News,* May 1, 1945; "Defend Treatment of War Prisoners," *New York Times,* May 1, 1945, p. 9; "Investigations of the National War Effort," June 12, 1945, pp. 10–11; and Lerch, "The Army Reports on Prisoners of War."

64. "Nazi Prisoners 'as Fat as Hogs' Are Reported at Arizona Camp," *New York Times,* April 23, 1945, p. 3; and U.S. Congress, House, "Representative Harless speaking on German Prisoner of War treatment," 79th Cong., 1st Sess.,

February 9, 1945, *Congressional Record,* XCI, pp. 1278–82.

65. Bryan, "Re-Education Program for German Prisoners."

66. "German Prisoners Re-Educated Here," *New York Times,* June 15, 1945, p. 5, and "Reorientation Program for German Prisoners of War to Be Extended to All Camps," Ibid., section IV, p. 7.

67. Benjamin Fine, "Plan to Reorient German Prisoners," *New York Times,* July 8, 1945, p. 1; "Re-Education Program for German Prisoners in Effect Here," *Publishers Weekly,* 147 (June 23, 1945), p. 2439.

68. Peter Edson, "Here's the Army Plan for 'De-Nazifying' German Prisoners," *Fort Smith Times Record,* July 7, 1945, p. 1.

69. "Prisoners in U.S. Bid Reich Yield," *New York Times,* April 8, 1945, p. 16.

70. Gansberg, *Stalag: U.S.A.,* p. 116.

71. Petition, POW Heinrich Carstens, Pvt., 31 G–13215, Branch Camp #7, to Major General A. Lerch, June 25, 1945, typewritten, 5 pp. RG 389, 383.6 General. MMB–NA.

72. *See:* "Captives Would Fight Nazis," *New York Times,* October 14, 1943, p. 3. The War Department thanked the Italians for their enthusiastic offer but politely rejected the plan.

73. As discussed earlier in this study, more than 4,900 such POWs were isolated by the PMGO in American camps and shipped back to their respective countries as combat replacements. *See also:* (unsigned) "Prisoners of War: Non-Germans Want to Go Back and Fight," *Military Police Training Bulletin,* 3, no. 1 (January 1945), p. 37.

74. Memo, Walter Schoenstedt, Captain, Chief, Programs Branch, to Director, Prisoner of War Special Projects Division. Subject: "The War Against Japan and the German Prisoners of War," February 2, 1945, p. 2. RG 389, 383.6 General. MMB–NA.

75. Ibid., pp. 3–4.

76. Memo, S. L. Scott, Brigadier General, Deputy Director, Plans and Operations, A.S.F., to General Somervell. Subject: "Employment of German prisoners of war on a volunteer basis as combat troops in the war against Japan," May 23, 1945, TOP SECRET. RG 160, OCG, Lt. G. Somervell's Desk File, 1945, Prisoners of War. MMB–NA.

77. Memo, Brehon Somervell, General, Commanding, to Chief of Staff, May 23, 1945, TOP SECRET. RG 160, OCG, Lt. G. Somervell's Desk File, 1945, Prisoners of War. MMB–NA.

78. *See, for example:* Lt. Paul V. Reed, Intelligence Officer, Camp Crowder, Missouri, to Commanding General, ASF, Hqs 7th Service Command, Omaha. Subject: "Enlistment of Aliens in American Army," June 9, 1945, SECRET. RG 389, POW Special Projects Division, 342.18. MMB–NA.

79. The candidates were selected by monitoring their mail for anti-Nazi statements or by substantiating their claims of early anti-Nazi activity or victimization. For examples of these lists, *see* Memo, Sgt. Carl J. Paschek, Marine Intelligence, HRPE, to C. T. Tucker, Major, Chief, Counterintelligence Section, Intelligence Division. Subject: "Offers of German PWs to assist the Allied Propaganda Effort," HRPE Report No. 515, File III–HRPE–d8008n, October 19, 1944, Confidential. Memo, Frederick W. Siegel, Major, Censorship Liaison Officer, to Chief, Domestic and Counterintelligence Branch, Intelligence Division. Subject: "German Prisoners of War Reveal Anti-Nazi Sentiment," November 4, 1944, Confidential, RG 389, 383.6 General. MMB–NA.

80. Letter from Dr. Howard Mumford Jones, September 12, 1977.

81. PMGO, "Re-education of Enemy Prisoner of War-Projects II and III" Historical Manuscript, War Department Special Staff, Historical Division File, No. 4-4.1, BA 2, Supplement 1, March 1, 1946, Office of the Chief of Military History, p. 11. *See also:* Speakman, "Re-education of German Prisoners of War," Chapter IV; "Captives Trained to Police Germany," *New York Times,* September 23, 1945, p. 27; "German Prisoners Trained Here," *New York Times,* October 21, 1945, p. 5; F. G. Alleston Cook, "Democratic ABC's for Nazi PW's," *New York Times,* November 11, 1945, IV, p. 8; and "German POWs Learn of Freedom," *The Rotarian,* 68 (March 1946, pp. 22–24).

82. Letter from Dr. Howard Mumford Jones, September 12, 1977.

83. Delbert Clark, "U.S. Training Held Help to Germans—Survey Shows Captives Have Higher Degree of Interest in Future Than Others," *New York Times,* February 16, 1948, p. 10-L.

84. See the official U.S. Army photographic files, SC 247285–SC 247221, U.S. Army Audio-Visual Activity, Room 5A518, The Pentagon. Washington, D.C.

85. *See:* "European Unity Architect, Walter Hallstein," *New York Times,* November 18, 1966, p. 10-L; and Dana Adams Schmidt, "German Captives Push Democracy," *New York Times,* June 9, 1946, p. 33.

86. PMGO, "Re-education of

Enemy Prisoners of War, Eustis Project, April 4, 1946." Unpublished Manuscript, War Department Special Staff, Historical Division, p. 2. Office of the Chief of Military History.

87. "Comprehensive Test," 10 pp. RG 389, POW Special Projects Division, 337 to 342.18. MMB–NA.

According to Dr. Henry Ehrmann, the examinations revealed that "the prisoners were generally ignorant of the liberal traditions in their own national history. To give but a few examples: ... 50 per cent were unable to identify either the Paulskirche in Frankfurt, symbol of the revolution of 1848, or Virchow, the liberal antagonist of Bismarck ...; 35 per cent revealed complete ignorance of the German Peasants' Revolt; 50 per cent neither had heard of Carl Schurz nor could name a single Social Democratic leader of the period before World War I. When tested about ... more recent events, such as salient events of the period of the Weimar Republic, the prisoners made hardly a better showing ..." Henry W. Ehrmann. "An Experiment in Political Education: The Prisoner of War Schools in the United States," *Social Research,* September 1947, pp. 315–16.

88. Quentin Reynolds, "Experiment in Democracy," *Collier's,* May 25, 1946, p. 41.

89. Letter from William G. Moulton, September 15, 1978.

90. Edwin Casady, "The Reorientation Program for PWS at Fort Eustis, Virginia," *The American Oxonian,* July, 1947, p. 149.

91. Ibid., p. 151.

92. Reynolds, "Experiment in Democracy," p. 41.

93. Ibid.

94. Letter from Judge Robert L. Kunzig, September 15, 1977.

95. William S. White, "German Prisoner Pledges New Life," *New York Times,* March 7, 1946, p. 18; "179 German Prisoners Graduated," *Providence* [Rhode Island] *Journal,* October 21, 1945; "160 in POW Class Get Certificates," *Providence Journal,* December 2, 1945.

96. Ibid.; "The PW University," *New York Times,* March 8, 1946, p. 20.

97. Gansberg, *Stalag: U.S.A.,* p. 160.

98. PMGO, "Poll of German Prisoner of War Opinion," "Re-Education of Enemy Prisoners of War," p. 30; Tollefson, "Enemy Prisoners of War," pp. 71–72; and "German Prisoners 74% 'Re-Educated,' " *New York Times,* July 29, 1946, p. 11.

99. Ibid.; "Poll of German Prisoner of War Opinion," p. 29.

100. Letter from Alfred Klein, July 15, 1977.

101. Letter from Heinrich Matthias, May 29, 1978.

102. Captain Robert Lowe Kunzig, "360,000 P.W.'s—The Hope of Germany," *American,* November, 1946, p. 133.

103. Quoted to Speakman, p. 16, n. 11.

104. Letter from Professor Harold Deutsch, May 21, 1977; July 18, 1977.

105. Quoted in Gansberg, *Stalag: U.S.A.,* p. 180.

106. Reynolds, "Experiment in Democracy," p. 13.

107. Henry W. Ehrmann, "A Reorientation Program Seen Through the Eyes of German Prisoners," Unpublished Manuscript, p. 22, quoted in Speakman, p. 114.

108. Office of Military Government for Germany (US), Information Control Division, report, "Former Special Prisoners of War," Berlin: June 26, 1947. Written by Dr. William G. Moulton.

109. Anna and Richard Merritt (eds.), *Public Opinion in Occupied Germany: The OMGUS Surveys, 1945–1959*, Report No. 92 (February 11, 1948) (Urbana: University of Illinois Press, 1970), pp. 200–201.

Chapter VII

1. Instrument of Unconditional Surrender of Germany, J.C.S. 623/9, RG 165, OPD 383.6, TS, Sec. I. MMB–NA.

2. Due, perhaps, to the relatively small number of POWs in their care, Britain was concerned less about the return of her prisoners than the fear that, under the 50/50 agreement, the United States might transfer at least 935,000 German POWs to British custody. *See:* Secret Cypher Telegram, Eisenhower to British Chiefs of Staff, June 1, 1945, FWD 23035, WO 32, 10721, ERD/1909. Public Record Office.

As late as September 26, 1945, Britain and Canada were still debating the logic of allowing ardent Nazis and unemployable POWs to be returned to Europe in the foreseeable future. *See:* Memo, E. S. H. Smith, War Office, to S. Morley Scott, Office of High Commissioner for Canada, September 26, 1945, WO/11132, 0103/5951. Public Record Office.

3. For information on such exchanges, particularly those carried out by the M. S. *Gripsholm, see* American National Red Cross, "Exchange of Pris-

oners," *Prisoner of War Bulletin* 1, no. 7 (December, 1943), p. 6; "Policy on Return of Prisoners of War," *Ibid.,* 2, no. 11 (November, 1944), p. 5; "Exchanges of Prisoners in France," *Ibid.,* 3, no. 6 (June, 1945), p. 13; and Graham H. Stuart, "Special War Problems Division," *Department of State Bulletin,* 11 (July 16, 1944), pp. 63–74.

4. *See, for example:* Memo, Major General Thomas T. Handy, Assistant Chief of Staff, Operations Division, to Provost Marshal General, June 16, 1944. Subject: "Repatriated Prisoners of War Serving in Armed Forces," OPD 383.6. Confidential Memo, Adolf A. Berle, Jr., Assistant Secretary, to Henry L. Stimson, Secretary of War, May 25, 1944, SWP 711.62114 Sick/357; Aide-Memoire, F. Gousev, Soviet Ambassador, to Anthony Eden, September 21, 1944, No. 1358–A, RG 165, OPD 383.6, Sec. VIII–A, Case 262. MMB–NA.

5. Memo, Representatives of the British Chiefs of Staff, to U.S. Combined Chiefs of Staff. Subject: "Proposed Exchange of Able-Bodied British and German Prisoners of War," March 23, 1945, C.C.S. 794 and 794/1. Memorandum by the U.S. Chiefs of Staff, March 23, 1945, RG 165, CCS 383.6, March 1945. MMB–NA.

6. Lewis and Mewha, *Prisoner of War Utilization,* pp. 90–91.

7. Memo, R. B. Lovett, Brigadier General, Adjutant General, to the Adjutant General, War Department, February 1, 1945. Subject: "Evacuation of Enemy Prisoners of War to the US," Top Secret, AG 513 TSCB (GA), RG 165 (Records of the War Department-General and Special Staffs), OPD 383.6, TS, Sec. I, Cases 1 through 19, p. 1. MMB–NA.

8. Bradley, *A Soldier's Story,* p. 545. For a depressing account of the problems involved in maintaining such huge numbers of prisoners, especially in the areas of sanitation and food, see Bayne-Jones, "Enemy Prisoners of War," *Preventive Medicine in World War II,* pp. 372–400. An excellent overview of the entire POW situation in the European Theater is to be found in Kurt W. Böhme, *Die deutschen Kriegsgefangenen in amerikanischer Hand-Europa,* Band X/2, Dr. Erich Maschke (ed.), *Zur Geschichte der deutschen Kriegsgefangenen des Zweiten Weltkrieges* (Munich: Verlag Ernst und Werner Gieseking, Bielefeld, 1973).

9. Memo, General Marshall, War Department, to General Eisenhower, European Theater of Operations, Main Echelon, Paris, October 27, 1944, Top Secret, CM-OUT-53129, RG 165, OPD 383.6, TS, S-c. I, Case 1. MMB-NA.

10. Memo, Brigadier General R. B. Lovett, Adjutant General, to The Adjutant General, War Department, February 19, 1945, Top Secret, AG 383.6 TS. Subject: "Status and Employment of Italian and German PWs on Collapse of Germany," p. 2. RG 165, OPD, 383.6, TS, sec. I, Case 1. MMB-NA.

11. Memo for Planning Committee, War Department. Subject: "Status and Employment of Italian and German PWs on Collapse of Germany," n.d., p. 6., Ibid. MMB-NA.

12. ASF Circular No. 191, May 29, 1945.

13. "Asks Rebuilding by Nazis," *New York Times,* May 1, 1945, p. 6; U.S. Congress, House, "Send German Prisoners Back to Europe," 79th Cong, 1st Sess., April 30, 1945, *Congressional Record: Appendix,* XCI, A1983–4.

14. U.S. Congress, Senate, 79th Cong., 1st Sess. July 13, 1945, *Congressional Record,* XCI, p. 7509.

15. "Early Return for Nazis," *New York Times,* September 4, 1945, p. 9.

16. U.S. Congress, "Resolution of Wisconsin Legislature," 79th Cong., 1st sess., September 10, 1945, *Congressional Record: Appendix,* XCI, p. A3821.

17. The War Production Board had anticipated this problem and had earlier tested the employment of furloughed American soldiers, but their lack of skill, time, and enthusiasm for the tasks and low wages only made the continued use of German prisoner labor more appealing. *See:* Memo, William Munger, Plant Productivity Division, War Production Board, to Joseph D. Keenan, Vice Chairman for Labor Production, March 10, 1945. Subject: "Use of Furloughed Soldiers in War Plants," RG 179, War Production Board, 241.1. MMB-NA.

18. Tollefson, "Enemy Prisoners of War," p. 73.

19. "Prisoners of War to Go Home Soon," *New York Times,* August 10, 1945, p. 7; "To End War Prisoners Jobs," *New York Times,* August 19, 1945, p. 34.

20. "50,000 'Useless' Nazi Prisoners and Fritz Kuhn Will be Sent Home," *New York Times,* May 19, 1945, pp. 1, 4; "War Prisoner Return to Begin Next Month," *New York Times,* June 27, 1945, p. 8; "1,482 Nazi Prisoners Will Embark Here," *New York Times,* July 26, 1945, p. 10; and "10,500 Captives to Return," *New York Times,* July 29, 1945, p. 34.

21. "Repatriates Seen as Threat in Reich," *New York Times,* July 30, 1945, p. 10.

22. Merrill R. Pritchett and William

L. Shea, "The *Afrika Korps* in Arkansas, 1943-1946," unpublished manuscript, University of Arkansas at Monticello, p. 24.

23. "Defends Assigning of War Prisoners," *New York Times,* May 18, 1945, p. 14.

24. *See, for example:* Letter, John W. Martyn to Senator Burnet Maybank, January 8, 1946, AGO, Decimal File, Box No. 2906. MMB–NA.

25. "Seek German Prisoners to Replace Farm Labor," *New York Times,* February 13, 1945, p. 9.

26. Letter, Marvin Jones, Administrator, War Food Administration, to James F. Byrnes, Director, Office of War Mobilization and Reconversion, February 23, 1945, RG 165, OPD 383.6, TS Sec. I, cases 1 through 19. MMB–NA.

27. Letter, James F. Byrnes, Director, Office of War Mobilization and Reconversion, to Robert P. Patterson, February 24, 1945, Ibid.

28. Radios CM–OUT 45235 (February 28, 1945) and CM–OUT 58755 (March 25, 1945); Draft of Cable, Marshall to Eisenhower, February 22, 1945, Secret, OPD 383.6, TS/72442. *See also:* Memo, Lieutenant General Somervell to AC of S, OPD, WDGS, February 20, 1945, comment no. 4/Gen. Lerch/ 76846. Memo, Lieutenant Col. Bernays, G–1, to AC of S, OPD, WDGS, February 22, 1945, comment no. 5/72234, RG 165, OPD 383.6 TS, sec. I, Cases 1 through 19. MMB–NA.

29. Memo, Major General J. E. Hull, Assistant Chief of Staff, OPD, February 23, 1945. Subject: "Evacuation of Enemy Prisoners of War to the U.S." Memo, Brigadier James H. Stratton, Assistant Chief of Staff, G–4, to General Bullard, P/W Div., SHAEF, January 26, 1945. Subject: "Capacity of Ships for Evacuation of P/W to US." RG 165, OPD 383.6 TS, Sec. I, Cases 1 through 19. MMB–NA.

30. Memo, G. C. Marshall, Chief of Staff (By Order of the Secretary of War), to All Commanding Generals, et. al., May 25, 1945, No. 580–45, AG 383.6. Farrand Collection, Hoover Institution.

31. Tollefson, "Enemy Prisoners of War," p. 74.

32. *See, for example:* "POWs are Kept Off Trains," *New York Times,* December 25, 1945, p. 2; "Movement of POWs at Shanks is Halted," *New York Times,* May 25, 1946, p. 4; and "Germans Being Returned Home," *New York Times,* June 9, 1946, p. 13.

33. "50,000 'Useless' Nazi Prisoners and Fritz Kuhn Will Be Sent Home," *New York Times,* May 19, 1945, pp. 1, 4.

34. "Return of Rabid Nazis Opposed," *New York Times,* May 31, 1945, p. 14.

35. "Prisoner Problem: Editorial," *Washington Post,* April 24, 1945.

36. "Return of Rabid Nazis Opposed," *New York Times,* May 31, 1945, p. 14.

37. "The First Fifty Thousand: A Proclamation to POWs," *Der Ruf,* July 15, 1945, No. 8.

38. "Army to Return German Prisoners to Mine Coal Europe Badly Needs," *New York Times,* July 22, 1945, pp. 1, 28.

39. "Deportees, POWs Head for Germany," *New York Times,* September 16, 1945, p. 20.

40. *See, for example:* "2,000 Germans Sail for Home Today," *New York Times,* September 21, 1945, p. 2; and "180 German War Prisoners Sail," *New York Times,* October 30, 1945, p. 9. For

an interesting examination of these POW returns at the camp level (Camp Grant, Illinois) see the following articles from the *Rockford Register Republic:* "PW's Want to Remain in US—First Shipped From Camp Grant," September 12, 1945; "Prisoners Head for Home Soon," September 12, 1945; "PW's at Camp on Way Home—65 in First Group," September 20, 1945; "871 Camp Grant PW's Shipped to California," October 5, 1945; "300 Camp Grant PWs Begin Trip Homeward," January 9, 1946; "997 Nazi PWs Begin Trip Homeward," January 9, 1946; "997 Nazi PW's to Leave Camp," March 20, 1946; "274 More Plus Start Back to Native Land," March 25, 1946.

41. "Speed Repatriation of Prisoners," *New York Times,* September 5, 1945, p. 9; "War Captives in U.S. to be Gone by Spring; Total of Prisoners Here is Put at 417,034," *New York Times,* September 13, 1945, p. 5.

For full information regarding the repatriation of the Italian prisoners, *see* "PMGO, A Brief History." In an interesting sidelight, a number of the more amorous Italian POWs managed to marry or propose marriage to American girls, many of whom followed the repatriated POWs back to Europe. *See for example:* "25 American Girls Sail to Wed Italians," *New York Times,* August 23, 1946, p. 37; and "White Plains Girl Announces Betrothal to Italian POW," *New York Times,* January 10, 1945, p. 20.

42. War Department Press Release, "Enemy Prisoners of War to be Returned by April," November 20, 1945. Farrand Collection, Hoover Institution.

43. "No Nazi Prisoners for 1946 Farming; To Leave by March," *Charleston News and Courier,* December 21, 1945.

44. War Department Press Release, "Transfer of German Prisoners to France to be Resumed," November 21, 1945. Farrand Collection, Hoover Institution.

45. Cable, Combined Chiefs of Staff, to Supreme Commander, SHAEF, 276/9, October 19, 1944; November 4, 1944, RG 165, CCS 383.6 (4–24–45) S.7. MMB–NA.

46. "France Aims to Use 2,000,000 Germans," *New York Times,* May 7, 1945, p. 9; "French Get 63,000 Prisoners," *New York Times,* June 22, 1945, p. 4; "Reich Captives in U.S. Slated for France," *New York Times,* September 5, 1945, p. 15; Statement by the War Department, "Repatriation of German Prisoners of War," SWNCC 317/D, SECRET, 18 pp., RG 165, CCS, 383.6, S.7. MMB–NA.

47. For a sampling of public opinion in this matter, see George Gallup, "Atrocities Make 8 in 10 Favor German Labor in Torn Russia," *Washington Post,* May 6, 1945.

48. Memo, War Department, "Prisoner of War Food Rations," No. 30-45, March 7, 1945; ASF Circular 150, Sec. II, Part Two. Sidney Shalett, "Sets Civilian Fare For War Prisoners," *New York Times,* March 13, 1945, p. 10. "Fresh Meat Ration of Prisoners of War Cut by Army to Hearts, Livers, Kidneys," *New York Times,* April 15, 1945, p. 9. "Menus for German Prisoners Here Are Cut Because of Food Shortage," *New York Times,* April 25, 1945, p. 5.

49. "Arrival of Two War Prisoner Groups," *New York Times,* May 14, 1945, p. 3.

50. "Anger at Nazi Atrocities is Rising, but United States Treats Prisoners Fairly," *Newsweek,* May 7, 1945, p. 58.

51. In truth of fact, however, the

entire issue of the POW diet was lost in the maelstrom of news flashes about the end of the war in Europe. Several outspoken union leaders claimed credit for the decision; a lone letter to the editor of the *Times* noted that "the scarce orange juice and milk available [to the German POWs] would be at its proper place in the stomachs of starving Belgian and Dutch children"; and, tucked away on page 25 of the *New York Times,* under the heading "War Is Hell Dept.," the Army announced the end of its sale of beer, cigarettes, and candy to nonworking German prisoners.

"Stops 5 Meals a Day for Nazi Prisoners," *New York Times,* April 12, 1945, p. 5; Letter to the Editor: "Would Curtail POW Menu," *New York Times,* April 16, 1945, p. 22; and "War Is Hell Dept.," *New York Times,* May 10, 1945, p. 25.

52. Gansberg, *Stalag: U.S.A.,* p. 40.

53. Letter from Heinrich Matthias, May 29, 1978.

54. Letter from John Schroer, December 1, 1977.

55. "Nazi Prisoner Labor Camps' Food Cut Hit," *Washington Post,* July 3, 1945; "Says Nazis Are Underfed," *New York Times,* July 3, 1945, p. 15.

56. Letter from Alfred Klein, August 4, 1977.

57. "Poll of German Prisoner of War Opinion," p. 13.

58. Letter, William O'Brien to PMG, February 18, 1945. Subject: German PWs, 383.6 Attitude, Special Problems Division, Box No. 1638. MMB-NA.

59. War Department Memo, No. 580-45, p. 3.

60. Costelle, *Les Prisonniers,* p. 241.

61. The War Department later increased the maximum weight limit for enlisted men to 55 pounds, with an additional 10-pound limit on printed matter if obtained from the camp canteen or if distributed by the War Department as orientation material. Since their baggage was seldom inspected, the prisoners universally used the 65-pound limit for their personal belongings.

62. "German POWs Weed Out Duffel to Haul Cigarettes," *New York Times,* February 28, 1946, p. 6.

63. McCarver, *Hearne on the Brazos,* p. 82.

64. Costelle, *Les Prisonniers,* p. 238; "PWs Want to Remain in U.S.," *Rockford Register Republic,* September 12, 1945.

65. "German Captain Commits Suicide in Camp," *New York Times,* March 28, 1946, p. 27; "3 POWs Escape, Caught at Shanks," *New York Times,* July 1, 1946, p. 32; and "German Captive Attempts to Quit Britain for Texas," *New York Times,* June 21, 1946, p. 9.

66. While there may have been several cases of POWs who were allowed to remain in the United States, only one case can be recalled by any of the scores of former prisoners contacted in the course of this study. A prisoner at Camp Opelika, Alabama, according to Alfred Klein, was given the opportunity to stay "because his uncle was an influential American Bishop" (Alfred Klein, August 4, 1977). Professor Pluth cites the single case known to him, a Lieutenant Max Coreth of the German Navy, incarcerated at Alexandria, Virginia. No other details are mentioned. (Pluth, *Administration of German Prisoner of War Camps,* p. 413, n. 43.)

67. "Prisoners Head for Home Soon," *Rockford Register Republic,* September 12, 1945.

68. "Farewell Dance Held Friday

Night at Kaufman Camp," *Kaufman Herald,* November 8, 1945, p. 5.

69. Pritchett and Shea, unpublished manuscript, "The *Afrika Korps* in Arkansas, 1943-1946," pp. 23–24.

71. ASF WD Monthly Progress Reports, sec. 11, Administration, in Lewis and Mewha, *Prisoner of War Utilization,* pp. 90–91.

72. Costelle, *Les Prisonniers,* p. 247.

73. "1,975 German PWs Leave for Reich," *New York Times,* December 8, 1945, p. 9.

74. Costelle, *Les Prisonniers,* pp. 233–35.

75. Captain Robert Lowe Kunzig, "360,000 P.W.'s—The Hope of Germany," *American Magazine,* November, 1946, p. 133.

76. Ibid.

77. Letter from Karl Schindler, November 15, 1977.

78. Letter from Alfred Klein, August 4, 1977.

79. Letter from John Schroer, December 1, 1977.

80. Letter from Alfred Klein, August 4, 1977.

81. Letter from Karl Schindler, November 15, 1977.

82. Letter from Heinrich Matthias, May 29, 1978.

83. "Retaining of War Prisoners May Imperil Future Peace," *World Dispatch,* October 8, 1946, pp. 10–11.

84. TWX, Hq ETOUSA, EX-94075, February 3, 1945. Memo, Hq. ETOUSA. Subject: "Employment of Prisoners of War to Neutralize or Remove Mines or Minefields," January 31, 1945. TWX, Hq ETOUSA, EX-92859, May 9, 1945, quoted in U.S. Army, *The Administration and Logistical History of the European Theater of Operations,* Part IX: *The Procurement and Use of Manpower in the ETO* (March, 1946), p. 285. Office of the Chief of Military History. Also Lewis and Mewha, *Prisoner of War Utilization,* p. 239.

85. Quoted in Lewis and Mewha, *Prisoner of War Utilization,* p. 245.

86. "Uncle Sam in the Slave Trade," *Christian Century,* June 12, 1946, p. 741; "Set These Slaves Free," *Christian Century,* July 31, 1946, pp. 933–34.

87. "U.S. to Free Last of Captives," *New York Times,* June 6, 1947, p. 6; "Last of 8,010,007 Captives Freed in Germany, Clay Says," *New York Times,* August 11, 1947, p. 1.

88. France's declaration that only 440,000 POWs remained in their care raised sharp questions in the War Department. An investigation of the number of prisoners lent to France, and those already repatriated, revealed a discrepancy of some 300,000 prisoners unaccounted for. While many American authorities strongly suspected that some had died of ill-treatment and that the majority were simply being held back for continued labor, they had no option but to accept the French explanation that "most of them escaped." "U.S. Doubts Captive Loss," *New York Times,* February 26, 1947, p. 5.

89. "French Fear Crippling Blow to Industry If U.S. Presses Early Return of Captives," *New York Times,* March 3, 1947, p. 8; "French to Confer on Prisoners," *New York Times,* February 27, 1947, p. 3; and "German Prisoners of War in France," *International Labour Review,* 56 (September, 1947), pp. 334–35.

90. Kunzig, "360,000 P.W.'s—The Hope of Germany," p. 134.

91. Letter from Alfred Klein, August 4, 1977.

92. Letter from Karl Schindler, November 15, 1977.

93. "Camp Shanks Ends War Mission as Last German PWs Start Home," *New York Times,* July 23, 1946, p. 27; "Last of the Supermen," *Newsweek,* August 5, 1946, p. 20.

94. Lewis and Mewha, *Prisoner of War Utilization,* p. 91. The remaining German POWs were later shipped to Europe in small groups assigned to vessels carrying replacements for the occupation areas. By August 8, 1947, only 24 escapees and 11 hospitalized cases remained. *See:* " 'Last' of 430,353 PW's to Leave the U.S.; Only Ones Remaining Are 'Escapees' or Ill," *New York Times,* August 8, 1947, p. 19.

Chapter VIII

1. "Investigations of the National War Effort," June 12, 1945, p. 13; "Fair Treatment is Causing Nazis to Surrender," *New York Herald Tribune,* May 1, 1945.

2. Ibid.; "Says Nazis Keep to Prisoners' Code," *New York Times,* December 1, 1944, p. 5.

3. ASF Circular No. 161, pp. 1–4. *See also:* "Released Americans Decry Prison Fare," *New York Times,* March 20, 1945, p. 8; and the following reports in the American National Red Cross' *Prisoners of War Bulletin:* "Repatriates Arrive Home from Germany," 1, no. 7 (December, 1943), p. 7; "German Camp Notes," 2, no. 6 (June, 1944), p. 2; "Repatriates from Germany," 2, no. 8 (August, 1944), p. 5; and "Reports from Camps in Germany," 2, no. 9 (September, 1944). pp. 1–3.

4. "Investigations of the National War Effort," June 12, 1945, pp. 18–19;

also "U.S. Sticks to Convention, Bars Prisoner Reprisals," *New York Times,* April 7, 1945, p. 6.

5. Memo, George C. Marshall, Chief of Staff, to President Roosevelt. Subject: German Reprisals Against American Airmen, December 29, 1943. Memo, President Roosevelt, to General Marshall, January 10, 1945. RG 165, OPD 383.6, Sec. V–B, cases 168–205. MMB–NA.

6. Letter, Henry L. Stimson, Secretary of War, and James Forrestal, Secretary of the Navy, to Fleet Admiral William D. Leahy, February 8, 1945, (SC) A16-2(3); JCS 1164/5, RG 218 (Records of the United States Joint Chiefs of Staff), CCS 383.6 (10–21–44) Sec. I. MMB–NA.

7. Henry W. Dunning, "How Relief Supplies Reach Prisoners of War," *Prisoners of War Bulletin,* 1, no. 2 (July, 1943), pp. 2–3; and "Life in a German Prison Camp," ibid., 2, no. 2 (February, 1944), pp. 6–7.

8. Tollefson, "Enemy Prisoners of War," p. 76; and "Defend Treatment of War Prisoners," *New York Times,* May 1, 1945, p. 9.

9. U.S. Army, Intelligence and Evaluation Branch, Psychological Warfare Branch, "Planning for the Effective Use of Soviet Prisoners of War," December 6, 1951, 23 pp. RG 319 (Records of the Army Staff), C1–3, 091 Russia, TS, Sect. 3, Case 46. MMB–NA.

10. W. Stanley Hoole, "Alabama's World War II Prisoner of War Camps," *Alabama Review,* 20, no. 1 (January, 1967), p. 112.

11. Edward S. Kerstein, "When POWs Stayed Here," *The Milwaukee Journal,* October 12, 1975.

12. Krammer, "When the *Afrika Korps* Came to Texas," pp. 280–81.

13. Pritchett and Shea, "*Afrika Korps* in Arkansas, 1943–1946," p. 22.

14. Moore, *The Faustball Tunnel,* pp. 245–46.

15. Costelle, *Les Prisonniers,* p. 242.

16. Collection of letters between Mrs. John E. Lane, Cedar Lane Farm, Kaufman, Texas, and Heinz Koppius, Altenburg, Thuringia. *See also:* J. W. Melton, "Ramblings," *Kaufman Herald,* May 6, 1976, p. 2.

17. Costelle, *Les Prisonniers,* p. 244.

18. Aaron G. Clark, "Ex-POW Greets General as 'Fellow Charlestonian,'" *Charleston News and Courier,* January 22, 1964.

19. "Poll of German Prisoner of War Opinion," p. 29.

20. "German Prisoner Wants to Return to Columbia," *The Columbia* [South Carolina] *Record,* June 13, 1949.

21. Ken Hand, "Offhand," *Dallas Morning News,* March 25, 1951.

22. Letter from James F. Greene, Deputy Commissioner, United States Department of Justice, Immigration and Naturalization Service, August 13, 1975, Reference CO 979–C, Table 13A.

23. Letter from John Schroer, December 1, 1977.

24. Ibid.; "Ex-POW Chooses Tampa for Home," *The Tampa* [Florida] *Daily Times,* January 14, 1952; Don White, "Ex-German Seaman and Prisoner of War Gets View of Democratic U.S. in Tampa," The *Tampa Daily Times,* January 31, 1952, p. 2.

25. Since the personnel records of all POWs in the United States were eventually returned to the Federal Republic of Germany, former prisoners can also locate one another by applying to the WAST Records Center, Eichborndamm 167-209, 1 West Berlin 52.

26. "Honorary Citizens!," *Mexia* [Texas] *Daily News,* October 5, 1971; Maryln Schwartz, "World War II POWs Come Back to Texas," *Dallas Morning News,* October 10, 1971, p. 33; and Gary Morton, "German Ex-POWs Return to Mexia Recall Prison Camp Experiences," *Waco* [Texas] *Tribune-Herald,* October 18, 1971.

27. McCarver and McCarver, *Hearne on the Brazos,* p. 82.

Bibliography

Books

Alanbrooke, Viscount. *Diaries.* Edited by Sir Arthur Bryant. Vol. I. London: Collins, 1957.

Arndt, John, ed. *Microfilm Guide and Index to the Library of Congress Collection of German Prisoner of War Newspapers Published in the United States from 1943-1946.* Worcester, Massachusetts: Clark University, 1965.

Bevins, Charles I. *Treaties and Other International Agreements of the United States of America, 1776–1949.* Vol. II. Washington, D.C.: Government Printing Office, 1969.

Blum, John Norton. *V Was for Victory: Politics and American Culture During World War II.* New York: Harcourt, Brace & Jovanovich, 1976.

Bosworth, Allan R. *America's Concentration Camps.* New York: Norton, 1967.

Bradley, Omar N. *A Soldier's Story.* New York: Henry Holt and Company, 1951.

Broadfoot, Barry, *Six War Years, 1939-1945: Memories of Canadians at Home and Abroad.* Toronto: Doubleday Canada Ltd., 1974.

Brown, Anthony Cave. *Bodyguard of Lies.* New York: Harper and Row, 1975.

Brown, John Mason. *Many a Watchful Night.* New York: McGraw-Hill Book Company, 1944.

Bullock, Alan. *Hitler: A Study in Tyranny.* New York: Bantam Books, 1967.

Cambray, P. G., and Briggs, G. G. B. *Red Cross and St. John: The Official Record of the Humanitarian Services of the War Organizations of the British Red Cross And Order of St. John of Jerusalem, 1939–1947.* London: n.p., 1949.

Cline, Ray S. *Washington Command Post, The Operations Division. United States Army in World War II.* Washington: Office of the Chief of Military History, 1951.

Cohen, B. M., and Cooper, M. Z. *A Follow-up Study of World War II Prisoners of War: Veterans Administration Medical Monograph.* Washington, D.C.: Government Printing Office, 1954.

Collins, J. Lawton. *War in Peacetime: The History and Lessons of Korea.* Boston: Houghton-Mifflin, 1969.

Cooper, Herston. *Crossville: How Did We Treat POW's?* Chicago: Adams Press, 1965.

Costelle, Daniel. *Les Prisonniers.* Paris: Flammarion, 1975.

Craven, Wesley F., and Cate, James L., eds. *The Army Air Forces in World War II: Plans and Early Operations, January 1939 to August 1942.* Chicago: University of Chicago Press, 1948.

Dalderup Leo, and Murdoch, John. *The Other Side: The Story of Leo Dalderup*. London: Hodder and Stoughton, 1954.

Faulk, H. *Group Captives: The Re-education of German Prisoners of War in Britain, 1945–1948*. London: Chatto & Windus, 1977.

Flory, William S. *Prisoners of War: A Study in the Development of International Law*. Washington, D.C.: American Council on Public Affairs, 1942.

Fooks, Herbert C. *Prisoners of War*. Federalsburg, Maryland: Stowell Printing Company, 1924.

Gansberg, Judith M. *Stalag: U.S.A.* New York: Crowell, 1977.

Gottschick, Johann. *Psychiatrie der Kriegsgefangenschaft; der Gestellt auf Grund von Beobachtungen in der USA an deutschen Kriegsgefangenen aus dem letzten Weltkrieg*. Stuttgart: Gustav Fischer Verlag, 1963.

Greenfield, Kent R., Palmer, Robert R., and Wiley, Bell I. *The Organization of Ground Combat Troops, United States Army in World War II*. Washington, D.C.: Government Printing Office, 1947.

Grodzins, Morton. *Betrayed: Politics and the Japanese Evacuation*. Chicago: University of Chicago Press, 1949.

Grunberger, Richard. *The 12-Year Reich: A Social History of Nazi Germany, 1933–1945*. New York: Ballantine Books, 1971.

Hinshaw, David. *The Home Front*. New York: G. P. Putnam's Sons, 1943.

Hornung, Manfred. *PW*. Vienna: Eduard Wancura Verlag, 1959.

Jackson, Robert. *A Taste of Freedom:*

Stories of the German and Italian Prisoners of War Who Escaped from Camps in Britain During World War II. London: Arthur Barker, Ltd., 1964.

Lerner, Daniel. *Psychological Warfare Against Nazi Germany: The Sykewar Campaign, D-Day to VE-Day*. Cambridge: M.I.T. Press, 1971.

Lewis, George, and Mewha, John. *History of Prisoner of War Utilization by the United States Army: 1776–1945*. Pamphlet No. 20-213. Washington, D.C.: Department of the Army, 1955.

McCarver, Norman L., and McCarver, Norman L., Jr. *Hearne on the Brazos*. San Antonio: San Antonio Century Press of Texas, 1958.

Maschke, Erich, ed. *Zur Geschichte der deutschen Kriegsgefangenen des Zweiten Weltkrieges;* Vol. X/1: Jung, Hermann, *Die deutschen Kriegsgefangenen in Amerikanischer Hand-USA;* Vol. X/2: Böhme, Kurt W., *Die deutschen Kriegsgefangenen in Amerikanischer Hand-Europa*. Bielefeld: Verlag Gieseking, 1972–73.

Merritt, Anna, and Merritt, Richard, eds. *Public Opinion in Occupied Germany: The OMGUS Surveys, 1945–1949*. Urbana: University of Illinois Press, 1970.

Millett, John D. *The Army Service Forces: The Organization and Role of the Army in World War II*. Washington, D.C.: Office of the Chief of Military History, Department of the Army, 1954.

Monroe, James L. (comp.). *Prisoners of War and Political Hostages: A Select Bibliography Report A10-1*. Springfield, Virginia: The Monroe Corporation, 1973.

Motley, Mary Penick, comp. and ed.

The Invisible Soldier: The Experience of the Black Soldier, World War II. Detroit: Wayne State University Press, 1975.

Nelson, Otto L. *National Security and the General Staff.* Washington: Infantry Journal Press, 1946.

Pabel, Reinhold. *Enemies Are Human.* Philadelphia: The John C. Winston Company, 1955.

Pogue, Forrest C. *George C. Marshall: Ordeal and Hope, 1939–42.* New York: Viking Press, 1966.

Richter, Hans Werner. *Die Geschlagenen (The Conquered)* (Munchen: K. Desch, 1949); or a French edition, *Les Vaincus.* Trans. Henri M. Thres. Paris: Editions de Flore, 1950.

Scotland, A.P. *The London Cage.* London: Evans Brothers, 1957.

Solzhenitsyn, Aleksander. *The Gulag Archipelago, 1918–1956.* New York: Harper & Row, 1973.

Swarthout, Glendon. *The Eagle and the Iron Cross.* New York: The New American Library, 1966.

Toppe, Alfred. *German Methods of Interrogating Prisoners of War in World War II.* Koenigstein: Historical Division European Command, 1949.

Victor, John A. *Time Out: American Airmen at Stalag Luft I.* New York: R. R. Smith, 1951.

Vulliet, Andre. *The YMCA and Prisoners of War: War Prisoners Aid YMCA During World War II.* International Committee of the YMCA, 1946.

Wehdeking, Volker Christian. *Der Nullpunkt: Uber die Konstituierung der Deutschen Nachkriegsliteratur (1945–1948) in den Amerikanischen Kriegsgefangenlagern.* Stuttgart: J. B. Metzlersche Verlag, 1971.

Wentzel, Fritz. *Single or Return: The Story of a German P.O.W. in British Camps and the Escape of Lieutenant Franz von Werra.* Trans. Edward Fitzgerald. London: William Kimber, 1954.

Wheeler, William Reginald, ed. *The Road to Victory: A History of Hampton Roads Port of Embarkation in World War II.* 2 vols. New Haven: Yale University Press, 1946.

Whittingham, Richard. *Martial Justice: The Last Mass Execution in the United States.* Chicago: Henry Regnery Company, 1971.

Wilcox, Walter W. *The Farmer in the Second World War.* Ames, Iowa: Iowa State College Press, 1947.

Journals

Ansbacher, Heinz. Attitudes of German Prisoners of War: A Study of the Dynamics of National Socialistic Fellowship. *Psychological Monographs* 62 (1948): 1–42.

Bondy, Curt. Observation and Re-education of German POWs *Harvard Educational Review.* 14 (January, 1946): 12–17.

———. Problems of Internment Camps. *Journal of Abnormal and Social Psychology* 38 (1943): 453–75.

Breycha-Vauthier, A.C. Reading for Prisoners of War as Seen from Geneva. *Library Quarterly* 11 (October, 1941): 442–47.

Brown, John Mason. Prisoners from the Master Race *Infantry Journal* 53 (December, 1943): 39–42.

———. German Prisoners of War in the United States. *The American Journal of International Law* 39 (April, 1945): 198–215

Burdick, Charles. Prisoners as Soldiers:

The German 999th Penal Division. *The Army Quarterly and Defence Journal* 102 (October, 1971–July, 1972): 65–69.

Busco, Ralph A., and Adler, Douglas D. German and Italian Prisoners of War in Utah and Idaho. *Utah Historical Quarterly* 39 (Winter 1971): 55–72.

Butler, Joseph T., Jr. Prisoner of War Labor in the Sugar Cane Fields of Lafourche Parish, Louisiana: 1943–44. *Louisiana History* 14 (Summer 1973): 283–296.

Casady, Edwin. The Reorientation Program for POW's at Fort Eustis, Virginia. *The American Oxonian* (July, 1947): 169–96.

Condition of Employment of Prisoners of War. *Monthly Labor Review* 56 (May, 1943): 891–95.

Conditions of Employment of Prisoners of War. *International Labour Review* 47 (February, 1943): 169–196.

Dalfiume, Richard M. The Forgotten Years of the Negro Revolution. *Journal of American History* 55 (June, 1968): 90–106.

Davis, Gerald H. Prisoners of War in Twentieth-Century War Economies. *Journal of Contemporary History* 12 (1977): 623–34.

Dicks, Henry V. Personality Traits and National Socialist Ideology. *Human Relations* 3 (June, 1950): 111–54.

Employment of Prisoners of War in Great Britain. *International Labour Review* 59 (February, 1944): 191–96.

Fay, Sidney B. German Prisoners of War. *Current History* 8, no. 43 (March, 1945): 193–200.

Fisher, Paul. Repatriation Labor—A Preliminary Analysis. *Quarterly Journal of Economics* 60 (May, 1946): 313–39.

Flynn, Eleanor C. The Geneva Convention on Treatment of Prisoners of War. *The George Washington Law Review* 11 (June, 1943): 505–20.

German Prisoners of War in France. *International Labour Review* 56 (September, 1947): 334–35.

Gottschick, Johann. Neuropsychiatrische Erkrankungen bei deutschen Kriegsgefangener in U.S.A. im Lichte Statistischen Betrachtungen. *Archiv für Psychiatrie und Zeitschrift Neurologie* 185 (1950): 491–510.

Hellman, Manfred. Deutsche Kriegsgefangenen des Zweiten Weltkriegs in Osteuropa. *Osteuropa* 27 (May, 1977): 413–26.

Hoole, W. Stanley. Alabama's World War II Prisoner of War Camps. *The Alabama Review* 20 (January, 1967): 83–114.

Hoover, J. Edgar. Alien Enemy Control. *Iowa Law Review* 29 (March, 1944): 396–408.

Humphrey, Yvonne E. On Shipboard with German Prisoners. *American Journal of Nursing* 43 (September, 1943): 821–22.

Hyde, Charles Cheney. Concerning Prisoners of War. *The American Journal of International Law* 10 (1916): 600–602.

Krammer, Arnold. German Prisoners of War in the United States. *Military Affairs* 40 (April, 1976): 68–73.

———. When the *Afrika Korps* Came to Texas. *Southwestern Historical Quarterly* 80, no. 3 (January, 1977): 247–82.

Kruse, Arthur M. Custody of Prisoners of War in the United States. *The Military Engineer* 38 (February, 1946): 70–74.

Levy, David M. The German Anti-Nazi: A Case Study. *American*

Journal of Orthopsychiatry 16 (July, 1946): 507–15.

Lunden, Walter A. Captivity Psychosis Among Prisoners of War. *Journal of Criminal Law and Criminology* 39 (1949): 507–15.

McKnight, Maxwell S. The Employment of Prisoners of War in the United States. *International Labour Review* 50 (July, 1944): 47–64.

Mau, Hermann. Die Zweite Revolution. *Vierteljahrshefte für Zeitgeschichte* 1 (1953).

Mazuzan, George T., and Walker, Nancy. Restricted Areas: German Prisoner-of-War Camps in Western New York, 1944-1946. *New York History* 59 (January 1978): 55–72.

Moulton, William G. Our Profession in Reverse: Teaching English to German Prisoners of War. *The Modern Language Journal* 42 (October, 1948): 421–30.

Peak, Helen. Some Observations on the Characteristics and Distribution of German Nazis. *Psychological Monographs* 59 (1947): 1–44.

———. Some Psychological Problems in the Re-Education of Germany. *Journal of Social Issues* 2 (August, 1946): 26–38.

Plassman, Clemens. Das Kriegsgefangenrecht und Seinen Reform. *Zeitschrift für Volkerrecht* 14 (1928): 521–41.

Pluth, Edward J. Prisoner of War Employment in Minnesota During World War II. *Minnesota History* (Winter 1975): 290–303.

Postwar Policies Regarding Foreign Workers and Prisoners of War. *Monthly Labor Review* 61 (November, 1945): 910–11.

Priorities in Allocation of Services of Prisoners of War. *Monthly Labor Review* 58 (June, 1944): 1189.

Pritchett, Merrill R., and Shea, William L., The Afrika Korps in Arkansas, 1943-1946. *The Arkansas Historical Quarterly* 37, no. 1 (Spring 1978), 3–22.

Radford, R. A. The Economic Organization of a POW Camp. *Economica* 11 (November, 1945): 189–201.

Rundell, Walter, Jr. Paying the POW in World War II. *Military Affairs* 22 (Fall 1958): 121–34.

Shils, Edward A., and Janowitz, Morris. Cohesion and Disintegration in the Wehrmacht in World War II. *Public Opinion Quarterly* (Summer 1948): 280–315.

Spidle, Jake W., Jr. Axis Invasion of the American West: POWs in New Mexico, 1942-1946. *New Mexico Historical Review* 49 (April, 1974): 93–122.

Stuart, Graham H. War Prisoners and Internees in the United States. *American Foreign Service Journal* 21 (October, 1944): 531, 568 +.

Tissing, Robert Warren. Stalag-Texas, 1943-1945: The Detention and Use of Prisoners of War in Texas During World War II. *Military History of Texas and the Southwest* 13 (Fall 1976): 23–24.

Tollefson, Martin. Enemy Prisoners of War. *Iowa Law Review* 32 (November, 1946): 51–77.

Tureen, L. L., and Palmer, J. O. Some Group Differences in Personal Values between American Soldiers and German Prisoners of War. *Journal of Social Psychology* 42 (1955): 305–13.

Wilson, Terry Paul. The *Afrika Korps* in Oklahoma: Fort Reno's Prisoner of War Compound. *The Chronicles of Oklahoma* 52, no. 3 (Fall 1974): 360–69.

Periodicals

"Anger at Nazi Atrocities is Rising, but United States Treats Prisoners Fairly." *Newsweek,* May 7, 1945, p. 58.

Arndt, Jessie Ash. "Prisoners of War on the Kansas Prairie." *The Christian Science Monitor Magazine,* October 16, 1943, p. 5+.

"Back from Bondage," *Newsweek,* December 13, 1943, p. 48.

"Back from Purgatory." *Newsweek,* December 18, 1944, pp. 47–48.

"Barbed Wire and Democracy." *Adult Education,* British Institute of Education, June, 1946, pp. 170–174.

Baum, Vicki. "Land of the Free." *Collier's,* August 19, 1944, pp. 11–12+.

"Behind the Wire." *Time,* June 21, 1943, p. 67.

Berding, Andrue. "Canada's 14,000 War Prisoners." *The Reader's Digest* 37, no. 224 (December, 1940), pp. 70–72.

"Boss of 200,000 Enemies." *American Magazine,* May, 1944, p. 131.

"Brave, Brave Warrior." *Commonweal,* June 29, 1945, pp. 261–62.

Britten, Marion Hale. "Newspapers in European Prison Camps." *American National Red Cross, Prisoners of War Bulletin,* September, 1943, p. 4.

Bruckner, Ferdinand. "Captured Into Freedom." *Soviet Russia Today,* May, 1942, pp. 20, 34.

Campion, Nardi Reeder. "West Point's 'Supe': No 'Potted Palm.' " *New York Times Magazine,* November 21, 1943, p. 12+.

"Captive Enemy." *Newsweek,* January 8, 1945, pp. 33–34.

Childs, Marquis W. "No Peace for the Swiss." *Saturday Evening Post,* May 1, 1943, pp. 14–15, 52–53.

Cook, F. G. Alletson. "Nazi Prisoners are Prisoners Still." *New York Times Magazine,* November 21, 1943, p. 12+.

Cross, Neal. "The New Axis Tourist Invasion." *School and Society,* February 26, 1944, pp. 148–49.

"Death and Treason." *Newsweek,* February 5, 1945, pp. 47–48.

"Democratizing Germans." *Science News Letter,* November 9, 1946, p. 293.

Derby, Stafford. "New Light for German POWs." *The Christian Science Monitor Magazine,* December 8, 1945.

Deutsch, Albert. "German PWs Living Better Than Our War Workers," *PM,* May 15, 1945, p. 6.

Devore, Robert. "Our 'Pampered' War Prisoners." *Collier's,* October 14, 1944, p. 144.

"Do We Pamper POWs?" *Collier's,* June 2, 1945, p. 78.

Dvorovy, Chaplain John. "Religion in Prisoner of War Camps." *The Army and Navy Chaplain,* July–August, 1945, pp. 17, 35.

Ehrmann, Henry W. "An Experiment in Political Education." *Social Research,* September, 1947, pp. 304–20.

"Enemy Prisoners of War." *Army and Navy Register,* February 17, 1945, p. 5.

"Escape in Arizona." *Time,* January 8, 1945, p. 16.

Fay, Sidney B. "German Prisoners of War." *Current History,* March, 1945, pp. 193–200.

Fisher, A. J. "394,000 German Prisoners of War." *The Central European Observer,* October 25, 1946, pp. 342–43.

Frost, Meigs O. "New Orleans Test Tube for German Democracy," *The Times-Picayune Sunday Magazine,* September 15, 1945.

———"*Afrika Korps* Veteran Flays Nazism, Tells of Torture," *The Times-Picayune Sunday Magazine,* September 23, 1945.

"German Prisoners." *Army and Navy Register,* April 28, 1945, p. 20

"German Propaganda." *Army and Navy Register,* April 14, 1945, p. 8.

"Good Samaritans." *Newsweek,* April 27, 1953, pp. 28–29.

Hauser, Ernest O. "German Prisoners Talk Your Ears Off." *Saturday Evening Post,* January 13, 1945, pp. 12–13, 61–62.

Herald, George W. "Our Nazi War-Prisoners." *Pic Magazine,* June 6, 1944, pp. 12–13, 45.

Herrick, Genevieve Forbes. "Behind Barbed Wire." *The Rotarian,* March, 1946, pp. 22–24.

Hirsh, Diana, "German Atrocities Raise Questions: Are Nazi POWs 'Coddled' Here?" *Newsweek,* May 7, 1945, pp. 60–61.

Hoover, J. Edgar. "Enemies at Large." *The American Magazine,* April, 1944, pp. 29–30.

"How War Prisoners Behave." *Science Digest,* April, 1944, pp. 29–30.

Janta, Alexander. "The German Ego in Defeat." *Plain Talk,* April, 1947, pp. 10–13.

Jones, John E. "PW." *Family Circle,* May 5, 1944, pp. 20–22.

Kirwan, William E., "German Prisoners of War." *Bulletin of the Bureau of Criminal Investigation, New York State Police,* August, 1944, pp. 1–6.

"Kriegsmarine Escape." *Newsweek,* January 8, 1945, pp. 33–34.

Kunzig, Robert L. "360,000 PW's—The Hope of Germany." *American Magazine,* November, 1946, p. 23 +.

Lang, Daniel. "A Reporter at Large: Dopes and Simple Joes." *The New Yorker,* November 10, 1945, pp. 65–75.

"Last of Supermen." *Newsweek,* August 5, 1946, p. 20.

"Legion of Despair." *Time,* March 19, 1945, pp. 20–21.

Lerch, Archer L. "The Army Reports on POWs." *The American Mercury,* May, 1945, pp. 536–46.

Leven, Stephen A. "A Catholic Chaplain Visits Our German Prisoners." *America,* June 24, 1944, pp. 320–21.

Liddell Hart, B. H. "The German Generals." *Harper's Magazine,* January, February, 1946, pp. 57–66; 187–92.

"Life in a German Prison Camp." *American National Red Cross, Prisoners of War Bulletin,* February, 1944, pp. 6–7.

"*Life* Visits a POW Camp." *Life,* November 13, 1944, pp. 121–25.

"Manpower Boost." *Business Week,* May 29, 1943, p. 20 +.

Margulies, Newton L. "Proper Treatment of War Prisoners." *Vital Speeches,* May 15, 1945, pp. 477–80.

Martin, Ralph G. "What Kind of Peace? The Soldiers' Viewpoint." *New York Times Magazine,* March 11, 1945, p. 5 +.

"Masquerader." *Time,* March 23, 1953, p. 25.

"Midnight Massacre." *Time,* July 23, 1945, p. 24.

"Military Police." *Fortune,* June, 1945, pp. 151–55.

Moore, John Hammond. "Hitler's Afrika Korps in New England." *Yankee,* June, 1976, pp. 82–88, 116.

Morse, Arthur D. "The Nazi Murder

Plot." *Look,* November 14, 1967, pp. 49–54+.

Murphy, Charles J. V., "Somervell of the S.O.S.." *Life,* March 8, 1943, pp. 83-4, 86, 88, 91-4.

"Nation—Enough Nazis." *Newsweek,* May 21, 1945, p. 38.

"Nazi Prisoners Are Nazis Still." *New York Times Magazine,* November 21, 1943, p. 38.

"Nazis Hoe Cotton." *Business Week,* June 19, 1944, p. 18.

"Nazis in the United States." *Time,* May 1, 1944, p. 64.

"No Converts." *Time,* December 11, 1944, p. 24.

"No Pin-Boys." *The New Yorker,* February 25, 1944, p. 16.

"On Pampering Prisoners." *Collier's,* August 12, 1944, p. 12.

"Our Growing Prison Camps; How United States Treats War Captives." *The U.S. News,* May 28, 1943, pp. 23–24.

"Our Prisoners of War." *The National Review,* January, 1941, pp. 31–32.

Pabel, Reinhold. "It's Easy to Bluff Americans." *Collier's,* May 16, 1953, pp. 20–23+.

Pate, Maurice. "A Report to Relatives of Prisoners." *American National Red Cross, Prisoners of War Bulletin,* February, 1945, pp. 1–4.

Peterson, Bernard. "What's Behind the American Salute by German Prisoners at Fort Devens." *Industry,* April, 1945, pp. 7-10, 22, 42-44, 52.

Pierson, Ralph. "The Barbed Wire Universities." *School and Society,* September 8, 1945, pp. 156–58.

"Points System in Prison Camps." *American National Red Cross, Prisoners of War Bulletin,* August, 1943, p. 30.

Porter, David. "Vocational Services for American War Prisoners." *Occupations,* May, 1945, pp. 453–56.

Powers, James H. "What to Do with German Prisoners." *Atlantic Monthly,* November, 1944, pp. 46–50.

"POWs, Non-Germans Want to Go Back and Fight." *Military Police Training Bulletin,* January, 1945.

"POWs Outbound." *Newsweek,* May 28, 1945, p. 34.

"Prisoner's Dues?" *Business Week,* February 19, 1944, p. 94.

"Prisoners of War." *Life,* May 31, 1943, p. 24.

"Prisoners Return." *Time,* November 8, 1943, p. 22.

"Profits: May Not." *Newsweek,* August 5, 1946, pp. 22–24.

"P.W. Camp 168," *New Statesman and Nation,* July 21, 1945, p. 4.

"PWs." *Life,* January 10, 1944, pp. 47–48+.

"Re-Educating the Nazis." *America,* August 26, 1944, p. 515.

"Re-Education Program for German Prisoners in Effect Here." *Publishers Weekly,* June 23, 1945, p. 2439.

"Repatriates." *Life,* March 27, 1944, pp. 41–44.

"Repatriates Arrive Home from Germany." *American National Red Cross, Prisoners of War Bulletin,* December, 1943, p. 7.

"Reports from Camps in Germany." *American National Red Cross, Prisoners of War Bulletin,* September, 1944, pp. 1–3.

"Retaining of War Prisoners May Imperil Future Peace." *World Dispatch,* October 8, 1946, pp. 10–11.

"Return from Reich." *Newsweek,* March 27, 1944, p. 50.

Reynolds, Quentin, "Experiment in Democracy." *Collier's,* May 25, 1946, pp. 12–13, 41–42.

Sagi, Douglas. " 'My Fuehrer, I Follow Thee,' " *The Canadian Magazine, Winnepeg Tribune,* January 4, 1975, pp. 4–6.

"Set These Slaves Free." *Christian Century,* July 31, 1946, p. 933–34.

"Seven by the Rope." *Newsweek,* July 23, 1945, p. 27.

Shafer, Jack. ". . . And Here's How We Treat Nazi Captives," *PM,* May 1, 1945, p. 9.

Shays, Eugene. "German Prisoners of War in the United States: Observations of a Soldier." *Fourth International,* December, 1945, pp. 366–71.

"Six Million POWs" *Fortune,* February, 1943, pp. 108-11 +.

Smith, Beverly, "Nazi Supermen Hit the Dirt." *American Magazine,* July, 1945, p. 45 +.

———. "The *Afrika Korps* Comes to America." *American Magazine,* August, 1943, pp. 28–29 +.

Snow, Edgar. "Russia's Antitoxin for Nazi Prisoners." *Saturday Evening Post,* April 14, 1945, pp. 20, 93–94.

Stenbuck, Jack. "German War Prisoner for Democratic Leadership." *Magazine Digest,* December, 1945, pp. 66–72.

Strong, Tracy. "Prisoners Under the Law." *Christian Century,* April 14, 1943, pp. 455–57.

Stuart, Graham H. "Special War Problems Division." *Department of State Bulletin,* July 15, 1944, pp. 63–74.

"Studies and Sports in German Prison Camps." *American National Red Cross, Prisoners of War Bulletin,* September, 1943, pp. 1, 5.

"Swastika Over Arizona." *Newsweek,* February 26, 1945, p. 58.

"Treatment of War Prisoners." *Army and Navy Register,* May 5, 1945, p. 8.

"Uncle Sam in the Slave Trade." *Christian Century,* June 12, 1946, p. 741.

"Utilize Prisoners of War." *Army and Navy Journal,* May 13, 1944, p. 96.

"War Prisoners." *Life,* October 23, 1944, pp. 37–38.

"War Prisoners Opposed." *Business Week,* January 15, 1944, p. 96.

"What Shall Be Done with Germany?" *See Magazine,* April, 1945, pp. 36–37.

"Writes William L. Shirer in the New York Herald Tribune." *The Reader's Digest,* January, 1945, p. 44.

Yackulic, George A., "Prisoners of War in Canada," *Canadian Business,* November, 1944, pp. 48–51, 124, 127.

Interviews and Correspondence

Coll, Thomas. Special Agent, F.B.I., Washington, D.C., March 31, 1977.

Corbett, Edward. Reserve, Louisiana, November 26, 1976.

Deutsch, Harold. U.S. Army War College, Carlisle Barracks, Pennsylvania, May 21, July 18, 1977.

Greene, James F. Deputy Commissioner, U.S. Immigration and Naturalization Service, Department of Justice, Washington D.C., August 13, 1975.

Griffin, Michael. Special Agent, F.B.I., Washington, D.C., April 15, 1977.

Hahn, William. Bryan, Texas, April 22, 1978.

Horn, Val. Mexia, Texas, March 10; November 23; December 5, 1976; August 15, 1977.

Jones, Howard Mumford. Cambridge, Massachusetts, September 12, November 7, 1978.

Kemper, Henry. Portland, Oregon, April 5, 16, 1978.

Klein, Lieutenant Colonel Alfred. Munich, Germany, January 15, April 22, May 22, 1976; August 4, 1977; February 18, 1978.

Kunzig, Robert L. Washington, D.C., September 15, 1977.

Lane, Mrs. John, Jr. Kaufman, Texas, June 22, October 11, 1977.

Link, Brigadier General Hans A. Washington, D.C., February 16, April 3, June 12, 1978.

Littmann, Walter Horst. Mexia, Texas; Koblenz, Germany, May 4, 29, July 24, 1978.

McCarver, Norman L., Jr., Hearne, Texas, October 15, 1975.

Matthias, Heinrich. Hamburg, Germany, May 29, July 13, 1978.

Meise, Robert. Düsseldorf, Germany, November 12, 1978.

Mellage, Guenter G. High Point, North Carolina, December 26, 1977.

Moulton, William G. Princeton, New Jersey, September 15, October 26, 1978.

Neumann, Robert G. Culver City, California, September 10, 1977.

Olive, Mrs. Selwyn A. Brownwood, Texas, March 3, 1977.

Pratt, Mrs. Gladden. Kaufman, Texas, November 1, 1977.

Richter, Werner. Mexia, Texas; Rosenheim, Germany, May 4, June 1, 1978.

Rordam, Peter. (Colonel, U.S. Army, Ret.), Brownsville, Texas, February 10–13, 1976.

Scheel, Eberhard. Mexia, Texas; Bad Vilbel, Germany, May 30, August 5, 1978.

Schindler, Karl. Cleveland, Ohio, November 15, 1977.

Schroer, John. Dallas, Texas; Los Angeles, September 29, December 1, 1977; April 10, 1978.

Smith, J. Fort. Mexia, Texas, March 10, 1976.

Staff, Richard. Lago Vista, Texas, September 15, November 12, 1976; June 5, 1977.

Theiler, Karl-Heinz. Kiel, Germany, January 5, 1976.

Ward, William Arthur. Fort Worth, Texas, March 23, 1978.

Wechmar, Baron Rüdiger von. New York, May 16, June 28, 1978.

Wiley, Mrs. Wilma. Bastrop, Texas, September 10, 1976.

Newspapers

Abilene [Texas] *Reporter-News*
Birmingham [Alabama] *Age-Herald*
Boston Globe
Bryan [Texas] *Eagle*
Charleston [South Carolina] *Evening Post*
Charleston [South Carolina] *News and Courier*
Chicago Sun
Chicago Tribune
Columbia [South Carolina] *Record*
Dallas Daily Times-Herald
Dallas Morning News
Dermott [Arkansas] *News*
Duluth [Minnesota] *Herald*
El Reno [Oklahoma] *American*
Fort Smith [Arkansas] *Times-Record*
Fort Worth [Texas] *Star-Telegram*
Hearne [Texas] *Democrat*
Huntington [West Virginia] *Herald-Dispatch*
Huntsville [Texas] *Item*
Kansas City Star
Kaufman [Texas] *Herald*
Mexia [Texas] *Daily News*
Milwaukee [Wisconsin] *Journal*

Nashville [Tennessee] *Tennessean*
Neue Volkszeitung
New Orleans Times-Picayune
New York Daily Mirror
New York Herald Tribune
New York Times
Providence [Rhode Island] *Journal*
Rockford [Illinois] *Morning Star*
Rockford [Illinois] *Register Republic*
St. Louis Globe-Democrat
Tampa [Florida] *Daily Times*
Tulsa [Oklahoma] *World*
Waco [Texas] *Tribune-Herald*
Washington Daily News
Washington Post

Archival Sources

UNITED STATES:

Records of Headquarters, Army Service Forces. *Prisoners of War Report No. 141,* Sept., 1943; General Somervell's Desk File. RG 160, Modern Military Branch, National Archives. (MMB-NA.)

Records of the War Department: General and Special Staffs. Combined Chiefs of Staff; Office of War Mobilization and Reconversion, RG 165. (MMB-NA.)

Records of the Office of the War Production Board, RG 179. (MMB-NA.)

Records of the Office of War Information, RG 208, NC-148, Entry 407. Box No. 2192. Washington National Records Center.

Records of the War Manpower Commission, Central Correspondence File, RG 211, Industrial and Social Branch, National Archives.

Records of the United States Joint Chiefs of Staff, RG 218. (MMB-NA.)

Records of the Army Staff, Intelligence and Evaluation Branch. Psychological Warfare, Russia, RG 319. (MMB-NA.)

Records of the Provost Marshal General's Office, Prisoner of War Division, 1941–1946; Special Projects Division, 1943–1946. RG 389. (MMB-NA.)

Records of the Army Adjutant General's Office, Operations Branch. Classified Decimal File; Decimal File, 1940–1945. RG 407. (MMB-NA.)

Department of State unpublished records, 1942–1944. World War II: German Prisoners of War. File Number 711.62114, RG 59. National Archives.

Stephen M. Farrand Collection, Hoover Institution of War, Revolution, and Peace, Stanford, California.

Public Information Division, Office of the Chief of Information, Department of the Army, The Pentagon, Washington, D.C.

Walter Schönstedt Collection, Department of Special Collection, the University Library, University of California, Davis, California.

GREAT BRITAIN:

Imperial War Museum, London.

Institute of Contemporary History and Wiener Library, London.

War Office Records, W.O. 32, Public Records Office, London.

GERMANY:

Wissenschaftliche Kommission für Deutsche Kriegsgefangengeschichte, Munich.

Government Documents

GERMANY. Wehrmacht. Oberkommando. *Vorschrift für das Kriegsgefangenenwesen.* Berlin: Reichsdruckerei, 1939.

U.S. CONGRESS, HOUSE. *A Bill Relating to Escapes of Prisoners of War and Interned Enemy Aliens.* H.R. 4108, 78th Cong., 2d sess., 1945.

A Bill Relating to Escapes of Prisoners of War and Interned Enemy Aliens. H.R. 1525, 79th Cong. 1st sess., 1945.

Committee on Military Affairs. *Investigations of the National War Effort.* H.R. 1992, 78th Cong., 2d sess., November, 1944.

Committee on Military Affairs. *Investigation of the National War Effort.* H.R. 728, 79th Cong., 1st sess., June, 1945.

Copy of speech by General Lerch on criticism of War Department. 79th Cong., 1st sess., March 5, 1945. *Congressional Record: Appendix,* XCI, A1024.

Extension of Remarks of Representative Goodwin on treatment of Prisoners of War. 79th Cong., 1st sess., February 22, 1945. *Congressional Record: Appendix,* XCI, A784.

Representative Curtis speaking on employment of war prisoners. 78th Cong., 1st sess., December 7, 1943. *Congressional Record,* LXXXIX.

Representative Dickstein speaking on German war prisoners. 79th Cong., 1st sess., February 14, 1945. *Congressional Record,* XCI, 1100–06.

Representative Gearhart speaking on pampering of war prisoners. 79th Cong., 1st sess., February 19, 1945. *Congressional Record; Appendix,* XCI, A3359.

Representative Harless speaking on German prisoner of war treatment. 79th Cong., 1st sess., February 19, 1945. *Congressional Record,* XCI, 1278–82; and July 5, 1945, 7217–19.

Representative Hope speaking on war prisoners policy. 79th Cong., 1st sess., May 4, 1945. *Congressional Record,* XCI, 4176.

Representative Larcade speaking on prisoner of war farm labor. 79th Cong., 1st sess., February 20, 1945. *Congressional Record: Appendix,* XCI.

Representative McDonough speaking on treatment of German war prisoners. 79th Cong., 1st sess., February 19, 1945. *Congressional Record,* XCI, 1280.

Representative McKenzie speaking on prisoner of war farm labor. 79th Cong., 1st sess., February 20, 1945. *Congressional Record: Appendix,* XCI.

Representative Murdock speaking on treatment of German war prisoners. 79th Cong., 1st sess., February 19, 1945. *Congressional Record,* XCI, 1280.

Representative Short speaking on treatment of war prisoners. 79th Cong., 1st sess., February 19, 1945. *Congressional Record,* XCI, 1280.

Representative Sikes speaking on treatment of prisoners of war. 79th Cong., 1st sess., February 9, 1945. *Congressional Record,* XCI, 980.

Resolutions of Wisconsin Legislature. 79th Cong., 1st sess., September 10, 1945. *Congressional Record: Appendix,* XCI, A3281.

U. S. CONGRESS. SENATE. *Report Relating to Escapes of Prisoners of War and Interned Enemy Aliens.* S. Rept. 180, 79th Cong., 1st sess., 1945. *Senate Miscellaneous Reports,* Vol. 1.

Senator McFarland speaking on treatment of German prisoners of war. 79th Cong., 1st sess., February 12, 1945. *Congressional Record,* XCI, 998-99.

Senator Maybank speaking on return of aliens and POWs to their homes. 79th Cong., 1st sess., July 13, 1945. *Congressional Record,* XCI, 7509.

Special Committee Investigating the National Defense Program. *Investigation of the National Defense Program Hearings* before a Special Committee Investigation of the National Defense Program pursuant to S. Res. 71, 77th Cong., 1st sess., through 79th Cong., 2d sess., Parts 1-34, 1941-46.

U.S. DEPARTMENT OF THE ARMY. Office of the Adjutant General. *Army Battle Casualties and Nonbattle Deaths in World War II, Final Report, 7 December 1941-31 December, 1946.* Washington, D.C.: Government Printing Office, June 1, 1953.

Office of the Chief of Military History. *U.S. Armed Forces: Middle Pacific and Predecessor Commands During World War II, 7 December 1941-2 September 1945.* Volume XXIV, Washington, D.C.: Government Printing Office, 1960.

Office of the Surgeon General, Medical Department. *Preventive Medicine in World War II.* Volume IX: Special Fields, Washington, D.C.: Government Printing Office, 1969.

The Administrative and Logistical History of the European Theater of Operations, Part IX, Washington, D.C.: Government Printing Office, March, 1946.

Army Service Forces Manual: Safe Work Practices For Prisoners of War (German), M805. Washington, D.C.: September, 1944.

Staff Officers' Field Manual, FM 101-10, Washington, D.C., June, 1941.

Technical Manual, TM 19-500, Washington, D.C., October, 1944.

U.S. DEPARTMENT OF DEFENSE. *POW: The Fight Continues After the Battle. The Report of the Secretary of Defense's Advisory Committee on Prisoners of War.* Washington, D.C.: Government Printing Office, 1955.

U.S. DEPARTMENT OF STATE. *Repatriation and Liberation of German Prisoners of War. Understanding between United States of America and France.* United States Treaties and

Other International Acts, Pub. 2405 (1947).

U.S. DEPARTMENT OF WAR. Army Service Forces, Control Division. *Statistical Review: WWII. A Summary of ASF Activities.* Washington, D.C.: War Department, 1946.

General Staff. *Reports of the Commander-in-Chief, A.E.F. Staff Sections and Services, The United States Army in the World War, 1917-1919.* Volume XV. Washington, D.C.: Government Printing Office, 1948.

United States Strategic Bombing Survey, Morale Division. Volumes I, II. Washington D.C.: Government Printing Office, December, 1946, May, 1947.

U.S. Statutes at Large. Volume LIX, Washington, D.C.: Government Printing Office, 1945.

Unpublished Materials

Corbett, Edward C. "Interned for the Duration: Axis Prisoners of War in Oklahoma, 1942-1946." Master's Thesis, Oklahoma City University, 1967.

Office of Military Government for Germany (US), Information Control Division, report, "Former Special Prisoners of War," Berlin: 26 June, 1947. Written by Dr. William G. Moulton. Copy presented to the author by Dr. Moulton.

Pluth, Edward. "The Administration and Operation of German Prisoner of War Camps in the United States During World War II." Ph.D. Thesis, Ball State University, 1970.

Pritchett, Merrill R., and Shea, William L. "The Afrika Korps in Arkansas, 1943-1946." University of Arkansas at Monticello, 1977.

Provost Marshal General's Office. "Office of the Provost Marshal General; World War II. A Brief History." Pt. III: "Prisoners of War." File, Office of the Chief of Military History, Dept. of the Army, Washington, D.C., January 15, 1946.

————. Prisoner of War Division. "Prisoner of War Operations." 4 vols. File, Office of the Chief of Military History, Dept. of the Army, Washington, D.C., August 31, 1945. All 4 volumes have recently been made available on microfilm through the Library of Congress (L.C. Shelf Number 51437).

————. "Prisoner of War Operations: Supplement." File, Office of the Chief of Military History, Dept. of the Army, Washington, D.C., April, 1946.

————. Special Projects Division. "Re-Education of Enemy Prisoners of War." File, Office of the Chief of Military History, Dept. of the Army, Washington, D.C., November 1945.

————. Special Projects Division. "Re-Education of Enemy Prisoners of War—Projects II and III." File, Office of the Chief of Military History,

Dept. of the Army, Washington, D.C., March 1, 1946.

————. Special Projects Division. "Re-Education of Enemy Prisoners of War—Eustis Project." File, Office of the Chief of Military History, Dept. of the Army, Washington, D.C., April 4, 1946.

Reiners, W. O. "Soviet Indoctrination of German War Prisoners, 1941– 1946." Center for International Studies, Massachusetts Institute of Technology, Cambridge, Mass.

Speakman, Cumins E. "Re-Education of German Prisoners of War in the United States During World War II." Master's Thesis, University of Virginia, 1948. Copy in Office of the Chief of Military History, Washington, D.C.

Addendum to Bibliography

Books

Choate, Mark. *Nazis in the Piney Woods* (Lufkin: Best of East Texas Publishers, 1989).

Koop, Allen V. *Stark Decency: German Prisoners of War in a New England Village* (Hanover: University Press of New England, 1989).

Powell, Allan Kent. *Splinters of a Nation: German Prisoners of War in Utah* (Salt Lake City: U. of Utah Press, 1989).

Journals

Billinger, Robert D. Jr. "Behind the Wire: German Prisoners of War at Camp Sutton, 1944-1946," *North Carolina Historical Review,* 61 (October 1984), pp. 481-509.

Fickle, James E. and Ellis, Donald W. "POWs in the Piney Woods: German Prisoners of War in the Southern Lumber Industry, 1943-1945," *The Journal of Southern History,* Vol. LVI, No. 4, November 1990, pp. 695-724.

Jepson, Daniel A. "Historical and Archaeological Perspectives on the World War II Prisoner of War Camp at Fort Carson, Colorado," Report to the National Park Service and the U.S. Army, Fort Collins, Colorado: Centennial Archaeology, Inc. August 1990

Krammer, Arnold. "American Treatment of German Generals During World War II, " *The Journal of Military History,* 54 (January 1990), pp 27-46.

————."In Splendid Isolation: Enemy Diplomats in World War II," *Prologue,* 17 (Spring 1985), pp. 25-43.

————. "Japanese Prisoners of War in America," *Pacific Historical Review,* 52 (February 1983), pp. 67-91.

Moore, John Hammond. "Nazi Troopers in South Carolina, 1944-1946," *South Carolina Historical Magazine,* 81 (October 1980), pp. 306-315.

O'Brien, Patrick G., Isern, Thomas D., and Lumley, R. Daniel. "Stalag Sunflower: German Prisoners of War in Kansas," *Kansas History,* 7 (Autumn 1984), pp. 182-198.

Parrish, Michael. "Soviet Generals in German Captivity: A Bibliographical Inquiry," *Survey,* 30, 4 (June 1989), pp. 66-86.

Paschal, Allan W. "The Enemy in Colorado: German Prisoners of War, 1943-1946," *Colorado Magazine,* 56 (Summer/Fall 1979), pp. 119-142.

Richter, Anton (ed.). "A German P.O.W. at Camp Grant: The Reminiscences of Heinz Richter," *Journal of the Illinois State Historical Society,* 76 (Spring 1983), pp. 61-69.

Shea, William L. and Pritchett, Merrill R. "The Wehrmacht in Louisiana," *Louisiana History,* 23 (Winter 1982), pp. 5-20.

"Some Thoughts on Prisoners of War in Iowa, 1943 to 1946," *Palimpsest,* 65 (March/April 1984), pp. 68-73.

Spencer, Ralph. "Prisoners of War in Cheyenne County, 1943-1946," *Nebraska History,* 63, (Fall 1982), pp. 438-449.

Walker, Chip. "German Creative Activities in Camp Aliceville, 1943-1946," *The Alabama Review,* 38 (January 1985), pp. 19-37.

Walker, Richard P. "The Swastika and the Lone Star: Nazi Activity in Texas POW Camps," *Military History of the Southwest,* 19 (Spring 1989), pp. 39-70.

Warner, Richard S. "Barbed Wire and Nazilagers: PW Camps in Oklahoma," *The Chronicles of Oklahoma,* Vol. 64, No. 1, (Spring 1986), pp. 37-67.

Worrall, Janet E. "Prisoners on the Home Front: Community Reactions to German and Italian POWs in Northern Colorado, 1943-1946, " *Colorado Heritage* 1990, pp 32-47.

Periodicals

Cook, Dave. "Fort Robinson Prisoner of War Camp Revisited," *The Crawford Clipper's Northwest Nebraska Post,* (September 1987), pp. 2-5, (October 1987), pp. 3-6.

Unpublished Materials

Keen, James Richard. *The Captive Enemy? Italian Prisoners of War in Texas During World War II,* Masters Thesis, University of Texas at Permian Basin, 1988.

Schott, Matthew J. and Foley, Rosalind. *Bayou Stalags: German Prisoners of War in Louisiana* (Pamphlet) Lafayette: 1981.

Webber, Pamela Sue. *German Prisoners of War in Colorado During World War II,* BA Thesis: Colorado College, 1982.

Index

(*n* indicates chapter note reference)